ETHICS, LAW AND SOCIETY

Ethics, Law and Society

Volume I

Edited by

JENNIFER GUNNING and SØREN HOLM
Cardiff Law School, Cardiff University, UK

Routledge
Taylor & Francis Group
LONDON AND NEW YORK

First published in paperback 2024

First published 2005 by Ashgate Publishing

Published 2018 by Routledge
4 Park Square, Milton Park, Abingdon, Oxon OX14 4RN

and by Routledge
605 Third Avenue, New York, NY 10158

Routledge is an imprint of the Taylor & Francis Group, an informa business

Publisher's Note
The publisher has gone to great lengths to ensure the quality of this reprint but points out that some imperfections in the original copies may be apparent.

British Library Cataloguing in Publication Data
Ethics, law and society
Vol. I
1. Professional ethics 2. Law and ethics 3. Bioethics 4. Social ethics 5. Human rights
I. Gunning, Jennifer II. Holm, Søren
174

Library of Congress Cataloging-in-Publication Data
Ethics, law and society / edited by Jennifer Gunning and Søren Holm.
p. cm.
Includes bibliographical references and index.
ISBN 0-7546-4583-5
1. Applied ethics. 2. Law. 3. Civilization. I. Gunning, Jennifer. II. Holm, Søren.

BJ1581.2.E85 2005
170--dc22

2005007351

ISBN: 978-0-7546-4583-2 (hbk)
ISBN: 978-1-138-27330-6 (pbk)
ISBN: 978-0-429-29260-6 (ebk)

DOI: 10.4324/9780429292606

TJI Digital, Padstow, Cornwall

Contents

PART II: ETHICS AND SOCIETY

List of Figures and Table

Figures

Table

List of Contributors

Dr Roberto Andorno is Visiting Professor of International Bioethics in the Department of Medical Ethics of the University of Goettingen, Germany. Dr Andorno has also been a member of the UNESCO International Bioethics Committee since 1998. He received his doctorates in law from the Universities of Buenos Aires (1991) and Paris XII (1994) and has published extensively in the field of international biomedical law, including articles and book chapters on the human genome and human rights, ethics and medically assisted reproduction, the notion of human dignity, genetic privacy, the moral and legal status of the human embryo, human cloning, the UNESCO Declaration on the Human Genome and the European Convention on Human Rights and Biomedicine.

Professor Robin Attfield is Professor of Philosophy at Cardiff University, where he has taught philosophy since January 1968. He has also been Visiting Lecturer in Philosophy, University of Ife, Nigeria (1972-1973) and Inter-University Council Visiting Lecturer in Philosophy, University of Nairobi, Kenya, 1975. In the late 1980s he became one of the founding members of the Cardiff Centre for Applied Ethics. He is the joint editor of *Values, Conflict and the Environment* (1989 and 1996), of *International Justice and the Third World* (1992), and of *Philosophy and the Natural Environment* (1994). In September 2003 he published *Environmental Ethics: An Overview for the Twenty-First Century*, with Polity (Cambridge).

Professor Roger Brownsword is Professor of Law at King's College London and Honorary Professor of Law at the University of Sheffield (where he was one of the founding members of the Sheffield Institute of Biotechnological Law and Ethics). He is the co-author, with Professor Deryck Beyleveld, of *Law as a Moral Judgment* (1986), *Mice, Morality and Patents* (1993), *Human Dignity in Bioethics and Biolaw* (2001), and *Consent in the Law* (2004). He co-edited (with Professor Cornish and Dr Llewelyn) *Law and Human Genetics: Regulating a Revolution* (1998) and, supported by a Leverhulme Trust Fellowship, he recently started work on a new book for Oxford University Press entitled *Rights, Regulation, and the Technological Revolution.* Professor Brownsword acted as a specialist adviser to the House of Lords Select Committee on Stems Cells and his recent journal papers in this general area include: 'Stem Cells, Superman, and the Report of the Select Committee' (2002) 65 *Modern Law Review* 568-587; 'Bioethics Today, Bioethics Tomorrow: Stem Cell Research and the "Dignitarian Alliance"' (2003) 17 *University of Notre Dame Journal of Law, Ethics and Public Policy* 15-51; 'An Interest in Human Dignity as the Basis for Genomic Torts' (2003) 42 *Washburn Law Journal* 413-487; 'Regulating Human Genetics: Dilemmas of Form and Substance, Doctrine and Design' (2004) 12 *Medical Law Review* 14-39; and 'Reproductive Opportunities and Regulatory Challenges' (2004) 67 *Modern Law*

Review 304-321. In addition to his interest in law, ethics and technology, Professor Brownsword has written extensively about the law of contract, including *Contract Law: Themes for the Twenty-First Century* (2000); he is the general editor of the *Understanding Law* series of books in which he has co-authored two titles with Professor John Adams; and he is co-editor of a four-volume set on *Global Governance and the Quest for Justice* published by Hart (2004).

Professor Arthur Caplan is currently the Emmanuel and Robert Hart Professor of Bioethics, Chair of the Department of Medical Ethics and the Director of the Center for Bioethics at the University of Pennsylvania in Philadelphia. Prior to coming to Penn in 1994, Caplan taught at the University of Minnesota, the University of Pittsburgh, and Columbia University. He was the Associate Director of the Hastings Center from 1984-1987. Born in Boston, Caplan did his undergraduate work at Brandeis University, and did his graduate work at Columbia University where he received a Ph.D. in the history and philosophy of science in 1979. Caplan is the author or editor of twenty-five books and over 500 papers in refereed journals of medicine, science, philosophy, bioethics and health policy.

Luke Clements is Co-Director of the Traveller Law Research Unit at Cardiff Law School and a consultant solicitor with Scott-Moncrieff Harbour and Sinclair (London) specialising in judicial review and human rights litigation. He has been involved in a number of European Court of Human Rights cases on behalf of Roma and British Travelling People. He is a member of the Legal Committee of the European Roma Rights Centre based in Budapest and a member of Advisory Board of the Georgian Human Rights organisation 'Article 42 of the Constitution'. He has written widely; his books include *European Human Rights* (Sweet & Maxwell) 1999 [2nd ed] *Human Rights: Changing the Legal Culture* (as joint editor) (Blackwell) 1999 and *Disabled People and European Human Rights* (Policy Press) 2003.

Professor Gillian Douglas is Professor of Law at Cardiff Law School. She is the author of *Law, Fertility and Reproduction* (1991), *An Introduction to Family Law* (2001) and co-author of *Bromley's Family Law*, 9th ed (1998).

Juanita Elias is a lecturer in International Politics in the School of Social Sciences at The University of Manchester. She is author of *Fashioning Inequality: The Multinational Company and Gendered Employment in a Globalizing World* (Ashgate, 2004). Her research interests include gendered political economy, the regulation of multinational corporations and Malaysian political economy.

Professor Margaret Esiri is Professor of Neuropathology at Oxford University. She divides her time between providing a diagnostic service (for example, providing tumour diagnoses on living subjects undergoing neurosurgical operations and post mortem diagnostic work), research and teaching of medical and neuroscience students. Her research is currently on multiple sclerosis, dementia and schizophrenia. She has written three textbooks and numerous original papers on her research.

Dr Berit Andersen Faber has an LLM from the University of Copenhagen in 1985, multidisciplinary courses in the Department of Education, Philosophy and Rhetoric 1982-83 in philosophy of science and argumentation theory. She has been Executive Director of the Danish Council of Ethics from 2002, acting executive director 1997-2000. She has previously worked as, Special consultant at the Centre for Bioethics and Risk Assessment, the Royal Veterinary and Agricultural University, consultant for the Management Secretariat at the University of Copenhagen – committee work on university faculty networking in connection with biotechnology, The University of Copenhagen, senior consultant for the Danish Central Scientific Ethical Committee and head of department in the Danish Ministry of Health. She is co-author with Prof. dr. jur., Rector of University of Copenhagen, Linda Nielsen of the report 'Ethical principles in European regulation of biotechnology – possibilities and pitfalls', The Danish Biotik-project 2002, The Ministry of Economic and Business Affairs. She is author of the juridical parts of the Danish Council of Ethics' reports on the ethical questions regarding the beginning of life, donor anonymity in relation to sperm and egg donation and reports regarding end of life decisions and has participated in negotiations on the administrative level in expert committees in the EU and The European Council regarding the authorisation system for medicinal products and The Council of Europe's Convention on Human Rights and Biomedicine (Oviedo-Convention). She has participated in EU – High-level workshop on public participation in debate on biotechnology and bioethics, and has been speaker at workshops on public participation in relation to biotechnology and bioethics at the biotechnology-conference 'Cordia 2003', December 2003, Vienna. Speaker at the Future Panel – Conference in The Danish Parliament in March 2004 on juridical and ethical aspects regarding donation of human sperm and eggs.

Professor Martha J. Farah is currently the Bob and Arlene Kogod Tern Professor of Psychology and Director of the Center for Cognitive Neuroscience at the University of Pennsylvania in Philadelphia. Prior to coming to Penn in 1992, Farah taught at Carnegie Mellon University in Pittsburgh. Born in New York City, Farah did her undergraduate work at the Massachusetts Institute of Technology and earned her Ph.D. in Psychology from Harvard University. Farah is the author of 2 books and over 100 refereed articles, and editor of several books and journal special issues. Her work has been honoured by awards from the American Psychological Association, the Cognitive Science Society, and the National Academy of Sciences, and is a former Guggenheim Fellow.

Dr Mark Fish is research fellow with the department of Geriatric Medicine, Cardiff University. He is a member of the Cardiff Community Memory Team and his research interests are cognitive impairment and dementia. He did his undergraduate studies at U.C.L. and completed his basic medical training in Wales.

Dr Christian Gamborg is a Senior Researcher at the Center for Forest, Landscape and Planning, and a Senior Research Fellow at at the Centre for Bioethics and Risk Assessment (CeBRA). He holds a Ph.D. in bioethics and natural resource management from the Royal Veterinary and Agricultural University (KVL). Since 1998 the majority of his research has been within bioethics and sustainability aspects of natural resource, forest and landscape management, farm animal breeding and reproduction and science-policy-dissemination interaction.

Jennifer Gunning originally trained as a scientist. She was for three years Secretary of the Voluntary Licensing Authority for Human In Vitro Fertilisation and Embryology. Subsequently she wrote a report for the UK government on human IVF and embryo research and related issues to provide information for Parliament during the passage of the Human Fertilisation and Embryology Bill. She has since written and spoken widely on regulatory issues in assisted reproduction. She has also worked on ethical issues relating to the use of human stem cells and to agriculture, animal welfare and sustainability. She is now a Senior Research Fellow in bioethics and law at Cardiff Law School where she co-ordinates the Cardiff Centre for Ethics, Law & Society.

Professor Ian Hargreaves is Professor of Journalism at Cardiff University. He was Director of the Cardiff Centre for Journalism Studies from 1998-2002. Before that, he was Editor of the *New Statesman*; Editor of the *Independent*; Deputy Editor of the *FT* and Director of News at the BBC.

Dr Søren Holm is Professorial Fellow in Bioethics and Director of the Cardiff Centre for Ethics, Law & Society at the University of Cardiff, UK, as well as Professor of Medical Ethics at the Centre for Medical Ethics at the University of Oslo, Norway. He holds degrees in medicine, philosophy, and health care ethics, and two doctoral degrees in medical ethics. He has written extensively on reproductive ethics, cloning, genetics and research ethics.

Professor Richard Gardner FRS is Henry Dale Professor of the Royal Society at the University of Oxford. Completing the Natural Sciences Tripos in Cambridge with a First in Physiology Richard Gardner did a Ph.D. at the Cambridge Physiological Laboratory under the supervision of Dr Robert Edwards who, with Patrick Steptoes, pioneered the development of human IVF. Appointed to Oxford University as a Lecturer in 1973, Richard was appointed Henry Dale Professor in 1978 and elected a Fellow of the Royal Society in 1979. He has chaired the Royal Society Ad Hoc Committees on Human Fertilisation and Embryology, on Ovarian Donation and most recently on Stem Cells and Therapeutic Cloning. In 1999 Richard was awarded the March of Dimes International Prize in Developmental Biology and in 2001 was awarded the Royal Society's Royal Medal.

Dr Ian Kenway is currently Director of the Centre for the International Study of Cyberthethics and Human Rights (CISCHR) and Honorary Research Fellow in Ethics and ICT at Cardiff University. Previous positions have included Assistant

Secretary of the Church of England's Board for Social Responsibility at Westminster, where he exercised a brief for legal affairs and edited its journal Crucible (1988-1993), and Director of Studies at the Centre for the Study of Theology – later renamed the Centre for Theology and Society – at the University of Essex (1993-99). During 1999-2001 he was engaged in independent research in Southern Nevada in ethics and information and communication technologies. CISCHR is a not-for-profit organisation, dedicated to promoting the international study of cyberethics, through quality research, teaching, publication and advocacy. In particular it seeks to extend informed public debate on human rights issues that relate to the actual or potential misuse of information and communication technologies as well as relevant issues concerning social inclusion.

Professor dr. Rick Lawson holds the Kirchheiner Chair on Protection of the Integrity of the Individual, Department of Public Law, Leiden University, the Netherlands. He teaches international human rights law, EC law and public international law. His specialisation is the European Convention on Human Rights; he is a member of the EU Network of Independent Experts on Human Rights and editor of *NJCM-Bulletin/Nederlands Tijdschrift voor de Mensenrechten*, the leading Dutch human-rights review. In 1999 Rick Lawson obtained a doctorate degree *cum laude* in Leiden for his PhD thesis *The European Convention on Human Rights and the European Communities – Towards a Responsibility Regime Relating to the Conduct of International Organisations.* The thesis was awarded the Study Price of the Foundation 'Preamium Erasmianum' in Amsterdam. In the same year he wrote a key note paper, concerning the position of international judgments in the Dutch legal order, for the annual meeting of the Dutch law association.

Professor Guy Lebeer Ph.D. Sociologist, Professor at the Université Libre de Bruxelles, Brussels, Belgium. He has worked for several years on topics related to ethics in medicine. His main research fields: clinical or research ethics committees, euthanasia and palliative care, genetic testing in the workplace, health and safety at work, personal data protection in biomedical research. He is member of the Belgian Advisory Committee of Bioethics and of the Bioethics Commission of the Belgian Human Rights Association.

Professor Robert Lee was Head of the Law School from 1995-1998, and is currently a Co-Director of the ESRC Centre on Business Relationships, Accountability, Sustainability and Society (BRASS). He is an environmental lawyer and an acknowledged expert on contaminated land and on waste management. He is General Editor of Laurence's *Waste Management Law* (Butterworths, 1999). Bob is Chair of the multi-disciplinary Cardiff Foundation of Environmental Research which seeks to generate funding for Environmental Research across all disciplines at Cardiff University. He is editor of *Environmental Law Monthly*, and *Commercial Liability Law Review* as well as the Environmental Editor for the *Journal of Business Law*. His interest in regulatory issues has led to a recent book with Derek Morgan entitled *Human Fertilisation & Embryology – Regulating the Reproductive Revolution* (Blackstone Press, 2001). Bob has spent time in practice with Denton Wilde Sapte and Hammond Suddards Edge. He now works with the Environment, Products and Regulation Group of Freshfields Bruckhaus Deringer, and continues to have an active interest in legal practice. This has led to the publication of a research study on large law firms (*Firm Views: The Work of and Work in Large Law Firms*, Law Society, 1999) and a recent essay on the ethics of staffing policies in such firms ('Up or Out – Means or End' in Thomas, P., *Discriminating Lawyers* (Cavendish, 2000). Bob is a Member of the Training Committee of the Law Society for which he works as both an external examiner and a reporting assessor for institutions offering the Legal Practice Course. He is a Member of the QAA Benchmarking Panel for Law, and the Lord Chancellor's Standing Conference on Legal Education. In the summer of 2001, he spent time in Queensland at Griffith University as a visiting Professor to the Law School.

Professor Ben Mepham is Professor of Applied Bioethics in the School of Biosciences at the University of Nottingham. A former research physiologist, he began teaching bioethics 20 years ago. His text book 'Bioethics for the Biosciences' is due to be published by OUP in Spring 2005. He has been a member of the Government's Biotechnology Commission (AEBC); Executive Director of the Food Ethics Council, which he co-founded in 1998; and is a Board member of the European Society for Agricultural and Food Ethics, of which he was a co-founder in 1999.

Professor Ruud ter Meulen is Director of the Institute for Health Ethics at the University of Maastricht and Director of the Institute for Bioethics in Maastricht. He studied psychology at the Catholic University of Nijmegen and graduated (1988) on the history of the reception of psychology and psychiatry among Catholics in The Netherlands. He has been senior researcher at the Institute for Bioethics since 1989 and Director since 1995. His professorship in health ethics and philosophy started in 1992. His main research areas are ethical issues of resource allocation and health policy, ethical issues of human experimentation, medical ethics committees, autonomy in the care for dependent persons, teaching of ethics, ethical pluralism and the problem of consensus. He has published a large number of articles, chapters and books on issues of justice and solidarity. He was the editor-in-chief of the volume *Solidarity in Health and Social Care in Europe*, published by Kluwer Academic Publishers (2001). Professor Ter Meulen has a large international experience and has directed several European projects. At the moment he is the co-ordinator of the Project Ethical Issues of Evidence Based Practice in Medicine and Health Care (EviBase) (2000-2003), which is financed by the European Commission within the Program Quality of Life and Management of Living Resources of the Fifth Framework Program. This project has resulted in a special issue of *Health Care Analysis* (December 2002) on Ethical issues of EBM in Health Policy.

Dr Peter Mills joined the HFEA staff in 2000 and is currently Policy Development and Co-ordination Manager. Since joining the HFEA he has been Secretary to the

Ethics and Law Committee (formerly the Ethics Committee) and has managed the development of HFEA policies on, among other things, PGD, aneuploidy screening, preimplantation tissue typing, and sex selection.

Dr.polit Hilde Wisløff Nagell is Director of the National Committee for the Social Sciences and the Humanities in Norway (NESH). Nagell has a doctorate in political philosophy. Her particular fields of expertise are research ethics, applied ethics, and ethics and public participation. Her present research project is on the question of responsibility in research. The National Committees for Research Ethics in Norway (www.etikkom.no) are appointed by the Ministry of Education, Research and Church Affairs, and have been active since 1990. The three independent but coordinated national committees for research ethics cover all scientific disciplines: The National Committee for Research Ethics in Science and Technology (NENT), The National Committee for Medical Research Ethics (NEM), and The National Committee for Research Ethics in the Social Sciences and the Humanities (NESH). The committees do not only deal with issues within the more narrowly defined field of research ethics, but include the broader field of the ethics of science. This includes issues of scientific responsibility for larger social concerns, like for instance biotechnology and genetic engineering, information technology, privacy, safety and security issues – risk and safety – environment, sustainability and resource allocation.

Shaun D. Pattinson is a Lecturer in European, Comparative, and International Law at Sheffield University, UK. He has published widely in the area of medical law and ethics, and is the author of *Influencing Traits Before Birth* (Ashgate, 2002).

Professor Ken Peattie is the Director of BRASS, Research Centre for Business Relationships, Accountability, Sustainability and Society, and also a Professor of Marketing and Strategy at Cardiff Business School. He holds a BA in Management and Geography from the University of Leeds, and before becoming an academic, he worked in marketing and systems analysis for an American paper multinational, and as a strategic planner within the UK electronics industry. His research interests include impact of environmental concern on marketing and corporate strategies, corporate social responsibility and social marketing.

Professor Jules Pretty is Director of the Centre for Environment and Society and member of the Department of Biological Sciences at the University of Essex. His books include *Guide to a Green Planet* (edited, 2002), *Agri-Culture: Reconnecting People, Land and Nature* (2002), *The Living Land* (1998), *Regenerating Agriculture* (1995), *Fertile Ground* (1999, co-authored), *The Trainers Guide for Participatory Learning and Action* (1995, co-authored); *The Hidden Harvest* (1992, co-authored); and *Unwelcome Harvest* (1991, co-authored).

He is Deputy-Chair of the government's Advisory Committee on Releases to the Environment (ACRE), and has served on government advisory committees for DEFRA, DFID, the Cabinet Office and DTI. He is a regular speaker, contributor to media, and presenter of the 1999 BBC Radio 4 series *Ploughing Eden* and contributor and writer for the 2001 BBC TV Correspondent programme *The Magic Bean.* He received a 1997 award from the Indian Ecological Society for 'International Contributions to Sustainable and Ecological Agriculture', and was runner-up for the 2002 European Sicco Mansholt Prize for agricultural science.

He was appointed A.D. White Professor-at-Large by Cornell University for six years from 2001. He is a founding member of the Agricultural Reform Group and the Neighbourhood Think Tank, editorial advisor to academic journals, vice-president of Suffolk-ACRE, member of the Institute of Biology and British Agricultural History Society. He was appointed to the International Jury for the Slow Food Award in 2002, and is Chief Editor of the *International Journal of Agricultural Sustainability.*

Dr Gregory Reichberg is Leader of the Ethics, Norms and Identities Programme and a Senior Researcher at the International Peace Research Institute in Oslo. His current research focuses on the ethics of war and peace (with special attention to the just war tradition), international business ethics, and selected themes in medieval philosophy. He is planning and conducting seminars and lectures on international ethics and military ethics and editing (with Henrik Syse) an anthology of classical texts on the ethics of war and peace. He studied philosophy at the University of Toulouse and obtained his Doctorate at Emory University (Atlanta, Georgia). Subsequently he was an Associate Professor at The Catholic University of America (Washington DC) and at Fordham University (New York City).

Dr Sam Salek is a Senior Lecturer and Director of the Centre for Socioeconomic Research at the Welsh School of Pharmacy, University of Wales, Cardiff as well as being the co-director of the internationally recognised UWC/BrAPP Postgraduate Course in Pharmaceutical Medicine. He is a member of a number of management and policy boards including the Centre for Applied Ethics, University of Wales. He is also a member of several national and international professional organisations, including honorary life membership of the British Association of Pharmaceutical Physicians; the Royal College of Physicians of the United Kingdom, Faculty of Pharmaceutical Medicine; and Professor of Pharmacy Practice, School of Pharmacy, Texas Tech University, USA. He speaks regularly at national and international scientific meetings and in the last decade he has given over 70 lectures related to his research areas. His main research interests are the development and clinical applications of health-related quality of life instruments. Examples of his developmental work are: United Kingdom Sickness Impact Profile (UKSIP); Renal Quality of Life Profile (RQLP); Community Dementia Quality of Life Profile (CDQLP); and palliative care specific quality of life instrument, the Cardiff Short Form McGill Quality of Life Questionnaire (MQOL-CFS). His areas of interest also include pharmacoepidemiology, pharmacoeconomics, drug safety evaluation and pharmacovigilance, drug profiling and patient knowledge, communication and patient information need. Dr Salek is author of over 280 journal articles and book chapters, as well as being on the editorial board of the *Journal of Clinical Therapeutics*, the *Journal of Applied Therapeutic Research*, the

Journal of Outcomes Research and the *Journal of Medical Economics*. His books include *The Ethical QALY*, the five volume *Compendium of Quality of Life Instruments, Pharmacoeconomics and Outcome Assessment: A Global Issue, Pharmaceutical Ethics* and *Dilemmas and Solutions in Global Drug Development: Your Questions Answered.*

Peter Sandøe was educated at the University of Copenhagen and at the University of Oxford. From 1992 to 1997 he was Head of the Bioethics Research Group at the University of Copenhagen. He is now Professor in Bioethics at the Royal Veterinary and Agricultural University in Copenhagen and director of the interdisciplinary Centre for Bioethics and Risk Assessment. Since 1992 he has served as Chairman of the Danish Ethical Council for Animals and has been president of the European Society for Agricultural and Food Ethics.

Professor Loane Skene came to the University of Melbourne in 1992 after working as a solicitor in Melbourne and England; and a policy adviser in Canada and Melbourne (10 years with the Victorian Law Reform Commission). She specialises in Health and Medical Law and is a Professor of Law in the Faculty of Law and an Adjunct Professor of Law in the Faculty of Medicine, Dentistry and Health Sciences. She is the author of two books: *Law and Medical Practice: Rights, Duties, Claims and Defences* (Butterworths, 1998); and *You, Your Doctor and the Law* (OUP, 1990). She has also published numerous chapters in books and articles in Australian and overseas legal, medical and scientific journals. Loane has served on many federal and state policy committees, especially in relation to the legal regulation of genetic testing. Her research interests also include the legal regulation of assisted reproductive technology and euthanasia. She is Deputy Director of the Centre for Law and Genetics at the University of Tasmania and the University of Melbourne; and Program Director, Medical Ethics, Centre for Applied Philosophy and Public Ethics (CAPPE), Charles Sturt University and The University of Melbourne. Her other University responsibilities include Deputy Vice-President of the Academic Board of the University and Council member, Queens College.

Elen Stokes graduated from the University of Bristol with an LL.B (Hons) degree in July 2002. In October 2002, she won a scholarship to undertake her Ph.D. at Cardiff Law School. She works in association with the ESRC-funded centre for Business Relations, Accountability, Sustainability and Society (BRASS). Her Ph.D. is supervised by Professor Bob Lee, and her thesis focuses primarily on the role of the precautionary principle in securing responsibility for long-term impacts of environmental decision-making. She is particularly interested in assessing the practical implications of the 'definitional deficit' of the precautionary principle; examining the bearing of risk society literature on the operation of the precautionary principle; and determining the role (potential and actual) of the precautionary principle in the UK BSE episode. More broadly, her thesis has a strong focus on the marginalisation of scientific uncertainty, and the inherent tensions between risk regulation and factual incertitude. She has recently been appointed co-editor of the UK Environmental Law Association (UKELA) *E-Law* journal.

Dr Norman John Vetter is a Reader in the Department of Epidemiology, Statistics and Public Health at the University of Wales College of Medicine and an Honorary Consultant in Public Health Medicine with Bro Taf Health Authority. He is a College of Medicine nominee as a Non Executive Director to North Glamorgan NHS Trust. He has written a number of books on health policy has at various times driven a Mobile Coronary Care Unit, worked with the WHO Smallpox Eradication Campaign and led a Welsh Office research group looking at the needs of elderly people.

Professor Celia Wells has held the post of Professor of Law at Cardiff University since 1995. Her research has mainly focused on criminal law, in particular the criminal liability of corporations (*Corporations and Criminal Responsibility*, OUP, 2nd edition 2001). With Nicola Lacey, she is co-author of *Reconstructing Criminal Law* (Butterworths 2003, 3rd edition), a student text adopting an explicitly feminist perspective. Celia has also published a number of articles in medical law on topics such as maternal-foetal relations and court-ordered caesareans. Through her role as founder of the Women Law Professors Network, she has developed a research interest in women in legal education and recently held the PricewaterhouseCoopers Legal Visiting Chair in Women and Law at the University of Sydney. Celia is a member of the editorial board of the Criminal Law Review and joint editor of Legal Studies. She is a member of the Cardiff University ESRC Centre for Business Relationships, Accountability, Sustainability and Society.

Professor Peter Whittaker served for 23 years as Head of Biology in the National University of Ireland, Maynooth. His main research interest during that period was the molecular genetics of pathogenic fungi. He took early retirement from this position in 2001 to pursue his interest in Bioethics. He is at present a Professorial Fellow at Lancaster University in the Centre for Economic and Social Aspects of Genomics. He is a member of the European Group for Ethics in Science and the New Technologies (which advises the European Commission on ethical aspects of developments in Biotechnology) and is Vice President of the Irish Council for Bioethics.

Stephen Wilkinson (Centre for Professional Ethics) has been at Keele since 1994. He was initially appointed to teach courses in Logic, Philosophy of Mind and Philosophy of Science, but soon became heavily involved in the University's professional ethics programmes and, since 1997, has taught almost exclusively on these. With Eve Garrard, he designed and launched (in 1997) the country's first MA programme in the Ethics of Social Welfare, and directed the development of the UK's first professional doctorate in Medical Ethics (DMedEth) which started in 2002. Stephen's recent research papers have addressed topics including: the allocation of health service resources, the commercialisation of the human body, pre-implantation genetic diagnosis, euthanasia, and the nature of mental illness. A paper on the latter won the 1999 Philosophical Quarterly International Essay Prize. He has just published a book called *Bodies for Sale* (Routledge 2003).

Professor Paul Root Wolpe is currently a Senior Fellow of the Center for Bioethics, and the Director of the Psychiatry and Ethics Program in the Department of Psychiatry, at the University of Pennsylvania, and Chief of Bioethics at the National Aeronautics and Space Administration (NASA).

Born in Charleston, S.C., Wolpe did his undergraduate work at the University of Pennsylvania and earned his Ph.D. in the Sociology of Medicine at Yale University in 1987. Wolpe has been at the University of Pennsylvania since 1987, and spent a four year stint as Director of Research in the Department of Psychiatry at Jefferson Medical College. Wolpe is the author of over 75 articles and chapters, and is the author of one book and editor of another. He is on the Editorial Board of a number of journals, and the Boards of institutions such as the American Society for Bioethics in Israel and the Medical Committee of Planned Parenthood Federation of America. He is also on the Pennsylvania State Ethics Advisory Board.

Acknowledgement

In putting this volume together we would like to acknowledge, first of all, the encouragement and support of Professor Andrew Grubb that led to the creation of the Cardiff Centre for Ethics, Law & Society. We would also like to thank Angela Groom, Kate Reeves and Sarah Kennedy for their help in gathering material and putting this book together.

Jennifer Gunning
Søren Holm

List of Abbreviations

ACRE	Advisory Committee on Releases to the Environment (UK)
AEBC	Agriculture and Environment Biotechnology Committree (UK)
AIDS	Auto-Immune Deficiency Syndrome
ALRC	Australian Law Reform Commission
ASPECT	Analysis of Spatial Planning and Emerging Communication Technologies
ATCA	Alien Tort Claims Act
BMA	British Medical Association
BRASS	Centre on Business Relationships, Accountability, Sustainability and Society
BSE	Bovine Spongiform Encephalopathy
CAP	Common Agricultural Policy (EU)
CAPPE	Centre for Applied Philosophy and Public Ethics (Melbourne)
CCELS	Cardiff Centre for Ethics, Law & Society
ccTLD	country code Top Level Domain
CDQLP	Community Dementia Quality of Life Profile
CeBRA	Danish Centre for Bioethics and Risk Assessment
CEC	Clinical Ethics Committee
CFC	Chlorofluorocarbon
CISCHR	Centre for the International Study of Cyberethics and Human Rights
CNR	Cell Nuclear Replacement
CT	Computerized Tomography
DBA	Diamond-Blackfan Anemia
DEFRA	Department of the Environment, Food and Rural Affairs (UK)
DFID	Department for International Development (UK)
DG SANCO	European Commission Directorate General for Health and Consumer Protection
DNA	Deoxyribonucleic Acid
DTI	Department of Trade and Industry (UK)
EBM	Evidence Based Medicine Evidence Based Medicine
ECHR	European Convention on Human Rights
ECJ	Court of Justice of the European Communities
EFSA	European Food Safety Agency
ELSA	Ethical Legal and Social Aspects
ERDF	European Rural Development Fund

ES cells	Embryonic Stem cells
ESRC	Economics and Social Research Council
EU	European Union
FAIP	Farm Animal Industrial Platform
FMRI	Functional Magnetic Resonance Imaging
FT	*Financial Times*
GDP	Gross Domestic Product
GM	Genetic Modification/Genetically Modified
GMO	Genetically Modified Organism
GSK	GlaxoSmith Kline
HCFC	Hydrochlorofluorocarbon
HFEA	Human Fertilisation and Embryology Authority
HGC	Human Genetics Commission(UK)
ICANN	Internet Corporation for Assigned Names and Numbers
ICC	International Criminal Court
ICT	Information and Communication Technologies
IMF	International Monetary Fund
INSALUD	Spanish National Institute of Health
IPCC	International Panel on Climate Change
ITU	International Telecommunications Union
IUCN	World Conservation Union
IVF	In Vitro Fertilization
KVL	Danish Royal Veterinary and Agricultural University
MARAN	Multi-Agency Rural Area Network
MGM	Metro-Goldwyn-Meyer
MNC	Multi-National Corporation
MQOL-CFS	Cardiff Short Form McGill Quality of Life Questionnaire
MRI	Magnetic Resonance Imaging
NASA	National Aeronautics and Space Administration
NATO	North Atlantic Treaty Organization
NESH	Norwegian National Committee for the Social Sciences and Humanities
NGO	Non-Governmental Organization
NHS	National Health Service (UK)
NICE	National Institute for Clinicl Excellence (UK)
OECD	Organization for Economic Co-operation and Development
Oftel	UK regulator of the communications industries (now Ofcom)
OHE	Office of Health Economics
OPCS	Office for Public Censuses and Surveys (UK)
PET	Positron Emission Tomography
PGD	Preimplantation Genetic Diagnosis
QALY	Quality Adjusted Life Year
RCT	Randomized Controlled Clinical Trial
RQLP	Renal Quality of Life Profile

SARS	Severe Acute Respiratory Syndrome
SC	Security Council of the United Nations
SCAN	Scientific Committee for Animal Nutrition
SCNT	Somatic Cell Nuclear Transfer
TB	Tuberculosis
TEU	Treaty of the European Union
TIERRAS	Telematics Applications Programme
TMS	Transcranial Magnetic Stimulation
UKELA	United Kingdon Environmental Law Association
UKSIP	United Kingdom Sickness Impact Profile
UNCED	United Nations Conference on Environment and Development
UNESCO	United Nations Educational, Scientific and Cultural Organisation
WCED	World Commission on Environmental Development
WHO	World Health Organization
WMD	Weapons of Mass Destruction
WSIS	World Summit on the Information Society
WTO	World Trade Organization

INTRODUCTION

Chapter 1

Introduction

Jennifer Gunning and Søren Holm

Ethics as a discipline has begun to escape the theoretical domains of philosophy and to pervade many fields of activity both academic and professional. This broadening ethical perspective began with the growth of medical ethics in the 1970s, and accelerated with the rapid advances in the biomedical and genetic technologies in the 1980s. Assisted reproductive technologies and genetic modification raised the level of discussion about humans, humanity, biodiversity and the environment. Sustainable rather than intensive development became a more common objective and the Precautionary Principle has become enshrined in a number of international treaties, starting with the Rio Declaration of 1992.

Following a number of environmental and financial disasters involving large or multinational corporations business ethics and corporate social responsibility have taken a higher profile, and have moved from academia to the board room. The issue of Human Rights has also grown in prominence with the UK eventually enacting its own Human Rights legislation in 1998. But Human Rights problems remain with regard to minority groups, refugees, deprived sectors of society and in many areas of everyday societal activity.

Finally, research ethics has become more prominent not just in medicine and the sciences but also in the social sciences and humanities. Nonetheless, elements of the research community remain skeptical of ethical scrutiny seeing the involvement of ethicists as inviting 'a spy on the shoulder' rather than as valuable research colleagues. But ethics has become an interdisciplinary field. Scratch an ethicist and you will often find underneath a former scientist, clinician, economist or lawyer, for instance. Many of those working in ethics truly span the divide between the arts and the sciences.

In the light of all this, Cardiff Centre for Ethics, Law & Society (CCELS) was established in 2003 to provide an interdisciplinary resource for those interested in ethics and, in particular, with a view of stimulating real collaboration on investigating ethical issues between people coming from different fields of interest. The Centre's aims are

- to foster interdisciplinary collaboration under the three themes of Bioethics, Ethics & Society and Business & Professional Ethics;

- to provide a resource for researchers seeking partners to address the ethical, social and legal aspects of their work;
- to provide a resource for policy makers seeking expert advice;
- to provide a forum for discussion of topical ethical, social and legal issues;
- to provide a resource which is both useful and attractive to academics, professionals, policy makers and citizens;
- to provide an educational resource.

Principally, CCELS operates as a virtual centre and, as part of meeting these aims, tries to publish on line original papers and commentaries about topical ethical issues. However, we consider it important that, as on line contributions are progressively archived, these papers should be made more widely available as a published series of volumes.

This first volume of Ethics, Law and Society represents a selection of papers and commentaries which have appeared on the website during the first year of CCELS together with a selection of papers which were presented at the first CCELS conference held in Cardiff in June 2004. The papers pre-published on line have been revised, where appropriate, to bring them up to date for publication in this volume. The conference papers appear here for the first time. The commentaries, which are short opinion pieces, appear in the final part of the book and were written in response to ethical issues which hit the news in one way or another and they are dated to indicate their topicality.

The papers that have been included in this volume have been grouped thematically. Part I, Bioethics, groups together papers addressing issues arising in biomedical and medical ethics. These range from issues at the cutting edge of assisted reproductive technologies to the role of clinical ethics committees. Part II, Ethics and Society, looks at broader societal issues particularly those relating to sustainability and the environment. The chapter on Food Ethics develops an ethical matrix which allows analysis of the impacts of any production system from a number of different perspectives. Other chapters address issues in business ethics and access to ICT. Part III, is devoted to issues of human rights in current global contexts.

Finally, Part IV brings together the commentaries which address news items arising during 2003. These cover a wide range of ethical issues including the legitimacy of the war in Iraq; the right to physician assisted suicide (following from the Reginald Crewe and Diane Pretty cases in the UK); the right to select tissue matched offspring to act as donors to sick siblings (following the Whitaker and Hashmi cases in the UK) and the separation of conjoined twins (of which there were two controversial cases in 2003). Although responses to topical events, the commentary in these papers remains valid.

The aim of this series is to provide a resource in ethics which will engage the attention of those working in number of fields as practitioners or academics. We hope that this volume will provide interest and enlightenment to those seeking to engage in ethics not only in their own disciplines but more broadly.

Jennifer Gunning
Søren Holm

PART I
BIOETHICS

Chapter 2

Therapeutic and Reproductive Cloning - A Scientific Perspective

Richard Gardner

Introduction

Few scientists and clinicians have publicly voiced dissent from the view that reproductive cloning in the human should not be undertaken at the present time. While many within these communities share similar ethical concerns to other professionals and to the public, their call for a moratorium, or even an outright ban, of this mode of cloning is motivated primarily by unresolved issues of risk that have become apparent through its application to other mammals. Nevertheless, statements of intent to clone humans, and even claims to have succeeded in this endeavour, have been made recently, but invariably through the media rather than the scientific press. The originators of such statements have not exposed to peer-review either their justification for embarking on human cloning at this juncture or, indeed, evidence of their competence to undertake it. In a very recent claim by a representative of Clonaid that cloned babies have been born, the work was said to have been done on its behalf by appropriately qualified people who wished to remain anonymous. If true, it implies that scientists and, particularly clinicians, are prepared to engage in practices with which they are unwilling to identify themselves. This is hardly likely to dispel growing public disquiet about the extent to which doctors and scientists can be trusted to act responsibly.

The lamentable state of secrecy regarding reproductive cloning contrasts starkly with the development of in vitro fertilisation (IVF) as a treatment for infertility. Here, through numerous articles in the popular press, Robert Edwards made strenuous efforts to inform the public about what he hoped to achieve and why, thereby stimulating sustained and sometimes acrimonious public debate. Such efforts began even before Edwards and his colleagues provided the first unequivocal evidence of vitro fertilisation in the human via a peer-reviewed publication in a respectable scientific journal (Edwards et al., 1969). Thereafter, both advances and reverses in the efforts to bring this technology to the stage of clinical application were fully documented in the scientific literature.

Relevant Scientific Developments

Before focusing on specific concerns relating to human cloning, it is appropriate briefly to consider the three different strands of scientific investigation that have made the application of this technology to the human possible. The first was the development of human IVF which, aside from offering entirely new approaches for treating infertility, rendered human gametes and early stages of development accessible to observation and experimentation. As noted earlier, the initial key step was the demonstration in 1969 by Edwards and colleagues that normal fertilisation of human eggs could be achieved outside the body (Edwards et al., 1969). This was followed less than 10 years later by the successful culture of such fertilised eggs through early cleavage and their replacement in the womb to produce normal healthy children. Subsequently, and particularly pertinently, improvements in the culture of IVF conceptuses enabled their continued development without loss of viability to the so-called blastocyst stage.

The second strand originated with the demonstration in the mouse that the growth of a cluster of uncommitted cells present in the early mammalian conceptus could be uncoupled from their further specialisation to produce indefinitely sustainable cultures of what have come to be known as embryonic stem (ES) cells (Evans and Kaufman, 1981). This meant that it was possible to maintain in vitro in large numbers cells that have the potential to form all the specialised types of cell of which the adult body is composed. Unaccountably, the concept of using cells from early human conceptuses for therapeutic purposes took a long time to gain momentum. It unquestionably originated with Robert Edwards who first mentioned it in a popular account of the development of human IVF (Edwards and Steptoe, 1980). Two years later, he raised this prospect more explicitly in the proceedings of a conference in which he discussed two options that were open at the time (Edwards, 1982). The first was to obtain organized postimplantation development of human IVF conceptuses in vitro to a stage when organ primordia would be available for transplantation. This option was, of course, closed in the United Kingdom with the introduction of the Human Fertilisation and Embryology Act (1990) that limited growth in vitro of human conceptuses to 14 days or to the stage of formation of the primitive streak, which marks the onset of development of the fetus as opposed to its investing membranes. The other option, prompted by Edwards' own much earlier work (reviewed in Gardner, 2002) and the then very recent success of Evans and Kaufman (1981) in obtaining ES cells from mice, was to derive cell lines from preimplantation stages that could be made to undergo the desired differentiation in vitro. It is curious that it took a further 15 years or so for the notion of embryonic stem cell therapy to be embraced by the biomedical community. Consequently, derivation of the first human ES lines was not reported until 1998 (Thomson et al., 1998).

The roots of the third strand lay in experiments started in amphibians in the late 1940s to address a fundamental question about the nature of cellular differentiation, namely whether genes that are not active in specialised cells are nonetheless all retained in a potentially functional state. However, contrary to the impression given in many texts books, no adult frog was ever obtained using nuclei from adult as opposed to larval cells. Similar studies were initiated in mammals in the 1970s culminating in 1996 in the birth of Dolly the sheep which was reported the following year (Wilmut et al., 1997). The important point about the Dolly experiment, once doubts about the provenance of the nuclear donor cell were eventually settled (Signer et al., 1998), was that it showed that when injected into unfertilised eggs deprived of their own complement of genes, nuclei from adult mammalian cells could support development through to adulthood.

Embryonic Versus Adult Stem Cells?

The notion of using ES cell for therapeutic purposes had hardly captured the enthusiasm of the biomedical community before an unsuspected complexity emerged. First there was a trickle and then a spate of papers suggesting that cells from a variety of adult tissues retain much wider options for differentiation than had been assumed hitherto. In most cases the work is still at the stage of intriguing phenomenology, so its significance remains difficult to assess. However, there are now some well documented examples of plasticity and interconvertibility of adult cells which have prompted claims that use of human blastocysts to derive lines of ES cell can no longer be justified. Many promoting this viewpoint have exaggerated the virtues of adult stem cells to an extent that has engendered alarm or dismay among scientists whose work they cite in support of it. Since it is likely that ES cells will be found to be more appropriate for some therapeutic uses and adult cells for others, there is a pressing need for a dispassionate appraisal of the merits and drawbacks of both. Cord blood, especially, merits concerted study as a relatively non-contentious source of stem cells that would offer the greatest scope for precise tissue matching. However, this depends critically on defining conditions that would enable its stem cells to be grown in vitro.

Particularly using spare human blastocysts and cord blood, the prospect can be envisaged of establishing banks of tissue-typed, virus free, stem cells in anticipation of patients needs. Depending on the size of such banks, and hence the genetic diversity they encompass, more or less good tissue matching would be achievable. However, while this might reduce need for immunosuppression of graft recipients, it would not obviate it altogether. A strategy which would, in principle, consistently yield a perfect match between graft and patient entails combining the 'Dolly' and 'ES cell' technologies. This strategy, which has come to be known rather prematurely as 'therapeutic cloning', entails transplanting nuclei from cells of patients into eggs whose own genes had been removed, and then activating the eggs to initiate development in culture. Those developing to the blastocyst stage would then be converted into cell cultures appropriate for the derivation of ES cells. The resulting ES cells, which would in essence be genetically identical to the patient, could then be directed to form whatever type of specialised cell or tissue the patient required. This strategy is obviously not appropriate for patients whose need for stem cell therapy is a direct consequence of genetic disease since in such circumstances it would be vital to ensure that the donor cells did not carry the gene defect in question.

Is Therapeutic Cloning a Realistic Option?

Short-term nuclear transfer is unquestionably a valuable way of gaining insight into how the reprogramming of gene expression may be achieved. What remains a more contentious issue within the biomedical research community is whether therapeutic cloning will prove to be a viable procedure clinically. Here, various issues have served to fuel the debate. Prominent among these is its low efficiency and consequent doubt as to whether, especially in view of the competing demand for egg donation in infertility treatment, an adequate supply of human eggs can be guaranteed. By capitalising on work in cattle, maturing oocytes from biopsied or post-mortem ovarian tissue may provide a way of enhancing their supply. Furthermore, introduction of technical refinements to the procedure is also likely to yield some improvement in its efficiency, though whether this will be sufficient to make it practicable is still a matter of conjecture. Even so, the technical complexity of therapeutic cloning is likely to militate against its being adopted widely in clinical practice. Moreover, the consistent occurrence of anomalous development in studies on reproductive cloning in animals inevitably raises concern as to whether ES cells produced via cloning would be safe to graft into patients. Here, opinion is rather sharply divided with some feeling that the perceived risks are likely to prove unfounded (Gurdon and Colman, 1999; Byrne and Gurdon, 2002), and others arguing that they are very real (Jaenisch and Wilmut, 2001). Hence, the question whether transfer of nuclei to eggs will simply remain a valuable research tool or find clinical application cannot be answered at present. If the former, there would be little reason to use precious human eggs as opposed to those from animals for undertaking basic studies on what the reprogramming of nuclei entails. Once an understanding had emerged from animal studies, there would be a case for limited work on human material to confirm the extent to which the findings apply to our own species. A safeguard that operates in the United Kingdom to ensure that human material is not used frivolously is that the relevant statutory body, the Human Fertilisation and Embryology Authority, is empowered to authorise research on human gametes and embryos only where it is persuaded that there is no alternative.

Reproductive Cloning in Man

From a technical point of view, therapeutic and reproductive cloning differ only in the way in which the resulting embryos are treated, namely whether they converted to a tissue culture or transplanted intact to the womb. Thus an obvious concern is whether permitting therapeutic cloning, as the UK Government has done recently, will make reproductive cloning more likely. It will certainly do so in the sense of generating the know-how necessary for improving the efficiency of obtaining healthy cloned conceptuses. And, of course, since such technical advances are normally published in the open scientific literature, this information will be just as freely available in countries that do not have relevant legislative controls as in those that do.

The reason why the Royal Society advocated a global moratorium on human reproductive cloning rather than outright prohibition is that a full and open discussion of the issues that it raises might lead to recognition of circumstances in which its use was considered appropriate. Among these issues there were particular concerns arising from experience of reproductive cloning in other mammals regarding its safety. So far, however, those who claim to have already embarked on human reproductive have shown little inclination to expose to public scrutiny either their reasons for doing so or what measures they have used to address the perceived risks. It is this that prompted the Royal Society to issue a statement focusing on 10 questions that are pertinent for evaluating both the credibility and the acceptability of claims of human reproductive cloning (Royal Society, 2002). These questions were not confined purely to scientific matters such as what tests had been carried out to establish that it was safe to transfer cloned embryos to the womb, but include more general concerns such as whether informed consent and ethical approval had been obtained.

The high rates of attrition and of malformation seen in mammalian reproductive cloning are generally thought to be due to perturbations in modifications to genes which, unlike mutations, are limited to the life cycle of an individual. These modifications, which are vital for the normal development and functioning of the body, are termed 'epigenetic' in recognition of the fact that they are not normally heritable from one generation to the next. One such epigenetic modification is imprinting which involves stable silencing of the maternally-inherited copy of some genes and the paternally-inherited copy of others. Several imprinted genes have been implicated in control of growth and large offspring syndrome is a common feature of reproductive cloning, at least in larger domestic mammals. Hence perturbations in imprinting are widely regarded as a likely cause of at least some of the anomalies that are common in cloned embryos and offspring. In some species, the 'large offspring syndrome' has also been reported following culture of embryos produced by fertilisation. This suggests that sub-optimal conditions of culture per se may affect gene imprinting, and evidence for perturbed expression of an imprinted gene has been found in these circumstances (Young et al., 2001). However, since the incidence of this syndrome is raised by cloning, it cannot be accounted for entirely by the need to culture cloned embryos in vitro. Nevertheless, it has been argued that the human may be less susceptible than animals to anomalies associated with reproductive cloning on two counts (Byrne and Gurdon, 2002). First, that media devised for culture of human conceptuses may be superior to those for conceptuses of other species. Second, one gene implicated in growth control that is imprinted in Rodentia and Artiodactyla is not imprinted in the human (Killian et al., 2001). There is, nonetheless, growing evidence for a link between in vitro assisted reproduction and perturbed imprinting in the human (RBM Online, 2003). Moreover, while the mouse, for which even more optimisation of culture conditions has been achieved than in the human (Summers et al., 1995, 2000), does not show large offspring syndrome, it nevertheless exhibits various anomalies following cloning that have not as yet been linked to perturbed imprinting (Tanaka et al., 2001). Furthermore, the most pervasive feature of reproductive cloning in animals is abnormality of the placenta with respect to both its morphological development and pattern of gene expression (e.g. Hill et al., 2000; De Sousa et al., 2001; Ono et al., 2001; Humpherys et al., 2002). Given that the human seems uniquely prone to derangements of placental trophoblastic growth that can manifest as frank malignancy (Gardner, 1983), there are grounds for concern that reproductive cloning may pose a particular risk to women carrying cloned embryos. Hence, even studies on non-human higher primates might not provide an accurate indicator of what to expect in the human. So far, cloned offspring have been obtained in the rhesus monkey only with nuclei from cells of very early embryos (Meng et al., 1997; Wolf et al., 1999). Moreover, given the exorbitant cost of purchasing and maintaining higher primates and growing public disquiet about using them in research, harnessing such animals for cloning studies that are extensive enough to furnish definitive results may well be unrealistic.

Why Clone Humans?

Finally, it is worth briefly considering reasons that have been given for embarking on human reproductive cloning. One is replacing a dead child. Here, considerable thought needs to be given to what one is seeking to achieve thereby. While the clone would probably bear a striking resemblance to the original physically, it would not do so in other important respects such as personality (Gardner, 1998). This is likely to engender unfulfilled expectations that could complicate or even blight relationships. Another justification is to enable people suffering from infertility due to the complete absence of eggs or sperm to produce offspring. In this case it would be very important to know the reason for their infertility. Animal studies have revealed an increasing number of genes whose mutation results in complete absence of mature germ cells. Cloning of humans whose sterility was due to a gene defect would result in the production of offspring which could themselves only reproduce by cloning, and would thereby form distinct lineages that were isolated reproductively from the rest of mankind.

Except for those resulting from spontaneous division of embryos to yield identical twins, we have all enjoyed a unique shuffling of our parental genes and it is this that accounts for our immeasurable diversity. Reproductive cloning entails imposing the genetic constitution of an existing individual on one or more future individuals. Since this is a much more intrusive application of genetics to medicine than has been attempted hitherto, it should not be contemplated until the many issues it raises have been properly addressed.

Acknowledgements

I wish to thank Professor Kenneth Bagshawe for helpful discussion and both the Royal Society and Wellcome Trust for support.

References

Byrne, J.A. and Gurdon, J.B. (2002), Commentary on Cloning, *Differentiation 69*, 154-157.

De Sousa, P.A., King, T., Harkness, L., Young, L.E., Walker, S.K. and Wilmut, I. (2001) Evaluation of Gestational Deficiencies in Cloned Sheep Foetuses and Placentae, *Biol. Reprod.* 65, 23-30.

Edwards, R.G. (1982), The Case for Studying Human Embryos and their Constituent Tissues in Vitro, *In Human Conception in Vitro*, (Ed. R.G. Edwards and J.M. Purdy), pp. 371-388. Academic Press: London.

Edwards, R.G. and Steptoe, P.C. (1980), A Matter of Life, Hutchinson: London.

Edwards, R.G., Bavister, B.D. and Steptoe, P.C. (1969), Early Stages of Fertilisation in Vitro of Human Oocytes Matured in Vitro. *Nature 221*, 632-635.

Evans, M.J. and Kaufman, M.H. (1981), Establishment in Culture of Pluripotential Cells from Mouse Embryos, *Nature 292*, 154-156.

Gardner, R.L. (1983), Origin and Differentiation of Extraembryonic Tissues in the Mouse, *Int. Rev. Exp. Path*, 24, 63-133.

Gardner, R.L. (1998), Cloning and Individuality, In 1998 *Oxford Amnesty Lectures: The Genetic Revolution and Human Rights*, (Ed. J. Burley), pp. 29-37, *Chicago University Press*, Chicago.

Gardner, R.L. (2002), Stem Cells: Potency, Plasticity and Public Perception. J. Anat. 200, 277-282.

Gurdon, J.B. and Colman, A (1999), The Future of Cloning, *Nature 402*, 743-746.

Hill, J.R., Burghardt, R.C., Jones, K., Long, C.R., Looney, C.R., Shin, T., Spencer, T.E., Thompson, J.A., Winger, Q.A. and Westusin, M.E. (2000), Evidence for Placental Abnormality as a Major Cause of Mortality in First-Trimester Somatic Cell Cloned Bovine Foetuses, *Biol. Reprod*, 63, 1787-1794.

Humpherys, D., Eggan, K., Akutsu, H., Friedman, A., Hochedlinger, K., Yanagimaachi, R., Lander, E.S., Golub, T.R. and Jaenisch, R. (2002), Abnormal Gene Expression in Cloned Mice Derived from Embryonic Stem Cell and Cumulus Cell Nuclei, *Proc. Natl Acad. Sci. USA 99*, 12889-12894.

Jaenisch, R. and Wilmut, I (2001), Developmental Biology, Don't Clone Humans! *Science 291*, 2552.

Killian, J.K., Nolan, C.M., Wylie, A.A., li, T., Vu, T.H., Hoffman, A.R. and Jirtle, R.L. (2001), Divergent Evolution on M6P/IGF2R Imprinting from the Jurassic to the Quaternary, *Hum. Mol. Genet.10*, 1721-1728.

Meng, L, Stouffer, R.L. and Wolf, D.P. (1997), Rhesus Monkeys Produced by Nuclear Transfer. *Biol. Reprod*, 57, 454-459.

Ono, Y., Shimozawa, N., Ito, M. and Kono, T (2001), Cloned Mice from Foetal Fibroblast Cells Arrested at Metaphase by Serial Nuclear Transfer. Biol. Reprod. 64, 44-50.

RBM Online (17 January 2003).

Royal Society (2002), Royal Society Checklist to Assess Claims about Human Reproductive Cloning, Media Release 31 December 2002.

Signer, E.N., Dubrova, Y.E., Jeffreys, A.J., Wilde, C., Finch, L.M.B., Wells, M., Peaker, M. (1998), DNA Fingerprinting Dolly, *Nature 394*, 329-330.

Summers, M.C., Bhatnagar, P.R., Lawitts, J.A., Raffin, M. and Biggers, J.D. (1995) Fertilisation of Mouse Ova from Inbred and Outbred Strains: Complete Preimplantation Embryo Development in a Glucose-Supplemented KSOM Medium, *Biol. Reprod. 53*, 431-437.

Summers, M.C., McGinnis, L.K., Lawitts, J.A., Raffin, M. and Biggers, J.D. (2000), IVF of Mouse Ova in a Simplex Optimised Medium Supplemented with Amino Acids, *Hum. Rep,. 15*, 1791-1801.

Tanaka, S., Oda, M., Toyoshima, Y., Wakayama, T., Tanaka, M., Yoshida, N., Hattori, N., Ohgane, J., Yanagamachi, R. and Hiota, K. (2001), Placentomegaly in Cloned Mouse Concepti Caused by Expansion of the Spongiotrophoblast Layer, *Biol. Repro,. 65*, 1813-1821.

Thomson, J.A., Iskovitz-Eldor, J., Shapiro, S.S., Waknitz,, M.A., Swiergiel, J.J., Marshall, V.S. and Jones, J.M. (1998), Embryonic Stem Cell Lines from Human Blastocysts, *Science 282*, 1145-1147.

Wilmut, I., Schnieke, A.E., Mc Whir, J., Kind, A.J. and Campbell, K.H. (1997), Viable Offspring Derived from Foetal and Adult Mammalian Cells, *Nature 385*, 810-813.

Wolf, D.P., Meng, L., Ouhibi, N., Zelinski-Wooten, M. (1999), Nuclear Transfer in the Rhesus Monkey: Practical and Basic Implications, *Biol. Reprod*, 60, 199-204.

Young, L.E., Fernandes, K., McEvoy, T.G., Butterworth, S.C., Gutierrez, C.G., Carolan, C., Broadbent, P.J., Robinson, J.J., Wilmut, I. and Sinclair, K.D. (2001), Epigenetic Change in IGF2R is Associated with Foetal Overgrowth after Sheep Embryo Culture, *Nature Genet*, 27, 153-154.

Chapter 3

Stem Cells, Patents and Ethics

Peter Whittaker

If we are to believe everything that medical scientists and cell biologists are telling us, stem cell research heralds a major revolution in medical therapy for many diseases and injuries. These include Parkinson's Disease, Alzheimer's Disease, diabetes, heart disease, diseases of the immune system and spinal injuries. Stem cells can be thought of as an elixir for the 21st century. They promise cures for so many different ailments but there is very little concrete evidence at this stage that they are going to work. Nevertheless, commercial interests clearly believe that stem cells are going to be 'big'. Where there is major commercial potential, we find a requirement for patents to protect the interests of companies that develop the associated technology.

Just how acceptable are stem cell patents? In this respect there are many questions that we might ask. Some of these questions, such as the ethical acceptability of patenting living cells, in particular living human cells, have been left behind as patenting such cultured cells is now so well established a practice that it would be almost impossible to turn back.

This paper considers the acceptability of patents involving stem cells and particularly human stem cells that require the destruction of embryos for their production. The paper presents.

a) A little background information on stem cells as a basis for the patenting discussion. This will include mention of the various types of human stem cells and the different ways in which they can differentiate.
b) Something on the various types of patents that have been sought and may be sought in the future.
c) A reminder of what a patent is – and what it is not.
d) A mention of the European Biotechnology Directive of 1998 and its relation to the patenting of human stem cells, particular reference being made to the ethical exclusions from patentability in Europe.

Human stem cells can be derived from 3 main sources, from early embryos, from aborted foetuses and from adult tissues.

Embryonic stem cells are isolated from the early embryo stage known as the blastocyst. At the present time this can only be achieved with the concomitant destruction of the embryo although it is possible that it might, in the future, become possible to remove the stem cell precursors without destruction of the embryo. The blastocyst embryos that are used for stem cell isolation can be grown in vitro from embryos produced by IVF. These are generally embryos that are surplus to requirements for reproductive use (supernumerary embryos) but may also be produced especially for stem cell derivation.

The blastocyst embryos may also be grown from embryos produced by the process known as somatic cell nuclear transfer (SCNT) – the technique used in producing Dolly the sheep. In this the nucleus of a mature cell is removed and inserted into an egg cell from which the nucleus has been removed.

In principle at least, embryonic stem cells can be directed to differentiate into any type of body cell – that is, they are pluripotent.

Aborted foetuses are potential sources of several types of stem cell. The most widely used are embryonic germ cells isolated from the developing gonadal tissues of the foetus and neural stem cells, which can be isolated from foetal brain and are under investigation as possible treatment for Parkinson's Disease. Embryonic Germ Cells are pluripotent but neural stem cells are multipotent – they have lost some of their differentiation potential and can only give rise to a limited range of neural cell types.

Umbilical cord blood is a source of multipotent blood cell forming stem cells. It is now possible to store a new born baby's umbilical cord blood with intention of using this as a source of stem cells for treatment should the baby, or later the child, develop diseases such as leukaemia. Several companies have been set up to provide this service on a for profit basis.

Many types of stem cells can be isolated from adult tissues. In this context adults would include children and even newly dead persons. It may become possible in the future to become a stem cell donor post mortem. Adult stem cells are generally multipotent or unipotent – able to give rise to only one type of cell. There have been reports however of small numbers of pluripotent stem cells in adult bone marrow although this is far from widely accepted.

An important feature of stem cells is their ability to differentiate into the various types of mature cell found in the human body. At the present, any therapy would require that the stem cells undergo differentiation before they are transplanted because of the danger of unrestricted growth of undifferentiated stem cells. Scientists are only just beginning to understand the techniques necessary to encourage cells along particular differentiation routes.

In addition to the process of differentiation, it is also possible that differentiated stem cells may be able to undergo: Retrodifferentiation (or dedifferentiation) where stem cells may regress to a higher level of potency (e.g. multipotent cells becoming pluripotent). Transdifferentiation where differentiated stem cells of one type might give rise to stem cells of a different type (e.g. neural to blood).

With respect to stem cells, patenting may involve either products (stem cells themselves) or processes involved in their isolation, culture or modification. Stem cell patents could be for newly isolated stem cells, undifferentiated stem cell lines, differentiated stem cell lines or genetically modified stem cell lines.

Patents for stem cell processes could involve:

- Enrichment of stem cells – stem cells isolated from foetal or adult tissues are usually contaminated by the presence of other types of cell.
- Culturing stem cells – newly isolated stem cells will require a particular culture regime for them to be useful.
- Genetic modification of stem cells – for stem cell cultures to be useful it may be necessary to modify the genetic characteristics of the cells for example to make them less likely to be rejected by the immune system of a recipient.
- Differentiation of stem cells – to modify the cells to affect a particular therapy.
- Retrodifferentiation or Transdifferentiation – to improve the range of types of cells which can be obtained from a particular stem cell line.
- SCNT (somatic cell nuclear transfer) for stem cell production to produce stem cells immunologically-identical to those of the potential recipient.
- Non-embryo processes for making stem cells – attempts are being made to produce pluripotent stem cells using a variety of techniques that do not require embryo destruction.

Patenting of stem cell processes and products is well underway. There are about 200 patents granted to date involving embryonic stem cells but only about 10 of these refer to human stem cells. There have been 3 or 4 times this number of patent applications filed.

There are four requirements for a patent, which are agreed more or less world-wide:

- Novelty. The invention must be something that was not available before the patent application was made.
- Inventiveness. The invention should not be obvious to someone familiar with the particular field.
- Industrial applicability. The invention should have an industrial application. Medicine is included as an industrial application.
- Adequate disclosure. The application must contain sufficient detail of the invention that a person skilled in the art should be able to reproduce it.

A patent is an agreement to limit commercial exploitation of an invention to the inventor for a fixed period of time in exchange for publication of details of the invention. It is important to remember that a patent is not a permission to exploit an invention. The inventor may commercially exploit the invention even if a patent is not awarded. It is just that he or she does not have legal protection from exploitation by competitors.

As mentioned earlier, all patents relating to human pluripotent stem cells to date have been from the USA. These include product patents on embryonic stem cells and embryonic germ cells and some processes associated with these. The award in Europe of patents associated with stem cells has been slowed down at least in part because of the ethical exclusion from patentability incorporated into the European Biotechnology Directive of 1998. Article 6 of the European Biotechnology Directive requires the exclusion from patenting of inventions that were 'contrary to ordre public or morality'. This article reflected Article 53 of the European Patent Convention of 1973, which established the European Patent Office.

Article 6 of the European Biotechnology Directive went further than the European Patent Convention in specifying certain inventions, which should not be patentable. These were:

- Processes for cloning human beings.
- Processes for modifying the germ line identity of human beings.
- Uses of human embryos for industrial or commercial purposes.
- Processes for modifying the genetic identity of animals, which are likely to cause them suffering without any substantial medical benefit to man or animal and also animals resulting from such processes.

It was clear from the explanatory documentation provided with the Directive that this list was not the last word. Recital 38 of this stressed that the list was 'to provide national courts and patent offices with a general guide to interpreting the reference to order public and morality ..... and obviously cannot presume to be exhaustive'.

It may or may not have been prudent for the European Parliament to include this ethical exclusion in the Directive but it does mean that the Patent Offices and Courts of the EU states have to work within its framework. Strictly speaking the list of exclusions need not apply to the European Patent Office as this is not an EU institution. Nevertheless the European Patent Office is constrained by the European Patent Convention, which has a similar exclusion if only presented in broad terms.

It is questionable whether it was appropriate to have this ethical exclusion in a situation where withholding a patent does not prevent commercial exploitation. The ethical exclusion could certainly handicap EU countries in the development of stem cell medicine. How are developments in embryonic stem cell research affected by the patent exclusions? Let us first look at the human cloning exclusion. There are important reasons for developing what has been referred to as 'therapeutic cloning'. In this a nucleus from a cell of the patient to be treated is inserted into an enucleated egg cell. The 'pseudoembryo' so formed may be caused to divide to the blastocyst stage from which a stem cell line may be isolated. The importance of this is that the stem cell line may be used to treat the patient without the risk of rejection inherent in the use of stem cell lines derived from IVF embryos. The problem is that the first steps in this process are identical to what would be done (and may already have been done) for reproductive cloning. Consequently, research in therapeutic cloning might be paving the way for developments in reproductive cloning. Does this contravene the ethical exclusion on cloning? One view would be that it is rather like arguing that we should not patent a new type of camera because it might be used in the production of pornographic images.

The second exclusion that might impact on human stem cell research relates to the industrial use or commercialisation of human embryos. Does the production of embryonic stem cell lines from human embryos constitute commercialisation of human embryos? Clearly, if someone were to invent a technique for using embryos directly to produce a commercial product (e.g. an anti-cancer drug,) no one could deny that this would represent the commercialisation of human embryos. In the case of embryonic stem cells, an embryo is being destroyed to produce a stem cell line that could, following a process of differentiation, be used to cure or alleviate an illness of some kind. Here the commercialisation of embryos is less clear. Sight cannot be lost, however, of the fact that embryos, no matter how produced, represent potential human beings and should be afforded an appropriate respect. Whilst it might be suggested that the use of an embryo to provide stem cells is ethically more acceptable than non-productive destruction of an embryo, it could also be argued that it would be better to nudge research in the direction of adult stem cells in order to circumvent the ethical questions surrounding the production of embryonic stem cell lines.

Overall it was probably not a good idea to include these ethical exclusions in the patenting process. Patent Offices will be required to make fine ethical judgments without the benefit of advice of suitably qualified ethicists. To provide for ethical advice for every patent applied for could be unwieldy and expensive. It would probably be better to regulate human cloning, embryo research, gene therapy etc. by national or European law clearly stipulating what is and is not permissible.

Chapter 4

Recent Issues in Assisted Reproduction: Evolutions in Science, Law and Ethics

Peter Mills

Beginnings

The Human Fertilisation and Embryology Authority (HFEA) is the UK's statutory regulator of assisted conception and human embryo research. It was established in 1991 by an Act of Parliament, the Human Fertilisation and Embryology Act 1990, following a lengthy period of consultation and reflection, beginning with the much admired and frequently cited report of the Committee of Enquiry chaired by Dame Mary, now Baroness, Warnock.

Early in 2004 the Minister for Public Health, Melanie Johnson, announced that the Government intended to review the framework legislation that governs assisted reproduction in the UK. This will undoubtedly also involve a public consultation.[1] As we gather ourselves in anticipation of this new beginning it is useful also to look back at the experience of regulating assisted reproduction over the last thirteen years. In doing so we cannot fail to appreciate the distance travelled during this comparatively short time. But in charting the course of assisted reproduction it is insufficient merely to consider distance travelled — one has also to consider the direction of travel and this, when one recognises that it is not determined merely by a 'natural' unfolding of its internal potentialities , must itself be thought as a problem. Issues in assisted reproduction draw together a number of different disciplines, each of which are subject to their own structural evolutions; for the practice of assisted reproduction, at the most basic level the privileged disciplines are those of ethics, science and the law, all of which have themselves experienced significant evolutions since 1990. Developments can, and in certain cases must, be thought in the relation between these canonical discourses, or between these and the practical exercises through which they are expressed – the clinical treatment of infertility, for example – making it difficult to speak simply of 'progress' in an abstract or 'teleological' sense. If this is the case it makes at least as much sense to examine developments in assisted reproduction as unfolding within, and often according to, particular alignments of these disciplines, as it does to see these developments as provoking such alignments or establishing consistencies between these canonical discourses as their conditions of possibility.

This becomes clearer when it is a question not of the accomplishments but of the frustrations of assisted conception, for example when the implementation of a new reproductive technology is inhibited by legal constraint, or by moral disapproval. As an analysis of this sort is necessarily somewhat philosophical, requiring not merely an examination of the recent history of ideas but rather a critique of epistemologies,[2] I shall touch on only one instance in the course of this paper. My main aim will be to focus on the way in which legislation, on the one hand, and regulation, on the other, have, over the course of thirteen years, mediated the relationship between folk morality and scientific advance in this area.

'Barriers that are not to be Crossed'

In the foreword to the Warnock report it is observed that:

> What is common (and this too we have discovered from the evidence) is that people generally want some principles or other to govern the development and use of the new techniques. There must be some barriers that are not to be crossed, some limits fixed, beyond which people must not be allowed to go. [...] A society which had no inhibiting limits, especially in the areas with which we have been concerned, questions of birth and death, of the setting up of families, and the valuing of human life, would be a society without moral scruples. And this nobody wants.[3]

The ethical framework, embedded in the 1990 Act by a series of requirements and prohibitions, lays out the broad parameters of what is acceptable in practice – that is, activities which may be conducted by licensees – and as purpose – that is, the reasons why such activities may be carried out.[4] The acknowledgement that the licensing of assisted conception treatments should have regard to the purpose for which they are to be used involved, already, a recognition that the work of the HFEA would, indeed must, have a juridical function, and one of a particular kind: one that combines or completes the simple function of administration with ethical reflection. This is important because whilst the technologies in use in assisted conception may be, from a scientific perspective, innocent, the uses to which they may be put, or the circumstances in which they may be used, can be evaluated in a variety of ways.[5] The constitution of the Authority, the composition of its board and the comprehension of a policy function within its remit reflects this. Before going any further, however, it must be emphasised that the exercise of this function should always be constrained by the established legislative parameters, by the existence of 'barriers that are not to be crossed.' Where these barriers are clearly codified, publicly understood and generally respected, the provision assisted reproduction treatments can proceed with relative confidence.

Legal Challenges

If it is possible to pose questions about the proper regulation of assisted conception and human embryo research – in other words, questions about the exercise of the juridical function of the regulator – in terms of the relation between the disciplines of ethics, law, and (bio) medical science, it is necessary to do so with reference to a particular moment in their histories and in relation to a particular problem. Inasmuch as these questions identify genuine problems, such problems often relate to inadequacies in the conceptual schemes of the disciplines, not so much for each discipline 'on its own terms' but rather when they are orientated towards a common problem: whilst they appear to be speaking a common language they sometimes find themselves unable formally to comprehend one another. Many concepts could perhaps furnish a demonstration but one suggests itself above all others, being in a sense foundational for the idea of regulation[6] and the one on which many of the important evaluative questions in assisted conception are focussed. This privileged concept is that of the 'embryo'.

If this conjecture is correct, it should be possible to show, by reference to the recent Pro-Life Alliance judicial review, how advances taking place within the science of embryology can expose inadequacies in the relation between the science of embryology and the legislation that is intended to comprehend it. The case, as is well known, essentially raised the question of whether 'embryos' created by the technique of cell nuclear replacement (commonly glossed as 'cloning') were capable of being regarded as embryos within the meaning of the 1990 Act, and therefore subject to regulation by the HFEA.[7] This development posed a genuine problem: either some novel argument (i.e. one that was not analytically present in the original formulation of the legal provisions) was needed to demonstrate that embryos created by this process could be accommodated within the existing framework after all or they would fall outside regulation. Their moral value, as well as their scientific description and legal status, was in the balance. From the point of view of the Government, which was a party to the case, if 'CNR embryos' fell outside the scope of regulation two responses were possible: to leave them outside the legal framework (and unregulated) or to reconfigure the framework, through new legislation and a return to Parliament.

It is worth noting, briefly, that the evolution of this case is interesting: the Government's response, when the Pro-Life Alliance application was successful at first instance, was to divide the question according to the ethical considerations it threw up, in other words, according to the purpose for which the new object, the 'CNR embryo' was created. It therefore adopted both of the strategies mentioned above: it laid emergency legislation, The Human Reproductive Cloning Act 2001, 'to prohibit the placing in a woman of a human embryo which has been created other than by fertilisation' whilst leaving other, supposedly less contentious, uses of these 'CNR embryos' unregulated for the time being.[8] Clearly it did not intend for research into what is known as 'therapeutic cloning' to remain unregulated but the alternative of unpicking, perhaps unravelling, the framework legislation was not one that could be contemplated at that time. This strategy appeared to have paid off when, at appeal, the first instance judgement was set aside and it was held, and subsequently confirmed by the House of Lords, that the 'CNR embryo' was, after all, an embryo for the purposes of the 1990 Act. Despite the Government's success on this occasion, however, it would be complacent to imagine that as science advances in the future, throwing up new objects for consideration, the courts will be able consistently to shore up the current legislation.

Regulatory Responses

So the regulation of assisted conception in the UK has two aspects. On one side are the broad parameters, concepts and rules laid down by Parliament – and interpreted from time to time by the Courts – which are independent of circumstance and even of technical possibility. On the other side are the policies, processes and decisions of the HFEA which are sensitive to circumstances in which, and purposes for which, assisted conception technologies may be used. Unlike the laws laid down by Parliament, the Authority's decisions must often have regard to the circumstances of an individual case or class of cases, certainly to the current state of development of the technology (including the latest evidence regarding its safety and efficacy), the experience and expertise of those proposing to use it, and also, among other things, to recent developments in case law and relevant ethical arguments.

All this may mean that over time, in response to changing circumstances, the appropriate answer to two ostensibly similar questions will differ. Techniques which were once regarded as unsafe or ineffective may become more-or-less routine. The opposite may also be true. Practices which were once regarded as unacceptable, even horrifying, may come to be seen as beneficial, even routine. The regulatory solution allows an answer to be given to the following sort of question: if something is permissible in law (this is often the first question to be determined) should it be permitted now, in these circumstances, in the light of present knowledge (accepting that knowledge emerging in the future may cast the answer in a significantly different light)?

This arrangement means that the HFEA can respond in a timely fashion to new developments in the field. Indeed the Authority has the obligation to do so: in many cases there will be an urgency because patients' treatment will depend on an application to the Authority and an unreasonable delay could seriously affect the prospects of a successful outcome.[9] In rare cases, lives – the lives of those already living rather than those who have yet to be conceived – may even be at stake.[10]

'What People Want'

So far I have discussed the relationship between science and the law. But there is one more thing. Again I return to Warnock: in Chapter One the report tells us the enquiry found that:

> Society's views on the new techniques were divided between pride in the technological achievement, pleasure at the new-found means to relieve, at least for some, the unhappiness of infertility, and unease at the apparently uncontrolled advance of science, bringing with it new possibilities for manipulating the early stages of human development.[11]

This is a very rich passage, but two brief observations will suffice for now. First, whilst the flow-tide of technological progress is explained in some detail in the report, the undertow of ethical hesitation is described is an unarticulated 'unease'.[12] The pragmatic response to this state of affairs, was to manage this 'unease' by appointing a body to regulate, and therefore to control, the 'advance of science' and its application, but also to provide accountability and reassurance. Second, this 'unease' is a moral unease; and generally (again perhaps pragmatically) issues of morality have not typically been regarded as the preserve of technical experts in the United Kingdom (in the way that the science sometimes has) but rather as issues for society as a whole. Hence the management of this unease must continually have reference to the views and interests of 'society'.[13]

This paper was originally presented in a session entitled 'The Ethics of Humanity'. Without wishing to labour the ambiguity of the genitive in this phrase, one thing might be noted: construed as a subjective genitive – that is, the 'ethical outlook that humanity has towards developments in science' – this title is particularly relevant to the ongoing debate on assisted conception in the UK. Since Warnock this has proceeded not always, or even not principally, on the basis of abstract reflection on ethical principles and their application to the current state of technology but through a discovery of pragmatic principles abstracted by reference to 'what people want':[14] the 'ethics of humanity' or at any rate of that portion which is domiciled in the UK. Like the science that has given rise to cell nuclear replacement, 'what people want' also has a discernible history in the course of which significant developments have occurred whilst the framework legislation has remained essentially the same. These developments are due partly to underlying social and cultural shifts and partly, in the case of assisted conception, to moral argument, some of which has been of a high quality, some less so.

What is interesting in this area, as in many others areas of applied ethics, is that when what is at stake is legislating for a range of future possibilities or deciding to permit or prohibit a novel and unprecedented application many of the arguments to consequences advanced to support or oppose that innovation are to a high degree speculative. In cases of this sort, in the absence of an evidence base that would determine the issue, much more important will be the answers to questions about how we should balance individual freedoms against possible prejudice against others, about how precautionary or adventurous we should be in implementing technical developments, about the degree of trust we have in clinicians, scientists, regulators and legislators, and about the value we choose to place on certain ways of treating patients, their gametes, embryos and children.[15]

In a pluralistic society such as that of the UK, it is impossible to assume that there could be a consistent set of answers to these questions that would command the support of all, or even of a majority, in relation to any given issue. However it is important to know what these answers are. Public consultation exercises help as a means of discovering what values and arguments are in play in relation to the question at issue. They do not help in the sense that they provide a mandate for a particular decision or initiative (the samples are often small and self-selecting, and it is impossible to know how truly informed respondents may be). Rather, their value is in ensuring that all arguments and points of view may be represented and that, being represented, they are all addressed.

Two Recent Examples

From the outset, the technologies of assisted conception developed rapidly and the questions they raised already reached beyond the relatively unproblematic project of circumventing infertility. For example, in chapter nine of the Warnock report, entitled 'The wider use of these techniques,' we find the following observation:

> So far in this report we have been concerned with the alleviation of infertility. The processes we have considered can, however, also been seen as a facility, a service available to anyone, whether infertile or otherwise, to enable them to have a child in a particular way.[16]

Or to have a particular kind of child, as the report then goes on to discuss the perennial issue of sex selection. This, it should be noted, is one area that the report recommended should be left to the statutory regulatory body (whose establishment it proposed) to keep under review. In the light of new innovations that would enable families to select a child of a particular sex (sperm sorting) and at the same time without clear evidence relating to the health or psychosocial effects of these techniques, in 2003 the HFEA conducted a second consultation on the use of assisted reproductive technologies for the purpose of sex selection.[17]

The main focus of this consultation quickly became the extent to which difficult-to-quantify concerns about the possible consequences of the treatment for a child who may be born as a result of the treatment were capable of supplying a sufficient reason to frustrate the (moral) claims of prospective parents to express their preference for a child of a particular sex. In the event, and although the likelihood of an undesirable outcome was almost universally acknowledged to be low, these concerns were thought to be sufficient to restrict access to the technology. It is unfortunate that this conclusion was somewhat overshadowed by the attention that was given to the numerical preponderance of those respondents who had opposed sex selection for non-medical reasons, which some (mis)took for a decisive argument against the practice.

Another example, one which shows how the acceptability of certain conditions under which fertility treatment is provided has evolved since the 1990 legislation, concerns the anonymity of gamete and embryo donors. As is widely known, new Regulations requiring that gamete and embryo donors registering after April 1, 2005 should be identifiable to people conceived as a result when they reach the age of 18, completed their passage through Parliament earlier in 2004.

When the 1990 Act was originally debated there may have been an assumption that because infertility was an intensely private, and potentially stigmatising, affair people would want treatment using donor gametes to be buried in secrecy. It may have been thought that this was the best approach: for donors, who did not have to confront any consequences or ongoing responsibilities as a result of their donation; for parents of donor-conceived people, who did not have to reveal the truth about their infertility to their friends and family; and for the children who would never have to come to terms with an 'identity confusion' arising from circumstances of their conception. Since then a new and growing constituency of people have begun to make their interests known: donor-conceived people and their parents. Many of these now assert that there is significant interference with their interests if information about donors remains undisclosed. Their arguments have been persuasive.

Following a protracted period of consultation, and having listened carefully to the strong arguments put forward by interested parties (parents, donor-conceived people, donors, clinicians and others) the Government reached a decision that, notwithstanding evidence that there would very likely be a drop in the number of people donating, at least initially, the most important principle now was that donor-conceived people should be able to have access to knowledge of identity of their donors.[18] It is important to recognise that, despite the small number of donor-conceived people and families who put the case very forcefully in favour of an end to anonymity, the decision could not have been based on sound evidence about the effects of anonymous donor conception, since the voices of the vast majority of donor-conceived people were absent. Nor indeed could that evidence plausibly have been obtained: this was a decision on a matter of principle, which the consultation had served to discover and to clarify. And this principle was not one which was revealed or taken to be decisive in the 1980s.

It was a striking finding of a recent piece of research into public opinion formation commissioned by the HFEA – specifically into the use of preimplantation testing to produce tissue donors for an existing family member – that in considering difficult moral questions about the application of 'cutting edge' techniques, members of the public referred repeatedly to the fact that a quarter of a century ago IVF itself had been commonly viewed with suspicion. The fact that it was now regarded as routine, led them to conclude, by extrapolation, that whatever they felt about them at present, the new technologies they were discussing would inevitably come to be seen as acceptable if they were implemented. Clearly, this acceptability would depend on the techniques being demonstrated to be effective and unlikely to produce adverse consequences for those involved. But this in turn, of course, depended on them actually being used. Their argument for allowing them to be used at all was, implicitly, that this was a step towards a situation which would vindicate that initial decision.

Why did they think that? How does one escape from or excuse this apparent circularity? The answer is, I think, that the participants in this research were applying a form of inductive reasoning, the conviction that past experience provides a reliable guide to the future. Clearly, on one level this reasoning exhibits a fallacy: the consequences that will result from the introduction of new technologies that are significantly different from previous ones cannot be predicted by analogy to the consequences of those different technologies with which we are familiar. On another level, however, this approach may be rational in that what is appealed to is not the similarity of past and future technologies but rather a confidence in the continued probity of scientists, clinicians, regulators and lawmakers in the face of technically and morally complex questions. This is the responsibility up to which those reviewing the legislation in the next few years must live when they take the opportunity afforded by what promises to be a vigorous public debate – beginning with the current Science and Technology Committee and the Department of Health review – to re-think the parameters within which regulation can continue to foster scientific and clinical advance in a climate of public confidence.

Notes

1 Since this paper was originally presented the Government has, as a result of its review of Arm's length bodies, announced its intention to merge the HFEA with the yet-to-be-established Human Tissue Authority to form RAFT, the Regulatory Authority for Fertility and Tissues. It is expected that the merger will be take place in 2008.

2 Since signposts have their uses in orientating oneself, I am thinking of an enterprise in the tradition of Bachelard, Foucault and, particularly, Serres.

3 *Warnock Report*, Foreword (emphasis in original).

4 For example, Schedule 2 to the 1990 Act, which governs the type of licences the Authority may issue contains a mixture of activities and purposes. We find that treatment licences may be issued for (a) bringing about the creation of embryos *in vitro*, (b) keeping embryos, (c) using gametes, (d) practices designed to secure that embryos are in a suitable condition to be placed in a woman or to determine whether embryos are suitable for that purpose…

5 A recent example (see below), on which the HFEA has recently consulted, is sex selection. Sex selection embraces a number of technologies all of which can be used, with greater or lesser effectiveness, to select the sex of children that will be born (to select children of a particular sex). Whilst this can be used to avoid serious, sex-linked genetic conditions, it can also be used to give expression to parental preferences or even to prejudices.

6 See, for instance, the quotation from the Warnock report, reproduced below (note 11).

7 *R. v. Secretary of State for Health ex p. Quintavalle (on behalf of Pro-Life Alliance)* [2003] UKHL 13.

8 One may wonder whether, in reacting in this way, the Secretary of State went too far – might there not be cases in which 'the placing of an embryo created other than by fertilisation in a woman' (although perhaps not for a long time a cloned embryo) might be desirable for morally acceptable reasons? The second gamble was, probably, that reliable alternatives to fertilisation would not be on the scene until an opportunity to give full consideration to the issues, and to produce new legislation, had been found.

9 I am thinking of cases in which the fertility of the woman to be treated may decline due to advancing age, or cases in which, for example, gametes of which patients wish to make use may be nearing the end of their permitted storage period.

[10] I am thinking here of the topical issue of 'saviour siblings', where parents wish to make use of IVF to allow the testing of preimplantation embryos for the purpose of conceiving a tissue donor for an existing, seriously-ill sibling.

[11] Warnock Report, *Chapter 1, The General Approach*.

[12] The anatomy of this unease is discussed elsewhere in Warnock [e.g. Ch.11], although not in great depth.

[13] 'Doctors and scientists work within the moral and legal framework determined by society. They do not and should not depart radically from that framework.' *Warnock*, p.75.

[14] See quotation above (note 1) from the 'Foreword' to the *Warnock* report.

[15] The hypothesis is this: where the value of an action or a practice cannot be established in relation to consequences, and where these possible consequences include highly desirable, as well as undesirable, sates of affairs such that not acting is itself potentially undesirable, it is tempting, and, to avoid aribtrariness, in some cases indispensible, to seek some normative principle or other as a guide.

[16] *Warnock*, p.48.

[17] The first was in 1993.

[18] This is not to say that the same applies retrospectively – in this case the interests of the donor, to whom anonymity had been guaranteed, are significant. In the future, however, donors can elect not to donate if they are not content to be identified.

I am thinking here of the [illegible] 13
use of IVF to allow the testing of [illegible] embryos [illegible]
a tissue donor for an existing, seriously ill sibling.
Warnock, Report of the [illegible] *The Observer*, [illegible]
The [illegible] of this [illegible] 14
but in great depth.
'Doctors and scientists work within the law [illegible] 15
[illegible]
[illegible]
See [illegible] 16
The [illegible] 17

Chapter 5

Why do Research on Human Brains?

Margaret Esiri

Introduction

There has been a sea-change in our attitudes to the study of human organs, particularly the brain, after death. This change commenced long before the recent British publicity surrounding the revelations about organ retention at the Bristol Royal Infirmary and Alder Hey hospitals in the 1990s. It started when technological developments in the 1970s made it possible to routinely obtain images of the brain in people who are alive. Before that the only opportunity available to us to examine a brain thoroughly was when it could be removed after someone's death and studied in such a way as to reveal any pathology that might have affected it such as a stroke, a tumour or a more subtle disease such as Alzheimer's disease. This was the traditional method of learning about diseases that affect the brain and in the period from the late 19th to the late 20th centuries an enormous amount of information was obtained in this way. This information was not acquired primarily to satisfy intellectual curiosity but to improve understanding of brain diseases so that they could be better managed to the benefit of living people afflicted by them. Examples of important discoveries that have borne fruit in better management of brain diseases are the realisation that Parkinson's disease is due to death of nerve cells that produce dopamine, a chemical that can be substituted for with an oral medicine; and that strokes are often the result of partial blockage of blood vessels in the neck that can be successfully operated upon.

Recently the value of this traditional approach to examining and investigating human brains after death has been questioned. Three major factors are responsible for this questioning. First, technological advances that have enabled us to 'see' living brains; second, the development of new methods of investigating brain diseases based on genetics; and third, recognition of the need to raise the standard of ethical consent given to allow examination of a brain after someone's death to take place. I will consider each of these developments below.

Technological Advances

Although the initial CT (computerized tomography) images obtained from living peoples' brains were a bit fuzzy the technology has progressed so that really stunning pictures of living brains can now be obtained with MRI (magnetic resonance imaging). Such images can demonstrate abnormalities in brains that are of great diagnostic value where the abnormality is quite large, i.e. visible with the naked eye. What is more, obtaining the images is safe, painless and convenient, requiring nothing more onerous than lying still for up to half an hour or so with your head in an enclosed space. However, it is expensive, currently at least £150 a time. More importantly, demonstrating pathology like this is only the start of the process of understanding what caused it and what can be done about it. To uncover answers to these questions usually requires the abnormal tissue to be examined at the microscopic level to reveal changes in cells and the expression of molecules that make up cells. Thus, molecules make cells which make organs. Images of brains (one type of organ) enable diagnoses to be made of many (but not all) brain diseases. However, *understanding* disease requires exploration of the brain at the cellular and molecular levels. In general, that is still not possible without extracting a small sample of the abnormal tissue in an operative procedure when the person is alive or by examining the whole brain after the person has died. In the future we may find ways of 'examining' cells and molecules in the brain without needing to remove tissue from it but such attempts are only just beginning. Meanwhile, post mortem rates have been dropping in most countries since the 1980s.

More recently even newer technological developments have made it possible to produce images of changes in metabolic activity and blood flow in the brain in living subjects. The techniques of positron emission tomography (PET) and functional MRI show us which parts of the brain are active when a particular task is undertaken. This has increased understanding of how the normal brain works and of how it adapts to ageing or to disease such as stroke or multiple sclerosis. As yet it does not provide useful diagnostic information but it has great potential and has already taught us much about normal brain function. It suffers from the same drawback of CT and MRI that it does not allow investigation of specific cells and molecules.

Impact of Genetics

Another change that has come about recently which has a bearing on the question posed in the title of this article is the realisation that our genes play key roles in many diseases, including those that affect the brain. Even if a pathological process is going on that is too subtle to see with brain imaging we may be able to diagnose the problem and gain an understanding of it by looking at a sample of DNA prepared from blood or a scraping of cells lining the mouth. If the disease is caused by genetic mutation (a fault in the inherited genetic material) there is no need to study the brain to detect it. All that is required is a simple blood test. This is true, for example, of brain diseases such as Huntington's chorea and inherited ataxia (unsteadiness). Furthermore we can use this knowledge about genetic mutations that cause human diseases to create animal models of the disease by inserting into an animal genome the mutation that causes the human disease. The animal model can then be manipulated to find new methods of treating the disease or, better still, preventing its expression. This is a tremendously powerful means to study inherited brain diseases even though, as yet its potential has not been fully realised for many diseases. Already in some diseases, such as those caused by single enzyme defects like Fabry's disease, a method has been found that prevents disease expression in the animal model and at least ameliorates the human disease. Some diseases are, in most cases, not the direct result of a faulty gene but in a few familial cases are caused by such a gene. Animal models of such diseases can be generated based on the gene mutations in the rare familial cases and these can have value for understanding sporadic cases as well. In an animal model of Alzheimer's disease based on insertion of a disease-causing mutation in mice an immune intervention was found to remove one of the pathological microscopic features of that disease. However, the same approach attempted in some human patients led to unforeseen complications and the trial of this treatment had to be abandoned. Nevertheless, further investigation may lead to ways to circumvent this complication in future. Whether or not this turns out to be the case this example brings home the importance of continuing to carry out post mortem brain examinations to see how novel treatments have affected a disease process.

Consent Issues and Ethical Concerns

The findings of the Kennedy and Redfern enquiries into the Bristol Royal Infirmary heart surgery cases and organ retention at Alder Hey Hospital, Liverpool, respectively led to a census being taken of all the organ and tissue collections throughout the UK. The size of these collections, amounting to thousands of organs, many of them brains, came as a surprise to the general public. Of great concern was that many of these organ and tissue collections had been built up without the fully informed consent of relatives. For example, in my own hospital, most relatives giving consent for a neuropathological post mortem examination were aware that a brain would need to be retained for full diagnostic work-up and if it was to be used for research. However, the wording on the post mortem consent form referred to 'use of tissue for research' without mention of brain retention. For post mortem examinations performed at the request of the Coroner the position was even less satisfactory as shown in the recently published Metters report which investigated the circumstances surrounding the unauthorised use of a brain for research following a Coroner's post mortem examination in the 1980s.

It has become clear that great ignorance surrounds the procedures involved in post mortem examination and that those people who were involved in obtaining consent from relatives were sometimes themselves hazy about what it entails. Following the very adverse publicity surrounding the publication of the Kennedy and Redfern reports some clinicians have been put off even asking relatives for permission for a post mortem examination, afraid that they might not have explained things in sufficient detail to allow consent to be deemed to be properly 'informed'. Relatives are also less likely to agree to a post mortem examination being carried out. In the desperately hard-pressed NHS doctors also lack the time needed to obtain such consent as it takes considerable time to explain the details and answer questions. This has resulted in a dramatic further reduction in the numbers of post mortem examinations being performed to investigate disease in many (though not all) hospitals. Those hospitals where such examinations have remained fairly frequent have been those, such as my own, where research involves longitudinal studies of people with incurable neurological or dementing diseases. People with such diseases (if judged sufficiently capable) have expressed the generous wish to contribute to research by donating their brain for examination after their death. If they are not judged capable of giving informed consent their relatives often wish to give consent.

What has emerged from much turmoil is the recognition of the need for new legislation that takes account of new and higher standards of explicit consultation and consent about post mortem examination. This will enable trust and confidence to be restored both in members of the general public and among doctors and other health staff. Currently we are using more detailed government-approved consent forms and pathologists are generally pleased to explain their work in more detail. Relatives usually respond with interest to discussions of post mortem findings with pathologists – a group of health professionals who have in the past been too hidden from the public. There is a greater recognition of the need to educate the public and health professionals about the purposes of, and procedures involved in, post mortem examinations. People need to be more aware of the benefits of such examinations not only for research, which may ultimately help others, but also for their own families. One of the points to arise from the increase in knowledge about the role of genes in disease is that diseases run in families even more frequently than had been recognised before. Detailed knowledge of the cause of a fatal illness in a baby, for example, may point up the dangers of another baby being similarly affected –.something that prenatal testing in another pregnancy may help to clarify to the benefit of the parents and sometimes more distant family members.

A wider issue is the extent to which members of society should be encouraged to assist with the progression of medical research that entails post mortem examination and organ retention. By giving their consent they are essential partners in this endeavour. People alive now are benefiting from treatment and management of their diseases that stems from the knowledge acquired from earlier post mortem examinations, as well as other investigations, performed last century albeit with what is now considered to be inadequately informed consent. Diseases change with time, some dying out and new ones arising. New forms of treatment bring new complications. Recognising new disease and new complications as soon as they arise is an important form of surveillance and post mortem examinations contribute to this. For example, the new variant form of Creutzfeldt-Jakob disease that arose in the wake of the BSE epidemic in the UK depends for its diagnosis, in part, on post mortem examination of the brain. In my view there is an urgent need to educate people so that they understand the importance of continuing to perform post mortem examinations. I find it encouraging that when such explanation is provided even to bereaved families who are passing through a phase of great stress, they often do agree to help in this way.

There is another aspect to the value of post mortem examinations – their value in teaching the next generation of doctors. Every person looked after in hospital has a team of doctors and nurses (and others) helping to look after them. Some of the staff are highly experienced and may have seen many similar cases before but others are just starting out on their careers. There may also be students learning about disease for the first time. I know from my own experience that the biggest impact in one's medical education comes from personally studied cases. Sad though it is, when a patient you have been helping to look after dies, a thorough demonstration of the pathology after their death remains vivid in one's memory and helps build up the experience that forms the best qualified health staff. Post mortem examinations are also essential to the training of the next generation of pathologists who are needed to diagnose disease in the living even more than in the dead. Thus, findings on post mortem examination need to be shared first of all with the family (if this is what they wish) and next with the staff who helped look after the person who has died, as well as with medical students and doctors training to be pathologists. Finally, by adding an individual case, anonymously, with others that suffered from the same disease, more can be learnt about the nature of that disease and the results can be written up in a report that can be read by interested persons worldwide. It is mainly to allow similar cases to be collected together that large archives of brains are maintained. Another reason for doing this is to allow new techniques to be applied that can cast new light on a death that occurred years earlier. It is partly by such laborious steps, taken countless thousands of times, that medical understanding has reached its current level. Translating such understanding into effective treatment may take many years. For example, the current modestly effective treatments for Alzheimer's disease, introduced widely only in the last few years, built on research that was reported in the mid-1970s. We need to keep the research impetus on brain diseases moving energetically forward if we are to be able to manage the huge expected case loads suffering from neurological and neurodegenerative diseases that are predicted in many who now live well into old age.

Where do We Go from Here?

We need to be able to maintain and add to brain archives with fully informed consent. Such archives need to acquire not only brains from those with neurological and psychiatric diseases but also brains from those with no such diseases since these are needed for comparison with diseased brains for research. Even for diagnostic purposes brains need to be retained for a limited period of about three months because the natural, jelly-like consistency of the brain makes it very difficult to examine properly. The first step that needs to be taken in examining a brain is to immerse it for four weeks or so in preservative. This hardens (or 'fixes') its structure and makes it more amenable to careful dissection. Small samples may, however, be removed before fixation, for example, to attempt to culture organisms from it or to allow the examination of frozen material for sensitive molecules that might be altered or destroyed by the chemical preservatives. Once the brain has been fixed, depending on the type of disease thought to be present, selected small samples are subjected to microscopy for diagnosis and, if relatives agree, for research.

Next we need to take steps to educate the public about why post mortem examinations are needed. A website like this helps to do that, as do TV programmes, videos, books and articles for a general readership and visits by researchers and pathologists to groups of interested people such as those brought together by a medical charity. For dealing sensitively with issues of consent at the time of someone's death we need specially trained bereavement staff as well as properly informed doctors who are able to discuss openly with relatives the need for post mortem examination. These people need to interact with officers in the Coronial system as well as with hospital staff and relatives.

Brain Banks

A third need is to organise archives of brains that have been donated for research in such a way that the brains collected in them can be used to greatest effect. Some brain diseases are rare and there can be great value in making brains from such cases accessible to researchers wherever in the country (or even the world) they are working. Other brain diseases are less rare but archived brains affected by them are rare. An example here is autism, a disease that desperately requires better understanding but for which very few brains are, as yet, available for study in this country. To improve availability of brains for research in such cases takes not only good organisation but also very sensitive discussion with parents and care-givers about the need for such research. Another disease where brains are badly needed for research is schizophrenia. It can be hard to arrange for archiving of brains from this condition because people live for very many decades with the disease and may lose touch with their close relatives from whom consent would need to be obtained after their death. To some extent this difficulty can be circumvented by carrying out studies on MRI images of the brains of living subjects. Such studies have the advantage that more clinical and neuropsychological information is likely to be available about each case, and the imaging can be done early in the disease course. However, such studies suffer from the difficulty mentioned earlier that MRI cannot provide information on cellular or molecular changes.

In general, the efficient use of brain banks for research is best carried out through networks that utilise a common, anonymised, database that enables tissue to be shared for particular lines of research that have received ethics committee approval. Brain banks are already in existence in many UK medical centres but they lack networked database facilities and their financial support is often inadequate or insecure. This needs to be remedied so that people who generously donate brains can know that the funding is there to ensure full use of those brains as intended.

Conclusion

Death and all the circumstances that surround it, including post mortem examinations, are taboo subjects in our society today. The reasons are entirely understandable but it would be better for us all if we could break down the taboos, at least a little. Death is never going to be a pleasant subject to think about but I firmly believe we can enjoy our lives and fulfil our potential better if we can learn to contemplate and come to terms with our own inevitable deaths. To help us do that we need people who are able to talk comfortably and openly about the subject. It is going to take time but all the concern and the soul-searching that has gone on recently in this country about consent to post mortem examination provides us with an opportunity which I believe we should grasp. We shall all benefit in the long run if we do this. Part of the benefit will come from research, freely consented to, on human brains. It is vital to the future understanding of brain diseases, which account for an enormous amount of disability and mortality, that research on human brains continues with the full consent of relatives and society in general.

Chapter 6

Bioethics in Europe

Berit A. Faber

Technologies within the field of bioscience and biotechnology have created new possibilities internationally as well as nationally. We no longer live in a technological society, we stand on the threshold of entering into 'Bio-Society' where Society must deal with the possibilities and pitfalls created by new developments within the field of biotechnology i.e. biomedicine, human health, foods and animal and plant production.

In the last decade new biotechnologies have emerged and there are many doubts on how to handle them both from a political, ethical and legal point of view. Biotechnology crosses many boundaries, including national, cultural and for some also ethical borderlines. Currently, we see a change in global political and legal frameworks. In the past it was possible for each country to take its own stand in different issues involving ethics but as the international legal framework is getting more detailed and developed, it is of greater and greater importance for the different countries to find a way to co-ordinate the international legislation and the administrative practises springing from this legislation. The decision-makers are also faced with the difficulties of balancing the freedom and rights of individuals with the need to reduce the risk of adverse effects to the environment, human health and ethical values.

Biotechnology, bioethics and biolaw are important issues seen as well from a national as an international perspective and especially in relation to the EU. Biotechnology raises hopes for the future development in science but at the same time makes us worry about what pitfalls and especially what breaches of fundamental ethical values it might entail. The new technologies raise the question on how to put the beneficial aspects of technology into use and to avoid the undesired aspects and consequences. In this process the operationalization of ethical principles in European legislation of biotechnology becomes essential.

Bioethics can contribute to the process of drawing the map of what use and what consequences of biotechnology we should consider as wanted and unwanted. If the ethical evaluation is carried out by securing democratic values as dialogue justice and informed decision-making in the process, the legislation will contribute to the operationalization of the bioethical principles in society, science and risk-assessment.

Important Questions

How do we develop this new concept of Bio-Society in order to secure 'Bio-Democracy' – to secure the crystallization, implementation and operationalization of bioethical principles – What policy commitments do we need in order to secure good governance, good conduct of marketing and good conduct of trade?

The EU has a central role in the process, both by virtue of its directives and its ethics committees and debates in the European Parliament. Matters of especial importance include the EU's role vis-à-vis the moratorium on GM products, the precautionary principle, the Charter of Fundamental Rights and regulation of the marketing of foods and medicinal products. At the same time, in recent years, regulation has been introduced in a large number of EU member states, which, with varying aims and intensity and employing different means, has sought to strike a balance between promoting and controlling biotechnology.

By employing models that contain both robust international 'brake pads' at the all-essential level, and also flexible regulatory models, such as debate models and national framework legislation, ethical principles can yet be operationalised. This will enable social responsibility to be assumed, which will prevent privatisation of ethical issues and hence ensure that core ethical principles are observed.[1] These thoughts and ideas have been developed and deepened through inspiring talks between Linda Nielsen, Derek Morgan and me during the fall of 2002.

If we turn to some of the EU directives, we find that there are differences in which ethical principles they take into account. The EU directive on clinical trials on medicinal products for human use require an ethical evaluation to be carried out, and require that this must be performed on the basis of predefined ethical considerations (balancing of benefits and integrity). The directive also meets the requirement for ethical evaluation to be concrete in relation to each individual trial. Against this, the directive does not require the involvement of lay people following an open consultative process.

In the latest review of the directive on deliberate release, the preamble states that ethical considerations concerned with approval of the release of GM crops are to be incorporated. However, the directive on deliberate release makes no direct reference to ethical considerations and does not stipulate the involvement of lay people following an open consultative process.

Biodiplomacy

It should be feasible from a legal point of view to incorporate ethical criteria in EU regulation of the application of gene technology.

Consequently while incorporation of ethical criteria in EU regulation is feasible it is also associated with considerable challenges. Furthermore it may be noted that regulation will to a large extent amount to procedural standardisation, and that the consequences of a decision-making process at the EU or national level will be significant. The essence of the conclusions may also be expressed to say that the incorporation of ethical consideration in EU regulation concern dialogue with the public and decision-making processes just as much as they do the legal technicalities of regulation.

Thus it should be expected that there will be a need for both regulation proper – social ethics from the top down – and acceptance from stakeholders in the broadest sense – i.e. ethics from the bottom up. Top-down and bottom-up will, however, be equally important. Biodemocracy is one of the new concepts in the area. The art of establishing and maintaining an open dialogue between the stakeholders will be essential in order to ensure the process of openness and co-determination.

Debate: Polycentrism and Timing

Elements from many different discourses and contributions are involved in ethical debate and in the decision-making process concerning regulation.

Polycentism: The generation of a form of ethical consensus is a process akin to theories concerning polycentrism in law. Law is created not only within a single forum, but in many different centres. The formation of laws is therefore not a monocentric process, but is polycentric in that it goes on in several spheres and is the object of dynamic exchange among different centres and levels. The legal experts Henrik Zahle and Hanne Petersen in Denmark have explored this theory of polycentrism in legal science.

The ethical process is characterised by the same polycentrism. Ethics are no longer formulated by a single proponent (for example the church) but are evolved in an interaction of forums and actors. If a legislator or authority wishes to promote ethical debate it is therefore important to analyse out the actors in order to initiate an ethical debate among their ranks (for example, in the particular sector that will be affected such as the food industry, agriculture or pharmaceutical industry). It is then also important to link up the debate ongoing at the different centres – who will be talking to whom so that we can be sure that an opinion is generated on the issue to be settled? Moreover it is important to sustain public debate and dialogue – how do we ensure that debate and dialogue do not peter out – how is momentum sustained?

A polycentric debate should be a phase devoted to settling issues and discussing them and thereby the precursor of a process to arrive at an enhanced regulation strategy based on a clear perspective of the general public's and the actors' attitudes to an issue prior to legislation. The debate phase calls for both an interdisciplinary component and recourse to the wisdom embodied by the general public. In this context the media have an important role to play, and the various forms of debate models can be employed depending on culture, traditions and so forth.

Timing: Timing is an element that is essential to stress in connection with ethical debate. The Danish Council of Ethics has adopted the motto 'Ethics Just In Time'.

As the words suggest, this means that ethical debate must not happen to late, but nor must it start too early. If ethical debate comes too late, products will already be placed on the market, and the risk is that there is no issue left to debate.

If it happens to early the risk is that no one will have any feel for the issues. The questions will not be taken seriously and ethical debate will fall by the wayside.

Prospects and Challenges

In the area of human health a number of ethical principles have now been adopted, but often after a quantum leap from general matters of principle to concrete interpretation and evaluation, in which dialogue and debate forums have often been lacking. There is therefore a need for:

1. National implementation of international conventions
2. Concrete guidance for administrators
3. Dialogue-fora among the different actors
4. Further scope for public debate

It is difficult to prescribe formulae for ethics that will allow them to be operationalized – but it is important to do so – if necessary by practising on different models of dialogue and regulation.

Note

1 Some of these themes are outlined in Derek Morgan: Issues in Medical Law, London, Cavendish Publishing, 2001, Chapters 1-3 and in Linda Nielsen and Berit A. Faber, 'Ethical principles in European regulation of biotechnology – possibilities and pitfalls', BioTIK, The Ministry of Economic and Business Affairs, Denmark 2002 www.biotik.dk

Chapter 7

A Penny for Your Thoughts – Ethics in Sponsored Research

Hilde W. Nagell

Introduction

Expressions like "production of knowledge" or "knowledge economy" are now frequently used also in relation to science. There is a general worry that universities are beginning to resemble commercial companies, and that research has become just another commodity (Bok 2003). Some fear that we are witnessing "the Dawn of McScience", to quote a headline from New York Review of Books (Horton 2004). One aspect of this commercialisation of research is a greater emphasis on sponsored research. Problems related to sponsored research are well known, such as a higher degree of secrecy, conflicts of interest, manipulation of data, selective use of results, and loss of autonomy on behalf of the research community. In the face of this development, it is interesting to address whether we can still trust the results from research even when it is done on commission. Recently, the National Committees for Research Ethics in Norway published a report on the ethical challenges of sponsored research (Forskningsetiske komiteer 2003), initiated by the Norwegian Parliament (Dok.nr.8:58). The report is only available in Norwegian, and this paper will give a brief summary of the report, and present some of its main conclusions.

The paper is organised as follows: First, two main functions of scientific research will be addressed: Science should be socially responsible and it should be trustworthy. Second, the main content of the Norwegian report will be presented. The term "sponsored research" will be outlined and a background of the report, its research design, and some of its methodological limitations will be presented. Finally, there will be a brief summary of the main conclusions alongside a discussion of further measures and recommendations.

The Social Responsibility and Credibility of Science

It is important to distinguish between two aspects of science that one may suspect will be under pressure in sponsored research. First, science has a special commitment towards society. We may call it the social responsibility of science.

Science should be truth-seeking, and have as its main goal to reach higher levels of inquiry. In the long run, research can only be of use if it also seeks knowledge for its own sake. This is not to say that research should not serve the public interest. Research adds to our understanding of our objectives and our culture, and it serves to supply premises on which society bases decisions and judgements. However, if science is to be able to serve this purpose, it is of the highest importance to keep some areas of research clean in the sense that they are not biased by financial, political or social interests.

A second aspect of research that deserves special attention is its credibility. In order to be called research at all, the activity in question must live up to certain standards related to what science is in relation to other activities such as consultant work, journalism, etc. When society's decision-makers base their decisions on scientific results, they are at the same time expressing confidence in scientific methods and practice. This confidence needs special protection, and it is vulnerable in situations of external or internal social, financial or political pressure.

In their report, the National Committees argue that the following three basic norms are crucial in order to protect the social responsibility and the credibility of science:

The first norm is transparency. Transparency serves to grant the public access to research. However, the highest possible degree of openness is also an important norm in order for the public to have confidence in the results from research. General information about the project, what methods are applied, and what kind of data is used should be easily accessible. Transparency also implies that the results should be published, preferably in a peer-reviewed journal.

The second norm is *quality*. Quality can or should not be judged according to a single standard. Good quality may for instance be defined as the best quality possible given the nature of the project. Consequently, the definition of good quality is relative, which also makes it all the more difficult to define when its standards have been breached. When institutes and research groups compete over scarce resources, projects can move away from a traditional scientific approach and over to something less ambitious. However, the essence of the quality-norm is that the research in question should comply with and be in accordance with basic scientific standards, such as validity, reliability and relevance.

The third norm is integrity. Researchers on contracts do not only sell the results from their research, they also sell their credibility as researchers. Researchers and research institutions have a responsibility as to how the results of their research are put into use. They should be responsible, not necessarily to avoid conflicts of interests or bias all together, but the norm of integrity at the very least demands disclosure of potential bias or conflict of interests. The practice of these norms in sponsored research is put under closer scrutiny in the report.

Sponsored Research: Transparency, Quality and Integrity

The report asks whether we can have confidence in research when it is done on commission. Sponsored research is defined as an activity which is externally financed, the research question is defined by the commissioning party, the research is mainly for instrumental use, and it involves a transfer of user rights to the commissioning party. More specifically, the question is whether or to what extent this kind of research violates basic norms defined as transparency, quality and integrity.

The report consists of a survey and a focus group study where researchers have been asked to report on their experience with sponsored research. Among the questions asked, was whether they have experienced problems due to conflicts of interests, manipulation of data, secrecy or biased results. The focus is on the individual researcher and how he or she perceives the entire research process. This involves a limitation of the study, as researchers may have a tendency to present their own work in a favourable light, and minimize the dilemmas and problems experienced by the commissioning party or the public. Nevertheless, researchers are considered to be reliable sources of information about the different stages of a commissioned project, from initiation to implementation and closing.

The survey was conducted on E-mail, and the informants were university and institute based researchers, both with and without experience from sponsored research. The total number of registered researchers (both research and development) in Norway is approximately 40,000. The question form was distributed to 3,879 addresses; 3,338 went through. We received 1,729 answers which constitutes a response rate at 52%. 1,288 of these answered the entire questionnaire (39%).

The questions were framed in a general fashion to avoid predisposed sentiments to influence the answers. The respondents were asked questions such as: Do you use a standard contract, or do you know whether such a contract exists in you institution? Does your institution have a policy on publishing all results? What are the routines for quality assessments? Have you ever experienced conflict with the commissioning party? What was the reason for the conflict? The answers were analysed in three main categories: 1) Whether the sponsored research in question was directed towards the government or trade and industry, 2) Whether the researcher belonged to a university, a school of higher education, or a research institute, and 3) What field of academic work the researcher belonged to (medicine, natural sciences, social sciences etc). Those who reported no experience with sponsored research were asked to answer the last part of the questionnaire, and give their opinion (agree, partly agree, disagree) on common statements such as: "Sponsored research is not as credible as other research due to unfortunate ties between the researcher and the commissioning party" and "sponsored research is not as credible as other research because the system of quality control is not good enough".

The survey was supplemented by a focus group study. This study consisted of 5 groups with 3–4 participants in each group. The respondents were selected from both research institutes and universities, and covered different fields of academia: medicine, the natural sciences and technology, and the social sciences and the humanities. One of the advantages of using focus groups is that the dynamics of a conversation often reveals aspects that are not possible to detect from a survey. Although the data are not equally representative, we gained information in these qualitative interviews that would have been impossible to distract from a quantitative survey.

Main Findings and Further Recommendations

The overall impression from asking researchers about their experience with sponsored research in Norway is that this research is better than its reputation. The results of the survey indicate a widespread use of standard contracts. Few reported to compound with his or her scientific competence during the introductory period of the project. A majority of the researchers report that their institutions have good routines for quality assessment. There seems to be a real possibility to turn down unwanted commissions. A majority reported that the contact with the commissioning party was entirely positive. Only a small minority reported of conflicts during the commission. Interestingly enough, the scepticism was most palpable among researchers who had not themselves been engaged in commissioned research. However, the report also uncovered more problematic aspects of sponsored research, and although these problems may not be large in terms of quantity, they are nevertheless serious they arise.

First, our findings indicate a limited use of contracts. This was particularly the case in medical research, where interestingly enough only 35% reported using standard contracts. Moreover, there was a significant difference between the research institutes – where 77% reported that they have developed their own contract – and universities and schools of higher education – where the same number was only 35%. Not surprisingly, the institute sector, where sponsored research constitutes a large part of the activity, has the most developed system for both the use of contracts and measurements of quality. However, a recent development involving closer ties between trade and industry and research, necessitates a higher awareness and alertness also in the universities, as it is likely that more university based researchers will be engaged in sponsored research in the near future.

Second, from the results of the survey one may question whether the existing contracts are good enough. Conflicts are more frequent in projects where contracts are used. This result may be taken to indicate that contracts give researchers the necessary backing and support they need in order to confront the commissioning party in cases of disagreement. However, the same results may be interpreted in yet another way: Contracts may not be suitable to solve the problems that caused the actual conflict. One of our recommendations is that contracts should be more specific with regard to important aspects such as reporting, publication, ownership to data, etc.

Third, our findings suggest that some researchers have experienced problems related to manipulation of data and method. Of the 27% who reported that they had experienced conflict, 37% stated disagreement on questions of data and method as the reason for the conflict. The researcher should be responsible for aspects concerning method and data. When a commissioning party intervenes in these aspects of the research process, one may suspect it is with the intention of manipulating the results or push the researcher towards certain conclusions. Consequently, conflicts on these issues are serious. It is important to stress that the researcher should have the final word in cases of conflict concerning data and method.

Fourth, there seems to be considerable room for improvement with regard to the policy for publication of the results from sponsored research. More than half of the researchers did not make sure that their institution had guidelines for publication. This is a troubling result considering that publication is a frequent issue of conflict. More than half of the researchers that had experiences conflicts, reported publication to be the point of controversy. The recommendation from the National Committees is that, as a general rule, all results from research should be published. This implies that research institutions and universities should have publication of all results as their official policy. Furthermore, the report recommends that data and background material should be easily accessible, and that researchers should be free to participate in the public debate and to contribute to the interpretation and analysis of the results of his or her research.

Fifth, the report displays pour or lacking routines for quality assessment in some areas, especially in the universities and within the social sciences. Unclear or conflicting practice with regard to publication also weakens the possibility of quality control. The report recommends that all research institutions have transparent and functioning systems for quality control and assessment, first of all based on internal routines. However, extended versions of quality control involving affected parties should also be considered.

Concluding Remarks

This paper has displayed problematic aspects of sponsored research experienced by Norwegian researchers. Nothing indicates that these problems are restricted only to Norwegian research. Unfortunately, we have not been able to find systematic in-depth studies that could be used to compare the findings in our report. In itself the report is a limited investigation, both in terms of scope and range. Further research is clearly needed on these issues. In order to follow up on the recommendations in the report, the National Committees for Research Ethics in Norway is currently developing a standard procedure for sponsored research. This procedure is intended to be a useful tool for all parties involved in commissioned research, addressing important aspects such as publication, conflicts of interest and property rights.

References

Bok, D. (2003), 'Universities in the Marketplace – the Commercialization of Higher Education', *Princeton University Press*, Princeton and Oxford.

Dok, Nr. 8:58 (1996-97), Forslag fra stortingsrepresentantene Sigurd Maneråk, Jon Lilletun og Lars Sponheim om å oppnevne et utvalg med mandat til å vurdere forskningens åpenhet, frihet og uavhengighet.

Forskningsetiske, K. (2003), Oppdragsforskning: Åpenhet, kvalitet og etterrettelighet. Oslo, Publikasjon nr. 4.

Horton, R. (2004), 'The Dawn of McScience', *New York Review of Books*, March 11, 2004, pp. 7–9.

Chapter 8

Ethical Issues of Evidence-Based Medicine

Ruud ter Meulen

In clinical care and health care policy-making one can notice an increased effort to base decisions on the outcomes of empirical studies. Instead of so-called 'opinion-based' decision-making, health care policy and clinical practice, in this view, should become more 'evidence based' by the use of the best available scientific evidence. The best evidence is evidence that is produced in randomised controlled clinical trials (RCT), where the association between a specific intervention and its outcomes is researched within very strictly controlled conditions. An important part of the EBM movement is the so-called Cochrane Collaboration, founded by Archie Cochrane, which by pooling and reviewing evidence tries to disseminate the best available evidence from clinical and health outcomes research. While focusing primarily on RCTs, the Cochrane Collaboration also gives attention to 'second-best' evidence, when RCTs are not available or possible, such as cohort studies and case-controlled studies.

The moving idea behind Evidence-based Medicine (EBM) is that doctors should only make use of therapies that have been proved to be effective, instead of making use of unproven therapies which may be ineffective or even harmful to the patient. From an ethical point view, one could argue what could be debatable about these efforts? What could be wrong to enhance the scientific quality and the efficiency of medical care by making use of the best available evidence? In fact the only normative issue at stake here is the resistance to such efforts and the alleged lack of co-operation of clinicians to improve the quality of care by the use of evidence-based guidelines. However, there are some concerns that the neutrality and impartiality of the evidence produced by the RCT and of the guidelines based on this evidence is not as objective and 'value-free' as it looks like. There is a growing belief, that in the production of evidence as well as the application in clinical practice and health policy, moral values play a hidden, but decisive role. For example, the definition of effectiveness of medical treatment or health care service is heavily dependent on individual or social views about the goals of the particular treatment or service. There is a serious concern too, that the rationalisation of the rationing process will be at the expense of widely shared social values like solidarity and equity.

In our project Ethical Issues of Evidence-based Practice in Medicine and Health Care (EviBase) which was sponsored by the European Commission within the Fifth Framework Program, we have tried to uncover and analyse the hidden values that are guiding the process of rationalisation of medical care and health policy on the basis of scientific evidence. In a number of workshops, organised by the core-group, researchers, philosophers, policy-makers and clinicians discussed the ethical issues of EBM in various disciplines and contexts like medical research, health economy, hospital care, policy-making, medical education and so on. In my presentation, I will give a short overview of the ethical issues that the project participants thought to be relevant and to be discussed in a wider audience.

EBM and the Individual Patient

While EBM was originally a reaction against the overload of information on medical research in the many medical journals, increasingly it has become a kind of guidance of clinical practice by way of guidelines and recommendations. The idea was that the best way to promote the use of evidence in clinical practice and health policy is to construct guidelines which prescribe carefully which steps doctors or policy makers should take in view of the systematic reviews of the RCT or other kinds of available evidence. This process of rationalisation, also called 'regulatory EBM', has raised a number of ethical concerns and criticisms. An important part of these concerns has had to do with the alleged gap between abstract measures and guidelines on the one hand and the situation of the individual patient on the other. The data of evidence-based medicine, it was said, are based on ideal populations and have little relevance if any in the encounter between the physician and the patient. (Sweeney, 1998; Van Weel and Knottnerus, 1999). In clinical practice the patient plays a central role: it is the patient who decides whether a treatment is beneficial or appropriate by assessing his or her own values and beliefs. Such situations are often ambiguous: what are the complaints of the patient, what diagnosis can be made, what therapeutic alternatives are available, what benefits and harms are to be expected for the patient, what harms can the patient bear, what does the patient actually want? (Culpepper and Gilbert, 1999).

As an example, one can point at psychiatric practice, where so-called patient-specific factors play an important role in the treatment of individual patients. Patient-specific factors determine for a large part the effectiveness of treatment. Examples of such factors include a patient's values, expectations and interactions with others, social-economic background, and trust of the psychotherapist. For example, patients from lower income groups tend to stop treatment prematurely. The reason for this lack of compliance is often sought in their different social and cultural lifestyles, incorporating a specific value system and use of language that are is difficult to reconcile with psychotherapeutic styles and methods. However, such subjective factors are very difficult to quantify. As guidelines are based on explicit and quantitative information, subjective factors lose ground. Nonetheless they can be shown to have an inevitable influence on the outcome of psychiatric and psychotherapeutic treatment. The emphasis on scientific evidence in mental health care then, could eventually result in a retreat of subjective, non-scientific values, such as the meaningfulness of a treatment for the individual. What is meaningful for an individual cannot be answered from a scientific perspective. However, in the process of standardization of psychiatric treatment, effectiveness and meaningfulness are constantly entangled.

Some proponents argue that this 'regulatory' use of EBM is not in fact 'real' EBM, as real EBM tries to provide the individual doctor with the best evidence for the care of his or her individual patient. For example, David Sackett, the founding father of the EBM movement, stressed that doctors should make a 'judicious' use of the data of systematic reviews. In his words, EBM can be defined as 'the conscientious, explicit and judicious use of current best evidence in making decisions about the care of individual patients', which 'integrates the best evidence with individual clinical expertise and patients' choice' (Sackett, 1996). However, one of the ethical criticisms regarding EBM also concerns the strong belief in the RCT as the only road to wisdom. The argument here is that the methodology of the RCT, which forms the core of the EBM movement, excludes many other kinds of research, such as observational studies and qualitative research. Although proponents stress the idea that EBM should be based on the best available evidence, there is, according to the critics, an inherent tendency to focus on randomised controlled clinical trials and even more on services and treatments that lend themselves to such research. There is a fear that if the RCT is considered the gold standard for research and the best road to evidence, researchers and their sponsors will focus more on drug trials, which provide the 'natural environment' for the RCT model. If policy decisions, particularly reimbursement decisions, are based on the 'best available evidence', drug-based treatment regimes could derive an unfair advantage over other kinds of treatments. For example in mental health care, drug-based treatment regimes could derive an unfair advantage in mental health care over other kinds of treatments, such as psychotherapy. Such treatments will be limited in terms of reimbursement, and in the end they could disappear from the public health system. The variety of mental health services will be decreased by cutting alleged 'unsuccessful treatments', even if many patients have benefited from such treatments.

EBM and Rationing of Treatments

While Sackett and his colleagues wanted to restrict EBM to the context on individual patient care, other advocates of EBM have extended the range of EBM to the area of health care systems and policy-making (Muir Gray 1997) Evidence-based medicine is seen not only as an important means to improve the quality of medical care, but also as an instrument to control costs. In view of the scarcity of health care resources, decisions on the allocation of care will have to be made more explicitly and should be made more transparent and accountable. As pressures on the health care systems are increasing, the call for more explicit decision-making and for more rationalisation by the use of empirical evidence will become louder. EBM stands now for a combined approach to improve the quality of clinical care as well as to control the costs of care by the use of the best available evidence.

An example of this rationalisation process is the effort to sharpen the indications for access to scarce medical treatments by the use of cost-effectiveness analysis. This approach results in many ethical problems. In a research project by the Royal Dutch Physicians' Organisation, aimed at investigating how guidelines for appropriate medical care should be construed on the basis of cost-effectiveness analysis , some of these ethical problems were analysed (Berg et al, 2001). In this project, the attitudes of specialist physicians (psychiatrists and cardiologists) concerning guidelines and cost-effectiveness analysis were confronted with the attitudes of researchers who were producing cost-effectiveness analysis as the basis for guidelines and other regulating instruments. It appeared that both groups, specialists and researchers, had conflicting definitions of effectiveness. For cardiologists and psychiatrists, an intervention is effective when it fits an individual patient's complaints, possibilities, expectations and so forth: it is a multi-dimensional measure of the 'match' between the intervention and the specific situation and history of an individual case (Dickenson, 1999). For the researchers, however, an intervention is 'effective' when it has been proven to increase e.g. (quality adjusted) life-years in well-designed clinical trials. For these groups, then, the concept of 'effectiveness' is more narrowly defined and refers to categories of patients. In order to allow comparison between studies, it does so ideally in identical ways: the definition of 'effectiveness' should be as independent of individual cases as possible.

In regard to the allocation of resources, the specialists generally accepted the need to include economic considerations in the decision making processes and seemed to agree with the utilitarian logic that characterizes cost-effectiveness analysis. However, their normative considerations differed significantly from the considerations and attitudes of the researchers. If what is 'effective' differs between clinicians and researchers, then what is 'cost-effective' will likewise differ: the apparent clear-cut recommendations that well-designed cost-effectiveness analysis-based guidelines might clash with the clinician's search for optimal individual efficiency (Berg et al, 2001). In practice, CEAs conflict with the perspective of the doctor, who values the individual's quality of life most.

In addition, clinicians and economists may disagree regarding the way CEAs calculate costs of medical services. The costs can be divided in direct costs, that is the direct financial costs of a treatment, and the indirect costs, that is the broader, social costs of (not treating) the disease. In the Dutch project mentioned above, the specialist doctors argued that it was crucial to include not only the costs of the intervention itself, but also the costs that the patient and his/her environment had to make, the costs to the patient's employer, and so forth (Berg et al, 2001). However, non-medical, indirect costs, however, are much harder to include in cost-effectiveness analysis than the direct costs. For example, it is unclear what to include in indirect costs and what not, and how to calculate e.g. the partial loss of someone's access to the labour market, or the costs of informal care. Not including them makes the calculations more robust – but it also creates yet another point at which the assumptions embedded in the cost-effectiveness analysis design may diverge.

The application of cost-effectiveness measures to allocation decisions may also affect the position of the weaker groups in our society. Patients who are expected to benefit in a low degree from particular treatments, such as the elderly and the chronically ill, may be excluded from access to such treatments, particularly when such treatments are expensive. Moreover, certain groups, like the elderly, are excluded from research, because they are not interesting enough, do not represent reliable data (because of co-morbidity) or are not able to participate in research. There is a serious concern, then, that the rationalisation of the rationing process will be at the expense of widely shared social values like justice, solidarity, equity and solidarity with the elderly population. (Maynard, 1997; Dickenson, 1999) Access for the elderly will be jeopardised when access to treatment is based only on cost-effectiveness analysis (or cost-utility analysis), since in general younger patients will have a more positive response to medical treatments.

EBM and External Control

But there are more problems with 'regulatory' EBM than the possible exclusion of weaker patient groups. Policy-makers and other third parties (like insurance companies) are often tempted by guidelines and cost-effectiveness analysis as an ideal way to control clinical practice and health care delivery and thus to control the costs of health care. Managed care is an example of such a system: in managed care a third party tries to control the use of medical and health care services by influencing the decision-making of the patient as well as that of the service provider. Managed care often joins decisions about the reimbursement of care and the delivery of care together in one agency. Such a system will have a profound influence on the professional autonomy of the physician and of the autonomy of the patient (Berger, 1996). Managed care already dominates U.S. health care and raises tremendous ethical problems for health care providers, in respect of access to care. In European health care systems that are based on health insurance (like Germany, The Netherlands and France), managed care is expected to gain a strong influence in the coming years. In The Netherlands and Germany for example, insurance companies will have to bear higher financial risks in the coming years, which is the reason why they are exerting a strong pressure to gain more control over the way in which medical care and health care are delivered.

Professional organisations have rather mixed feelings about the increasing emphasis on evidence-based guidelines, particularly those intended to ration scarce or expensive medical treatments. In Germany, for example, the health care system has undergone major reforms in the last years, which have attempted to respond to the increasing need to allocate limited resources. One example of these ongoing changes is the recent development of a list of medications that will be paid for by insurance companies However, within the medical community there is a fundamental disagreement on how and to what extent economic considerations can and should influence health care policy and medical practice. The majority of clinicians are very sceptical about these developments, as they fear they may lose their therapeutic freedom.

In the same way as subjective patient factors are excluded from the development and application of guidelines, subjective professional factors such as intuition and experience may become less important. Such factors lack scientific value and are therefore not useful for clinical practice. According to Redman (1994), clinical practice guidelines may eventually limit patients' and providers' autonomy by accepting without question the values contained within scientific research as the only basis on which judgements can be made by further codifying these values in reimbursement decisions.

EBM and Patient Autonomy

Evidence-based medicine is welcomed by some as a critical response to the inadequacies of traditional medicine, in part as a reaction to the authority (of doctors and other health professionals. (Hope, 1996) With the outcomes of systematic reviews in their hands, patients and their representatives could claim a more central role in medical decision-making. However, it is rather questionable whether EBM will indeed result in a medical democracy. There is a serious concern among doctors and other health care practitioners that the increasing dominance of evidence-based medicine may lead to a shift of power from doctors (and their patients) to managers and purchasers. Policy-makers and insurance companies are often tempted by guidelines and cost-effectiveness analyses as an ideal way to control clinical practice and health care delivery and thus to control the costs of health care. In theory, evidence-based guidelines could improve the position of patients in clinical decision-making. In practice, however, third parties are gaining more power to control the delivery of care services and will in fact determine which kinds of treatment and how many will be reimbursed. In continental health care systems, for example, the introduction of market approaches in the health care system will result in a shift of power towards insurance companies. Because those companies bear greater financial risks, they will force health care providers and institutions, to make use of the most cost-effective treatments.

Evidence-based criteria are increasingly expected to guide clinical decision-making and the allocation and rationing process in European health care systems. However, when the values and assumptions of managed care and other evidence-based systems remain hidden and implicit, such systems can be a serious challenge to the values of European societies in respect of the quality of delivery of medical care and health care. One of the reason for the Royal Dutch Physicians Organisation to conduct a research project into ethical problems of evidence-based was that, if clinical decisions increasingly come to be guided by evidence on their cost-effectiveness, it is better to have insight into the ethical assumptions and problems behind the use of this kind of evidence. In that case doctors, policy-makers and patients could reach a common ground for the implementation of such a policy.

Conclusion

The participants of our project took a critical attitude towards EBM, but none of them condemns EBM as altogether 'wrong' or 'bad'. They all agree that EBM can make an important contribution to the quality and allocation of medical care. However, they also emphasized that EBM can only do so by being transparent about its own hidden moral assumptions and values. This transparency is needed to enable a professional and political debate about the contribution such tools and systems can make to the quality and allocation of health care. Such a debate will help us to accept on a clinical level as well on the level of society the positive contribution these rationalising instruments might make.

Acknowledgement

The author wishes to thank the participants of the project Ethical Issues of Evidence-based Practice in Medicine and Health Care (EviBase) and the European Commission who sponsored this project within the Fifth Framework Program (Project QLG6-CT-2000-00964).

Other outcomes of the project:

Health Care Analysis, Special Issue on Evidence Based Medicine, Vol. 10, 2002, pp. 231-337.

Journal of Medical Ethics, Symposium on Evidence-based Medicine, Vol. 30, 2004, 119-175.

Meulen, R.H.J. ter, N. Biller-Andorno, Ch. Lenk, R. Lie (eds.), Ethical Issues of Evidence Based Medicine, Springer Verlag, Berlin, 2004 (in press)

References

Berg, M., Burg, M. van den, Meulen, R.H.J. ter (2001), Guidelines for Appropriate Care, The Importance of Empirical Normative Analysis, *Health Care Analysis 9*, 77-99.

Berger, J.F., Rosner F. (1996), The Ethics of Practice Guidelines Archives Internal Medicine;156, 2051-2056.

Cochrane, A. (1999), Effectiveness and Efficiency London: RSM Press.

Culpepper L., Gilbert T.T. (1999), Evidence and Ethics Lancet, 353, 829-831.

Dickenson, D.L (1999), Can Medical Criteria Settle Priority-Setting Debates? The Need for Ethical Analysis Health Care Analysis, 7, 131-137.

Hope, T. (1995), Editorial: Evidence-Based Medicine and Ethics Journal of Medical Ethics, 21 (5), 259-260.

Maynard, A. (1997), Evidence-Based Medicine: An Incomplete Method for Informing Treatment choices, Lancet, 349, 126-128.

Muir Gray J.A. (1997), Evidence-Based Healthcare, How to Make Health Policy and Management Decisions Edinburgh: Churchill Livingstone.

Redman, B.K. (1994), Clinical Practice Guidelines as Tools for Public Policy: Conflicts of Purpose, Issues of Autonomy and Justice Journal of Clinical Ethics 5(4), 303-309.

Sackett, D.L, Rosenberg, W.M., Gray, J.A, Haynes, R.B, Richardson, W.S. (1996), Evidence Based Medicine: What it is and What it isn't, *British Medical Journal* 312(7023), 71-72.

Sweeney, K.G., MacAuley D, Gray D.P. (1998), Personal Significance: The Third Dimension, Lancet, 351, 134-136.

Weel van Ch., Knottnerus J.A. (1999), Evidence Based Interventions and Comprehensive Treatment, Lancet, 353 916-918.

Chapter 9

Health Economics and Access to Treatment

Sam Salek

There has been a continuing increase in healthcare expenditure world-wide, particularly in the past three decades. Paradoxically, awareness of resource scarcity relative to need and introduction of rationing mechanisms into healthcare policy making is occurring at the same time as expenditure is rising.

The magnitude of this rise in expenditure can be seen in the case of the UK where a 30% increase was seen from 1973 to 1995 (OHE, 1995). Furthermore, review of the relative increase in healthcare expenditure as a percentage of GDP for the UK, USA, Europe and more globally for countries belonging to the Organisation for Economic Co-operation and Development (OECD), show a major increase in the relative share of total available resources being spent on healthcare (OHE, 2004).

Expenditure on pharmaceutical products constitute approximately 10% of the total healthcare expenditure (OHE, 2004), yet it is the first target to be hit by any rationing or cost saving programme. Due to its non-complexity, it is often looked upon as a soft target by purse holders and policy-makers.

Evidently, the situation of increasing healthcare expenditure together with the problem of resource scarcity must be largely due to increasing healthcare needs at a higher rate creating greater demands.

The Concept of Need and its Dynamic Nature

'Need' is regarded by economists as 'capacity to benefit' from a given resource (Williams, 1988). On the other hand, philosophers define need as a resource that is required, instrumentally, as a precondition to any other human action (Daniels, 1980; Ramsay, 1992). Daniels (1980) argues that social provision for the satisfaction of healthcare needs is a necessary condition for ensuring fair equality of opportunity and thus justice within a society. Nevertheless, the claim that healthcare should be given to patients according to their clinically determined needs is attractive, precisely because it has the superficial appearance of resolving complex moral dilemmas of allocation through appeal to an objective and quantifiable phenomenon.

From an economist's perspective, Williams dismisses the appeal to needs as a 'red herring'. He reduces the philosophy of need to the proposition that someone would be better off with the 'needed' treatment than without it. This leaves open the issue of whose values determine whether that person will be better off and how one person's 'needs' (i.e. potential benefit) are to be weighted against another's (Williams, 1988). Williams raises two important points here. First, the assumption that needs claims are inherently objective is challenged and as such to be distinguished from less morally pressing subjective claims, such as desires, wants, wishes or demands. To suggest that there is an issue as to whose values should determine the respective weighting of two competing needs claims, is to suggest that even needs claims entail some element of subjective evaluation. So that the complexities of moral decision making are not avoided after all. Second, needs are ultimately reduced to the ability of each patient to benefit from treatment. Given the scarcity of healthcare resources it is not possible for all healthcare needs to be satisfied immediately. Competing needs claims will therefore have to be prioritised. According to Williams' view, the ultimate criticism of priority for needs will be the patients' respective ability to benefit (e.g. in terms of QALY gain) from the available medical resources.

Based on the above premise, need is perceived to be very dynamic and healthcare needs increase with every new medical advance including new medicines for old diseases (Walker, 2002). For example, very low birth-weight babies, short children and infertile couples were not in 'need' until the development of neonatal intensive care, growth hormone therapy and fertility treatment. However, without a commensurate increase in resourcing this trend will lead to a widening in any existing gap between total need and net need. While there are numerous examples of new technologies being less costly than those which they replace (e.g. by allowing procedures formerly requiring in-patient stays to be performed on a day case basis), most new technologies allow people to benefit more but at a positive cost. Indeed, as the pace of technological advances show no sign of slowing, the ability of any healthcare system to 'meet all needs' becomes an increasingly difficult task.

Apart from technological advances, changes in population demography have also contributed to the dynamism of need for healthcare services. For example, a boy born in the UK during 1948 could expect to live for 66.4 years, whereas in 1994 this life expectancy had increased to 74.3 years. Furthermore, 36 out of each 1000 children born in the UK during 1948 died in the first year of life, whereas the infant mortality rate in 1988 was only 8.9 deaths per 1000 live births. Realistically, one of the consequences of this success is that healthcare systems have to care for an increasingly elderly population (OHE, 2004). Older people tend to have greater healthcare needs (OPCS, 2003) and receive a relatively large share of overall healthcare resources (OHE, 2004).

Prioritisation - Is it Ethical?

Choices for healthcare have to be made whether on clinical or ethical grounds. However, introducing cost into the decision-making process is inevitably unpleasant but it is argued that it is a necessary part of the pursuit of a health service's broad objectives that it is ethical and in any case it is unavoidable. 'Health Economics' is about the efficient use of scarce resources and logically, based on this, 'efficiency' becomes the best criterion for choice.

The outcomes of healthcare come in many different forms and guises. Pain relief, anxiety reduction, mobility improvement and life extension are all examples of successful outcomes/achievements of healthcare. What is sought is a measure which can express all these different aspects of achieved health improvement in common units. Such measure is referred to as QALY. The basic thinking behind QALY is that health has two main dimensions: length and quality. Effective healthcare must either extend life or improve its quality or preferably some combination of the two. So, in theory, all effective healthcare will produce Quality Adjusted Life Year or QALYs which is also used to express healthcare achievement.

QALYs are advocated as an aid to resource allocation decision-making on the basis that priority setting and/or rationing are a necessary feature of these types of choices. The term 'priority' has positive connotation with its focus on the extra benefits that will be conferred on some patient group (e.g. the elderly), disease group (e.g. cardiovascular disease), or through the expansion of some related health care activities (e.g. prevention). The term rationing on the other hand has negative connotation with its focus on denial of potentially achievable benefits. However, regardless of which term is used, for reasons of ever increasing demands on scarce resources, the reality is that the unpleasant choices cannot be avoided. Of course, in an ideal world of infinite resources neither prioritising nor rationing would be necessary and sufficient resources would be available to meet all health needs fully and immediately. Unfortunately, we do not live in such an ideal world but rather in one where resources for healthcare are now and always will be scarce. If this statement is accepted then the need to make choices about how to allocate healthcare resources – to whom, when and in what quantity – is inescapable. However, the technical issues of how to design construct and execute some form of systematic mechanism to address the resource allocation choices cannot be separated from questions of ethics. Thus, any allocation mechanism that is proposed or implemented must be morally defensible.

Increased Spending on Healthcare and Demand – Can We Afford It?

Too many, including Hancock (1993) the problem is not one of infinite demand but of insufficient resources being available to meet finite demand. So why not just spend more? What if the UK spent as great a Proportion of its GDP as the USA? (The basic premise of health economics is that resources are finite while demand for healthcare is infinite (Mooney, 1986). While demand is increasing, there are many who dispute this, arguing that there is a finite limit on how large demand can grow and therefore there is some level of resourcing which would eliminate the need to make choices in healthcare on the basis of cost. In contrast to this hypothesis, in practice, demand has increased year-on-year.

Indeed, there are significant differences in the percentages of GDP which different countries choose to spend on healthcare. For example, in Europe, the percentage of GDP varies from 5% in Greece to almost 9% in Germany. In recent years European countries have tended to spend more than other OECD countries (e.g. Switzerland or the USA). On this basis those countries towards the bottom of the spending league table could spend more, although this would have opportunity costs in terms of foregone benefits from other areas of economic activity (OECD, 2004).

A decision to increase the proportion of GDP devoted to healthcare cannot, however be made in isolation. Health creation has opportunity costs in that the benefits from alternative uses of these resources are foregone. For example, if healthcare is publicly funded, then the opportunity cost will be in the form of foregone benefit from other areas of public activity such as education, defence, transport, social services or protecting environmental quality. These too have moral value, and indeed many of them can also have direct and indirect impacts on health. In the case of the UK, over the last decade the proportion of public spending allocated to healthcare has been increasing, with funding being diverted from, among others, housing and defence (OHE, 2004).

Access to Medicines – Who Should Decide?

At one time the British National Formulary classified medicines as A, B or C, depending on the Joint Formulary Committee's assessment of the medicine's therapeutic usefulness. Doctors were discouraged from prescribing other than class A or B medicines and preferably only class A. Some members of this Committee were also members of the Committee on Safety of Medicines appointed to advise the government on the licensing of new medicines under the 1971 Medicines Act. Thus the prescribing of medicines already granted marketing authorization by the government could still be restricted by this classification. However, the classification had no statutory power and fell from use by 1976, although medicines which cannot be prescribed on the NHS are still marketed.

The system has now been reinforced in the form of the National Institute for Clinical Excellence (NICE), set up by government to advise on best medical practice. This Institute tells medical practitioners what therapeutic guidelines they should follow and which medicines they may prescribe on the National Health Service. It thus basically decides which medicines will be reimbursed by the government and which will not. It is difficult to understand how on the one hand the government can license a medicine as safe and effective and then decide on the other hand that it is not therapeutically justified and refuse to pay for it. There are many examples of medicines not being prescribable on the National Health Service (NHS). Sildenafil was licensed by Pfizer for treatment of male impotence. NICE decided that this use was not justified on the NHS. Strong protests caused NICE to change its mind and allow it for certain patients with a chronic underlying disease such as diabetes mellitus. NICE also decided that GlaxoSmithKline (GSK) recently approved antiflu tablet did not qualify for reimbursement, then again changed its mind, apparently due to consideration of further evidence following strong political pressure from GSK. It is difficult to understand how clinical judgements can vary so rapidly on consideration of apparently the same clinical evidence. Other countries approach the rationing of state-funded medicines in different ways.

Should the state be deciding which patients get appropriate treatment and which do not, unless they can afford it themselves? In an ideal social order, no such distinction should be made, but in the real world of practical socialism, there has to be rationing and expensive new remedies cannot be exempt from this. But should the decision be made centrally for all doctors and patients by one committee such as NICE, or should it be left to individual hospitals and practices to set their own prescribing policies? At present in the UK we have both systems, so that even those medicines approved for reimbursement on NHS prescription may not be approved by the local therapeutic prescribing committee as items to be stocked or dispensed. There is yet another level of control exercised by the government on doctors' prescribing habits. Each year general practice doctors' prescribing costs are analysed and compared in such a way that individual doctors can be advised that their costs are higher than average and must be reduced. This should have the net effect of reducing the average annual prescribing cost, since high prescribers are constantly being advised and disciplined.

It is a dangerous policy to limit treatment only to those considered deserving patients. Do they include those wanting plastic surgery breast implants, plastic nose jobs, or only heart transplants for non-smokers? If limited to those not taking part in hazardous pursuits, we should have to exclude not only all smokers, all alcoholics, all drug addicts and those injured during criminal activities, etc., but also all vehicle drivers and all those doing sporting activities. The situation becomes absurd. It is impossible to draw a line between acceptable and unacceptable activities or illnesses. Healthcare and provision of medicines cannot by judgemental and dependent on following a centrally decided acceptable lifestyle. Who makes the rules as to who is eligible for treatment? Those in authority may not always be in the best position to decide.

Surely such delicate and individual decisions cannot be taken empirically by a central committee, which clearly has political remit to make sure that state which medicines are sufficiently safe and effective in specific indications to support its medical culture, and grant marketing licences accordingly. It also has the absolute right to determine how much it is prepared to pay for such remedies in the state health care system. Thereafter any decision about which patients should be treated has to be taken by the patient and administering doctor at the time, with the patient's best interests at heart. Only at this level can a rational and ethical decision be taken as to who may or may not benefit and have access to treatment.

However, regrettably, emotional arguments usually appeal more strongly to most people than logical arguments. The Licensing Authority was set up as a result of the emotional outburst in the wake of the thalidomide-provoked phocomelia epidemic. The public did not want unscrutinised medicines going on the market. They want well tried and tested medicines with proven efficacy and safety, especially when other effective remedies are already available for that disease. The conflict between emotion and logic becomes particularly acute with possible treatments for diseases for which there is no effective treatment. To be compellingly tenable, ethical decisions should always apply across the whole spectrum of activities.

Concluding Remarks

Resource scarcity, access to treatment and the need for choice are universal problems, but are by no means universally accepted. It is demonstrated here that rationing, prioritising or more simply making choices has always been a feature of healthcare and cannot be avoided. However, economic techniques and their systematic mechanisms such as QALYs facilitate resource allocation decision-making and could assist in the moral defence of the whole process, providing transparent, explicit and logical policies for access to treatment.

References

Daniels, N. (1980), Health-care needs and distributive justice, *Philosophy and Public Affairs*, 10(1), 147-176.

Hancock, C. (1993), Getting a Quart Out of a Pint Pot, *Rationing in Action*, London, BMJ Publishing Group.

Mooney, G. (1986), Economics, Medicine and Healthcare, London, Harvester Wheatsheaf.

OECD (2004), OECD Health Data 2004: First Edition. Paris, OECD.

OECD (1993), OECD Health Systems: Facts and Trends 1960 - 1991. (Volume 1) *Health Policy Studies No 3,* Paris, OECD.

Office of Health Economics. (1995) Compendium of Health Statistics. London, Office of Health Statistics.

Office of Health Economics, (2004), Compendium of Health Statistics, London, Office of Health Statistics.

Office of Population Census and Surveys, (OPCS) (2003), General Household Survey 2001, *Series GHS No 24*, London, HMSO.

Ramsey, M. (1992), Human Needs and the Market, Aldershot, Avebury.

Walker, R. (2002), Can We Afford the Medicining We Need: An Ethical Dilemma? In Salek, S. & Edgar, A. (editors) *Pharmaceutical Ethics*, John Wiley & Sons, Chichester, UK, 2002.

Williams, A. (1988), Creating a Healthcare Market: Ideology, Efficiency, Ethics and Clinical Freedom, NHS White paper, Occasional Paper 5, York, Centre for Health Economics.

Chapter 10

Clinical Ethics Committees in Europe: Assistance in Medical Decisions, Fora for Democratic Debates, or Bodies to Monitor Basic Rights?

Guy Lebeer

This article is primarily based on the final report of the BIOMED II project Ethical Function in Hospital Ethics Committees (European Commission's concerted action).[1] The report discusses the question of hospital ethics committees in nine countries: Belgium, Denmark, France, Greece, Italy, Norway, Spain, Sweden and the United Kingdom.[2] The purpose of the project was to set up and organise a European-wide reflection on the practice of ethics in hospitals. It appeared especially heuristic to base this general reflection on a study of the concrete activities of hospital ethics committees whatever their form, but taking into account their concern for both research ethics and clinical ethics.

This text presents a summary comparing the various situations of clinical ethics committees in our European reference area as well as the main debates this comparison elicited in our small circle of experts. We will not report all the questions under discussion in this field, nor a fortiori all those possible. Nevertheless the differences that sparked lively discussions in our group, I feel, highly reflect current issues in the institutionalisation of ethics in medicine. Indeed, all the questions whether they concern, for instance, the composition of ethics committees or training for their members revolve around the more fundamental issue of the role, attributions and responsibilities of ethics committees and thus their present and future capacity to effect deep-seated transformations in medical practice.

This article will only deal with clinical ethics committees or related forms.[3] Although our concerted action also looked into research or national ethics committees, we will not discuss these areas here due to space limitations, despite the considerable influence the various types of committees have on one another. Moreover, as the comparative data date from 2001/2002 there may have been major changes in the ensuing time, especially in legal areas.

Institutionalising Clinical Ethics: the Diversity Found in Europe

Denmark is the only partner country that does not have clinical ethics committees (CECs). The eight others do have CECs although only two have accorded them legal status: Belgium and Greece. In these two countries, in fact, the hospital ethics committees are 'mixed', with a dual mission to supervise research and address questions raised by clinical activities.

The other countries vary in the extent these structures have been institutionalised. In Spain, a Commission of INSALUD (the Spanish National Institute of Health, a network of 80 public hospitals) had approved some 20 hospital committees by the end of the concerted action period. In Norway, the creation of regional ethics committees in 1985 resulted in the disappearance of the hospital committees. A gap in the system, however, became apparent and the Ministry of Welfare and Health decided to conduct a study based on a triple experience with clinical ethics committees. This study, lasting from 1993-1998, led to recommendations to establish a CEC in each major hospital.

Elsewhere (France, Italy, Sweden, UK) the CECs seem to have been established spontaneously. They may be 'specialty' committees, like some in France and Italy. Our Italian partners, for instance, were members of the ethics committee in the paediatrics department of the University of Padova hospital. Similarly, some British assisted conception centres have their own ethics committee. Nevertheless, the 'spontaneous' committees are usually 'trans-specialty' dealing with the range of healthcare practices and hospital policy.

France holds a special place in the clinical ethics landscape. The network of Parisian public hospitals (Assistance Publique – Hôpitaux de Paris or AP-HP) in 1995 set up an innovative and trans-hospital structure: the Espace Ethique (Ethics Forum). It is an original place of study, analysis and comparison that focuses on thought about the ethics of care and hospital practices, with all the economic and social issues involved. In particular it fosters the creation of thematic reflection groups ('Groupes Miramion') composed of healthcare professionals and outside experts to think about the hospital. These groups exist for the period of the reflection process, then they disband, start up again or are replaced by other groups. The Espace Ethique also fulfils an educational mission, and in this area are similar to many other European clinical ethics committees.

Multiple Functions

While the scopes of the research ethics committees do not seem burdened by ambiguity and are relatively homogenous throughout Europe, the same cannot be said for the clinical ethics committees. But what are CECs exactly? The European CEC is first and foremost a body for reflection and is thus primarily available for the hospital's practitioners, occasionally families (for example the CEC in a paediatrics department), and sometimes – but this is rare – for patients. This last case was cited in Spain. In some Spanish hospitals the patients can apply to an ethics committee, but most often only after a filtering-body has sorted the patients' requests into those admissible for an ethics reflection and others assimilated to complaints which are heard by a completely different body. The CEC audience rarely goes beyond the hospital grounds – only when it has itself been established on an external basis, such as the French Espace Ethique.

A CEC can also fulfil other functions, essentially drawing up guidelines in hospital policy and, more rarely, direct assistance in decisions. In Belgium where, we recall, the CECs are inseparable from RECs, the law of 1994 entrusts these committees with both types of missions in addition to evaluating protocols. Recent statistics on the activity of Belgian hospital committees show that over four out of five questions handled concern the examination of protocols, and that only a small portion of the questions deal with assistance to decisions.[4] In the 'mixed' Belgian – and Greek – committees, clinical ethics has drastically receded, literally overwhelmed by tasks related to research ethics. To counteract this effect, some hospitals doubled up the function by creating a sub-committee dealing more specifically with matters of clinical ethics. This 'demotion' of clinical ethics or the fear of this happening is not felt solely in Belgium and it leads many observers to recommend a clear distinction between the two structures. This separation would thus not be founded on principles – there is no fundamental difference in the ethical goals pursued by research and clinical ethics committees – but rather on the practical experience of the 'mixed' committees.

Drawing up Guidelines

CECs frequently work to draw up guidelines. This is particularly true for the CECs created at the initiative of hospital management. In some countries, such as Belgium, management is a persona non grata in the CECs. Neither the administrative management, nor the medical or nursing directors can belong, so as to not inhibit the expression of the committee members. In Norway, management participation was under discussion. In Italy, however, particularly in the ethics committee of the Padova University paediatrics department, management is closely associated with the work of the committee. This involvement is justified by the idea that you can never truly expect to modify hospital practices without the practical and symbolic support of management, on the one hand in terms of realism and organisational competence and on the other for political legitimacy. This management involvement does not necessarily have to be as full-fledged committee member, which experience shows can also adversely affect the freedom of discussion. Other schemes exist, the most usual being to invite management at strategic points of the discussion and thus to preserve the committee's autonomy in the opinions it hands down.

Ethics Consultation

The mission of a priori assistance in medical decisions is fairly rare in the European CECs. This does not mean, however, that it cannot be ensured in another form such as an 'ethics consultant'. This institution is well-known in the United States but also found in some European countries, Sweden in particular. The 'ethics consultant' institution has its proponents and detractors. The proponents see the ethics consultant as a lightweight, mobile structure that can be mobilised at any time, especially in an emergency. It is thus favoured by those who conceive a hospital's 'ethics' function as directly associated with medical decision-making. This formula usually has a major implication: the ethics consultant is a specialist in medical ethics. This is why the partisans also favour professional specialist training. This view, dominant in the United States, is far from unanimous in Europe.

The detractors of 'ethics consultation' – whether entrusted to one person or a committee – hold up several reasons. Some feel that proclaiming a specific competence in ethics runs the risk of encouraging clinicians to consult the expert(s) on any occasion, especially in the present context of increasing pressure by society regarding the responsibility of the medical corps. This itself entails the risk of divorcing medical practice from its essential ethics component, calling into question the time-honoured relationship between the doctor and patient founded on the therapeutic pact. Others also state that the doctor's power of decision, as a power, is thus considerably undermined. Refusing the 'ethics consultation' function and the notion of ethics expertise that it implies is thus justified by the concern to recognise the doctor's ethical competence or even moral authority. Another category of detractors advocate the same type of arguments but this time – and the difference is essential – not from the doctor's perspective but from the ordinary citizen's. For these critics, ethics is not the domain of specialists but is a matter for us all since ethics deals with the wish to say something about the final meaning of life, as Wittgenstein stated.[5] Consequently the designers of the Norwegian project considered it crucial to recognise a 'non-expert grounding' for ethics: the ethical review is primarily based on a non-expert foundation in regard to experience and virtue. In their eyes, training in ethics is nevertheless important but cannot be a sine qua non. This perspective is clearly more consistent with a notion of the ethics committee as a reflection body (possibly on an individual medical decision but in this case a posteriori) and/or as the producer of general guidelines rather than a partner in medical decisions in vivo.

Diverging Views on the Committees' Composition and Training

The antagonism between the positions for or against a concept of the ethics committee assisting medical decisions and ethics as a specialised competence has repercussions at two levels: training for committee members and the role they accord themselves in this area, and the composition of the committees, in particular the participation of lay people.

We can thus describe initially the divergence between two types of stances: one favourable to specialised ethics competence at the service of a medicine in quest, the other favouring a collective non-specialised competence built on discussion and addressing the equally collective issues of a medicine questioned first from the outside. In the first stance the committee members are doctors, nurses and paramedical staff providing support to an ethicist who must be present. A legal expert may participate as well but this is not obligatory. In the second stance the committee is open to multiple points of view – philosophers, sociologists, legal experts, psychoanalysts... along with lay people or 'public representatives'. This last category is nevertheless problematical, even for those in favour. For who exactly can 'represent the public'? Members of political parties, as in Denmark and Sweden? But in this case the notion of personal membership as a representative of humanity is replaced by a collective membership representing special interests. The 'man in the street'? But how to choose such a person? Haphazardly or on the basis of criteria, and then which criteria? These questions are still open.

We could then schematically group the following positions under one category: first, the view that an important function of an ethics committee is to offer assistance in medical decisions that remain to be taken, the recognition of a specialised ethics competence, the need for ad hoc qualifying training, the ethics committee's contribution to the training process, the presence of a duly trained ethicist and discounting the need for a lay point of view, in other words outside scientific, clinical, philosophical or even legal references. This schematic type can then be opposed to a second set of positions: that an ethics committee is first a body for reflection on the generalities of medical practice, especially in relation to its social, political and economic context, the position of principle whereby ethics cannot be the territory of a particular social group, an interest in training but not as a condition for ethical reflection, an ethics committee not seen as a forum for ethical expertise and which can thus not claim to be one of specialised training – in this case the term would rather be 'awareness function' – the concern for the broadest diversity in viewpoints, with the presence of lay members symbolising the points of view of other members of society on the whole.

This schematic description certainly offers a pertinent grid to interpret the reality of the European CECs. But it is merely schematic and only reflects broad types of positions. The divergence it illustrates only quite partially covers the variations actually found among the partner countries of our concerted action. In some countries the divergence can be pertinent, not to describe and compare in block one national system with another, but to illustrate the internal tensions within a single country. In Belgium, in fact, the two opposite positions can be found: although regulated by law the ethics committees can actually serve two contradicting purposes. The 'spontaneous' nature of the way clinical ethics committees were created in some countries obviously means that their goals and activities can reflect highly diverse concepts – this is highly probable in France and also likely in the UK as well.

A hypothetical relationship could be seen between strong medical authority and resistance towards forming an ethical expertise that proposes – or even claims the right – to intervene in medical decisions, and inversely between contested medical authority and affirming an ethics specialty, as in the United States. In Europe the situation is more complex. For instance, the Spanish committees set up by the INSALUD Commission are quite comfortable with a medical context that is still extremely dominant, as Freidson explains.[6] As it happens, however, when these committees were set up one condition was that the creators follow a clearly specialising training. This is still a prerequisite for any new ethics committee. In this system, ethics expertise is thus clearly affirmed and assumed. In other countries, however, the medical establishment is extremely cautious about forms of institutionalised ethics that would undermine its dominance. Denmark has no clinical ethics committees. France has local committees that are not recognised by law where doctors are largely in the majority. Belgian law recognises hospital ethics committees, but almost all of them merely deal with the bureaucratic aspects of protocols. As such, some may say that the European ethics committee structures are either barred to the outside or at best co-managed by a homey alliance between a strong medical authority and a new group becoming professionalised: the ethicists.

Paths to Ethical Inventiveness

Analysis, however pertinent it may seem to some people, nevertheless does not fairly reflect two concomitant processes. In the first place, in the interstices of the various institutionalised ethics systems we can find extremely innovative initiatives under development, spawned more by premises of a political nature than drawn from the specialised corps of medical ethics. Furthermore, at the heart of the medical profession, practitioners are increasingly open to a critical reconsideration of their practice, a reconsideration which both draws from and leads to an ethical reflection. In some countries, like Belgium, hospitals over recent years have set up new bodies for ethics reflection, in parallel with the official committees. The professionals behind these new bodies are disappointed in the official committees and many hold what sociologists term 'dominated' positions in the hospital structure: nurses, psychiatrists, geriatrists, palliative care staff, etc. In France, the doctors participating in the Espace Ethique's 'Groupes Miramion' accept, in a context other than that of their workplace, to place themselves on equal footing with other hospital professionals and with actual or potential patients – something they are hardly used to in their daily practice. The subjects raised in these groups frequently touch on macro-social dimensions extending beyond hospital walls. And we should not forget that the Espace Ethique was created by the Parisian public hospital system. A recent work by the Espace director is entitled 'The hospital revolution. Democracy in healthcare'[7]... a programme and manifesto. Training for hospital staff is at the heart of the Espace Ethique's mission. This training consists in a series of conferences primarily cultural in scope; the aim is not strictly qualification in terms of acquiring operational skills. The UK is experiencing an exponential rise in the number of CECs, a phenomenon that intrigues us. Our British partners see this 'spontaneous generation' of ethics bodies as the sign of a constant degradation in the treatment of British patients; not only in medical treatment, but also – and especially – in their rights. It may well be that the CECs in the UK can gradually grow into bodies for emulation and monitoring, and someday possibly even mandated to guarantee the respect of people's basic rights.

Patients' Rights

We have here a totally new notion of the clinical ethics committee. No longer a body at the service of the patient through the auspices of a medical profession wishing to become more ethical, or via a public debate forum on the aims of hospital practice, but rather a place for observation and incitement at the service of the patient in the respect of their basic rights. This vision obviously calls into question the consultative nature of the clinical ethics committees, a task on which the countries of Europe have pragmatically agreed until now. Indeed, it is somewhat hard to imagine how a committee observing major infringements on basic rights would not have the possibility, in other words the authority, to impose respect of these rights. If the committee is to have this authority, however, it must receive a public mandate along these lines which ensures at least a minimal degree of independence from the hospital structure. And Europe is far from taking this step. As we have seen, few countries have granted a legal status to the CECs. Many observers feel that this mission, if granted to CECs one day, is in total contradiction with a mission of reflection. Few practitioners would be ready to submit an ethical problem for discussion by a committee that would then have a direct or indirect legal authority to sanction, in other words to what could well be called a potential 'medical practices court'. The concerted action debate on this question was quite lively.

A Biomedical Citizenship?

Europe presents a mosaic of situations. This variety in the extent to which clinical ethics has been institutionalised cannot be explained simply. It is a combination of several causes: power of the medical corps, weight of religion, legal system, cultural representations about medicine, the political and economic organisation of the health care system... This analysis is still largely to come.

The disparities between the various models of clinical ethics committees have arisen from different concepts regarding the institutionalisation of ethics in medicine: assistance to medicine, reflection beyond the strict medical field, protecting the rights of patients. Neither do the partner countries of the concerted action clearly line up along either side of the issue. The disparities tend rather to illustrate internal tensions, as if all the partner countries experienced this conflict in the different notions, albeit to various extents and in variable configurations. The clinical ethics committees, at the onset seemed full of inventive promise, opening the hospital to external and multiple points of view, thus renewing with the with age-old concern to recompose a humanist project for medicine. Some people have seen hospital ethics committees as opportunities to render reflections more democratic, to establish public fora for thinking on medical ethics. And on this subject, they spoke of possibilities for a 'biomedical citizenship'.[8] The time does not seem ripe for an optimistic response to these questions.

Notes

1 G. Lebeer (ed.), *Ethical Function in Hospital Ethics Committees*, IOS Press, Amsterdam/Oxford, 2002. See also G. Lebeer, M. Moulin (eds), *Ethical Function in Hospital Ethics Committees, Working papers Worshop 1 & 2*, Université Libre de Bruxelles, Bruxelles, 2000 and 2001.

2 This article is based on contributions from the following participants: Prof. M. Moulin, S. Carbonnelle, A. Perissino and Prof. Y. Englert (Université Libre de Bruxelles – Belgium), Prof. M.-L. Delfosse (Facultés Universitaires Notre-Dame de la Paix – Belgium), Prof. J.D. Rendtorff (Roskilde University – Denmark), Prof. I. Arnoux (Université Bordeaux III – France), Prof. P. Dalla-Vorgia and T. Garanis (University of Athens – Greece), Prof. C. Viafora, D. Gobber and P. Drigo (University of Padua – Italy), Prof. K. Ruyter (University of Oslo – Norway), A. Sainz-Rojo (INSALUD – Spain), Prof. Th. Achen (Linköping University – Sweden), Prof. G. Hermeren (Lund University – Sweden), Prof. J. Gunning (Cardiff University – United Kingdom), Prof. D. Beyleveld and Prof. R. Brownsword (Sheffield University – United Kingdom) and also Fr. Crawley (European Forum for Good Clinical Practice – International Organisation) and A.-M. Prieels (Tech-Know Consultants – Belgium).

3 I wish to thank Sylvie Carbonnelle for her helpful criticism and wise judgements.

4 Rapport d'activité des Comités d'éthique locaux (Activity report of the local ethics committees) 1998-2001, Document du Comité Consultatif de Bioéthique de Belgique (Belgian Advisory Committee of Bioethics), p.8.

5 L. Wittgenstein, *Leçons et conversations suivies de Conférence sur l'Ethique*, Gallimard, Folio, Paris, 1992, p.155.

6 E. Freidson, *Professional Dominance*, New York, Atherton, 1970. An analysis that is still quite timely.

7 E. Hirsch, *La révolution hospitalière. Une démocratie du soin*, Bayard, Paris, 2002.

8 B. Cadoré, *L'éthique clinique comme philosophie contextuelle*, Fides, Québec, 1997, p.16.

Chapter 11

Human Dignity and the UNESCO Declaration on the Human Genome

Roberto Andorno

Introduction

The United Nations Educational, Scientific and Culture Organization (UNESCO) made in 1997 a first important step towards common standards on genetic issues with the adoption of the Universal Declaration on the Human Genome and Human Rights. Although this instrument dates back to seven years ago, its significance and future perspectives have been until now little explored in the legal literature. This is surprising, since this is not just another document on ethics and genetics, but the most complete global initiative aimed at protecting human rights with regard to genetic technologies.[1] Furthermore, according to one of its drafters, this instrument represents a 'futuristic advance' in international human rights law.[2] For those reasons, the UNESCO Declaration deserves to be analysed in a more detailed, focused way. The purpose of this paper is precisely to explore one of its most noticeable features: the very central role it gives to the notion of human dignity. More specifically, this paper aims to distinguish two different dimensions of human dignity that result from the UNESCO Declaration: the dignity of the individual and the dignity of humanity as such.

The Two Dimensions of Human Dignity

The emerging international biomedical law assigns a key role to the notion of human dignity, which is presented as the ultimate rationale for the rules settled in this area. This trend, particularly visible in the instruments relating to bioethics adopted since 1997 by UNESCO and the Council of Europe, is impressive enough to lead scholars to present dignity as 'the shaping principle' of international bioethics.[3] Perhaps the main reason for this strong appeal to human dignity lies in the fact that this notion is regarded as a last barrier against the alteration of some basic human characteristics that could result from techniques such as reproductive cloning or genetic engineering. It is noteworthy that the traditional understanding of human rights as a means of empowerment for existing individuals (or groups of individuals) seems unable to address the new concerns raised by biotechnological developments, because the notion of 'rights' can hardly cover the interests of future generations or of humanity as such. Therefore, international instruments dealing with biomedical issues have recourse to the idea of human dignity with the hope that it can provide an ultimate theoretical reason to prevent a misuse of emerging biotechnological powers.

Certainly, the reference to human dignity in international law is neither new nor specific to instruments dealing with biomedicine. On the contrary, this notion is at the cornerstone of the international human rights movement that emerged in the aftermath of the Second World War. The expression appears in the Universal Declaration of Human Rights of 1948, which proclaimed the 'inherent dignity (...) of all members of the human family.' References to human dignity are to be found in most international human rights instruments adopted during the last half-century, including Conventions to protect prisoners of war and civilian persons in time of war, to eliminate racial discrimination and discrimination against women, to prevent torture and other inhuman and degrading treatments, to promote the rights of the child and to protect persons with physical or mental disabilities, among many others. Nevertheless, the fact is that instruments relating to biomedicine emphasize the notion of human dignity in a very powerful way. Indeed, the contrast between the background role assigned to human dignity in the founding international instruments of human rights and the foreground role assigned to it in the emerging international biomedical law could not be more striking.[4]

On the other hand, it is noteworthy that international law refers to human dignity without providing any clarification about the meaning of this concept. This lack of explanation leads some scholars to argue that dignity is a purely rhetoric notion, without any specific content, or even a 'useless concept' that should be simply abandoned.[5] This latter conclusion seems, however, too simplistic. It is true that the bioethical discussion shows an inflationary use of the notion of human dignity that should be avoided, especially when no additional explanation is given to say why a particular practice is regarded as being in conformity (or not) with human dignity. Nevertheless, this situation should not lead us to throw out the baby with the bath water. It would be an exaggeration to conclude from this phenomenon that the concept of dignity itself is empty. Rather on the contrary, it can be argued that, in spite of the apparent vagueness of this notion, the central role assigned to it in international biomedical law is not the result of a merely rhetoric strategy, but reflects a real concern about the need to protect the integrity and identity, not only of existing individuals, but also of humanity as such.

In fact, the task of providing, if not a very precise definition, at least a minimal explanation of what 'dignity' means is not so difficult as it might seem. In a few words, two different meanings can be attached to this notion: a basic meaning and an extended meaning:[6]

a) The basic meaning of dignity, which is the primary, most common and stronger expression of this idea, refers to the intrinsic worthiness of human beings, irrespective of age, sex, physical or mental ability, religion, ethnic or social origin. The word 'intrinsic' is used to indicate that such a dignity does not rely on a particular feature or capacity of persons but only on their human condition. This is why dignity cannot be gained or lost, and it does not admit of any degrees. In other words, the idea of dignity relates 'to the intrinsic importance of human life'[7] and requires that 'people never be treated in a way that denies the distinct importance of their own lives'.[8] Again, if we want a more precise account of the notion of dignity we can turn to Kant for help. According to the German philosopher, this idea means that persons should always be treated as an end in themselves and never as a means only.[9] Thus, dignity is exactly the opposite of 'price', the kind of value for which there can be an equivalent, whereas 'dignity' makes a person irreplaceable. Therefore, according to the Kantian explanation of dignity, this notion can be equated with a requirement of non-instrumentalisation of persons.

b) The extended meaning of dignity relates to a more abstract notion, which refers to the value of humanity as a whole, including future generations. If all human beings have a dignity and should be respected unconditionally, it is reasonable to maintain that the larger group they belong to (humanity) possesses also, in a derivative way, an intrinsic value. This broader concept of dignity covers, on the one hand, the preservation of a sustainable environment for our descendants (a task for environmental ethics) and, on the other hand, the protection of the identity and integrity of the human species (a task for biomedical ethics). It should be pointed out that the Kantian imperative already contains, in some way, this extended notion of dignity because it literally says that it is humanity ('die Menschheit'), whether in our own person or in that of another, that should never be used only as a means.

Does the idea of a dignity of humanity necessarily mean that it is entitled to a right to its own existence or to its own identity? The answer to this question is controversial.[10] Perhaps a distinction should be made between property rights and the most fundamental human rights, which are those related, not to external things, but to the human body itself. On this basis, it can be argued that, on the one hand, humanity is entitled to a right to ownership of all those natural and cultural elements that are included in the category of 'common heritage of humanity'.[11] On the other hand, it is extremely difficult to conceive humanity, including future generations (that is, people who have not even been conceived), as a subject of rights dealing with physical integrity without distorting the notion of 'right' as an entitlement of existing individuals. Therefore, if we use the word 'right' with the latter meaning, we can conclude that humanity is probably more an object of obligations of the present generation, rather than a subject of rights. In support of this understanding, it is interesting to recall that during the discussions at UNESCO for the elaboration of an international instrument for the protection of future generations, between 1994 and 1997, one of the preliminary drafts included an explicit mention the 'rights' of future generations. Nevertheless, this expression was removed from the draft because it was considered as being in conflict with the notion of rights, which always refers to existing persons. For that reason, the final instrument adopted on 11 November 1997, was entitled 'Declaration on the

Responsibilities of Present Generations Towards Future Generations' and avoids any reference to the 'rights' of future generations.[12]

Dignity of the Individual

Some provisions of the UNESCO Declaration on the Human Genome and Human Rights are clearly oriented towards the protection of the dignity of the individual. In this respect, the basic premise is formulated by Article 2 (a), which states that 'everyone has a right to respect for their dignity and for their rights regardless of their genetic characteristics'. This is a specific application of the general principle of equality between individuals and reminds us that this principle does not admit any exception due to predisposition to genetic diseases. Article 2 (b) explains in a negative way the same principle. For that purpose it provides that 'dignity makes it imperative not to reduce individuals to their genetic characteristics and to respect their uniqueness and diversity.' It means that the dignity of the human person is the expression of philosophical ideals and convictions that transcend biology or genetics. Human dignity is not the result of a particular combination of DNA, even of a very complex one. We know, from the first results of the Human Genome Project, that humans have approximately 99% of their DNA in common with chimpanzees. However, it would be absurd to deduce from this fact that the human specificity lies in that 1% of peculiar genetic information. On the contrary, it can be argued that this discovery shows that what makes us human cannot be found only at the genetic or biological level. Because the most specific feature of human beings is not their genetic make up or their bodily structure (both of which are not very different from those of some non-human animals), but their spiritual dimension. This is precisely what makes them 'persons', that is, individuals belonging to a rational (i.e. spiritual) nature, according to the classic definition of this notion.[13] In sum, the discovery of our genetic similarity with non-human animals, far from refuting the inherent dignity of human beings, confirms a contrario what philosophers of every age, from Plato and Aristotle onwards, have always maintained: that humans, given their intellectual capacities, are essentially spiritual beings.[14]

Let us consider now some other provisions of the UNESCO Declaration that are based on the idea of dignity of the individual: Articles 5, 7 and 10.

Article 5 relates to the respect for individual's autonomy, which is a direct corollary of the principle of human dignity. Paragraph (b) embodies a fundamental principle of medical ethics according to which a biomedical intervention may only be carried out after the patient has been informed of its purpose, nature, risks and consequences, and has freely consented to it. The principle of informed consent has its origins in the 'Nuremberg Code' of 1947, having thereafter been included in the Helsinki Declaration of 1964. At present, virtually all medical ethics guidelines and research codes hold that physicians and researchers must obtain the informed consent of patients and subjects prior to any substantial intervention. Paragraph (c) recognizes both the right to know and the right not to know the results of genetic tests. Both claims, despite their apparent opposition, can be seen as different expressions of autonomy. Individuals may indeed have a legitimate interest in not knowing their genetic make-up to avoid serious psychological consequences. This interest may constitute an enhancement of autonomy, in the sense that the decision to know or not to know is not taken out of the hands of the patient by the doctor. Of course, the right not to know, as in fact most rights, is not an absolute but a relative right, because it may be restricted when disclosure is necessary to prevent serious harm to third persons (especially, family members), which means that some form of prevention or treatment is available.[15]

Article 7 sets out the principle of confidentiality of genetic data, which is not but a specific application of the general principle of confidentiality of personal health information. This solution is justified since, as an increasing volume of personal genetic information becomes available, it may be a source of harm to people, especially resulting in any kind of discrimination or stigmatization. In addition to this, a regulation of confidentiality in this specific area is needed on account of the uniqueness of genetic information: first, genetic tests have implications not only for the individuals who have been tested, but also for their blood relatives; second, this information has an almost uniquely identifying nature, including its capacity to confirm, deny or reveal family relationships; third, genetic tests not only concern the past, but also the future of people and therefore, may have a significant predictive value; fourth, genetic information could be obtained from a very small amount of material, possibly secured without the donor's consent.[16] The most difficult issue is of course to identify precisely what practice may constitute a violation of confidentiality of genetic data. Since Article 7 is formulated in very general terms and does not provide any guidance in this respect, UNESCO has adopted on 16 October 2003 an International Declaration on Human Genetic Data that regulates this issue in more detail.[17]

Article 10 embodies another direct corollary of the principle of human dignity by providing that 'no research (…) should prevail over respect for human rights, fundamental freedoms and human dignity.' The primacy of the human person over the sole interest of science and society is a classic principle of medical ethics that also appears with a very similar formulation in the Declaration of Helsinki on medical research on human subjects (World Medical Association, 1964-2000): 'Concern for the interests of the subject must always prevail over the interests of science and society' (Article 5). In both cases, the idea is the same: individuals should not simply become instruments for the benefit of science, because science is not an absolute, but just a means at the service of persons. This is why non-therapeutic research is only permitted by ethical guidelines when some conditions are met, in particular, when: a) the free and informed consent of all participants has been obtained, b) the risks to subjects are minimized and proportionate to anticipated benefits, and c) the research proposal has been approved by an independent committee, after review of its scientific merit and ethical acceptability.

Dignity of Humanity

The principle of respect for human dignity in its extended meaning, the dignity of humanity as such, constitutes the main originality of the UNESCO Declaration. One of the central concerns of the drafters of the Declaration was indeed the need to protect the human genome from improper manipulations that may endanger the identity and physical integrity of future generations. To respond to this concern, Article 1 provides that the human genome 'is the heritage of humanity'. This notion is inspired by the concept of 'common heritage of humanity', taken from international law, which aims to preserve the world's natural and cultural resources for the benefit of humankind as a whole. When applied to the human genome, this expression means that genetic research engages the responsibility of the whole of humanity and that its results should benefit present and future generations.[18] At the same time, it indicates that the human genome is not suitable for appropriation by any State or private entity.[19]

It should be noted that with the UNESCO Declaration, humanity as such is regarded for the first time as a common heritage to be protected.[20] Certainly the notion of 'crimes against humanity', the clearest example here being genocide, has been part of international law since the end of the Second World War. However, the category of crimes against humanity aims to avoid inhumane acts committed against a particular ethnic, social or religious group and therefore does not cover the protection of the human species as such, or indeed the preservation of its genetic structure, which is precisely the main purpose of the UNESCO Declaration.[21]

A further issue arises in relation to Article 1, because its first sentence is somehow misleading. It reads: 'the human genome underlies the fundamental unity of all members of the human family, as well as the recognition of their inherent dignity and diversity'. This article could be interpreted in a crude materialistic way, as if the eminent value we attach to the human person were solely based on the genetic information that characterizes our species. But this interpretation would be contrary to the intent of the drafters of the Declaration, as it results from other provisions of this instrument, in particular, Articles 2 and 6, which stress the idea that people cannot be reduced to their genetic make-up. What is then the purpose of Article 1? In my view, this provision just aims to stress the fact that, from a genetic perspective, there is a deep interrelatedness between all members of the human species. Human genes are common to all past, present and future generations because the same genetic structure is inherited from one generation to the next.[22] Therefore, and independently of any changes that might evolve, which are recognized by Article 3, each individual inherits the same basic genetic structure of those that preceded him or her. Thus, it is fully appropriate to consider the human genome as a 'common heritage of humanity' and consequently to protect it from irresponsible manipulations.

It is important to point out that the UNESCO Declaration did not confine itself to lay down very general principles for the protection of the integrity and identity of the human species. It also dared to adopt some exceptionally precise provisions to this purpose. This is the case with Articles 11 and 24 that declare human reproductive cloning and germ-line interventions, respectively, as 'contrary to human dignity'.

Regarding human cloning, the UNESCO Declaration is consistent with the worldwide condemnation of human reproductive cloning.[23] The most fundamental objection against this practice is that it gives those who create the clone unjustifiable powers over that individual, who would be deliberately produced to resemble an existing individual (or even a dead one) just to satisfy the desires of third persons. In this way, cloning would become a new and radical form of instrumentalisation of people and therefore, of a practice contrary to human dignity. In addition, it is worth remembering that the cloned child would be produced without genetic parents and would therefore be irreversibly deprived of the possibility to relate his or her existence to a 'father' and a 'mother' in the normal sense of these terms.[24] In sum, two fundamental features of the human species (the non-predetermination of genetic characteristics and the sexual or biparental reproduction) are at stake in this issue.

The rejection of germ-line interventions, included in Article 24 of the UNESCO Declaration, is also in conformity with international guidelines dealing with the issue.[25] It is important to stress that, unlike the alteration of the genes in the somatic cells, which affects only the individual treated, any alteration in the germ cells (gametes) or in the early embryo would be passed to the next generation. This fact raises enormous concerns about the risks of irreversible harm to future generations. In addition, in the case of genetic engineering for enhancement purposes, the objections against this procedure are based on the idea that we do not have the right to predetermine the characteristics of future individuals.[26] That means that people should be free to develop their potentialities without being biologically conditioned by the particular conceptions of 'good' and 'bad' human traits that were dominant at the time of those who preceded them. In other words, genetics should not become the instrument for an intergenerational tyranny.[27]

Conclusion

The notion of human dignity relates primarily to the inherent worthiness of every individual, and, with an extended meaning, to the intrinsic value of humanity as such. The UNESCO Declaration on the Human Genome and Human Rights, which adopts this notion as a key concept, covers adequately both dimensions of dignity. The dignity of the individual is especially addressed by those provisions dealing with the rejection of genetic reductionism (Article 2) and genetic discrimination (Article 6), with the requirement of informed consent (Article 5), of confidentiality of personal genetic information (Article 7) and no instrumentalisation of individuals for the benefit of science (Article 10). The dignity of humanity as such is covered by the recognition of the human genome as a 'heritage of humanity' (Article 1) and by the rejection of human reproductive cloning (Article 11) and germline interventions (Article 24) as being 'contrary to human dignity'.

Notes

1 A. L. Taylor, 'Globalization and Biotechnology: UNESCO and an International Strategy to Advance Human Rights and Public Health', *American Journal of Law and Medicine*, 1999, n° 4, p. 479-541.

2 N. Lenoir, 'La Déclaration sur le génome humain, avancée futuriste', *Le Monde*, 9 December 1998.

3 N. Lenoir and B. Mathieu, *Les normes internationales de la bioéthique*, Paris, PUF, 1998, p. 16.

4 D. Beyleveld and R. Brownsword, *Human Dignity in Bioethics and Biolaw*, Oxford, Oxford University Press, 2002, p. 11.

5 R. Macklin, 'Dignity is a useless concept', *British Medical Journal*, 2003, vol. 327, p. 1419-1420. See several replies to this paper in subsequent issues of the same journal.

6 This distinction is suggested by D. Birnbacher in 'Ambiguities in the concept of Menschenwürde', in: K. Bayertz (ed.), *Sanctity of Life and Human Dignity*, Dordrecht, Kluwer, 1996, p. 107-121.

7 R. Dworkin, *Life's Dominion. An Argument About Abortion, Euthanasia and Individual Freedom*, New York, Vintage, 1994, p. 236.

8 R. Dworkin, *ibid.*

9 This idea is expressed in the second formulation of the categorical imperative: 'Act in such a way that you treat humanity, whether in your own person or in the person of another, always at the same time as an end and never simply as a means (I. Kant, *Grundlegung zur Metaphysik der Sitten [Groundwork of the Metaphysics of Morals]*, Berlin, Akademie-Ausgabe, vol. IV, 1911, p. 428).

10 In favor: H. Gros Espiell, 'Droits de l'homme et droits de l'humanité', in: Federico Mayor (ed.), *René-Jean Dupuy. Une œuvre au service de l'humanité*, Paris, UNESCO, 1999, p.15-32; A. Tarantino, 'Diritti dell'umanità e giustizia intergenerazionale', *Rivista internazionale di filosofia del diritto*, n° 1, 2002, p. 88-124. Against: B. Mathieu, *Génome humain et droits fondamentaux*, Paris, Economica, 2000, p. 93.

11 Since collective entities, such as associations, societies and even States, are entitled to a property right, why humanity as such could not be entitled to an analogous right? In favor of recognizing humanity as the owner of commons: A.-Ch. Kiss, 'La notion de patrimoine commun de l'humanité', in: *Académie de Droit International, Recueil des Cours*, 1982, II, vol. 175, The Hague, Nijhoff, 1983, p. 235-237. However, it is widely admitted that there are still serious practical obstacles for considering humanity as entitled to a property right: Who may act as the representative of humanity? Every State? A particular State specifically committed by the international community for that purpose? International organizations? An Ombudsman of humanity? See: M. A. Fitzmaurice, 'International Protection of the Environment', in: *Académie de Droit International, Recueil des Cours*, 2001, II, vol. 293, The Hague, Nijhoff, 2002, p. 192.

12 See: C. Zanghi, 'Pour la protection des générations futures', in: *Boutros Boutros-Ghali. Amicorum Discipulorumque Liber. Paix, Développement, Démocratie*, Bruxelles, Bruylant, 1998, p. 1459-1478.

13 The classic definition of 'person' is that given by the philosopher Boethius in the 6th century AD: *Naturae rationalis individua substantia* (an individual substance of a rational nature).

14 For Aristotle, not only humans, but also plants and non-human animals, as living beings, are by definition *animated* by a principle of life. But the intellectual faculty (mind, *nous*) that characterizes human soul distinguishes it radically from the souls of other living beings. The human soul is *immaterial* in the full sense of the word, that is, it is unmixed

with the body (*De Anima*, III, 4, 429a 25). Aristotle deduces that from the typical function of the intellect: the *knowledge*. Through their cognitive faculties human beings are able to assimilate the 'forms' (or essences) of the things they know without the 'matter' that constitute those objects. Thus, while remaining physically distinct from other material things, persons can through their knowledge unite themselves with objects in a nonmaterial way. Thanks to knowledge, persons become a *microcosmos*, reflecting the nature of all things in their minds. This is only possible insofar as the intellect is in no way a material entity, that is, just the faculty of a corporeal organ. In other words, the *soul*, since it thinks all things, should be unmixed with any (*id.*, III, 4, 429a 18).

15 R. Andorno, 'The right not to know: an autonomy based approach', *Journal of Medical Ethics*, 2004 (forthcoming).

16 J. K. Mason and A. McCall Smith, *Law and Medical Ethics*, 5th ed., London, Butterworths, 1999, p. 167; UK Human Genetics Commission, *Inside Information. Balancing interests in the use of personal genetic data*, May 2002, p. 28-32.

17 See especially Article 14 of the International Declaration of Human Genetic Data.

18 H. Gros Espiell, *Genèse de la Déclaration universelle sur le génome humain et les droits de l'homme*, Introduction, Paris, UNESCO, 1999, p. 3.

19 R. Ida, 'Human Genome as Common Heritage of Humankind', in: N. Fujiki and D. Macer (eds.), *Bioethics in Asia*, Tsukuba, Eubios Ethics Institute, 1998, p. 59-63.

20 Ch. Byk, 'A Map to a New Treasure Island: The Human Genome and the Concept of Common Heritage', *Journal of Medicine and Philosophy*, 1998, n° 3 p. 235.

21 B. Mathieu, *op. cit.*, p. 92.

22 E. Agius, 'Patenting Life: Our Responsibilities to Present and Future Generations', in Emmanuel Agius and Salvino Busuttil (eds.), *Germ-Line Intervention and our Responsibilities to Future Generations*, Dordrecht, Kluwer, 1998, p. 76.

23 See for instance: WHO Resolutions WHA50.37 (1997) and WHA51.10 (1998); World Medical Association Resolution on Cloning of 1997; Charter of Fundamental Rights of the European Union of 2000 (Article 3.2); Additional Protocol on Human Cloning to the European Convention on Human Rights and Biomedicine of 1998.

24 G. J. Annas, 'Why We Should Ban Human Cloning' 1998, 339 (2) *New England Journal of Medicine*, p. 122-125.

25 See: Australian National Health Medical Research Council (NHMRC), Guidelines for Ethical Review of Research Proposals for Human Somatic Cell Gene Therapy and Related Therapies, 1999; Austrian Gene Technology Law, 1994 (Section 76); Brazilian Law n° 8974 on Genetically Modified Organisms, 1995, Article 13.1; French Civil Code, Article 16-4; German Embryo Protection Law, 1990, Article 5; Swiss Constitution, Article 119a; UK Human Fertilisation and Embryology Act, 1990, Schedule 2, Articles 2(4), 3(4); US National Institutes of Health (NIH), Guidelines for Research Involving Recombinant DNA Molecules, 1998, Appendix M.

26 H. Jonas, *Technik, Medizin und Ethik*, Frankfurt, Insel, 1985, p. 162-203; J. Habermas, *Die Zukunft der menschlichen Natur. Auf dem Weg zu einer liberalen Eugenik?*, Frankfurt, Suhrkamp, 2001.

27 R. Andorno, 'Biomedicine and international human rights law: in search of a global consensus', *Bulletin of the World Health Organization*, 2002, vol. 80, n° 12, p. 959-963. Available online at: www.who.int/bulletin.

PART II
ETHICS AND SOCIETY

Chapter 12

Theft of DNA: Do We Need a New Criminal Offence?

Loane Skene

The UK Human Genetics Commission (HGC) – and also the Australian Law Reform Commission (ALRC) – have recently proposed that a new criminal offence should be created in relation to the 'non-consensual or deceitful obtaining and/or analysis of personal genetic information for non medical purposes' (HGC)[1] or that 'Criminal liability should attach to any individual or corporation that, without lawful authority, submits a sample for genetic testing, or conducts genetic testing on a sample, knowing (or recklessly indifferent to the fact) that the individual from whom the sample has been taken did not consent to such testing' (ALRC).[2] This paper considers the desirability of such an offence, in particular, the activities that might be considered criminally culpable; whether the criminal law rather than the civil law should be utilised to protect any legal interest that people have in their own bodily material and genetic information; and the terms in which the proposed offence might be phrased. The author concludes that the proposals of both the HCG and the ALRC for a new criminal offence are appropriate but there are likely to be difficulties in drafting a new statutory offence.

Activities that Might be Considered Criminally Culpable

There are three alternatives in criminalising activities related to non-consensual taking of genetic information:

- *Obtaining* genetic material without the 'donor's' consent;
- *Testing* genetic material without the 'donor's' consent;
- *Using* that material or information for 'reward' or 'benefit' without consent from the 'donor's' consent.

These options are considered in turn in relation to what might be covered by a new offence and its perceived culpability.

Obtaining Genetic Material without the 'Donor's' Consent

The first option is to criminalise non-consensual acquisition of a person's genetic information without any further testing or use of it. There are privacy and property arguments in favour of such an approach.

In relation to privacy, Edinburgh law academic, Dr Graeme Laurie, believes that privacy law must protect not only personal information (its current aim), but also a person's 'spatial privacy' – a 'general sphere of separateness from others', not having one's 'space' invaded.[3] Considering the concept of spatial privacy in the context of non-consensual acquisition of genetic material, one might say that a person's privacy interests may be infringed merely by someone acquiring their genetic material. Even if nothing further is done with it, the sample *could* later be tested and personal information obtained without consent from the person concerned. Or it could be placed at a crime scene or used in a way that would otherwise harm the person's interests. Thus, even if the sample is not tested or used, the knowledge that a sample has been obtained – and could be tested or used – may cause the person sufficient anxiety or distress to warrant criminal liability being imposed. One might draw analogies with offences of unlawful surveillance; computer hacking where the hacker does no more than read the material on the computer; and stalking, which are designed to protect a similar interest of personal privacy where there is also an element of distress about the invasion of privacy.

One may question whether such distress is a sufficient harm to warrant the imposition of criminal liability. Indeed, if the person whose genetic material has been taken without consent does not know about it, it is difficult to see how that person has been harmed at all. But, harm is not always needed to impose criminal liability. The criminal law is also used to punish or deter conduct the community thinks is 'wrong', as in the case of 'streaking' or desecration of a corpse. But is the mere taking of genetic material culpable in that way?

In relation to property arguments, one might contend that people should be regarded as having property rights in their own excised bodily material and that it should be theft if another person takes that 'property' with the intention of permanently depriving them of it. The common law to date has refused to recognise a general principle that people 'own' their excised bodily material. It is regarded at that point as not being property at all and so not susceptible to property rights in favour of anyone.[4] Thus, one cannot commit theft of material that is not property,[5] or that belongs to no-one, such as theft from the dead. It is only when others have expended 'work and skill' on excised bodily material that it becomes property and property rights arise in respect of it – but in favour of the person doing the work and skill, not the person from whom the material came.[6] Thus research scientists gain property rights by developing a new 'product' from genetic material – such as cell lines for use in diagnosis and treatment; but the 'donor' has no property rights.[7]

However, some commentators have suggested that the present law should be changed. Professor J.W. Harris said in 1996, 'Every person ought to be regarded as the owner of any separated part of his body'.[8] Professor Derek Morgan said in 2001, 'Lockean concepts of property and Kantian concepts of autonomy…suggest that my body may be my own to use and enjoy as I please; that it is my own to 'own''.[9] Professor Ian Kennedy said in his report on retained organs and tissue at the Bristol Royal Infirmary that parents or next of kin should be entitled to have the body, body parts and all bodily material of their dead children returned to them for burial or cremation.[10] This is a right to possession rather than 'full' ownership but a right to possession is a form of property right. Then, on the basis of these authors' arguments, one might say that people should have property rights in their own excised bodily material and that non-consensual acquisition of it by another person with the intent to keep it should be regarded as theft. Indeed, in a different context, the law has already recognised that non-consensual removal of body parts or bodily material from people who have acquired a property interest in it by 'work and skill' may be theft[11] (though it is theft from the person or institution in possession of them and not from the person whose body parts they were).

One may question, however, whether the privacy and property arguments set out above are persuasive; and also whether the mere acquisition of bodily material without consent is so culpable that it should be criminalised, even when it is deliberately taken and retained.[12] In relation to privacy, English Courts have been reluctant in civil actions to recognise a right of privacy either at common law or under the Human Rights Act, preferring to extend the equitable concept of breach of confidence as an appropriate remedy. Issues of privacy arose in the case of actors Catherine Zeta-Jones and Michael Douglas who alleged that their right to privacy was infringed when an unauthorised person photographed their wedding for a magazine.[13] The privacy issue was confused, however, by the fact that the two actors are public figures who had sold the photography rights to another magazine. In other cases, a convicted burglar and car thief, Gary Ellis, obtained an injunction banning Essex police from using his face on a 'wanted' poster as part of a crime prevention campaign; and the European Court of Human Rights decided that privacy rights of another man, Geoff Peck, under the European Convention of Human Rights were breached when a film of him carrying a knife after attempting suicide was shown on television, in which he was recognisable.[14] Deirdre Fottrell remarked after the latter case that 'approaches to the 'right to privacy' [in the UK] may need to be revisited or refined'.[15]

All of these cases, however, involved a publication of private information and clear harm to the person in question. They are different from A taking B's photo or even taking B's hair or saliva – and simply keeping it, which seems an insignificant breach of B's right to privacy, if there is such a right. Although one could confer a right of action in favour of B and assume that it will not be pursued if B suffers no real harm, or that a court would not award significant compensation in such a case, one could equally say that there should be no right of action at all in the absence of substantial injury or other harm; and a fortiori, that there is not a sufficient harm to justify making this conduct a criminal offence. Instead, if one wanted to provide a remedy for B in such a case, a more effective remedy might be an injunction preventing any use of the material that was taken (or, in the case of bodily material, preventing it being tested); or requiring it to be destroyed. Alternatively, if a common law right of privacy is ultimately accepted, then the remedy for breach should be a civil one (an order that the genetic material be returned and/or damages for distress).[16] It should not be a criminal offence.

In relation to property arguments, I have argued elsewhere that the law should not recognise as a general principle that people have property rights in their own excised bodily material.[17] But a more important issue here is the nature of what has actually been taken in an alleged theft of genetic material. What the 'donor' is really concerned about is not so much the taking of the bodily material (hair, saliva, semen etc), but rather the *information* that may be connoted by it. In other words, the 'donor's' interest is not infringed by the taking of the bodily material but by the 'de-encryption' of personal information from it by testing. If that is so, should the focus of the offence be on the testing – the de-encryption of the information – rather than the acquisition of the material?

That option is considered more fully in para 1.2 below, but, before leaving this section on acquisition of genetic material, one should note the consequences if the mere acquisition without the 'donor's' consent were to be criminalised. Hospitals and research institutes retaining tissue after surgical procedures could face prosecution unless they have obtained specific consent for retention.[18] So could museums holding human remains for public education and research. And research would no longer be possible on tissue taken for other purposes, such as Guthrie cards, even if it was done on a totally anonymised basis, and monitored by an ethics committee;[19] an ethics committee might provide a substitute authority to use the tissue without the person's specific consent but it could not override the person's property in the tissue, if such a property right existed.

Testing Genetic Material without the 'Donor's' Consent

The second option for a new criminal offence focuses on testing genetic material rather than the mere taking of it; and, as noted above, the emphasis is then on information, rather than the material itself. The Australian Law Reform Commission preferred this option in its Discussion Paper on Protection of Human Genetic Information.[20] Its proposed offence 'would apply where any individual or corporation, without lawful authority, submits a sample for testing, or conducts genetic testing on a sample, knowing (or recklessly indifferent...) that the individual from whom the sample was taken did not consent to such testing'.[21] Thus, the offence could be committed by a testing laboratory as well as the person submitting the sample. Lawful authority would presumably include forensic tests authorised by statute or court order.

The UK Human Genetics Commission proposed a similar offence, focussing on the 'non-consensual or deceitful obtaining and/or analysis of personal genetic information for non-medical purposes'.[22] It stated that police and court uses should be provided for, and that medical and scientific research should not be inhibited. It also noted that the proposed offence might need to be broadened to other personal information, perhaps as part of a wider review of the *Human Tissue Act* 1961 (UK).[23]

An offence of non-consensual testing, or non-consensual obtaining and/or analysing genetic information has the advantage of concentrating on what I have suggested earlier is people's main concern in this area – that someone may find out personal information about them that they may not wish others to know. There are several reasons why this conduct might be regarded as culpable.

First, it contravenes people's rights to privacy and to control information about themselves. As noted earlier, the common law has not yet recognised a general right to privacy but there is increased statutory protection of the privacy of personal information, including also who should have access to it and who should control it. Personal *information* has been regarded as the province of privacy law in a way that bodily material is not.[24]

Secondly, and associated with the right to control one's personal information, is a right *not* to know genetic information. A person who analyses another person's genetic material and tells that person the test results has infringed that person's right not to know. One might imagine a person concerned about the genetic status of a relative surreptitiously taking bodily material from the relative and having it tested, hoping to relieve the relative's worries about later developing the condition.[25] If the test is negative, the relative may be relieved but feel their privacy or autonomy has been wrongfully invaded. If the test is positive, the person who sought the test has a powerful weapon against the other if their relationship changes – or may blurt out or otherwise reveal the result unintentionally when the affected person has not had the preparation and support of genetic counselling. This is especially problematic given the uncertainty of tests for genetic susceptibility in particular – the penetrance of the gene; the interaction of lifestyle and environmental factors and the like.

Thirdly, if obtaining genetic information is to be an offence, there is an interesting commodification of this type of information in the process. Compare this with a proposal that plagiarism should be regarded as theft.[26] To be theft, the thing taken must be property – it must be commodifiable. With plagiarism, argues Professor of Law, Stuart Green, what is 'stolen' is not the words or the ideas of the author. One is permitted to appropriate these provided there is proper attribution. The plagiarist in reality 'steals the *credit*' to which the author is entitled in relation to the work (and also any benefits such as payment, prestige, promotion etc that follows from the credit). Stewart argues that this 'credit' is commodifiable – a 'thing of value'[27] and may be the subject of theft.[28]

By analogy, genetic information might be regarded as suitable for commodification (and so properly regarded as the subject of theft) because it may have 'value'. But, so far as that is so, the 'value' could arguably be the focus of the offence rather than obtaining the information. Plagiarism is an offence when I *publish* your article with my name as author, even in a limited way, such as submitting a university essay. If I keep your article with me as author in my drawer, there is no offence, even if I have technically 'stolen' your article.

Finally, if an offence is being considered of wrongful acquisition of genetic information, such conduct might be better regulated under privacy legislation than the criminal law. In Australia, merely collecting personal information about a person without that person's consent is a breach of the National Privacy Principles in the Privacy Act 1988 (Cth).[29] Similarly, personal information cannot be used or disclosed unless the individual has consented to the use or disclosure.[30] Perhaps the current laws on privacy, supported if necessary by Court Rules on illegally obtained evidence, may be sufficient to deal with this type of conduct.

Using Genetic Material or Information for 'Reward' or 'Benefit' without Consent from the Person Concerned

This brings us to the third option for a new offence, which would focus on potential *uses* of non-consensually obtained genetic material or information. One might think that this is the real crux of the culpability. Consider the three examples given by the Human Genetics Commission of situations constituting 'an unacceptable breach of privacy'.[31]

- X swipes Y's beer glass for DNA, analyses it and *sells information to a newspaper* that Y has a particular genetic condition;
- X de-crypts anonymised genetic information about Y from a research study and *uses it for wrongful purposes*;
- X obtains a sample from a child A for whom he has no parental responsibility,[32] [to see if] he is the father of the child [*and so avoid paying child support*] (emphases and words in parenthesis added).

It would seem that the 'unacceptable breach of privacy' in each case comes not from the acquisition of the information, or even from the testing and acquisition of personal information about a person, but from further *use* of it, indicated by the words italicised (the italicised words in the third sentence seem to be implied). If this is the culpability of the offence, perhaps the offence should focus on use, rather than acquisition and testing of genetic material. This is the subject of the next section.

The 'Culpability' of Non-consensual Acquisition of Genetic Material and Information

I have suggested to date that the intrinsic culpability of conduct in relation to non-consensual acquisition of genetic material and information arises essentially when it is used, or proposed to be used, by the person who acquired it. This can be illustrated by some examples.

Consider the story initially reported in the press about tennis player Boris Becker. Becker alleged that a woman '[stole] his sperm [by holding it in her mouth after oral sex] and inseminat[ed] herself to have his baby' so she could blackmail him.[33] Becker later withdrew the allegation and admitted paternity; but if that story had been true, it would seem warranted to impose criminal liability on the woman concerned. She would have acted 'in bad faith' to obtain a financial advantage for her child and, indirectly, for herself. Similarly, if Monica Lewinsky had initiated her encounter with the former President in order to obtain forensic evidence she could use against him if the occasion arose, she would seem to have acted culpably; but not if she merely hung up her dress in the wardrobe, albeit knowing the nature of the stain on it and being prepared to have it tested later in the event of an investigation. And the private investigators who took the trash from MGM millionaire, Steve Bing, and removed and analysed material on used dental floss to establish that he was the father of a baby born to the wife of the investigator's client could also be regarded as having acted culpably. The gist of culpability is surely the *use* of the test information. If the investigator had simply retained the dental floss, Bing would probably not have complained, even if he knew about it and found it distasteful. Even if the DNA were tested and no further action was taken – for example, if it did not match – he would probably not have complained. The essence of the offence is the use or potential use of genetic material obtained without his consent in legal proceedings against him.

A Criminal Offence or the Civil Law? Difficulties in Drafting a New Offence

Thus, if the essence of criminality is culpability in addition to mere harm, one might argue that non-consensual *use* of genetic material should be the offence, rather than taking or testing it. The appropriate remedy for obtaining the material or information from testing it may more properly be the subject of a civil claim or a complaint about the invasion of privacy.

The number of criminal offences has proliferated in recent years and one may question the ready utilisation of the criminal law merely on the basis that someone has been, or may be, harmed, especially where the harm in question is relatively slight. If the issue is punishing or preventing wrongful collection or use of genetic material or information, then, as suggested earlier, that may be better dealt with by the civil law, either through actions in conversion; equitable claims for breach of confidence; or the complaint system established by privacy legislation.

It must be remembered, however, that civil actions require individuals to bear the costs and stress of gathering evidence and initiating and proving claims. Many people will choose not to proceed; offenders will not be punished; and there will be little disincentive for others not to undertake non-consensual tests.

On the other hand, criminal prosecution is at the discretion of prosecution authorities and injured parties cannot compel the state to initiate it. It may seem appropriate that people who have been harmed should gain a remedy directly and that would not occur if the offence were prosecuted by the state in the criminal courts.

There are also difficulties in drafting a new criminal offence. What mental element would be required? The Human Genetics Commission (HGC) suggested an offence of '*non-consensual or deceitful* obtaining and/or analysis of personal genetic information for non medical purposes (emphasis added)'.[34] This would make my hairdresser guilty of a crime if the hair was swept up and discarded without my consent – or is consent to be implied in such a case? And, if so, is there implied consent to use my Guthrie card, or my surgically removed tissue, in research? If the mental element were limited to 'deceitful', how is that different from non-consensual? Does it suggest that the collection of the genetic material is furtive, as well as non-consensual? And why should 'non-medical' use be the subject of the offence? If it is wrong for a person to take my genetic material without my consent or 'deceitfully', surely it is equally wrong if they break into the hospital and take away my stored tissue. Even if the hospital holds property rights over the tissue and not me personally, this taking would seem to be theft (as the courts have already held[35]). Or is this situation excluded because it is already covered by the common law; and if so, why can the common law not be interpreted to cover the cases envisaged for the proposed new offence?

The Australian Law Reform Commission (ALRC) suggested an offence of testing '*knowing (or recklessly indifferent* to the fact) that the individual from whom the sample has been taken did not consent to such testing' (emphasis added).[36] This seems equally difficult to apply in practice. How is the testing laboratory to know if consent has been given by 'the individual from whom the sample has been taken' unless that person is physically present and consents at that time? What will happen to the current system of pathology testing where samples are sent by courier or post for testing? Although testing for medical reasons could be excluded, as in the UK, that was not the proposal when the ALRC published its discussion paper.

I have suggested that a new offence could focus on the wrongful use of genetic material or information but I face as many difficulties as the HGC and the ALRC in framing an offence. It might be an offence of knowing or recklessly using genetic material or information for a purpose other than that for which it was acquired without the consent of the person concerned. 'Use' would cover publication of genetic information, or sale or transfer of such information to another person, and threats to do so; as well as placing genetic material at a crime scene or other place, to produce an adverse effect on the person concerned (for example, an embittered wife might put her husband's semen on their baby's bib, suggesting child abuse, to persuade a court to deprive him of access to the child).

Conclusion

On balance, it may be wise to expand the potential civil actions for wrongful taking and testing of genetic material and also to create a new criminal offence. The civil actions might be in conversion; equitable claims for breach of confidence; or complaints under privacy legislation. I have argued that the criminal offence should consist of more than mere taking and testing of genetic material but I acknowledge the difficulty of drafting such an offence. We may gain some guidance on this when Human Genetics Commission and the Australian Law Reform Commission have completed their projects on genetic privacy.

Notes

1 Human Genetics Commission, *Inside Information: Balancing Interests in the Use of Personal Genetic Data* (2002), London, 62, para [3.61]; http://www.hgc.gov.uk/insideinformation/iichapter3.pdf

2 Australian Law Reform Commission, *Protection of Human Genetic Information, Discussion Paper 66*, August 2002, p 194, Proposal 5-5, or http://www.austlii.edu.au/au/other/alrc/publications/dp/66/. The Commission's Report has been completed but it not yet publicly available.

3 Graeme Laurie, Genetic Privacy, *A Challenge to Medico Legal Norms*, Cambridge Uni Press, UK, 2002 pp 250-1.

4 *Doodeward v Spence* (1908) 6 CLR 406 (HCA); *Williams v Williams* (1982) 20 ChD 659.

5 Brent Fisse, *Howard's Criminal Law*, 5th ed. Law Book Co. 1990, pp 258ff.

6 Loane Skene, 'Proprietary rights in human bodies, body parts and tissue: regulatory context and proposals for new laws' (2002) 22(1) *Legal Studies* 102, especially text accompanying notes 16-22.

7 *Moore v University of California* 793 P 2d 479 Cal SC (1990).

8 *Property and Justice*, Clarendon Press, Oxford, 1996, p 351.

9 'Where do I own my body (and why)' in *Issues in Medical Law & Ethics*, Cavendish, London, 2001, pp 83-104.

10 Interim Report of the Inquiry into the management of care of children receiving complex heart surgery at the Bristol Royal Infirmary) Chair, Professor Ian Kennedy), May 2000; available at http://www.bristol-inquiry.org.uk/index.htm Recommendation 60 p 49.

11 *R v Kelly* [1999] QB 521 in which the English Court of Appeal upheld the conviction for theft of an artist who removed body parts from the Royal College of Surgeons to draw them; *R v Rothery* [1976] RTR 550, in which a defendant who removed a blood sample after a blood test was found guilty of theft; *R v Welsh* [1947] RTR 478 in which urine was held to be 'property' and capable of being stolen.

12 To be theft, the intention to take and retain the material would need to be contemporaneous. Even if there were a statutory offence of theft of DNA, Monica Lewinsky would commit no offence if she decided some time after the events in the Oval Office to keep the stain on her dress for later analysis and possible use in her defence in the event of an investigation.

13 *Douglas and others v Hello! Ltd and others* [2003] EWHC 786 (Ch), [2003] All ER (D) 209 (Apr), (Ch Div).

14 These cases are discussed by Deirdre Fottrell, 'When a private life is not public', The Times, 18 March 2003 'Law' p 8.

15 Ibid.

16 I discuss civil actions more fully below.

17 Loane Skene, 'Arguments against people legally 'owning' their own bodies, body parts and tissue' (2002) 2 *Macquarie Law J* 165.

18 Bodily material is quite properly retained by hospitals for quality assurance and audit as well as research and other purposes: see Skene, note 17 above.

19 In Australia, research on retained genetic material is permitted without consent from the people concerned if it is not practicable to get consent; there is a clear public benefit; and the research is monitored by a Human Research Ethics Committee: NHMRC *National Statement on Ethical Principles for Research involving Human Subjects*, Commonwealth of Australia 1999, http://www.health.gov.au/nhmrc/publications/humans/contents.htm para 14.4.

[20] Australian Law Reform Commission, *Protection of Human Genetic Information, Discussion Paper 66, August 2002*, Commonwealth of Australia, 2002, p 194, Proposal 5-5; or http://www.austlii.edu.au/au/other/alrc/publications/dp/66/

[21] Id, p 33.

[22] Human Genetics Commission, *Inside Information: Balancing Interests in the Use of Personal Genetic Data* (2002), London, 62, para [3.61] http://www.hgc.gov.uk/insideinformation/iichapter3.pdf.

[23] Id, para [3.60].

[24] This is not always the case. The New South Wales Privacy and Personal Information Protection Act 1998 includes genetic material in its definition of 'personal information': s 4(2): 'Personal information includes such things as an individual's fingerprints, retina prints, *body samples* or genetic characteristics'(emphasis added).

[25] This testing would seem to be outside the offence proposed by the Human Genetics Commission as it is for 'medical' reasons.

[26] Stuart P Green, 'Plagiarism, norms and the limits of theft law: Some observations on the use of criminal sanctions in enforcing intellectual property rights' (2002) 54 *Hastings Law J* 167.

[27] Id, p 288.

[28] Id, p 221.

[29] Privacy Act 1988 (Cth), National Privacy Principle 1. Alleged breaches of privacy may be investigated by the federal Privacy Commissioner and there are enforceable remedies available if a person's privacy is found to have been infringed. These include the payment of compensation. Some staters have similar privacy legislation.

[30] National Privacy Principle 2.1(B).

[31] Human Genetics Commission, *Inside Information: Balancing Interests in the use of human data*, May 2002, para [3.51]; http://www.hgc.gov.uk/insideinformation/iichapter3.pdf.

[32] The Human Genetics Commission refers here to a man who has *no* parental responsibility. However, in the usual paternity case paternity is the issue when the sample is submitted. Until then, the man does not know if he is the father or not. The sentence might be better phrased: 'a child A in respect of when he questions his parental responsibility'.

[33] Luisa Dillner, 'Seminal Truths', *The Guardian*, 23 Jan 2001.

[34] Note 1 above.

[35] See *R v Rothery* [1976] RTR 550; *R v Welsh* [1947] RTR 478; note 11 above.

[36] Note 2 above.

Chapter 13

Environmental Ethics, Environmental Problems and the Ethics of Science

Robin Attfield

Introduction

After an initial expression of support for the 1984 Uppsala Code of Ethics for Scientists, and definitions of 'environment' and of 'ethics', I turn to the ethics of global warming, water resources and electricity generation. In reply to Björn Lomborg's suggestion that instead of seeking to mitigate global warming we should devote resources to projects like supplying humanity with fresh water I argue that mitigating global warming is necessary for a sustainable future, and that we should do both these things. I also suggest that international co-operation and scientific research are needed to ensure that the waters of major rivers are equitably shared. A possible basis for future international agreements on greenhouse gas emissions is put forward, based on the work of Michael Grubb and Henry Shue; emission quotas should be allocated to countries in proportion to their population, but an element of quotas earmarked for basic needs should be inalienable. The combined goals of adequate electricity supplies and of mitigating global warming, however, require an expansion of research into renewable sources of energy, with a view to tapping carbon-free sources such as solar energy in an environmentally-friendly manner.*

I am hoping to throw some light on the ethics of three major environmental topics involving scientific research: global warming, electricity generation and water resources. There are many other important topics relevant to the ethics of scientific research and to every region of the planet, including the use of human subjects in clinical trials, experimentation on animals, and military applications of science, and these I have to set aside (apart from citing a Pugwash Conference statement with approval). There are also certain more generic topics, such as the direction of scientific research and of its funding, on which what I have to say will perforce be fragmentary, but which I cannot ignore, since some of the global and local problems that I hope to discuss could require some refocussing or redirection of scientific investigation. Another such topic is the environmental sustainability of countries and continents, again a topic that cannot be ignored, but only some aspects of which can be addressed.

As compensation for my silence on some of these topics, and before I define some key terms, I would like to quote with approval from the 1984 Uppsala Code of Ethics for Scientists, which emerged from the Pugwash Conferences on Science and World Affairs, and was included in a background paper of the UNESCO Budapest conference of 1999:

Scientific research is an indispensable activity of great significance to mankind – for our description and understanding of the world, our material conditions, social life and welfare. Research can contribute to solving the great problems facing humanity, such as the threat of nuclear war, damage to the environment, and the uneven distribution of the earth's resources ... Yet research can also, both directly and indirectly, aggravate the problems of mankind. This code of ethics for scientists has been formulated as a response to a concern about the applications and consequences of scientific research. In particular it appears that the potential hazards deriving from modern technological warfare are so overwhelming that it is doubtful whether it is ethically defensible for scientists to lend any support to weapons development.[1]

With that I must leave most of these topics, to concentrate on the three issues mentioned earlier, relating to impacts of science and technology on the environment.

Instead of a detailed discussion of the concept of the environment, I will assume that 'environment' means 'nature and the natural systems of a country, a continent or of the globe'. Maybe I should apologise for not using 'environment' in the sense of 'the perceived milieu' of each one of us, or the environment as we each experience it; but even if such an apology is due, I could add that there would be no environments in this special, phenomenological sense of the term if there were no shared, interpersonal natural systems which precede and succeed each human generation and which make our existence possible, and which we need also if we are to talk about the environment in the individualised sense, particularly in an age when all the environments of our planet are plausibly being endangered by human action. In particular, there is a strong scientific consensus that global warming is caused by human activity (or is 'anthropogenic'), and besides affecting the climate is probably disrupting natural cycles, producing both droughts and flooding in different countries,[2] and is probably contributing to the northwards growth of deserts in the northern hemisphere. This already makes global warming a crucial topic for environmental ethics.

By 'ethics' I mean the critical study of normative claims, judgements and beliefs about value, morality, virtue, and obligation. Fortunately I do not mean the standards actually embodied in the actions of individuals, societies, corporations or countries (another widespread sense of 'ethics'). There is all too often a gap between what ought to be done and what is done, as the Pugwash statement reminds us. But this is a basis for hope, for ethics need not be confined to what has already happened, but can produce reasoned accounts of goals that should be aimed at and practices that would enhance social and international existence, and thus at policies both local and global. The study of ethics has been pursued for more than two millennia, but mainly with regard to inter-human relations, often at the individual level. However, the study of environmental ethics (like some of the other branches of ethics discussed in this conference) is a new development of the past thirty years, and involves the study of principles concerning obligations not only with regard to current human beings but also towards future generations and nonhuman species too (our fellow-creatures dependent like humanity on planetary ecosystems).

I have mentioned that there is a strong scientific consensus about global warming, its anthropogenic nature, its cumulative tendencies, and its probably deeply disruptive impacts. This consensus has been expressed in successive reports from the Intergovernmental Panel on Climate Change. There remain a few scientific sceptics about all this, and continuing research into these matters remains important. But without waiting for global unanimity, it is reasonable to take international action to curtail the emissions of gases likely to cause global warming, of which carbon dioxide is the most important. This is indicated by the widely-recognised Precautionary Principle, a principle of ethics relevant both to science and to public policy, which says that where there is a significant risk of serious or irreversible harm intervention should take place to prevent it, even in the absence of scientific consensus, and also that in these circumstances the absence of scientific consensus should not be treated as a reason for inaction. Fortunately this Principle was implemented in the matter of CFCs and HCFCs that were causing potentially fatal gaps in the ozone layer, and more importantly still, most nations recognise its applicability to global warming.

But even among those who accept the science of IPCC scientists, some argue that there is a strong economic case against applying the Precautionary Principle in this case and in favour of accepting global warming and planning around it, rather than seeking to curtail it and to alleviate or mitigate its effects. In particular, Cambridge University Press recently published Björn Lomborg's book The Skeptical Environmentalist, which argued that the costs of remediation are nearly as great as the costs of global warming itself, and that huge benefits to humanity could be attained by investing the resources required for mitigation and remediation instead in development projects such as supplying fresh water to all of humanity, cleaning up the atmosphere of cities, and other life-saving measures.[3] Lomborg's concerns were clearly restricted to human interests, as was apparent when he made unfavourable comparisons between efforts to conserve nonhuman species and investments that would save or prolong human lives, and this is already one important criticism of his position, since he seems to write as if numbers and length of human lives are the only values, and as if nothing else has any independent value whatever. But there is an equally important criticism. For to allow the ecosystems of the planet to be transformed, small islands and coastal plains to be inundated, and climatic zones and agricultural production to move significantly polewards is not an option that can be weighed against alternative national or international policies. Granted the scientific consensus, it is to opt for an unsustainable future, and to bequeath a natural environment to our successors and to such other species as survive in which the kind of sustainable development internationally recognised as vital at the Rio conference of 1992 becomes impossible. In some cases (such as low-lying islands and coasts) this is because the relevant environments would no longer exist; in others it is because fertile lands would have become deserts, and the kinds of human and nonhuman life that have up to now been possible would be no longer so. In the language of research, this would be like conducting an open-ended experiment at global level, but with foreseeably disastrous consequences.

Lomborg puts the costs of bearing global warming at five trillion US dollars, and goes on to suggest that this is a bearable cost. But his alternative projects presuppose some kind of stable environment in which (for example) enhanced water-supply could be supplied universally. Yet there could well be no stable environment if global warming is allowed to proceed unrestricted. In fact we find ourselves in an area of thought where costings are afflicted by paradox. When things are assigned a market value, it is because there is some moderately stable environment in which they could continue to be enjoyed by someone or other. But where this assumption breaks down, as it does when our ecosystems could well cease to function in any recognisable manner, all costings become meaningless.

There are some other problems with his proposals. He professes to be in favour of investment in clean water, but would have to recognise that the prospect of this option actually being selected for the alternative deployment of resources that countries might have been considering devoting to global warming is far from certain. So his position involves the risk of humanity neither resisting global warming nor supplying water to all that need it. What he can claim is that measures such as satisfying the universal need for fresh water would cost much less, hundreds of billions of dollars perhaps, rather than trillions, and much less, he suggests, than the aggregated costs to humanity of the mitigation of global warming. However, the estimates of those costs seem to take little account of the positive gains such as beneficial ways in which human ingenuity and creativity could treat the project of mitigation and remediation as an opportunity for devising new, greener technology, in which natural sources of energy could be tapped, and their benefits garnered, and in which the energy necessary to satisfy human needs would cease to depend on harmful carbon-related emissions. Besides, if 178 nations (the number participating in the recent Bonn agreement on global warming) are prepared for an effort on this kind of scale (although not necessarily costing what Lomborg suggests), there must be some possibility of combining this project with a serious international effort to supply clean water to the whole of humanity as well (as I have implicitly argued in a book that advocates doing both).[4] This might easily bring environmental problems of its own, but remains highly important in view of the avoidable human misery attributable to water-borne diseases and to lack of clean water for drinking, cleansing and sanitation, particularly in northern Africa and in places like the Gaza Strip, where the amount of water per person is at its lowest in the world.[5] The suggestion that attending to global warming and coping with the need for clean water are alternatives is entirely unnecessary.

Admittedly both of these international projects would depend on a considerable degree of international co-operation. Just for a moment, before I return to co-operation about global warming, I want to mention another aspect of the cross-boundary co-operation required. For away from coasts, where desalination plants are sometimes feasible, the supply of fresh water to those that need it depends on equitable sharing of the water of major rivers. This is another area for scientific research, which should be conducted before rivers are impounded and downstream countries deprived of customary flows, or of large parts of them. The risk should not be taken that farmers and communities downstream can no longer rely on rivers such as the Mekong, the Nile, the Euphrates or the Tigris. Hydrologists should be empowered and requested to study the effects of periods of lack of rain and of drought as well as of heavy rain and of floods before dams are constructed or large quantities of water are extracted for irrigation. Global warming seems to be exacerbating variations in rainfall, particularly in years of the El Niño effect, and we cannot afford to assume that we understand such patterns in current circumstances. Humanity has a bad record in such matters; for example the Aral Sea has been transformed by misconceived irrigation schemes along its two principal rivers in the Soviet period into an environmental disaster zone bestriding a whole region consisting of several countries. To generalise, even schemes to supply clean water to the citizens of one's own country need to observe international constraints, at least if considerations of ethics and of equity are to be heeded, and if the mutual dependence of different countries is to be recognised. (Incidentally the same applies to hydro-electric schemes, particularly with regard to the dams that sometimes accompany them.) Considerations of ethics and of equity require both upstream and downstream countries to co-operate for the good of all their peoples.

To return to global warming, I now want to outline some problems which will call for further international co-operation and scientific and technological research. Eventually, international agreements governing greenhouse gas emissions must involve the full participation of developing countries, since without this participation the problem cannot be solved. I welcome the fact that many countries of the South are now beginning to participate, as they were doing recently at Bonn. However, it would be unreasonable to expect developing countries to agree to limit their emissions to a scaled-down percentage of 1990 emission-levels (the central basis of the Kyoto and Bonn agreements). This is because developing countries are currently unable to satisfy the basic needs of some of their citizens, since doing so would involve generating more electricity than in 1990, and because in practice generating more electricity involves increases to greenhouse gas emissions. So some different basis from that of the historical emission levels of 1990 will be needed to facilitate the full participation of developing countries.

Besides, to restrict emissions to 1990 levels would be inequitable for developing countries, where per capita emissions have always been much lower than those of developed countries. Equity suggests that every person alive has the same entitlement as every other to access to the atmosphere with regard to greenhouse gas emissions; if so, we should seek to introduce, as Michael Grubb has been suggesting, emissions quotas proportioned to population[6] (and not to history). Countries desiring to exceed these quotas would then have to purchase them from those not fully using their own quota. The introduction of the population criterion could facilitate the full participation of developing countries in the international emissions regime of the future.

Even this apparently equitable solution has its problems, and not only through the foreseeable resistance of the big polluters, since unlimited emissions trading might mean that indebted countries would sell their entire quota by way of debt servicing, to the detriment of their inhabitants. A solution to this problem would be a limitation on international trading in emissions quotas. Part of each country's quota should be made inalienable, a part large enough to provide for enough electricity generation to supply the basic needs (with respect to energy) of the people of the country concerned.[7] While some amount of trading would be important to give developing countries an incentive to participate in the system, limitations of this kind would also be important to prevent unethical outcomes in terms of the availability of the energy that people need.

There is a further problem, whether the population criterion is adopted or not. This is the problem that far larger reductions in greenhouse gas emissions are necessary to tackle global warming than either the Kyoto or the Bonn Agreement would deliver. To halt global warming, reductions not of 5% nor of 3% or 2% are needed, but of more like 60%, or so IPCC scientists say.[8] But reductions of total emissions on anything like this scale are going to involve new methods of energy generation, using renewable sources not involving carbon emissions. I should rapidly add that such methods do not, in my view, include nuclear energy generation, granted the lack of safe methods of disposal of nuclear waste products for the many thousands of years of their continuing radioactivity. Granted the instability of most human systems, to risk the future of humanity on any such measures would be hazardous in the extreme.

What emerges as a significant part of any feasible solution is investment in the science and technology of renewable energy generation, whether from solar sources, perhaps the most promising kind in areas receiving a large amount of sunshine such as North Africa and most of India, or from wind-power, wave-power and tidal sources, more promising in countries with plenty of wind and extensive oceanic coastlines such as the UK,[9] or from hydro-electric sources, applicable wherever these methods are possible. Investment in such research would appear vital both for global warming to be seriously tackled, and for basic human needs to be supplied where energy supplies are in question. One advantage of an emissions regime involving quotas based on the population criterion is that it would produce a strong incentive for developed countries to invest in such research, with a view to reducing the need to purchase emission quotas. Another ethically relevant advantage of renewable energy generation is that the replacement of conventional energy generation offers a greatly enhanced future to the wild species that depend on current ecosystems remaining largely intact, or at least not becoming unrecognisably different through mining and mineral extraction and pollution.

Once again, there could be consequent environmental problems. It would, for example, be objectionable if all the wilderness areas of the warmer areas of the planet were to be occupied by solar receptors, leaving not even the deserts for their wild inhabitants. But fortunately there is little prospect that this would be necessary or sought after. So large is the continual stream of solar energy that only comparatively small areas would need to be dedicated to such technology. Admittedly wind-energy generation would currently involve very large areas dedicated to windmills, but investment in the relevant technology and/or off-shore wind farms may well overcome this apparent problem as well. Thus the introduction of renewable methods of electricity generation is likely to make a strong overall contribution to environmental sustainability.

I have omitted many aspects of global warming agreements, such as the issue of carbon sinks. Once again, research into the functioning of such supposed sinks will be needed to guide future agreements. I have also omitted certain areas to which scientific research needs to be redirected, such as tropical medicine and tropical agriculture, confining myself rather to topics centring on global warming, water-supply and energy-generation. But I hope this paper gives enough indication of the relevance of ethics as well as of science to the identification and solution of both regional and global environmental problems.

Notes

* These conclusions are also argued in Robin Attfield, The Ethics of the Global Environment, Edinburgh: Edinburgh University Press and West Lafayette, IN: Purdue University Press, 1999, and in Environmental Ethics, Cambridge: Polity, 2003.

1 Cited in 'Ethics and the Responsibility of Science', anonymous background paper for UNESCO World Conference on Science – Ethics and the Responsibility of Science, Budapest, 1999; see http://www.unesco.org/science/wcs/background/ethics.htm.

2 J.T. Houghton et al., Climate Change 1995: The Science of Climate Change, (published for the Intergovernmental Panel on Climate Change), Cambridge: Cambridge University Press, 1996.

3 Björn Lomborg, The Skeptical Environmentalist, Cambridge: Cambridge University Press, 2001.

4 Robin Attfield, The Ethics of the Global Environment, Edinburgh: Edinburgh University Press, and West Lafayette, IN: Purdue University Press, 1999, pp. 89 and 170f.

5 Michael Prest, 'Water, Water, Nowhere?', Review, London: Rio Tinto, 1997, pp. 15-19 at p. 17; Prest here cites World Bank estimates.

6 Grubb, Michael, The Greenhouse Effect: Negotiating Targets, London: Royal Institute of International Affairs, 1989; also Energy Policies and the Greenhouse Effect, Aldershot: Gower, 1990.

7 Henry Shue, 'Equity in an International Agreement on Climate Change' in Proceedings of IPCC Workshop, Nairobi, July 1994 (on 'Equity and Social Considerations Related to Climate Change'), Nairobi: ICIPE Science Press, 1995, 385-92.

8 An example is Robert T. Watson, Chair of the IPCC, commenting on their latest report in November 2000.

9 Gareth Thomas MP and Stewart T Boyle, At the Energy Crossroads: Policies for a Low Carbon Economy, London: Fabian Society, 2001. The commitment of the UK Prime Minister, Tony Blair, to increase the use of wind and wave power over the next 50 years, made in a speech of 24 February 2003, indicates that this has now become UK policy, at least in principle.

Chapter 14

Ecological Modernisation and the Precautionary Principle

Robert Lee and Elen Stokes

The precautionary principle is claimed as a component part of two influential streams of social science thinking. The first is the more optimistic message of *ecological modernisation*, and the second derives from the *risk society* thesis, offering a more sombre warning of dissolved traditional trust relationships and a social obsession with the distribution of 'bads' rather than goods.[1] We argue below that the ambiguity with which the precautionary principle is defined allows the continuing claim of both schools of thought to claim ownership of the precautionary principle.

The concept of ecological modernisation is founded on the possibility of environmental improvement and enhancement through technological development. As such, it has been described as 'an optimistic message'[2] and may be seen as a break away from traditional perceptions that economic development and environmental protection are necessarily inconsistent. Central to the notion of ecological modernisation is the claim that technological progress delivers cost savings as well as environmental gains. The introduction of new manufacturing or industrial process, such as the use of flue gas scrubbers to curb air pollution, or the recycling of otherwise 'waste' heat, for example, ensures increased economic efficiency as well as minimising environmental degradation. Other change is much more fundamental and structural in nature, and might be labelled 'industrial ecology'.[3] Thus, shifts to information products and the use of ICT may allow economic growth while leaving a much lighter environmental footprint than the heavy industry that it replaces.

As an optimistic message, ecological modernisation may be contrasted with the gloomier prognosis of Beck's *risk society* thesis,[4] notwithstanding attempts to link the two.[5] As Buttel[6] points out, Beck argues that reflexive modernisation has given rise to more fragmented social movements and a sub-political form of environmental action – often opposing the technologies for which environmental benefits are claimed, as arguments surrounding biotechnology illustrate.

There is a marked tension between the idea of a risk society based upon *manufactured* risk rather than *natural* hazards, and the notion inherent in ecological modernisation that *technological* rather than *societal* change is capable of delivering environmental gains.

On the other hand both analyses have a close relationship to precaution. In risk society, reflexive modernisation causes the modern condition to turn 'back on itself' to face problems of its own making. Technological progress creates as many uncertainties as it dispels, and the process of reflexive modernisation has exposed the disjuncture between the ability of modernity to create the future, and its inability to control it. As a result, in order to maintain a general ethos of security, salubrity and self-preservation, the offerings of science and technology must be forgone.

Links between ecological modernisation and the precautionary principle are said to be both historical and geographical – notions of ecological modernisation date back to the German Environmental Action Programme of 1971[7] which emphasises technological foresight in the hope of promoting longer term gains through process changes. Principles of prevention at source and of precaution were central to the Programme. It is worth noting that ecological modernisation envisages solutions to environmental degradation emerging from technological innovation. This fits with the wording of the precautionary principle (below) which demands that cost effective measures to curb pollution should not be postponed. From this viewpoint, technological developments will intervene to reduce environmental costs.[8]

However, not all of technological innovation is likely to be benign or to deliver the double dividend promised by ecological modernisation. Particularly at the industrial ecology level, not all changes may be welcomed and some may be resisted even by those people said to benefit from the 'advance'. It becomes a task then to separate out those technologies offering the win/win situation of ecological modernisation from those offering 'what no one saw and no one wanted - self endangerment and devastation of nature'.[9] Put another way, how do we decide whether to allocate technologies to ecological modernisation or to risk society? In order to try and answer this question, we now examine the notion of the precautionary principle and review a recent case which appears to be instrumental in shaping thinking about the application of precaution in the EU, before drawing some wider conclusions in answer to the question framed above.

The Precautionary Principle – A Profile

The precautionary principle finds itself operating in a lacuna between states of certainty and uncertainty – where a potential *threat* of environmental damage can be ascertained but the *actual* likelihood of the occurrence of that threat remains uncertain. Quintessentially, it is a symptom of the modern risk condition and is seen as a reaction to the problems encountered in policy formulation in the face of scientific uncertainty.[10] The underlying assumption is that 'the damaging effects of human activities may become irreversible before the scientific community can agree the precise nature or scope of their impact; taking precautionary action can help avoid this'.[11] Sociologists such as Beck and Giddens illustrate how characteristics of modern society spawn new models of political discord regarding risk issues.[12] The term 'risk society' has emerged to describe an emerging post-industrial society. Crucial to its understanding is a marked increase in suspicion of science as a result of a deep social malaise that is typical of modern society,[13] facing rapid scientific progress which provides the root of contemporary environmental risks. Accordingly, 'the sources of danger are no longer ignorance but knowledge',[14] and, people are depicted not so much as problem solvers, but rather as the problem itself.[15]

Since the 1970s, the precautionary principle has become a universally recognised concept. Suffice to say, there is an extensive body of literature tracing its development. The most commonly cited working definition of the precautionary principle is found in Article 15 of the 1992 UNCED Rio Declaration, which provides that:-

> ...where there are threats of serious or irreversible damage, lack of full scientific certainty shall not be used as a reason for postponing cost-effective measures to prevent environmental degradation.

The language of this definition generates a number of questions regarding the scope of the precautionary principle. First, it suggests that the principle is inapplicable in situations where there is no serious or irreversible damage to the environment. Not only are we left without any definition of thresholds such as 'serious', but neither are we told how to measure or identify them. Secondly, the concept of a threat of such damage raises alarm bells because it brings us into the risk debate; it is in the nature of a threat that it may not materialise, or may be averted. A threat is unwelcome, but it is also uncertain. Yet the notion of uncertainty is itself multifarious, and can exist in different circumstances. The chances of one surviving a train or bus journey at a given time and in a given space can be described as being uncertain, despite the fact that a probabilistic analysis of actuarial figures could undoubtedly be generated. On the other hand, in some situations the probability of a threat materialising may be unascertainable. This can also be described as uncertainty. The requirement that there must exist a threat of environmental damage creates a hypothetical threshold – which Article 15 allows to remain indistinct.

A third observation about the Rio definition is that it calls for some form of cost-benefit risk assessment by the acceleration of cost-effective measures. This is inconsistent with other visions of the precautionary principle promoted by NGOs and interest groups who call for an total ban on a proposed activity, in the event of scientific uncertainty. For example, the Commission Directorate for Health and Consumer Protection assert that:

> The Precautionary Principle is an approach to risk management that is applied in circumstances of scientific uncertainty reflecting the need to take action in the face of a potentially serious risk without waiting for the results of scientific research.[16]

This is a far cry from the implicit cost-benefit analysis propounded in Article 15, which would suggest that, should the cost of its application outweigh its effectiveness in preventing environmental degradation, the precautionary principle shall not be invoked. Of course, this leaves open the possibility of having regard to factors other than environmental protection, such as economic or social concerns, which might not necessarily secure environmental protection.

The precautionary principle has grown rapidly in status over the past three decades, yet a common understanding of its meaning, scope and application continues to elude us. It is currently at the forefront of EU environmental policy, and has been described as the 'cornerstone'[17] and 'the fundamental principle'[18] of the campaign for sustainable development.

It is enshrined in EC Treaty Article 174, paragraph 2, which states that EC environmental policy:

> ...shall aim at a high level of protection taking into account the diversity of situations in the various regions of the Community. It shall be based on the precautionary principle and on the principles that preventive action should be taken, that environmental damage should as a priority be rectified at source and that the polluter should pay.

It is important to note that the Treaty fails to define the precautionary principle. Having recognised the need for clarification, and in response to the WTO Beef Hormones litigation,[19] the Commission produced a written Communication in February 2000.[20] At the outset, it aims 'to inform all interested parties, in particular the European Parliament, the Council and Member States of the manner in which the Commission applies or intends to apply the precautionary principle when faced with taking decisions relating to the containment of risk.'[21] It also seeks to develop a common understanding of risk assessment, management and communication, and prevent the misuse of the precautionary principle in a protectionist manner. Should action based on the precautionary principle be deemed necessary, it ought to be proportionate, non-discriminatory, consistent with previous action, based on a cost-benefit analysis, and subject to future review.

Unquestionably, the Communication provides a useful tool for decision-making, and contributes to the ongoing debate on the issue. Yet the Communication is 'still thin on precise definition',[22] and fails to clarify thresholds that determine the point at which the precautionary principle is to be employed. The Environment Commissioner stated that 'there is a definition...in the communication'[23] – but when asked what that definition was, she answered 'it depends on the case it is being applied to'.[24] Instead, the Communication provides more general guidelines of application. And whilst this does not aid the quest for a concrete definition, it certainly leaves the door open for future manipulation and embellishment.

A European Legal Principle?

The European Communication provides information as to how the Commission intends to operate the precautionary principle. Inevitably then, and in the light of Article 174(2), the European Court of Justice will be drawn into determining the legality of Commission decision-making in accordance with the principle. Thus we see the precautionary principle begin to move from a statement of political principle at Rio to functioning a legal instrument. The review by the Court of Commission action is not necessarily unwelcome even by the Commission, for it is aware of wider challenges to the policies of the European Union[25] in the WTO Appellate Tribunals and elsewhere. In effect, the task of the European Court of Justice in developing the jurisprudence of the precautionary policy is a vital component in the legitimation of the Single Market programme. This role may be illustrated by a review of the significant decision of the Court of First Instance in relation to the banning of antibiotics in animal foodstuff.[26]

Additives to animal foodstuffs such as vitamins, trace elements, binders, preservatives, coccidiostats and antibiotics are currently controlled by Directive 70/524/EC which was last substantially amended by Directive 96/51/EC. Only additives on an authorised list can be used in animal feeds subject to certain conditions of use. The legal provisions permit a Member State to halt the use of an additive if it is thought to create a risk to animal or human health or the environment. In such circumstances, the Member State is obliged to inform the European Commission and other Member States of its action, and the Commission is required to seek advice from the Standing Committee on Foodstuffs. Should the Commission reject the advice from the Committee, it is obliged to consult the Council of Ministers. In addition, the Commission may seek guidance from the Scientific Committee for Animal Nutrition (SCAN), set up in 1976.

In 1998, relying on advice from a national scientific body, Denmark banned the use of virginiamycin, belonging to the streptogramin class of antibiotics, in animal foodstuffs. The Commission sought scientific advice from SCAN, and on 17 December 1998, following the Commission's guidance, the Council adopted Regulation (EC) No. 2821/98. This banned the use of four antibiotics – virginiamycin, bacitracin zinc, spiramycin, and tylosin phosphate – as additives in animal foodstuff for fear of the development of animal resistance to antibiotic and subsequent transmission of resistance to humans through consumption.

The contested regulation forms part of the CAP framework. It was adopted by the Council on the basis of Article 11(3) of Directive 70/524 – enabling the Commission to instigate an Article 24 procedure to alter the lists of authorised antibiotics in response to concerns by a Member State regarding the protection of human or animal health or the environment exposed. The Council relied upon Article 3a(e) of the Directive, which provides that authorisation of a foodstuff additive is only to be given if 'for serious reasons concerning human or animal health its use must not be restricted to medical or veterinary purposes'.[27] Authorisation for the use of four antibiotics as additives in feedingstuffs was withdrawn, and the Council was of the opinion that, in relation to virginiamycin in particular, this decision was justified on the grounds that the effectiveness of certain human medicinal products could be jeopardised.[28]

Pfizer Animal Health SA ('Pfizer') was the sole producer in the world of virginiamycin when the regulation was adopted. Pfizer lodged an application at the European Court of First Instance for judicial review of the Council's adoption of the regulation, challenging the legality of the provision.[29] Pfizer argued that there were eight grounds for annulment, which inevitably make this case exceedingly complex. Pfizer's principal claims essentially amounted to the contention that the Community institutions erred in their assessment and management of potential risks to human health posed by the use of virginiamycin in animal foodstuffs and in their application of the precautionary principle.[30] As both parties agreed that, when the contested regulation was adopted, the existence of the risk had not been scientifically proven, the Council relied on precautionary principle to justify the adoption of the regulation.[31]

However, although the parties agreed that the framework of Directive 70/524 provides that Community institutions may adopt a measure on the basis of the precautionary principle, they disagreed on its interpretation. Both parties agreed that such a measure withdrawing authorisation cannot legitimately be based on a 'zero risk' test, since it is impossible to prove irrefutably that a particular substance creates zero risk to human health either now or in the future. Pfizer maintained that the Community institutions are prohibited from invoking precautionary measures unless and until they have undertaken a scientific assessment of the risks, and have shown that any such risks are probable.[32] Pfizer contended that the Community institutions erred in their risk assessment. Although Pfizer accepted that the use of virginiamycin creates a 'hazard to human health', it argued that this is not enough to validate the withdrawal of authorisation on the grounds of the precautionary principle. Instead, Pfizer claims that a higher standard of proof should be imposed, and stated that 'it would be proven with the first dead man. It would be proven with the first infection, or with the first proof of colonization, or the first proof of transfer in a human'.[33]

The Court concluded that Pfizer's interpretation of the precautionary principle was incorrect, stating that:

> ...it must be borne in mind that, when the precautionary principle is applied, the fact that there is scientific uncertainty and that it is impossible to carry out a full risk assessment in the time available does not prevent the competent public authority from taking preventive protective measures if such measures appear essential, regard being had to the level of risk to human health which the public authority has decided is the critical threshold above which it is necessary to take preventive measures.[34]

The Court noted that the application of the precautionary principle is acceptable in situations where there exists a risk to human health, even if it cannot be fully demonstrated, but it cannot be based on a purely hypothetical approach to risk. In the circumstances, it was held that the Community institutions did not surpass the limits of the discretion bestowed upon them by the Treaty when they concluded that there existed a proper scientific basis for a possible connection between the use of virginiamycin in feedingstuffs and the occurrence of streptogramin resistance in humans.

The Community institutions decided that the use of virginiamycin created a risk to human health despite the fact that SCAN concluded that the use of virginiamycin did not create an immediate risk to human health in Denmark.[35] Even though Pfizer recognised that the Community institutions are not legally bound by SCAN's opinion, it claimed that it was impermissible for Community institutions to discount it. However, the Council considered there to be sufficient scientific evidence to conclude that a risk to human health did exist, and drew upon parts of the opinion to support their contention. The Court held that SCAN had not fully understood the application of the precautionary principle, and that it was open to the Community institutions to depart from elements of the SCAN opinion whilst relying on other aspects of the conclusions drawn.[36]

Furthermore, the Court recognized the significance of a scientific study on live rats carried out by the Danish authorities and various reports from international, Community and national bodies, and claimed that it amounted to 'major fresh evidence' that virginiamycin created a risk to human health.[37] The Court held that this additional information was undoubtedly based on the 'best scientific data available at international level'.[38] The Court concluded that, overall, the Community institutions neither made manifest errors of risk assessment and risk management nor breached the precautionary principle.

Managing Uncertainty

The decision in Pfizer is an important step in developing a process that allows for the application of the precautionary principle in risk assessment, but it is not without difficulties. To begin with there is little consideration in the case of issues of risk characterisation. Both parties accepted that measures could be adopted on a precautionary basis under the Directive, at least where there was more than a zero risk. However, the Court implicitly accepts that there exists some level of risk above a 'critical level' demanding preventative measures, without articulating the factors that allow such risk characterisation. SCAN's finding that virginiamycin did not create an immediate threat to human health might have allowed Pfizer to challenge the invocation of the precautionary principle in the first place. Had Pfizer done so, the Court might have shed some light on the degree of scientific uncertainty required to implement the precautionary principle.

Processes of risk assessment generally begin with some form of risk characterisation because identifying the type and nature of the risks helps to guide the risk assessment. Here, however, the critical stage of characterisation seems to be by passed on the basis that since a risk can be perceived, it ought to be assessed. Whilst not denying that risk perceptions may trigger legitimate demands for assessment, we might hope for something more concrete than this. Given that, in the nature of the process, this is the first stage in the exploration of something about which there is no full scientific knowledge, we cannot hope for too much. However, it ought to be possible to clarify the degree of uncertainty with which a potential hazard presents itself. Thereafter, the contingent and indeterminate nature of the perceived risk might allow a better focus for eventual risk assessment. Without something of this kind, we could oscillate between any perception of risk, however unlikely, being used to invoke precautionary assessment on one hand, and the continual denial of (mere) perceptions as relevant on the other. Put another way, it is useful to accept the risk society notion that life on 'a high technological frontier' will generate doubts about possible futures[39] without, on this ground alone, forgoing the gains of ecological modernisation where those futures may prove beneficial.

A second problem relates to the depiction of the processes of risk management, followed by risk assessment, depicted by the court in its judgment. The first stage assessment is a task for the scientists. Thereafter, politicians and bureaucrats may be charged with managing risk. This is not an uncommon understanding of shared but divided responsibilities in handling risk. Indeed it may be emerging as a preferred EU model. In BRASS, work is progressing on a study of the development of the European Food Safety Agency (EFSA). In the course of this work, DG SANCO expressed the hope that science-based decision-making in the EFSA would 'protect against political indiscretion especially regarding precautionary measures'. DG Trade felt that the EFSA could go a long way in helping to 'separate out science from legislation'. However, Eurocommerce, a major private interest umbrella organisation, bemoaned the lack of legislative capacity, stating that:

> the EFSA has a very important role to play but since it does not have any legislative powers, its impact will be somewhat similar to that of a scientific lobby body. Food safety policy itself will continue to be made by the European Commission with DG SANCO [at the heart of the process] whilst the EFSA will be responsible for communicating food risks to member states and the public.

Although the *Pfizer* decision has been welcomed as recognising that science does not trump, and that there may still be room for precautionary decisions even in the face of a scientific body finding little discernible risk, there are reasons to be cautious about the two-stage type of process outlined above. Eurocommerce's concern is that scientists can advise or lobby, but cannot decide. However, there is a parallel objection that other stakeholders may be able to influence the management process but will have little role in potentially influential assessments. There are a number of difficulties with this, and although these are well recognised within social science literature, they are nonetheless worth emphasising. The most obvious of these is the danger that the risk assessment process will revert to a reductive quantitative tradition, with ethical and social aspects of risk remaining irrelevant until the risk management process. This would be unfortunate since, as Wynne as argued, non-expert assessments may be instrumental in shaping the risk assessment process itself.[40] And certainly the worry is that when the European directorates talk of the scientific basis of decision making, the policy options have already been foreshortened by the discrete and limited nature of the assessment undertaken.

Moreover, the two-stage model propounded within Europe equates risk assessment with good science, and implicitly asserts a value neutral testing of hypotheses of the type undertaken in the laboratory. There are a number of reasons why risk assessment does not look like this. One is the necessity to make or frame assumptions given the task of determining magnitude and likelihood. Assumptions imply choice and deny the possibility of definitive answers.[41] An extension of this point is that risks will be played out not in laboratory conditions but in social, temporal and spatial conditions subject to considerable diversity and complexity. The depiction of the risk assessment process in the European model is that it should lead to a conclusion, which may or may not be followed in the later risk management stage. What it does not seem to allow for is the possibility of competing interpretations of the risk: the possibility of indeterminacy in the face of contradictory but plausible outcomes.

Finally one of the dangers of the ring-fencing of risk assessment is that insufficient room is left for ignorance.[42] As used in social science literature, the term is not referring to lack of knowledge but rather to knowledge that is not yet attainable.[43] This element of surprise may be discounted and even rejected because it disturbs scientific closure on issues, thereby undermining the political role given to science in the EU model of providing the 'scientific basis' for decision making by admitting wide ranging and divergent suppositions. For all of these reasons one might hope for a more integrated process of deliberation which is more widely inclusive of a range of interests and views.

However, similar remarks may be made of the risk management process. The fears of Eurocommerce should not be lightly dismissed. There are equally problems where there is no scientific involvement in the risk management process. If the role of risk assessment and of risk communication becomes the focus of 'lobbying' then there is a danger of closed and unaccountable risk management decisions. Moreover, if we seek the benefits of ecological modernisation then it would be folly to deny the utility of technology driven solutions at the risk management stage. Often the pattern will be even more complex, with claims made for technologies, but with divergent social attitudes not merely to the risk, which may be small, but also to the benefit claimed. There is a range of possibilities here. Objections may be raised to slight risk where the adverse consequences are irreversible. Or the risk may be disproportionate in its effect on particular social groups when one examines the distributional effects. Or society may find a potential outcome so repugnant that it would wish to forgo opportunity in the face of the possibility of the realisation of that particular risk. In all of these instances one would hope for wide-ranging debate, which would neither privilege scientific prognosis as determining the risk management pathway, nor isolate and marginalize it as an initial part of the process, but which would embrace it as integral to a deeper understanding of the possibilities presented. Indeed it may be yet another criticism of risk assessment processes to date that they exact threats to careful scrutiny without paying equivalent attention to the benefits claimed.

Conclusion

The juxtaposition of the risk society against notions of ecological modernisation helps us dwell on the role and significance of the precautionary responsibility, but it is somewhat artificial. In truth, technology has the capacity to bring both benefits and burdens. Indeed, this is why risk procedures are required. However, if we are to assess opportunities and threats in a holistic way, little is to be gained from dividing up the stages of risk handling and producing institutional separation between scientific processes of risk assessment and political decisions about risk management. There are necessary reasons why an integrated process must emerge in which both the scientific and social scientific dimensions of risk are understood, accepted and integrated into a meaningful process of decision-making based upon a plurality of approaches to precaution. It is perhaps ironic that only by engaging with elements of distrust will we restore trust in the scientific capacity for risk evaluation.

Notes

1 Lash, S. and Wynne, B. 'Introduction', in Beck, U. *Risk Society: Towards a New Modernity* (Sage; London; 1992).
2 Andersen, M. S. and Massa, I. 'Ecological Modernisation – Origins, Dilemmas and Future Directions' (2000) 2 *Journal of Environmental Policy and Planning* 337.
3 Buttel, F.H. 'Ecological Modernisation as Social Theory' (2000) 31 Geoforum 57.
4 Beck, U. (1992) *op. cit.* note 1.
5 Mol, A. *The Refinement of Production: Ecological Modernisation* (Van Arkel; Utrecht; 1995); and see the discussion in Buttel F.H. (2000) *op. cit.* note 3.
6 *ibid.*
7 Andersen, M.S. and Massa, I. (2000) *op. cit.* note 1 and Janicke M. *State Failure: The Impotence of Politics in Industrial Society* (Pennsylvania; Pennsylvania State University Press; Pennsylvania; 1990).
8 Boehmer-Christiansen, S., 'The Precautionary Principle in Germany' in O'Riordan, T. and Cameron, J. (eds) *Interpreting the Precautionary Principle* (Earthscan; London; 1994).
9 Beck, U., *Ecological Enlightenment* (Polity; Cambridge; 1995).
10 Stallworthy, M., *Sustainability, Land Use and Environment: A Legal Analysis* (Cavendish Publishing; London; 2002) at 48.
11 Holder, J., 'The Precautionary Principle Under UK Environmental Law' in Holder, J., *Impact of EC Environmental Law in the UK* (Wiley; Chichester; 1997) at 123.
12 See Grove-White, R. (1998) 'Risk Society, Politics and BSE', in Franklin, J. (ed) *The Politics of Risk Society* (Polity; London; 1998) pp.50-53, at 50.
13 Roberts, S., 'Future Directions in Green Political Thought – Welcome to Jurassic Park: Science, Marxism and the Domination of Nature in the Lost World,', www.psa.ac.uk/cps/1998/roberts.pdf, accessed June 2003, at p.6.
14 *ibid.* at 7.
15 *ibid.* at 8.
16 As cited in National Consumer Council, *Public Health and the Precautionary Principle* (NCC; London; 2000).
17 Bergkamp, L., 'Understanding the Precautionary Principle (Part I)' (2002) 1 Env. Liability 18-30, at 18.
18 Cameron, J. and Abouchar, J., 'The Precautionary Principle: A Fundamental Principle of Law and Policy for the Protection of the Global Environment' (1991) 14 B.C. Int'l & Comp. L. Rev. 1-27, at 2.
19 See WTO Appellate Body Report on EC Measures Concerning Meat and Meat Products (Hormones), complaint by the USA WT/DS26/ABAB/R.

[20] European Commission, *Communication on the Precautionary Principle*, 2 February 2000 COM (2000) 1 final.

[21] *ibid.* at 8.

[22] Lee, R.G, '(Pre)cautionary Tales: Risk, Regulation and the Precautionary Principle, in Lee, R.G. and Boswall, J. (eds) *Economics, Ethics and the Environment* (Cavendish; London; 2001) at 93.

[23] As cited in Bergkamp, L. (2002) *op. cit.* note 17 at 18.

[24] As cited in Stone, C.D., 'Is there a Precautionary Principle?' (2001) 31 Env. L. Rep. 10789-10799, at 10790.

[25] See, for example, EU chemicals policy and hazard assessment: European Commission, *White Paper Strategy for a Future Chemicals Policy* COM (2001) 88 final.

[26] *Pfizer v European Commission*, Case T-13/99, 11 September 2002.

[27] See Recital 5 of Regulation (ed) No.2821/98.

[28] *ibid.* at Recital 21.

[29] It is worth noting that an interim application to market the product pending appeal was rejected.

[30] *op. cit.* note 26 at para. 108. Note that a joint application was made by Alpharma in relation to bacitracin zinc (Case T-70/99).

[31] *ibid.* at para. 113.

[32] *ibid.* at paras. 129-130.

[33] *ibid.* at para. 379.

[34] *ibid.* at para. 382.

[35] *ibid.* at para. 188.

[36] *ibid.* at para 200.

[37] See Recital 20 Regulation 2821/98.

[38] *op. cit.* note 26 at para. 307.

[39] Giddens, A., 'Risk and Responsibility' (1999) 62 MLR 1.

[40] Wynne, B., 'May the Sheep Safely Graze', in Lash, S., Szerszynski, B., and Wynne, B. (eds) *Risk, Environment and Modernity: Towards a New Ecology* (Sage; London; 1996).

[41] Shackley, S. and Wynne, B. 'Representing Uncertainty in Global Climate Change Science and Policy' (1996) 21 Science Technology and Human Values 275.

[42] For a review of the social science literature in relation to this issue, see Stirling, A., 'Risk Uncertainty and Precaution' in Berkhout, F., Leach, M., and Scoones, I. *Negotiating Environmental Change* (Elgar; Cheltenham; 2003).

[43] Van Zwanenberg, P. and Millstone, E., 'Mad Cow Disease – 1980s-2000: How Reassurances Undermined Precaution', in Gee, D. *et al*, *Late Lessons from Early Warnings: The Precautionary Principle 1898-2000* (EEA; Copenhagen; 2001).

Chapter 15

Agri-Culture: Some Principles and Lessons for Sustainability

Jules Pretty

Agri-Cultures

Despite several decades of remarkable agricultural progress, the world still faces a massive food security challenge, with an estimated 790 million people lacking adequate access to food. Most agree that food production will have to increase in the coming years, and that this will have to come from existing farmland. But solving the persistent hunger problem is not simply a matter of developing new agricultural technologies. Most hungry consumers are poor, and so simply do not have the money to buy the food they need. Equally, poor producers cannot afford expensive technologies. They will have to find solutions largely based on locally-available natural, social and human resources. The key questions are, therefore, to what extent can agricultural systems become more productive whilst not causing harm to the environment, and do these offer any new hope for the hungry?

Something is wrong with today's agricultural and food systems. Despite great progress in increasing productivity in the last century, hundreds of millions of people remain hungry and malnourished. Further hundreds of millions eat too much, or the wrong sorts of food, and it is making them ill. The health of the environment suffers too, as costly degradation seems to accompany many of the agricultural systems we have evolved in recent years.[1, 2] Can nothing be done, or is it time for the expansion of another sort of agriculture, founded more on ecological principles, and in harmony with people, their societies and cultures?

In the earliest surviving texts on European farming, agriculture was interpreted as two connected things, *agri* and *cultura*, and food seen as a vital part of the cultures and communities that produced it. Today, however, our experience with industrial farming dominates, with food now seen simply as a commodity, and farming often organized along factory lines. To what extent can we put the culture back into agri-culture without compromising the need to produce enough food? And can we create sustainable systems of farming that are efficient and fair and founded on a detailed understanding of the benefits of agroecology and people's capacity to cooperate?

As we advance into the early years of the 21st century, we have some critical choices.[3, 4] Humans have been farming for some 600 generations, and for most of that time the production and consumption of food has been intimately connected to cultural and social systems. Foods have a special significance and meaning, as do the fields, grasslands, forests, rivers and seas. Yet over just the last two or three generations, we have developed hugely successful agricultural systems based on industrial principles. They in most cases produce more food per hectare and per worker than ever before, but only look so efficient if we ignore the harmful side-effects – the loss of soils, the damage to biodiversity, the pollution of water, the harm to human health.

Over these 12,000 years of agriculture, there have been long periods of stability, punctuated by short bursts of rapid change. These resulted in fundamental shifts in the way people thought and acted. We are at another such junction. A sustainable agriculture making the best of nature and people's knowledge and collective capacities has been showing increasingly good promise. But it has been a quiet revolution because many accord it little credence. It is also silent because those in the vanguard are often the poorest and marginalized, whose voices are rarely heard in the grand scheme of things. No one can exactly say where this revolution could lead us. Neither do we know whether sustainable models of production would be appropriate for all farmers worldwide. But the principles do apply widely. Once these come to be accepted, then it will be the ingenuity of local people that shapes these new methods of producing food to their own particular circumstances.

We know that most transitions involve trade-offs. A gain in one area is accompanied by a loss elsewhere. A road built to increase access to markets helps remote communities, but also allows illegal loggers to remove valuable trees more easily. A farm that eschews the use of pesticides benefits biodiversity, but may produce less food. New agroecological methods may mean more labour is required, putting an additional burden on women. But these trade-offs need not always be serious. If we listen carefully, and observe the improvements already being made by communities across the world, we find that it is possible to produce more food whilst protecting and improving nature. It is possible to have diversity in both human and natural systems without undermining economic efficiency.

How can Agricultural Sustainability Help?

A more sustainable agriculture seeks to make the best use of nature's goods and services as functional inputs. It does this by integrating regenerative processes (such as nutrient cycling, nitrogen fixation, soil regeneration and natural enemies of pests) into food production processes. It minimizes the use of inputs that damage the environment or harm human health. It builds on farmers' knowledge and skills, and seeks to make productive use of social capital, namely people's capacities for collective action for pest, watershed, irrigation, and forest management.

Agricultural systems emphasizing these principles are also multi-functional within landscapes and economies. They jointly produce food and other goods for farm families and markets, but also contribute to a range of valued public goods, such as clean water, wildlife, carbon sequestration in soils, flood protection, groundwater recharge, and landscape amenity value. As a more sustainable agriculture seeks to make the best use of nature's goods and services, so technologies and practices must be locally-adapted. They are most likely to emerge from new configurations of social capital, comprising relations of trust embodied in new social organizations, and new horizontal and vertical partnerships between institutions, and human capital comprising leadership, ingenuity, management skills, and capacity to innovate. Agricultural systems with high levels of social and human assets are more able to innovate in the face of uncertainty

Sustainable agriculture relies more on agro-ecological and organic approaches to food production. This is not to say that modern agriculture cannot successfully increase food production. Any farmer or agricultural system with access to sufficient inputs, knowledge and skills, can produce large amounts of food. But most farmers in developing countries are not in such a position. The central questions today are i) to what extent can farmers improve food production with cheap, low-cost, locally-available technologies and inputs, and ii) to what extent can they do this without causing environmental damage.

The success of modern agriculture in recent decades has often masked significant externalities (actions that affect the welfare of or opportunities available to an individual or group without direct payment or compensation), which affect both ecosystem services and human health, as well as agriculture itself. Environmental and health problems associated with agriculture have been increasingly well-documented, but it is only recently that the scale of some of these costs has come to be appreciated.

Recent Evidence

In recent research, we examined the extent to which farmers have improved food production in recent years with low-cost, locally-available and environmentally-sensitive practices and technologies.[5, 6, 7] We analyzed by survey during 1999-2000 208 projects in 52 developing countries, in which 8.98 million farmers have adopted these practices and technologies on 28.92 million hectares, representing 3.0% of the 960 million hectares of arable and permanent crops in Africa, Asia and Latin America.[8, 9]

We found improvements in food production occurring through one or more of four mechanisms:

i) intensification of a single component of farm system;
ii) addition of a new productive element to a farm system;
iii) better use of water and land, so increasing cropping intensity);
iv) improvements in per hectare yields of staples through introduction of new regenerative elements into farm systems and new locally-appropriate crop varieties and animal breeds. The 89 projects with reliable yield data show an average per project increase in per hectare food production of 93% (see Figure 15.1).

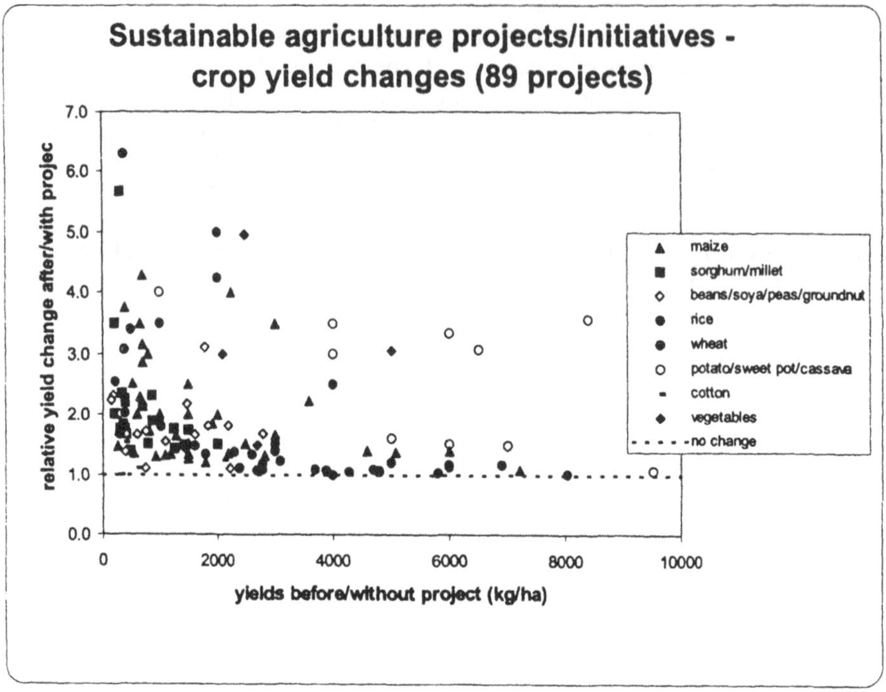

Figure 15.1 **Sustainable agriculture projects/initiatives – relative crop yield changes (89 projects, where 1.0 represents no change, and relative yields above 1.0 represent multiples) (from Pretty et al, 2003)**

There are several key practices and technologies that have led to these increases: increased water use efficiency, improvements to soil health and fertility, pest control using biodiversity services with minimal or zero-pesticide use, and social organization for collective action.[6, 10, 11, 12, 13] This research reveals promising advances in the adoption of practices and technologies that are likely to be more sustainable, with substantial benefits for the rural poor. With explicit support through national policy reforms, better markets, and more integrated and cross-disciplinary approaches to science, these improvements in food security could spread to much larger numbers of farmers and rural people in the coming decades.

Social learning is a vital part of the process of adjustment in sustainable agriculture projects.[5, 10] The conventional model of understanding technology adoption as a simple matter of diffusion, as if by osmosis, no longer holds. But the alternative is neither simple nor mechanistic. It involves building the capacity of farmers and their communities to learn about the complex ecological and biophysical complexity in their fields and farms, and then to act in different ways.

The process of learning, if it is socially-embedded, provokes wider changes in behaviour.

Farmers require timely information on pest-predator relationships, moisture and plants, soil health, and the chemical and physical relationships between plants and animals. These are subject to manipulation – and farmers who understand this, and who are confident about experimentation, are better innovators. The empirical evidence tells us two important things. Social learning leads to greater innovation together with increased likelihood that social processes producing these technologies are likely to persist.

On Policies for Sustainability

Several things are now clear with respect to sustainable agriculture[3]:

i) The technologies and social processes for local level agro-ecological improvements are well-tested and established;

ii) The social and institutional conditions for spread are less well-known, but have been established in several contexts (in particular social groups at local level and novel partnerships between external agencies;

iii) The political conditions for the emergence of supportive policies are the least established, with only a very few examples of real progress.

Most of the sustainable agriculture improvements seen in the past decade have arisen despite existing national policies. These will need major reform. Policies framed to deliver increased food production will have to be changed if they are to help deliver environmental and social benefits too. Food policies framed to help deliver cheap and abundant food regardless of quality will have to change too. And rural development policies and institutions focusing on 'exogenous' solutions to the economic and social problems of rural communities are ill-suited to the needs of community-based and participatory development.[6, 11]

Nonetheless, there has been increasing global recognition of the need for policies to support sustainable agriculture.[3, 8] Although almost every country would now say it supports sustainable agriculture, the evidence points towards only patchy reforms. Only three countries have given explicit national support for sustainable agriculture – putting it at the centre of agricultural development policy and integrating policies accordingly. These are Cuba, Switzerland and Bhutan. Cuba has a national policy for alternative agriculture; Switzerland has three tiers of support to encourage environmental services from agriculture and rural development, and Bhutan has a national environmental policy coordinated across all sectors.

Several countries have given sub-regional support, such as the states in southern Brazil supporting zero-tillage and catchment management, and some in India supporting watershed management or participatory irrigation management. A much larger number have reformed parts of agricultural policies, such as China's support for integrated ecological demonstration villages, Kenya's catchment approach to soil conservation, Indonesia's ban on pesticides and programme for farmer field schools, India's support for soybean processing and marketing, Bolivia's regional integration of agricultural and rural policies, Sweden's support for organic agriculture, Burkina Faso's land policy, and Sri Lanka and the Philippines' stipulation that water users' groups manage irrigation systems.

A much larger number of countries have reformed elements of agricultural policies through new regulations, incentives and/or environmental taxes, and administrative mechanisms, and these are having considerable though partial effect. These include catchment approaches for soil conservation, bans on selected pesticides, combined with national programme for farmer field schools and IPM in rice, support for soybean processing and marketing, and regional integration of agricultural and rural policies. But most countries have not yet explicitly put sustainable agriculture at the centre of their policy frameworks.

Agricultural systems can be economically, environmentally and socially sustainable. But without appropriate policy support, they are likely to remain at best localized in extent, and at worst simply wither away. We cannot, therefore, yet say whether a transition to sustainable agriculture, delivering increasing benefits at the scale occurring in these projects, will result in enough food to meet the current food needs of developing countries, the future basic needs after continued population growth, or the potential demand following adoption of more meat-rich diets. Even the substantial increases reported here may not be enough. However, there is scope for cautious optimism, as the evidence indicates that productivity can increase steadily over time if natural, social and human capital assets are accumulated.

References

1. Altieri, M. (1995), *Agroecology: The Science of Sustainable Agriculture.* Westview Press, Boulder.
2. Pretty, J., Brett, C., Gee, D., Hine, R., Mason, C. F., Morison, J. I. L., Raven, H., Rayment, M. and van der Bijl, G. (2000), An assessment of the total external costs of UK agriculture. *Agricultural Systems* 65 (2), 113-136.
3. Pretty, J. (2002), *Agri-Culture: Reconnecting People, Land and Nature.* Earthscan, London 261.
4. McNeely, J. A. and Scherr, S. J. (2001) *Common Ground, Common Future. How ecoagriculture can help feed the world and save wild biodiversity.* IUCN and Future Harvest, Geneva.
5. Röling, N. G. and Wagemakers, M. A. E. (eds), (1997), *Facilitating Sustainable Agriculture.* Cambridge University Press, Cambridge.
6. Uphoff, N. (ed) (2002), *Agroecological Innovations: Increasing Food Production with Participatory Development.* Earthscan, London.
7. Ye, X. J., Wang, Z. Q. and Li, Q. S. (2002), The ecological agriculture movement in modern China. *Agric., Ecosys. Environ.* 92, 261-81.

8 Pretty, J. and Hine, R. (2000), The promising spread of sustainable agriculture in Asia. *Nat.Res.Forum* 24, 107-126.

9 Pretty, J., Morison, J. I. L. and Hine, R. E. (2003), Reducing food poverty by increasing agricultural sustainability in developing countries. *Agric. Ecosys. Environ.* 95, 217-234.

10 Pretty, J. and Ward, H. (2001), Social capital and the environment. *World Development* 29 (2), 209-227.

11 Scott, J. (1998). *Seeing Like a State. How Certain Schemes to Improve the Human Condition Have Failed.* Yale University Press, New Haven.

12 Stoll, S. and O'Riordan, T. (2002) *Protecting the Protected: Managing Biodiversity for Sustainability.* Cambridge University Press, Cambridge.

13 Pretty, J., Ball, A. S., Li, Xiaoyun, and Ravindranath, N. H. (2002). The role of sustainable agriculture and renewable resource management in reducing greenhouse gas emissions and increasing sinks in China and India. *Phil.Trans. Royal Society Lond. A* 360, 1741-1761.

Chapter 16

Applying the Notion of Sustainability – Dilemmas and the Need for Dialogue

Christian Gamborg and Peter Sandøe

Abstract

This paper revisits the strained yet ubiquitous notion of sustainability to see where and how it can make a contribution to improved agricultural and natural resource management and policy making. The case of a three-year EU network on farm animal breeding and reproduction is used as a practical illustration. In this network, commercial breeders and breeding scientists were required, with professional assistance from philosophers and social scientists, to develop a definition of sustainable farm animal breeding.

The word 'sustainability' does not define a unique ethical perspective. At best it indicates a willingness to open an ethical agenda. However if the agenda is not specified in some detail, there is a real danger that necessary ethical discussion will be swept under the carpet. Even worse, the word may be used as a fig leaf in an attempt to legitimise projects which are ethically dubious.

Used conscientiously, the framework of sustainability has two benefits: First, it invites parties involved in the planning of future activities in a company or sector to take a comprehensive look at potentially conflicting concerns and to face any difficult trade-offs. Second, it encourages concerns to be presented within a framework (i.e. of sustainability) that is endorsed by society as a whole, and this enables the stakeholders to make room for communication to, and dialogue with, a broader audience than the rather narrow group of people directly involved.

Adapting the definition of sustainability to specific conditions and circumstances is more than a technical or scientific task. It requires us to address carefully underlying questions about values. The fundamental dilemmas that emerge when the notion of sustainability is considered have no easy solutions, but they can be addressed by taking into account four key characteristics of sustainability discussed in this paper.

Introduction

Recent decades have witnessed considerable change in the agricultural sector and more generally in all the activities and practices associated with land use in

Europe. Some practices that were considered defensible and rational fifty years ago are no longer looked upon by all as prudent or acceptable. While the earlier focus was on securing supply and making production more efficient, issues such as environmental protection, nature conservation, food safety and animal welfare now feature prominently on the land use agenda. With the rise in living standards and human well-being, at least in our affluent part of the world, a shift of values has occurred.

This shift has presented scientists and those who work in the agricultural sector with new scientific and technological challenges, but the considerable task of identifying and reflecting on the ethical issues involved in these challenges lies largely ahead. Sustainability can play a key role in this task by providing a conceptual framework, endorsed by society as a whole, within which the scientific, technological and, not least, the ethical issues can be crystallised (Gamborg et al., 2002).

The notion of sustainability has been widely embraced as something that allows for a common vision of the utilisation of renewable resources in land use systems – a vision that helps to discourage the sort of polarised discussion that has one-sided focus on productivity and profit on one side, and uncompromising demands for nature preservation and radical changes in agricultural production on the other.

The question remains, however, whether everyone really looks at this overarching ideal, this supposedly common frame of understanding, in the same way. Loading the notion of sustainability with all things desirable, we certainly need to make sure that we are not simply suppressing disagreement over priorities. Thus if we are to make continued use of sustainability as a conceptual framework in agricultural production and land use, we need to clarify that framework, examine its philosophical underpinnings, and scrutinise its implied priorities and value commitments. Below, we first trace the evolution of the notion of sustainability and look at its present relevance. We then turn to examine a recent network project on farm animal breeding (i.e. altering the hereditary constitution of livestock to better serve human needs). This project illustrates one of the ways of addressing the dilemmas embedded in sustainability.

Sustained Yield, Sustainable Development and Sustainability

The notion of sustainability brings together a set of ideas relating to resource use over time. It has been used for several centuries, and over this time it has evolved by encompassing an ever-wider set of concerns. To understand its present use, and its impact on politics and management, one needs a basic knowledge of its history.

Essentially, sustainability can be characterised as a state or process which, in theory, with the right kind of management, can be maintained indefinitely. Sustainability may be seen as an expansion of the concept of *sustained yield*. This latter concept was developed as a resource planning tool to be used in connection with problems associated with exploitation in the primary sector. It was described systematically for the first time more than 300 years ago in relation to German forest and mining activities; and at this time the criteria of sustained yield were biological.

Over the next two centuries, the interpretation of sustainability evolved. Greater emphasis was put on the maintenance of *economic* output. (This emphasis replaced the earlier focus simply on continued production of commodities such as wood.) Key objectives came to be described as 'procurement of goods', and later on, especially in the mid-twentieth century, 'wise use' of resources. The latter involved minimum standards of conservation designed to avoid deterioration that was considered too expensive, or indeed impossible, to reverse.

Gradually, in the wake of ecological stirrings, such as those evinced in Rachel Carson's 'Silent spring', published in 1962, attention turned to the conservation of nature, not just as a consumable resource, but also for the sake of its biological diversity. Thus at the Stockholm conference on the human environment in 1972, and especially at the 'World conservation strategy', released by the World Conservation Union (IUCN) in 1980, the ideal of sustainability was explicitly extended beyond issues concerned with immediate human livelihood to cover the *preservation* of species and ecosystems.

The report of the 'Brundtland' Commission, 'Our Common Future' (WCED), published and widely studied in policy circles from 1987, shifted the focus to *distribution* over time and talked about sustainable development. In a sense, Brundtland brought sustainability back to the notion of nature as a resource but expanded the time-frame. Sustainability was no longer a question just of immediately subsequent generations but covered the anticipated interests of several generations further down the line. Thus, famously, *sustainable development* was defined by the Brundtland Commission as 'development that meets the needs of the present without compromising the ability of future generations to meet their own needs' (WCED, 1987: 8).

With this definition a new dimension of sustainability emerged. The ethical thrust was now towards social justice and, in particular, social justice across generations (e.g. McNeill, 2000; Lee, 2000). Among the issues that needed to be resolved with the Brundtland definition of sustainability were: What do we owe future generations (Sikora and Barry, 1978)? How do we distribute these obligations among the present generation, and how should we define a 'fair' distribution between generations? Fairness can be seen as maximisation of utility across generations, or as something requiring strict equality, or as a matter of helping the worst off. These interpretations of distributive justice have been the subject of much dispute (Palmer, 1997).

The work of the Brundtland Commission and the IUCN was elaborated in 1992 in the 'Rio Declaration on Environment and Development'. In this declaration, issues of distributive fairness covered distribution not only *between*, but also *within*, generations – especially among rich and poor countries. Another notable outcome of Rio was the so-called 'Agenda 21', which set out a blueprint of how to ensure that development is economically, environmentally and socially sustainable.

More recently, the European Union treaty signed in Amsterdam in 1997 stressed the Union's commitment to 'harmonious, balanced sustainable development'. Again, in the Johannesburg Declaration of 2002 objectives from Stockholm through to Rio were reaffirmed, and a very broad notion of sustainability – one covering everything from clean water, animal welfare, and a good working environment, to profit for the farmer and corruption – was pressed into service.

Present Relevance of Sustainability

The ideal of sustainability we now have is broad and inclusive. It can seem, indeed, to offer something to everyone, and consequently it has reconciliatory appeal. It is difficult *not* to be in favour of development which (*i*) allows industry to prosper, (*ii*) gives a sustained yield of high quality products, (*iii*) protects the natural environment, (*iv*) respects the needs of future generations, (*v*) meets the needs of people living in poverty, and (*vi*) is sensitive to concern about animal welfare and other ethical concerns. Initially, this may appear attractive. However, it is clear that a process of conceptual erosion has set in (Dubgaard et al., 1999). In general concepts offer less clarity and guidance the more features they cover. Hence, the problem of sustainability now consists in taking into account a growing number of concerns, and in trying to balance these potentially conflicting ideals against each other.

It is no surprise, then, that when the idea of sustainability is applied to the main issues raised by agriculture and food production, dilemmas arise and priorities need to be set. One such dilemma involves *animal welfare*: the protection of animal health and well-being vs. human and environmental interests. Another involves *gene technology*: the precautionary principle vs. expected benefits. If sustainability is to be more than a buzzword, and if the task of balancing conflicting concerns is to be taken seriously, sustainability needs to be made more operational.

There are two main avenues here. The first has been taken in natural resource economics. Here the focus of sustainability has been considerably sharpened, and the relevant concepts have been clarified. This has created greater awareness of the role of underlying ethical assumptions, including beliefs about distributive justice and the value of nature. However, as result, sustainability has lost its role as an instantly recognizable denominator of all things good. An alternative approach is to operate with a broad notion of sustainability, but to make it clear that work is needed to adapt this general notion to specific conditions, agendas and priorities. In this approach, continuous dialogue and an open-minded willingness to explore conflict are needed. We propose to examine the second approach. We shall illustrate the approach with a three-year EU network on farm animal breeding and reproduction.

Specifying the Value Issues – the Case of Sustainable Farm Animal Breeding

Where the general consumer or citizen is concerned, farm animal breeding – i.e. the controlled propagation of domestic animals with the aim of improving qualities considered desirable by humans – is a largely unnoticed, yet economically vital part of the agriculture and food sector. But despite remarkable advances in productivity (that is, greater outputs and improved use of resources), farm animal breeding has had various negative impacts: for example, on animal health and welfare, and on genetic diversity. This raises the question of what limits to acceptable practice we should set in this area. Here, discussions of sustainability may open up dialogue on ethical issues and help to set an agenda (Gamborg and Sandøe, 2003).

In three projects in which we have taken part, ethical aspects of farm animal breeding and reproduction have been examined. In the first, 'ELSA' (which ran 1998-1999), ethical concerns and value foundations of farm animal breeding were characterised (FAIP, 1999). In the second, 'SEFABAR' (2001-2003), sustainability was used as a common framework within which connections were made between value foundations and practice (Liinamo and Neeteson-van-Nieuwenhoven, 2003). In the third, ongoing, project, 'CODE_EFABAR' (2004-2005), breeders are attempting to operationalise the results of SEFABAR by producing a code of good practice.

In the second of these projects, commercial breeders were required, with the professional assistance of animal scientists, social scientists, philosophers, and stakeholder representatives, especially from animal welfare groups, to develop a definition of sustainable farm animal breeding and reproduction which could be applied across four species groups (i.e. ruminants, pigs, poultry and fish). They were asked to identify their key concerns and priorities, to characterise any resulting dilemmas, and to suggest ways towards a meaningful operationalisation. In doing this, they were to bear in mind that many ethical concerns do appear relevant to modern farm animal breeding and reproduction (e.g. concerns about animal welfare, animal health, food quality and productivity), and that different stakeholders (from the industry, consumer organisations, animal welfare groups and so on) tend to emphasise different concerns. The aim was not to find a 'magical', stand-alone definition. It was to engage in a process in which underlying goals were reflected upon. The breeders worked through the issues using a 'concerns-criteria-indicator' model (see: Gamborg and Sandøe, in press).

The commercial breeders were readily able to set out the concerns they considered relevant to their species groups. They clarified key concerns equally easily. But they found it harder to identify the concerns they had chosen to exclude, and the translation of key concerns into criteria and indicators was more difficult still. Most difficult, perhaps, was the prioritisation of potentially conflicting concerns. Roughly speaking, there are two ways to overcome conflict here: (i) technological solutions, in which the relevant conflict is resolved through technological changes in breeding practice; and (ii) increased transparency, in which clear statements about the relative priorities, together with a willingness to enter into dialogue, are essential.

An interesting general lesson emerged from the SEFABAR project, namely: once the need for appeals to a concept like sustainability has been recognised, breeders (and, more generally, decision makers, resource managers and other stakeholders) may well look for a ready-made definition of sustainability that they can put to use. However, any expectation that such a definition will be available is for various reasons unrealistic:

- *Sustainability is not a single, easily measurable or readily tangible notion.* It should rather be looked upon as a more or less structured set of ideas, a notion which acts as an umbrella for different visions and different apprehensions held either collectively by society or by individual groups.

- *Translation or adaptation of the overall concept is needed.* Even when one specific idea or interpretation of the general notion sustainability has been singled out, much will remain to be said about how to proceed with farm animals, or within breeding and reproduction of farm animals.

- *Prioritisation of concerns is needed.* The general notion can be adapted within farm animal breeding and reproduction, but not all desirable things will necessarily be achievable. Potentially conflicting concerns will need to be identified. Moreover, there is no uniquely correct answer as to when (say) a 'sufficient' number of, say, animal welfare goals have been met.

- *Explanation is needed.* Whether a more operational concept of sustainability within the context of farm animal breeding and reproduction emerges is not entirely a matter for breeders alone. It also concerns the wider agricultural community, as well as the wider society they serve.

When we apply the notion of sustainability, tacit assumptions about the realistic alternatives will always be made: assumptions about the desirability of unregulated commercial development, a society built on organic production, no meat consumption, no use of fossil fuels, and so on. So sustainability will always be a matter of more or less: it can never be an absolute goal. The case of farm animal breeding shows the need to specify the value issues at stake when we use a broad, yet adapted notion of sustainability, and also demonstrates the need to explain any underlying ethical assumptions clearly.

Communicating Priorities

There are two main tasks when we appeal sustainability. One is to show to others that one (e.g. as a company, manager or organisation) has met, or is trying to meet, the objectives of sustainability. In this sense sustainability functions as a management tool. The other is to explain that it is not possible to do everything desirable simply by creating stakeholder understanding — or even acceptance — of the priorities. So long as we state carefully what is included, and what is deliberately not included, as a concern, sustainability can be used to convey the basis of priorities and goals to stakeholders. Stakeholders can then see relatively easily whether they share these values. In this latter task, mutual understanding can only be achieved on the basis of a dialogue.

The difference between using sustainability entirely as a management tool and using sustainability with a view to communication and the appeasement of stakeholders and society is considerable. The two key issues in the first case are usability and controllability. In the second case the key issues are accountability and credibility. So, for example, sustainability as a managerial instrument will involve only a few, clear, and preferably non-conflicting concerns. But in a communication setting many, conflicting concerns will probably appear. Of course, in the end, there must be a connection between what managers or companies say they want to do and what they actually do.

Conclusion

Sustainability once focused exclusively on the wise use of resources for the sake of future generations. It later developed to cover aims associated with nature preservation and intra-generational justice in the distribution of goods. Recently, the range of issues typically considered in connection with sustainability has expanded even more. Thus a very broad notion has emerged. This means that those who use the notion need to specify what, exactly, they mean when they say an activity is 'sustainable'.

Sustainability should not be seen as a readily prescribed cure for the problems facing modern agriculture, natural resource management and land use. It emphatically is not a short cut to the solution to the present-day and future challenges. It is an on-going process requiring careful thought.

Nor does the word 'sustainability' define a unique ethical perspective. At best it indicates a willingness to open an ethical agenda. However if the agenda is not specified in some detail, there is a real danger that necessary ethical discussion will be swept under the carpet. Even worse, the word may be used as a fig leaf in an attempt to legitimise projects which are ethically dubious.

Used conscientiously, the framework of sustainability has two benefits. First, it invites parties involved in the planning of future activities in a company or sector to take a comprehensive look at potentially conflicting concerns and to face any difficult trade-offs. Second, it encourages concerns to be presented within a framework (i.e. of sustainability) that is endorsed by society as a whole, and this enables the stakeholders to make room for communication to, and dialogue with, a broader audience than the rather narrow group of people directly involved. Thus the two most important aspects of sustainability in its modern form are to make explicit choices that have to be made in planning and policy formulation, and to create understanding in civil society, and among stakeholders, of the priorities and underlying values that underlie those choices.

References

Dubgaard, A. Gamborg, C., Larsen, A. and Sandøe, P. (1999). Bæredygtighed – økonomi, etik og energi [Sustainability – economics, ethics and energy], English summary. *Nationaløkonomisk Tidsskrift* 137: 256-283.

Farm Animal Industrial Platform (FAIP). (1999). Workshop on the future developments in farm animal reproduction and selection and their ethical, legal and consumer's implications. Proceedings. Utrectht.

Gamborg, C. and Sandøe, P. Sustainability in farm animal breeding: a review. *Livestock Production Science*. In press.

Gamborg, C. and Sandøe, P., (2003). Breeding and biotechnology in farm animals – ethical issues. In: *Key issues in bioethics*. Levinson, R., Reiss, M. (eds.). London: Routledge Falmer, pp. 133-142.

Gamborg, C., Madsen, K.H. and Sandøe P. (2002). Bæredygtighed – den værdimæssige dagsorden for jordbrugets udvikling [sustainability – the ethical agenda for agricultural development]. In: *Visioner for fremtidens jordbrug* [In Danish]. Jensen, E.S., Vejre, H., Bügel, S.H. & Emanuelsson, J. (eds.). København: Gads Forlag, pp. 13-32.

Lee, K. (2000). Global sustainable development: its intellectual and historical roots. In: *Global sustainable development in the twenty-first century*. Lee, K., Holland, A. and McNeill, D. (eds.). Edinburgh: Edinburgh University Press, pp. 31-48.

Liinamo, A.E. and Neeteson-van-Nieuwenhoven, A.-M. (eds.) (2003). SEFABAR Sustainable European Farm Animal Breeding and Reproduction. Proceedings. QLG7-CT-2000-01368. Final workshop Rome.

McNeill, D. (2000). The concept of sustainable development. In: *Global sustainable development in the twenty-first century*. Lee, K., Holland, A. and McNeill, D. (eds.). Edinburgh: Edinburgh University Press, pp. 10-30.

Sikora, R.I. and Barry, B. (1978). *Obligations to future generations*. Philadelphia: Temple University Press.

World Commission on Environment and Development (WCED) (1987). *Our common future*. New York: Oxford University Press.

Chapter 17

GM Resistant: Europe and the WTO Panel Dispute on Biotech Products

Robert Lee

Introduction

In May 2003, Argentina, Canada and the U.S.A. requested the WTO to constitute a Disputes Settlement Panel in pursuance of their complaints concerning the authorisation system for Genetically Modified Organisms (GMOs) and Genetically Modified foods (GM foods).[1] The three countries pointed to the apparent suspension by the EU of the application and approval process for these products arguing that there was in existence a de-facto 'moratorium' on new GM varieties. Since October 1998, no new GMOs had been authorised for release into the environment[2] on the basis that the EU's regulatory regime was being revised to better address the challenges posed by biotechnology. A new regulatory framework was adopted in March 2001[3] and entered into force in October 2002, but this did not immediately bring an end to the moratorium as further measures on tracing and labelling of GM products were planned.

The EU, through its Trade Commissioner, was to express regret at this 'unnecessary litigation' arguing that the legal action would confuse already sceptical European consumers. The Environment Commissioner stated that

> There should be no doubt that it is not our intention to create trade barriers. But my concern is that this request will muddy the waters of the debate in Europe. We have to create confidence among citizens for GMOs and then allow them to choose. [4]

The US authorities did not agree and went on to argue in the opening of the submission to the Dispute Panel that:

> The United States is confident that once the European Commission allows its scientific and regulatory procedures to reach their conclusion, it will once again approve new biotech products, benefiting EC consumers and biotech producers around the world.[5]

Very little separates these statements in their apparent concern for citizens and consumers and their fond expectation that, once filled with confidence, consumers would be free to choose these products to their benefit. This leads to three points that form the basis of this paper. The first is that notwithstanding the dispute, there is a shared philosophy of trade liberalisation and globalisation that does more to bind the parties to the litigation than to separate them. The second is that in pursuance of this agenda, there is little in the WTO framework that leaves room for wider cultural or ethical values of the citizens to be asserted as significant. Finally both sides assert that the reform (or re-formation) of regulation through science will clear the mud in the water and restore confidence to a doubting populace. In this model, 'sound science' is deployed as a weapon to combat consumer resistance in a manner that risks alienating rather than engaging with the European public.[6] This has significant dangers given existing levels of distrust in European Member States.

Europe – Union?

The GM moratorium, which lasted from 1998 to 2004, was hardly a planned move on the part of the EU. In October 1998 the EU authorised two biotech carnation varieties (to improve vase life and modify flower colour), and these became the last live GMO plants to gain approval – making 18 GMOs in total authorised for commercial release prior to the moratorium. In June 1999, France and Greece called for the moratorium on new GMO approvals at meeting of EU environment ministers and won backing from Italy, Denmark and Luxembourg. Later agreement to the moratorium by Belgium and Austria helped form a powerful bloc that could effectively vote down approvals in any case.

These moves signify the wider concerns of EU Member States, which in turn reflect the political pressure felt by the States in the face of considerable popular resistance. The EU was well aware of such concerns since these were apparent in the existing approvals system. Once approved in a Member State, a product is free to be marketed within the single market. In the case of GM products, however, Article 16 of Directive 90/220/EEC[7] provided that where a Member State has justifiable reasons to consider that a GMO, which has received written consent for placing on the market, nonetheless constitutes a risk to human health or the environment, it may provisionally restrict or prohibit the use and/or sale of that product on its territory. Member States had invoked the Article 16 restriction on nine separate occasions.[8] The scientific evidence provided by these Member States in justification was then submitted to the Scientific Committee(s) for opinion. In all cases, no new evidence was found that would justify overturning the original authorisation. In addition, Italy invoked the safeguard clause in the Novel Food Regulation[9] in August 2000 suspending trade in and use of products derived from four GM maize varieties, notwithstanding their approval as products 'substantially equivalent' to those already on the market. Again, the Commission immediately sought an opinion from the Scientific Committee for Food, which concluded, in less than one month, that the information provided by the Italian Authorities did not provide detailed scientific grounds for any restriction.[10] By this time (with effect from July 2000), the EU environment ministers had expressed support for the moratorium pending the development of proposals labelling and tracing GMO content.

The fact that in every one of these instances the invocation of a safeguard clause is dismissively rejected by the scientific committee suggests that Member States wished to reflect much more diverse and deeper seated unease about the genetic modification of crops by resort to precaution, and equally that, rather than face this dilemma squarely, the EU attempted to use the Scientific Committees as the institutional mechanism to override national objection. It did not work, however, and even when the WTO action had commenced, Austria sought to introduce national measures banning the use of GMOs in the region of Upper Austria for a three-year period.[11] The Upper Austrian Regional Government promoted this measure in an attempt to protect organic and traditional methods of agricultural production in its area because of fears regarding what it saw as cross contamination from GMOs. The European Food Safety Authority[12] concluded that the scientific information Austria provided in its request for exemption offered no new data to justify a ban. The Environment Commissioner expressed 'full respect for the concerns of the Austrian authorities' but, in striking down the measure, she said 'legally speaking, this seems a clear-cut case.'[13]

If charges of protectionism are to be levelled then, it should not be against the EU as such, for they can be seen both to have acted only under pressure from Member States, and to have acted whenever possible to order these States back into line. It is worth noting also that while the Dispute Panel action is against the European Union, these recalcitrant States know well enough that they will face the bill for compensation, which the USA claims is at least $1.8bn representing the loss of exports during the six years of the moratorium. Indeed when, in April 2004, the European Commission effectively overturned the moratorium with the approval of a modified sweetcorn developed by Syngenta, it did so following a refusal by agriculture ministers from the Member States to approve this product only one month earlier. The ending of the moratorium failed to end the WTO dispute, but it provoked widespread criticism in Europe that the move was anti-democratic. Consumer and Health Commissioner Byrne responded that:

> The fact that ministers were unable to make a logical response is a matter for them... (the decision was) fully in conformity with democratic systems we've put in place in the EU...the more the public realise they're protected and informed, this will filter through to elected representatives and it'll perhaps be easier in the Council.[14]

Thus, we see that rather than in opposition to the opening up of markets to GM produce, the Commission is adopts a role of selling such goods to a sceptical public.

The problem for the Commission is the extent of public resistance. Even in the USA there are calls for more effective regulation with an ABC News telephone poll of 1,024 adults, in July 2003 finding that 93 percent of Americans support labelling of genetically modified foods.[15] In Britain an unprecedented canvassing of public opinion, involving 675 public meetings and more than 36,000 written responses, The Report, 'GM Nation?'[16] in the Summer of 2003, found that: 'the more people engage in GM issues, the harder their attitudes and more intense their concerns.'[17] According to the Financial Times:

> Most people turn out to have an intelligent understanding of the issues, a rational scepticism about the benefits and a healthy mistrust of GM advocates.[18]

Headlines from the Report were that 85 per cent of respondents thought that GM crops would benefit producers not ordinary people; 86 per cent said that they were unhappy with the idea of eating GM food; 91 per cent thought that GM had potential negative effects on the environment; and 93 per cent felt that GM technology was driven more by the pursuit of profit than the public interest. Interestingly Monsanto now accepts that in marketing GM produce in Europe it made a number of errors including addressing the wrong stakeholders and bringing assumptions from the USA about the safety and benefits of the products, which created adverse reactions and opposition.[19]

Following the publication of the report the Environment Secretary famously stated: 'We said we would listen and we will.'[20] Yet five months later minutes of a cabinet sub-committee disclosed the Minister as stating that there was no case for an outright ban, even though many would support this, because, although the Report had revealed concerns, 'it was unclear whether participants in this part of the debate had received balanced information.'[21] The minute records that:

> The proposed approach was science-based, precautionary and sensitive to public opinion. While a ban was the easy way out, it was an irrational way for the government to proceed, particularly given the symbolic importance of the decision for the government's science policy and the UK science base.[22]

Again this places science (though we are really talking about technology) in opposition to popular opinion. Science must be both protected from an unthinking, luddite approach, and employed to defeat the irrationality of the majority view.

Science, Justification and the WTO

Deploying the science is posited here as presenting the facts to educate the public. Science can defeat the doubt because its objectivity can override the subjective misgivings of the public whose views are loaded and tainted by commitments to particular values. So it was that the Agricultural Biotechnology Council (the industry trade association) was able to decry 'GM Nation?' as a flawed exercise dominated by ideological opponents of GM, while expressing the hope that the public would see 'why GM crops are so widely grown in other countries.'[23] Ironically, in their very statement the Council reveals its own commitment to and aspirations for the technology that they advocate, making it difficult to share a faith in it. In the same way the Government miss the major message of Professor Grant's Report to them – their handling of the ongoing debate was not fostering trust but building scepticism. But there is a deeper issue at stake here than the somewhat trite observation that science itself is value laden, and it is about the role of social ethics in decision-making regarding technological advance.

Elsewhere, our work has argued, in the context of food risks, that linear models of risk governance in which risk management decisions are made in the shadow of scientific risk assessment need to be re-fashioned to allow the integration of cultural factors at every stage of the governance process.[24] To take a simple example, the propensity of certain foodstuffs to lead to obesity is not necessarily a social factor to be taken into account at the final risk management stage, but a major risk factor itself that, from the earliest stages of risk characterisation, should be addressed. We see from this that public engagement may be crucial not merely in the management of risks, but in the very definition of the hazards to be addressed. Equally deep societal divisions about technology may mean that the national context of risk assessment will vary to properly allow a range of strategies to focus on much needed consensus and resolution. It is clear, however, that models of risk assessment built into the fabric of the WTO framework show little understanding of this.

Put simply it could prove very difficult indeed for the EU to defeat the challenges before the Dispute Panel precisely because these limited models of risk assessment and narrow conceptions of ('sound') science are those recognised in the Agreement on the Application of Sanitary and Phytosanitary Measures (the SPS Agreement).[25] The essential argument, in relation to the general moratorium,[26] put by the USA[27] is that the moratorium constituted a measure under the SPS agreement likely to affect international trade. At the very least this amounted to undue delay under Article 8 of the agreement and procedurally this was flawed under Article 8 and Article 7 (in the latter case because of a failure to publish promptly details of the moratorium). The submission points also to the need for any moratorium to be based upon risk assessment in line with the requirements of Article 5.1. Alongside this the USA argue that the moratorium is not based on scientific principles and maintained without sufficient scientific evidence contrary to Article 2.2. Finally these measures are said to be discriminatory in their effect (infringing Article 5.50 and amount to disguised restrictions on imports contrary to Article 2.3 of the agreement.

Reviewing the requirements for risk assessment in this formulation, Article 5.1 demands:

> an assessment, as appropriate to the circumstances, of the risks to human, animal or plant life or health, taking into account risk assessment techniques developed by the relevant international organizations.[28]

Moreover any response (such as a moratorium) must be based on such an assessment. Risk assessments under this framework must address either threats of pests or disease or the effects of food or feed on human or animal health. This is narrowly drawn and does not encompass wider fears that might have engaged the European public. In the aftermath of a series of food risks, much more work may be needed in Europe to restore trust and confidence in the regulation of food risks.

This is unlikely to be gained by experts pronouncing the results of risk assessment, and may require the active support and participation of a dubious citizenry.[29]

More than that, however, those factors of genetic modification that trouble Europeans extend far more widely than human health concerns. There is a diverse collection of worries including threats to the environment other than simple questions of plant health, and wider uncertainties relating to technology and change. Indeed there is a culture that is more hesitant to see technological innovation as obviously beneficial and even outright opposition to the entire enterprise of agricultural biotechnology irrespective of questions of risk. Questions of the benefits of technology become important here if only because its advocates place the claimed benefits firmly on the scale in questioning opposition to the technology. Famously, according to George Bush:

> we can greatly reduce the long-term problem of hunger in Africa by applying the latest developments of science...Our partners in Europe are impeding this effort. They have blocked all new bio-crops because of unfounded, unscientific fears...[30]

This invocation of benefits forms a significant part of the debate. As we see opponents of the technology are castigated for denying the obvious benefits that the technology will bring. But problems of world hunger are not so simple that the production of yet more food presents an immediate solution, and the opening out of the argument to include the benefits said to follow from technology places the debate firmly in a political and social context. In this context, questions of whether fears are unfounded or unscientific are a minor element of the wider issue of what sort of world we want.

Europe possesses, in some States still, short food chains centred on local markets. For such States pressure to retain local sourcing of food may prove considerable because citizens view this as symbolic of wider aspirations connected to culture, lifestyle, and national difference that the World Trade Organisation will not and cannot accept. Rejection of GM produce may reflect a wish to reject not merely the product itself, but the intensification of agriculture and the dominance, through intellectual property rights, of fewer and fewer varieties of agricultural products at the expense of regional variation.

These are values that neither the EU nor the WTO can ultimately allow to stand in the way of the agenda of trade liberalisation, precisely because they are most decidedly protectionist.[31] But what they seek to protect is something more subtle and complex than economic advantage in the manner asserted by the applicants to the Dispute Panel. It is not a simple question of the EU engaging in some subterfuge that involves the pretence of a moratorium in order to forestall trade and protect markets. Notwithstanding the considerable lead that the Americas have developed in relation to agricultural biotechnology, there is little to indicate that the EU institutions are against the opening up of markets in these products. Rather, the opposite is the case. There are any number of statements from Commissioners that seem ill-advised and ill-timed in the context of the dispute, and that, while defensible, also reflect instinctive support for the enterprise. Commissioner Byrne is already on record as admitting that:

> There is no scientific proof that GM-Food is more dangerous per se than any other form of food.[32]

While Frits Bolkestein as Commissioner for the Internal Market reflected that:

> It's rather a saddening spectacle to see that 0.03 per cent of worldwide acreage producing GMs is within the confines of the EU compared to about 60 to 70 cent in the US...We want to hold our own and we want to lead in new technologies and this is a new technology of prime importance...[33]

Rather than seeing EU regulation as inhibiting the development of and marketing of GM crops, the simple fact is that it will permit these things to happen in the face of resistance from a highly sceptical European public. Regulation is the mechanism whereby GM crops can be grown and sold. Within this regulatory structure the European Food Safety Authority (EFSA) now provides a more centralised approach to approvals that will prove much less problematic than Member State scrutiny and that will assert scientific certainty as a first stage in an approval system. In describing this development one Commission Official told the BRASS Research Team that the creation of the EFSA took matters away from the Commission itself in a manner that:

> would hopefully lead to policy being made with other objectives in view than the economic interest of the sector including for example a very big emphasis on making policy which is science based, in a quite structured way.[34]

The aspirations for this approach are well summed up in the following statement again in a BRASS interview in Brussels:

> The science, basically the Food Safety Authority is going to be the key player for science I would say, so they are going to assess the risk; there is a piece of meat/wheat and we don't know if its harmful or dangerous, so the scientists are going to analyse and then they are going to send their scientific decision to the Commission.[35]

We see here a willingness to invest in what is seen as a neutral and untainted assessment of questions of harm in the hope of diffusing dispute and resistance. Interestingly, however, at a political level, the ultimate risk management decisions with the Commission. This would seem to be because the European Commission is better placed to gauge the public temperature and proceed at an achievable pace, albeit one that is rather more brisk on the back of scientific approval. It appears then that the Commission seek the best of both worlds: the accreditation of science based decision making where validity rests on its lack of outside influence, alongside the right to reject scientific findings in the face of political difficulty.

Conclusion

The EU moratorium on approvals was no simple matter. It was borne out of the capacity of GM products to create deep rifts between Member States and the EU institutions, as the manner of the ending of the moratorium and the stand off between the Commission and the Council indicates. Nonetheless the moratorium has gone and there is no reason to doubt that the EU will pursue its agenda of trade liberalisation in this area as for all other goods. The question is how not whether it will proceed in this direction. The EU view the mechanisms that have brought about the ending of the moratorium, tracing of GMOs and labelling of GM products, as the minimum assurances need to gain public acceptance of GM products. The American litigants may well yet take the view that these are further barriers to trade that:

> extend far beyond health protections for consumers and in fact create onerous and impractical regulatory barriers.[36]

There seems little appreciation of the tight spot in which the EU finds itself in coaxing reluctant Member States faced with widespread domestic opposition. It is in failing to grasp these essential truths that the American litigants are seen by a despairing Commission as 'muddying the waters'. A ruling against Europe for failure to conduct adequate risk assessment prior to the moratorium, although entirely explicable in terms of the SPS agreement, will do little to diffuse resistance to GM products. Indeed although Europe has now introduced mechanisms through EFSA that address questions of risk assessment in the manner promoted by the WTO with expert determination at the primary and leading phase in risk governance, these structures are more not less remote from European citizens. They are torn from a national context that may have been vital in shaping views of GM products. They are less likely to incorporate the range of concerns that will inevitably shape the development of the technology in Europe and which a holistic system of risk assessment ought really to embrace.

All of the evidence shows that social, cultural and ethical attitudes to the technology have driven the dispute from the outset. Any process that seeks to marginalize such concerns, re-educate towards a correct view of the value of innovation, or, for that matter, rule in favour of one side over the other runs the risk of deepening distrust in a way that, as the EU institutions have already witnessed, threatens the very goal of advancing world trade, as the WTO itself becomes the point of resistance.

Notes

1 For the background to the dispute in greater detail see O'Rourke R, 'US-EU Trade War looming over GM Foods' (2004) *1 Journal of International Biotechnology Law* 28.

2 Under Directive 90/220/EC.

3 Directive 2001/18 on the Deliberate Release into the Environment of GMOs.

4 EC Commission Press Release (IP/03/1165), 18 August 2003.

5 United States, *European Communities: Measures Affecting the Approval and Marketing of Biotech Products- First Submission of the United States (WT/DS 291,292 ,and 293) 21 April 2004 at paragraph 6.*

6 For a more extensive review of this last point see Busch et al 'Amicus Curiae Brief submitted to the Dispute Resolution Panel of the WTO in the case of *European Communities: Measures Affecting the Approval and Marketing of Biotech Products- First Submission of the United States (WT/DS 291,292 ,and 293) 21 April 2004*' (forthcoming Yale Journal of International Law). I am grateful for Brian Wynne for providing me with a copy of this submission.

7 Widely referred to as the safeguard clause; see now the safeguard clause provision of Directive 2001/18/EEC (Article 23).

8 Three times by Austria, twice by France, and once each by Germany, Luxembourg, Greece and the United Kingdom.

9 See regulation 12 of Regulation 1813/97 on Review and Approval of Novel Foods.

10 Opinion concerning a submission from the Italian authorities raising concerns for the safety of certain products approved under the notification procedure of Regulation (EC) 258/97, expressed on 7 September 2000, CS/NF/DOS/11 ADD 4 REV 2 Final; for a useful review see Dabrowska P, 'GM Foods, Risk, Precaution and the Internal Market: Did Both Sides Win the Day in the recent Judgment of the European Court of Justice?' (2004) 5(2) *German Law Journal* 151.

11 Request made in March 2003 under Article 95(5) of the EC Treaty, which allows Member States to derogate from European Union harmonisation measures, under certain strict conditions.

12 Which by this time was in place – see European Parliament and Council Regulation (EC) No 178/2002 of 28 January 2002.

13 Commission Press Release (IP/03/1194), 2 September 2003.

14 Commission Press Release (IP/04/663) 19 May 2004.

15 Cited by Hart K, 'Symposium: An Introduction to Genetically Modified Foods' (2003) 10 *Richmond Journal of Law and Technology* 6.

16 See *GM Nation: The Findings of the Public Debate* (2003) available at: http://www.gmnation.org.uk/docs/gmnation_finalreport.pdf.

17 Ibid at paragraph 6.

18 Leader, 'The Popular Verdict on GM Crops', *Financial Times*; 25 September 2003.

19 Frewen M, 'Responsible innovation: the use of GM food', Conference Presentation *CSR in the Food Industry* 21 September 2004 (Agra London).

20 Vidal, J. and Sample, I., 'Five to One against GM crops in biggest ever public survey' *Guardian* 25 September 2003.

21 'Balancing the benefits with the Public's Scepticism', *Guardian* 19 February 2004.

22 *Ibid.*

23 Quoted in Leader, 'The Popular Verdict on GM Crops', *Financial Times*; 25 September 2003.

24 Thankappan, S. et al., *Regulation, Science and the Management of Risk in the Food Chain*, Brass Working Paper No 22 (2004).

25 Although the moratorium arguably breaches both the Agreements on Agriculture, Technical Barriers to Trade, and the General Agreement on Tariffs and Trade (GATT1994) see for example Zedalis RJ, 'GMO Food Measures as 'Restrictions' under GATT Article XI (1)' (2002) 11 *European Environmental Law Review* 16. The arguments in the USA's submission focus particularly on the SPS Agreement.

26 Because there are also arguments about the product specific applications that were not processed and the marketing and/or import bans pursued by Member States themselves.

[27] All arguments here are taken from the fist submission of the United States (supra n. 4).

[28] Article 5.1 of the *Agreement on the Application of Sanitary and Phytosanitary Measures*15 April 1994.

[29] For an analysis of the arguments surrounding the debate on GM crops see: Toke D 'A Comparative Study of the Politics of GM Food and Crops (2004) 52 *Political Studies* 179.

[30] See for example the report at: http://www.newsmax.com/archives/articles/2003/5/22/144647.shtml.

[31] For an argument that a new Treaty would be required to encapsulate consumer preference see: Perdikis, N., Kerr, Shelburne W. and Hobbs, J. 'Reforming the WTO to Defuse Potential Trade Conflicts in Genetically Modified Goods' (2001) 24 *The World Economy* 379.

[32] 'Absolute Purity Does Not Exist' 39 *Die Ziet* 20 September 2001, reproduced at: http://europa.eu.int/comm/commissioners/byrne/interviews/zeit0901_en.htm.

[33] As reported in the *Daily Mail,* 20 November 2001.

[34] Quote from interview with EU Commission Official – Health and Consumer Protection Directorate, Brussels, 23rd July 2002.

[35] Interview with European Food Law Association, Brussels, 24 July 2002.

[36] As reported in 'United States expresses concern over New European Commission Food Labeling Regulations', *Food and Drink Weekly* 30 July 2001; and for a review of labelling issues see: Sheldon, I., 'Regulation of Biotechnology: Will We Ever Freely Trade GMOs?' (2002) 29 *European Review of Agricultural Economics* 155.

Chapter 18

Food Ethics

Ben Mepham

This paper has two main aims: to explore the meaning and significance of the term *food ethics*; and to propose a framework to facilitate the ethical analysis of issues in this field.

The Meaning and Significance of Food Ethics

As far as is known, the term *food ethics* was first used in 1996, as the title of a book of essays of which I was the editor.[1] Since then, the term has been taken up by others, and it is incorporated into the titles of at least two organisations – the European Society for Agricultural and Food Ethics (EURSAFE)[2] and the Food Ethics Council[3] in the UK.

Philosopher Elizabeth Telfer suggests that, in that ethics is a branch of philosophy, the apparent neglect of food as a suitable subject for philosophical consideration, at least until very recently, might be explained by its supposedly mundane subject matter.[4] For example, in 5th century BC Greece, Plato considered food to be of only transient and inferior concern; in the 18th century, Kant explicitly denied that dietetics could be regarded as a form of ethics; and even in 19th century Britain, the leading utilitarian philosopher John Stuart Mill was also dismissive of food, counting its pleasures far lower than those of the intellect. Latterly, however, attitudes have undergone much change, and Telfer argues that the importance of food now raises many ethical questions which are properly addressed by philosophy.

Applied Ethics, Bioethics and Food Ethics

Food ethics is evidently a branch of Applied Ethics, a field which has come to prominence over the last 20 years, after a period when the prevailing view of philosophers was that philosophy could not usefully be applied to ethical problems. Moral philosopher Ruth Chadwick suggests that there are different models of applied ethics, e.g. depending on whether it is a matter of 'applying' a particular theory to a specific ethical dilemma (a 'top-down' approach) or whether specific developments can affect the development of appropriate theory (a 'bottom-up' approach).[5] The central task might even be that of identifying the ethical dimensions of a novel situation. Food ethics, as much as any other branch of applied ethics, reflects these differences.

Indeed, one view is that the breadth of content of such a form of applied ethics denies it the status of a 'discipline.' Thus, philosopher Onora O'Neill opens a recent work with the words:

> Bioethics is not a discipline, nor even a new discipline: I doubt whether it will ever become a discipline. It has become a meeting ground for a number of disciplines, discourses and organisations concerned with ethical, legal and social questions raised by advances in medicine science and technology.[6]

According to this view, food ethics (which in many respects overlaps with bioethics) might have rather modest aspirations, as though simply facilitating the interchange of views of people with coinciding interests justified the denomination.

However, it might be argued that O'Neill claims too little, and that if deliberation in this field is to have productive outcomes there is a need to devise a more explicitly normative programme. In the Preface to *Food Ethics* (1996), I wrote:

> ... almost all the issues discussed in this volume relate to universal, pervasive, long-term concerns, which are most readily perceived as subjects of public policy decisions. They are all based on the biological requirement (often unmet) for safe, acceptable, nutritious food, which is produced in ways which respect (or fail to respect) the welfare of other sentient beings, alive and unborn. Hence the issues demand attention from philosophers, economists, sociologists and anthropologists, as well as medical, agricultural and food scientists. In the author's opinion, if real progress is to be made in resolving the numerous ethical concerns related to food, these separate fields of enquiry need to be welded together in a new interdisciplinary programme, for which he has coined the term 'food ethics.[7]

Clearly, there is room for debate over what constitutes a 'discipline' and an 'interdisciplinary programme',[8] but it is assumed here that 'food ethics' can, and ought, to aspire to a level of enquiry beyond that which characterises a talking shop.

Food Ethics in History

Having coined what I believed was a neologism, it came as something of a surprise to encounter, within a few years, the publication by the philosopher Hub Zwart of a paper entitled 'A short history of Food Ethics'. He wrote:

> With the publication of the volume Food Ethics by Ben Mepham in 1996, a new branch of applied or professional ethics was introduced, but a long tradition of dietetics and other forms of moral concern with food preceded it. Although the fact of this particular branch of ethics receiving a new name ('food ethics') rightly stresses its discontinuity with the past, some legacies and points of continuity can be indicated as well. [9]

Zwart identified a number of historical phases of moral concerns related to food. For example, in ancient Greece the Hippocratic tradition laid emphasis on temperance in food consumption, whereas Hebrew thought was dominated by a binary code according to which *permissible* foods were sharply demarcated from the *impermissible*. In medieval times, attitudes alternated between periods of abstention from excess intake (asceticism) and those of the 'celebration of plenty' during the Renaissance. In the post Renaissance period (and much more recently) increasing attention was paid to scientific assessments of food adequacy, safety and nutritional value. For example, in the 19th century, the production of food, and its treatment prior to consumption, raised critical concerns, such as i) Malthus' prediction that population growth would soon outstrip the Earth's ability to provide adequate food; ii) dangers from the microbial risks of retailed food; and iii) the ill effects of intentional food adulteration. Early in the 20th century, scientific advances led to a preoccupation with calories, proteins and vitamins.

Since the 1960s concerns have been raised over the environmental impacts of agrochemicals (notably identified by Rachel Carson[10]), animal welfare (highlighted in the UK by Ruth Harrison[11] and subsequently in the government enquiry chaired by Rogers Brambell[12]) and global climate change (e.g. by James Lovelock[13]). And recent years have seen the emergence of a new range of issues which relate to the increasing industrialisation and globalisation of food production, responses to which are often reflected in forms of ethical consumerism. Thus, consumer choice is now a means by which many people express their concerns over issues like: the adverse environmental impacts of intensive farming (and its effects on biodiversity and sustainability); animal welfare – and associated public health concerns (notably revealed, though Zwart does not mention them, by the effects of outbreaks of animal diseases such as BSE and FMD); and threats to social justice (to which 'fair trade' programmes are a response.)

Surprisingly, Zwart's analysis makes only an oblique, and passing, reference to vegetarianism, which many might consider a centrepiece of ethical deliberation on food. It is also an issue which indisputably has a 'history', as recounted in *The Ethics of Diet* by Howard Williams, the 1907 edition of which referred to the fact that the 'first editions appeared many years ago' – but did not provide dates.[14]

Food Ethics as Social Ethics

Zwart's characterisation of a 'virtual food ethics' evident throughout history provides a useful timeline of concerns about food, which inevitably reflect wider social and political norms, as well as religious and cultural influences. But does this historical, and primarily sociological or ethnographic, account capture the essential concept of food ethics defined above (in the Preface to *Food Ethics*)? For while Zwart instanced 'ethical concerns', like attitudes of temperance and fears of adulteration (many of which are addressed by other fields of endeavour, e.g. in these cases, theological prescriptions and measures to ensure food safety), food ethics as conceived here proposes an approach which, in the current jargon, attempts to integrate concerns for the elements of the whole food chain, from 'field to fork.' Rather than focusing on concerns of individuals, e.g. as consumers or farmers, the plane of analysis here is social ethics, especially concerning the implications for public policy. Clearly, people are entitled to use the term 'food ethics' as they see fit, especially when it is such a new field of enquiry. But in the following it will be viewed as a form of holistic, social ethics which is characterised by significant degree of interdisciplinarity.

An Analysis of Food Ethics

Despite being a still-emergent discipline, an attempt has already been made to characterise the structure and objectives of food ethics by analysis of papers presented at the congresses of EURSAFE held in Florence (2001) and Toulouse (2003), respectively.[15] As a result, Christoph Baumbauer and Marc Meinhardt, noting that of the total of 214 papers surveyed very few had a strictly 'philosophical content', concluded that 'there is a danger of replacing normative reflections about values and ideals by the observation and description of public opinion.' Such a conclusion might seem to lend support to O'Neill's view of bioethics – that it (and by implication food ethics) might be (merely) the 'meeting ground for a number of disciplines, discourses and organisations.' For Baumbauer and Meinhardt these considerations

> touch a crucial problem: the insufficient reflection on foundations, values and specific standards of rational justification put 'food ethics' at risk of being nothing else than an inconsistent conglomeration of various untied fields of research without any inner coherence.'

It is likely that this criticism overstates the case, because the database (conference proceedings which include many contributions from non-specialists, in an effort to expose this new field to a wider audience) is probably unrepresentative of committed food ethicists. I believe that a more authentic assessment would be obtained by reference to papers in journals such as *The Journal of Agricultural and Environmental Ethics* and *Agriculture and Human Values*, or to my contributions to encyclopaedias of applied ethics.[16, 17] Even so, the criticism is worthy of note, and the warning salutary.

A Framework to Facilitate Analysis of Issues in Food Ethics

On the assumption that food ethics has a pronounced normative dimension, if not focus, how ought its problems to be addressed? Is there a toolbox which might facilitate ethical decision-making in this field, irrespective of the specific nature of problems? The remainder of this paper outlines a framework for ethical analysis, called the *ethical matrix*, which was designed to facilitate the resolution of dilemmas over agricultural and food biotechnologies. As described below, it is envisaged as a framework to be used by a group of policy makers, seeking to arrive at, and justify, ethical decisions on a proposed innovation affecting (some) elements of the agri-food chain.

Some Background

Since the normal outcome of the exercise of human reason within democratic societies is 'a plurality of reasonable yet incompatible doctrines'[18] consensus on a moral orthodoxy is probably an unrealistic, if not a dangerous, objective. A sounder aim might be that of devising a social contract which benefits from social cooperation despite the differences of opinion between the contractors. Thus, the role of ethical theory in this process is not to determine *the* right policies but to act as a means of assessing whether specific proposed policies are ethically acceptable.

Typically, differences in ethical evaluation are reflections of differences in 'worldview' and are often bound up with cultural, religious and political perspectives. This has wide-ranging consequences because in a world in which increasing globalization of trade appears inevitable there are likely to be enormous costs (and not only financial costs) if international agreement cannot be reached on how critical issues should be regulated. After all the debate, there is a need for 'closure', i.e. for some mutually agreed course of action. Broadly speaking, ethical judgements on specific issues which have political consequences (e.g. whether to require labelling of a GM food product) depend on two factors:

- acknowledgement of general ethical principles (such as, 'people should be free to choose the type of food they eat') and
- agreement on scientific facts (e.g., to pursue this case, whether there is a significant difference between the GM food product and the non-GM product to which it might be claimed to correspond).

The Common Morality and a Principled Approach

With respect to the first of these factors, an approach I have been developing in recent years appeals to the notion of the *common morality*, as a starting point for ethical analysis. In the field of medical ethics, the *four principles* approach proposed by Beauchamp and Childress has achieved wide currency.[19] The approach recognizes *prima facie* duties to respect certain principles, viz. nonmaleficence, beneficence, autonomy and justice. Thus, in treating patients a doctor is regarded as having ethical duties to, respectively:

- cause no harm (enshrined in the Hippocratic Oath) [nonmaleficence]
- to effect a cure (or at least provide palliative treatment) [beneficence]
- to respect patients' autonomy (and not regard them merely as 'cases') [autonomy]
- to treat patients fairly (e.g. without sexual or racial discrimination) [justice].

It must be appreciated that this so-called 'principled approach' is not an ethical theory and does not aspire to be a decision making procedure. But, according medical ethicist Raanan Gillon, it provides a set of 'substantive moral premises upon which to base reasoning in health care ethics' and, moreover, 'offers a transcultural, transnational, transreligious, transphilosophical framework for ethical analysis' by allowing differences of emphasis within a scheme of universal applicability.[20] So, although the common morality is hardly likely to provide the last word in moral judgement it would be difficult to conceive of a better starting point for the development of ethical theory.

In recent years, I have extended the applicability of the Beauchamp and Childress principles in order to assess the ethical impacts of biotechnologies in the fields of agriculture and food technology (e.g.[21, 22]), and thereby provide a means of ethical analysis which might facilitate political decision-making. Despite sharing a common dependence on biological science, the agri-food industry differs substantially from medicine in the pervasive impact of its activities at the production, distribution and consumption stages, so that application of the principles to this different field requires that they be translated into terms appropriate to a wide range of different 'interest groups'.

Specification of Principles and Interest Groups in the Matrix

In Figure 18.1, suggested interpretations of the ethical principles as they apply to four such interest groups (treated organisms, producers, consumers and biota) are summarised in the form of an *ethical matrix*. The matrix permits analysis of the ethical impacts of any production system (e.g. application of a biotechnology) from the perspective of the different groups affected by its employment. In the manner of Rawls' *original position*,[23] actors (e.g. members of a regulatory committee) are asked to imagine themselves as belonging to each specified interest group in turn, and to assess the ethical impacts of the introduction of the proposed technology. The object here is simply to propose and illustrate a methodology: rigorous analysis would require much fuller treatment.

RESPECT FOR:	WELLBEING	AUTONOMY	FAIRNESS
TREATED ORGANISM	e.g. Animal Welfare	e.g. Behavioural Freedom	Intrinsic value
PRODUCERS (e.g. FARMERS)	Adequate income and working conditions	Freedom to adopt or not adopt	Fair treatment in trade and law
CONSUMERS	Availability of safe food; acceptability	Consumer choice (e.g. labelling)	Universal affordability of food
BIOTA	Protection of the biota	Maintenance of biodiversity	Sustainability of biotic populations

Figure 18.1 The ethical matrix

In the form of the matrix illustrated in Fig 18.1, the principles of beneficence and non-maleficence are combined as 'respect for wellbeing', partly because it simplifies the framework, but also because in terms of human stewardship over organisms used in agriculture these two principles are inextricably related: combining them in no way diminishes the importance which attaches to them separately. The, now, three principles may be considered to correspond to three major theories of ethics, viz. utilitarianism (wellbeing), Kantianism (autonomy) and Rawlsian theory (fairness).[24] However, in some circumstances it might be preferable to retain the original distinction between the two utilitarian principles.[25]

It is clear that principles employed in medical ethics need to be appropriately specified if they are to be effective in this different context. For example, in relation to animals treated in biotechnology, respect for wellbeing, autonomy and fairness are interpreted as: respect for welfare (freedom from pain and stress); freedom of behavioural expression; and respect for intrinsic value (i.e. as opposed to 'instrumental value'), respectively (see Figure 18.1). In the case of consumers of food produced by biotechnology, these principles are interpreted as: respect for food safety; consumer choice (e.g. by appropriate labelling) and affordability, respectively. By extending the number of affected groups an ethical matrix of any desired degree of complexity can be constructed.

The Aims and Limitations of the Matrix

Because some people have misunderstood the aims of the matrix, e.g. assuming that it is intended to be prescriptive,[26] it is important to appreciate its aims and limitations. These may be summarized as follows:

- The impacts defined for each of the separate 'cells' depend on rigorous examination of objective (often scientific) data.
- The duties described are *prima facie* duties: circumstances will frequently arise when there are conflicts of interest between different duties and compromises will have to be made.
- Construction of the matrix is in principle ethically neutral, i.e. it is an *analytical* tool. In accordance with Beauchamp and Childress's account, the principles 'are general guides that leave considerable room for judgement in specific cases and that provide substantive guidance for the development of more detailed rules and policies.' [27]
- By contrast, ethical *evaluation* (or *judgement*) requires a weighing or ranking of the different impacts, so that e.g. an animal rightist might consider *any* exploitation of animals inadmissible, while someone adopting a utilitarian view might accept that substantial human benefits outweigh minor harms inflicted on animals.
- The matrix records ethical impacts in one set of circumstances (e.g. the prospective introduction of a technology) with another set of circumstances (usually, the *status quo*). Hence, the impacts recorded are *relative* to a pre-existing condition – which itself might be less ethically acceptable than some other, actual or possible, condition.
- While it might guide individual ethical judgements, the principal aim of the matrix is to facilitate rational decision-making by articulating the ethical dimensions of any issue in a manner which is transparent and broadly comprehensible.
- Far from constraining ethical reasoning, the matrix should provide a means for the expression of the full range of ethical perspectives.

Evidence for the latter claim is provided by the fact that both people approving of use of a particular agricultural biotechnology and people opposing its use can use the ethical matrix to justify their differing opinions, as has been demonstrated in workshops conducted with experts.[28] This indicates two important points about the matrix: i) it provides a means of explaining and justifying different ethical positions; ii) it facilitates identification of the areas of agreement and disagreement.

Use of the Ethical Matrix in Public Consultations and Expert Committees

The matrix has been used in several other ways, both by the author and other groups. For example, Matthias Kaiser and Ellen-Marie Forsberg have used it in public consultations about the future of the Norwegian fishing industry. Typically, such exercises are organised to include representatives of the major stakeholder groups, or – if the interest group is a non-human one – then those with particular expertise and/or commitment to their cause are present, such as animal welfare and environmental groups. Kaiser and Forsberg ascribe the value of the matrix to a number of features, i.e. it: a) is liberal regarding the approach to be adopted, enabling it to be read equally as a utilitarian or a deontological approach; b) provides substance for ethical deliberation, guiding participants so that they do not stray into irrelevant paths; c) translates abstract principles into concrete issues of direct concern to participants who may have little acquaintance with, or interest in, ethical theory *per se*; d) facilitates extension of ethical concerns into fields benefiting from debate, such as democratic decision making; e) captures the basic fact that because different stakeholders will be affected differently by a decision their ethical evaluations may well differ – the object not being to downplay these differences but to search for an optimal solution in the light of the conflicts.[29]

The matrix has also served as a useful structure for professional bodies and organisations concerned with formulating policy. For example, the European Academy's investigation into the ethical and social issues associated with the development of functional foods employed the matrix to structure its deliberations,[30] while the Food Ethics Council has used the framework in several of its reports.[31]

The author has used the matrix to structure discussion of a wide range of bioethical issues in a textbook designed for bioscience students[32] (for whom competence in bioethical reasoning is a benchmarked criterion identified by the Quality Assurance Agency in Higher Education[33]); and it forms the basis of an interactive web-based exercise designed for school and college students in the age range 16-20 years.[34]

Summary

Food ethics is a new field of applied ethics, although there is evidence of ethical concerns over food throughout recorded history, especially from a dietetic perspective. As an emergent discipline, food ethics is in the process of establishing its identity. However, there is a danger that sociological accounts of 'public opinion' might assume too much importance in a field that would more appropriately be concerned with normative reflection on values.

The account given of food ethics here considers it to be a form of holistic, social ethics, which is characterized by a significant degree of interdisciplinarity. The paper outlines a framework, the ethical matrix, which has been designed to facilitate deliberation in this field, and to assist in transparent, rational decision making. While doubtless capable of refinement and improvement, the extensive use of the matrix in educational, policy-making and public participation contexts, suggests that it may be a useful tool in structuring ethical reflection.

References

1 Mepham, B. (1996), *Food Ethics* (ed.). Routledge, London.
2 European Society for Agricultural and Food Ethics (2004), www.theo.uu.nl/Eursafe.
3 Food Ethics Council (2004), www.foodethicscouncil.org.
4 Telfer, E. (1996), *Food for thought: philosophy and food.* Routledge, London.
5 Chadwick, R. (1998), 'Preface', in: R. Chadwick (ed) *Encyclopedia of Applied Ethics.* Academic Press, San Diego, vol 1, p xxxv.
6 O'Neill, O. (2002), *Autonomy and Trust in Bioethics.* Cambridge University Press, Cambridge, p.1.
7 Mepham, B. (1996), 'Preface', in B. Mepham (ed) *Food Ethics.* Routledge, London p xiv
8 Carson, R. (1963), *Silent Spring.* Hamish Hamilton, London.
9 Zwart, H. (2002), *Journal of Agricultural and Environmental Ethics.* A short history of food ethics. 12, 113-126.
10 Carson, R. (1963), *Silent Spring.* Hamish Hamilton, London.
11 Harrison, R. (1964), *Animal Machines.* Vincent Stuart, London.
12 Rogers Brambell, F. W. (1965), *Report of the technical committee to enquire into the welfare of animals kept under intensive livestock husbandry conditions.* CMND 2836, HMSO, London.
13 Lovelock, J. E. (1979), *Gaia: a new look at life on Earth.* Oxford University Press, Oxford.
14 Williams, H. (1907), *The ethics of diet.* Albert Broadbent, Manchester; Richard J. James, London.
15 Bambauer, C. and Meinhardt, M. (2004), 'Food ethics – Quo vadis? An empirical and philosophical analysis of methods and trends', *Science, ethics and society.* (Preprints of 5th EURSAFE Congress). Katholic Universiteit Leuven, Belgium. pp. 297-300.
16 Mepham, B. (1998), 'Agricultural Ethics', in R. Chadwick (ed), *Encyclopedia of Applied Ethics.* Academic Press, San Diego, vol. 1, pp. 95-110.
17 Mepham, B. (2001), 'Novel Foods', in R. Chadwick (ed), *The Concise Encyclopedia of the Ethics of New Technologies*, Academic Press, San Diego, pp. 299-313.
18 Rawls, J. (1993), *Political Liberalism*, Columbia University Press, New York.
19 Beauchamp, T.L. and Childress, J.F. (2001), *Principles of Biomedical Ethics*, 5th edition, Oxford University Press, New York.
20 Gillon, R. (1998), 'Bioethics, overview', in R. Chadwick (ed), *Encyclopedia of Applied Ethics*, Academic Press, San Diego, vol. 1, pp. 305-317.
21 Mepham, B. (1996), 'Ethical analysis of food biotechnologies: an evaluative framework', in B. Mepham (ed), *Food Ethics*, Routledge, London. pp. 101-119.
22 Mepham, T.B. (2000), 'The role of food ethics in food policy', *Proc Nutr Soc*, 59, pp. 609-618.
23 Rawls, J. (1972), *A theory of Justice*, Oxford University Press, Oxford.
24 Winkler, E.R. (1993), 'From Kantianism to contextualism: the rise and fall of the paradigm theory in bioethics', in E.R. Winkler and J.R.Coombes (eds) *Applied Ethics*, Oxford University Press, Cambridge, Mass, pp. 343-365.
25 Mepham, T.B., Moore, C.J. and Crilly, R.E. (1996), 'An ethical analysis of the use of xenografts in human transplant surgery', *Bulletin of Medical Ethics*, 116, pp.13-18.

[26] Mepham, B. (2004), 'A decade of the ethical matrix: a response to criticisms', *Science, ethics and society* (Preprints of 5th EURSAFE Congress). Katholic Universiteit Leuven, Belgium. pp.271-4.

[27] Beauchamp, T.L. and Childress, J.F. (1994), *Principles of Biomedical Ethics* (4th edition) Oxford University Press, New York, p. 38.

[28] Mepham, B. and Millar, K. (2001), 'The ethical matrix in practice: application to the case of bovine somatotrophin', in *Food safety, food quality, food ethics*, (Preprints of the 3rd EURSAFE Congress: Florence) A&C, University of Milan. pp. 317-319.

[29] Kaiser, M. and Forsberg, E-M. (2001), 'Assessing fisheries – using an ethical matrix in a participatory process', *Journal of Agricultural and Environmental Ethics*, 14, pp.191-200.

[30] Chadwick, R., Henson, S., et al (2003), *Functional Foods*, Springer-Verlag, Berlin.

[31] E.g. Food Ethics Council (2001), *After FMD: aiming for a values-driven agriculture*, FEC, Southwell.

[32] Mepham, B. (2005), *Bioethics: an introduction for the biosciences*, Oxford University Press, Oxford (in press).

[33] Quality Assurance Agency for Higher Education (2004), *Biosciences*, http://www.qaa.ac.uk.

[34] Mepham, B. and Tomkins, S. (2003), *Ethics and animal farming*. www.ethicalmatrix.net.

Chapter 19

The Ethics of Journalism: A Summing-up for Lord Hutton

Ian Hargreaves

Lord Hutton has retired to consider the voluminous evidence given to him during the two months of his inquiry into the circumstances of the death of Dr David Kelly, the Government scientist whose apparent suicide provoked the closest thing we are likely to get to a forensic inquiry into the decision by the Blair Government to go to war against Iraq.

The purpose of this commentary is to clarify and contextualize some of the principles which Lord Hutton might wish to bear in mind as he considers those aspects of the case before him which bear upon the ethics of journalism.

This leaves aside a number of large ethical matters germane to the Kelly affair and which have nothing much to do with journalism. These extend from the morality and legality of the war itself to the culture of the personnel department of the Ministry of Defence. It is also safe to say that Lord Hutton's examination of the behaviour of journalists in the Kelly affair is unlikely to help him illuminate the causes of Dr Kelly's death, the task with which he is officially charged.

But there is no doubt that Hutton's conclusions about journalism will reverberate because journalism is widely perceived to be in trouble; suffering from a long-run decline in trust intensified by a run of scandals, from fakery at the New York Times which cost the paper's editor his job to a persistent sense that self-regulatory bodies like Britain's Press Complaints Commission aren't up to the job of holding the line, let alone improving, journalists' behaviour.

In her 2002 Reith Lectures, Dr Onora O'Neill, the Cambridge philosopher, argued that today's news media have acquired such power that the foundation stone of liberal democracy, the idea of a free press, could no longer be considered "an unconditional good." Modern journalism, she suggested, was so unreliable that there was a danger that "the wells of public discourse and public life are poisoned."

This is the background against which Lord Hutton will make his own judgments, and against which those judgments will be read. His inquiry has already proved the most searching public examination ever of a single piece of journalism, considering as it has not only the work of the individual journalist at the centre of the controversy (Andrew Gilligan) but also the workings of the institution which employs him (the BBC) and the complex and controversial governmental communications machine his journalism was seeking to expose.

The specific journalistic issues under consideration by Lord Hutton are, however, relatively clear, even straightforward. The most striking concerns accuracy. What responsibility do journalists have to give an accurate account of events and what action should they take when they become aware that they have published an account which contains inaccuracies?

Sub-themes to this question of accuracy include the way that journalists use and refer to anonymous sources; their procedures for taking notes or recording interviews and the impact upon accuracy of certain broadcasting techniques, such as the wide-spread use of the informal conversation of "two-way" between a presenter and a reporter to bring out the facts of a report, rather than relying upon a scripted report. Then there is the issue, poignant in the Kelly case, of the journalist's responsibility to protect the identity of an anonymous source.

In terms of a news organization's responsibility to correct an inaccurate report, we enter a more complex sphere, since media organizations vary greatly in the way that they deal with complaints about accuracy.

The BBC's own procedures, based upon lengthy published "producer guidelines", provide an ambitious set of standards against which its reporting can be judged. The key text under scrutiny is the report of Andrew Gilligan, a BBC Defence Correspondent, on the Today Programme at 6.07am on May 29, 2003.

It is useful, however, to consider the BBC's standards of journalistic behaviour against a wider UK background, not least since Gilligan is himself a former *Daily Telegraph* reporter, rather than a journalist reared within the BBC's own culture.

This last point is brought into sharp focus by the fact that the Government's complaint about Gilligan's report was apparently given greater force by Gilligan's decision to follow up his work for the Today Programme with an article signed by himself in the *Mail on Sunday*, in which he named Alastair Campbell, then the Prime Minister's Director of Communications, as the individual behind the "dodgy" intelligence dossier which the Government used to make the case for war. In the May 29 broadcast, Gilligan did not name Campbell when he suggested that the Government had knowingly inserted a questionable claim that Iraqi weapons of mass destruction could be mobilized within 45 minutes.

The aim here is not so much to assess the detailed evidence given to Lord Hutton on these specific matters, as to identify how the questions and the discussion around them sit within a wider consideration of journalistic and media ethics.

If Onora O'Neill and many even more anxious commentators are right then we are courting great danger in a period when the news media are both more powerful and ubiquitous than before and yet also less reliable, less responsible and less worthy of trust.

Journalists themselves, especially British journalists, often find it difficult to take seriously such challenges to their behaviour. One of the more popular journalistic text-books introduces the subject of journalism with the following thought:

> To the outsider, journalism and ethics are about as incongruous a mixture as you can get. Even to put the two words in the same sentence is to risk reducing the listener to helpless laughter. To the insider on a mass-market tabloid, ethics are largely an irrelevance. Editors, pressured by intense competition for readers, demand that staff cut ethical corners; and competition among staff encourages some to respond. Lecturing these journalists about ethics is as pointless as advocating celibacy to sailors arriving in port after six months at sea.[1]

Or, as Kelvin Mackenzie, the legendary editor of the *Sun* in the 1980s, put it: "ethics is a place to the east of London where the men wear white socks."

This will strike some as an example of macho cultural bravado, in which the reflectiveness of the moralist is perceived as being too effeminate for the rough, tough reality of the world of the tabloid newspaper.

There is something in this – note only, in passing, the culture of journalism assumed in *Private Eye*'s long-running caricature of the "Street of Shame", but it also has a more serious and respectable origin in the view that British newspapers have their origin in the struggle for free speech and democracy which took root during the English Civil War, flowering and multiplying in the rapid industrialization of the century which followed.

English newspapers carried the torch for the enfranchisement of the working class and became a deeply embedded feature of a booming democratic industrial capitalism, more inclined to trust the disciplines of the market than the actions of state censors and regulators, against whose dictates the 18th century press defined its readers' interests.

If the British press has its cultural heart in an England of democratic industrial capitalism, its broadcasting organizations have theirs, by contrast, in a 20th century dominated by a struggle between post-Victorian society and the ambitious counter-forces of Bolshevism, Socialism and Fascism.

The BBC itself was born as a function of the Ministry of Posts, as Governments across the industrialized world realized that in dispensing the right to use radio waves for broadcasting they had acquired a level of power over public communication which the Church lost with the invention of the printing press.

Although the BBC was never exactly a "state broadcaster", it has always been obliged to struggle for an evolving definition of its own independence from the state, which to this day continues to determine the level of its public funding, the composition of its Board of Governors and its entitlement to the renewal of its Royal Charter and licence to broadcast.

At the end of the 20th century, the BBC found itself in a quite extraordinary position. Having stood its ground in the 1980s against aggressive pressure from Margaret Thatcher's Government, which was determined to bring new commercial forces into broadcasting on the back of the emerging technologies of cable and satellite television, the BBC found itself impressively well positioned to argue that it should be given significant additional funding to enable it to play a bigger role, as these technologies were jostled by the even more far-reaching opportunities of the internet and other broadband digital communications.

Then, as the commercial dot com bubble burst in 2001, leaving behind numerous casualties in the commercial communications sector, the BBC was able to continue to expand, against the economic cycle, establishing itself as, unequivocally, the largest force in UK television, radio and the internet.

Greg Dyke, who became Director General of the BBC in February 2000, was the inheritor of this fortunate situation, which has put him in such a strong competitive position that the BBC faces constant complaint from its commercial rivals that it is using its public licence fee to compete unfairly against them.

Politically, it should also be noted that Dyke himself had been a financial supporter of the Labour Party, as had the new chairman of the BBC Governors, Gavyn Davies. The Blair Government, worried like all previous Labour Governments, at the likelihood that the "capitalist" press would turn against it, must have felt unusually confident that it would be well served by this cash-rich BBC.

When Dyke gave evidence to the Hutton inquiry on September 15, he gave the inquiry some striking statistics about the scale of the BBC's journalistic operations. There were, he said, 3,400 staff working in BBC News, among a total of 27,000 working for the BBC as a whole. That makes BBC News larger, in terms of staff, than the whole of the national newspaper industry. It is the biggest news organization in Europe and, quite possibly, the biggest in the world.

So, how BBC journalists conduct themselves is a matter of very great importance. In response to this fact, the BBC has, over the years, evolved a set of ethical guidelines which are impressive in their range and detail.

The question for Lord Hutton, and then, later, for Greg Dyke and Gavyn Davies, is whether these standards were breached by Andrew Gilligan's reports and, if so, whether this was a regrettable, but inevitable, aberration in an otherwise soundly managed news department, or something more serious.

In the immediate aftermath of Dr Kelly's death, the BBC was in denial about its errors, but by the time that Mr Dyke gave evidence to the Hutton inquiry in September, he was ready to concede that things ought to have been handled differently.

He was particularly contrite about the failure of the BBC's complex programme complaints system to take up Alastair Campbell's complaint about Gilligan's 6.07am report. He has made it clear that once the Hutton Report is available, the BBC will be making changes to aspects of its producer guidelines, including the use and description of anonymous sources; the use of unscripted "two-ways" and the rules which govern BBC journalists when they write for newspapers.

These changes, he is implying, will be necessary if the BBC is to retain its proclaimed objective to be a "trusted guide" to those who use its services, in an increasingly competitive and untrustworthy media-scape.

The BBC's willingness to sharpen its guidelines and its accessibility to public complaint will be important advances, much more important than the issue of who, if anyone, will be forced to resign as a result of the scandal. An even more important question is to ask why it has required such a highly public affair to have these points fully and openly debated: the BBC may wish to think, for the future, how to make itself more responsive to the climate of public distrust in the news media, since it plainly has a task of high importance to stand against that climate.

Will these changes in guidelines be sufficient to restore confidence in the quality of BBC journalism? The short answer to that is probably "yes", since confidence in BBC journalism is rather high, certainly compared with confidence in newspaper journalism. By this measure, Hutton, in fact, will probably turn out to have done the BBC nothing but good.

Does Mr Dyke's agenda of learning points, however, cover all the necessary ground? Here, I'm not so sure. There is, for example, the rather basic issue of note-taking. It was evident from the Hutton Inquiry hearings that the Palm Pilot notes assembled by Andrew Gilligan during and/or after his conversations with Dr Kelly fell some way short of providing corroboration for the story as broadcast.

Yet, many reporters, and most broadcast reporters, are untrained in short-hand and, when working on background research, fail to use tape-recorders when conducting interviews. One difference between Gilligan's reports and those of Susan Watts, his colleague and rival on Newsnight, was that Watts had tape recordings of her conversations.

In a journalism school, such as the one we run at Cardiff, the debate about short-hand is one that never dies. Those studying newspaper journalism are obliged to have it – not least because it represents a standard required by the National Council for the Training of Journalists, an industry body. The pro-short-hand faction is often dismissed as hopelessly fuddy-duddy by its critics. Would-be broadcasters are not required to study shorthand and almost all never learn it. Magazine students are given the option – and mostly choose not to learn. It's an arduous technical task getting up to 100 words per minute or better.

This is one of many points where the world of journalistic ethics meets the world of journalism education. One of the most important functions of a great journalism school is to set the tone and standard which encourages its graduates in the sure belief that they must carry with them a set of personal standards of reliability and honesty in their work which are fire-proof against unscrupulous or merely over-pressured news editors and proprietors.

What else can we conclude from the Hutton hearings about the ethics of journalism? One conclusion is certainly the continuing and vital importance of journalists being able to work with sources on an agreed contract of anonymity, a principle which lies at the heart of whistle-blowing in open societies. This is something which the Kelly affair has, plainly, damaged, but let us hope not irrecoverably so. In international research on journalistic ethics, the anonymity principle is among the most strongly shared standards among journalists in a wide range of democratic countries.

We will also, I think, learn something about the regulation of those parts of journalism which have their roots in the 20th not the 17th century and which do have a formal regulatory relationship with the state and its agencies. Here, the evidence to Hutton suggests, we need to ensure that we have a balance between independence, expertise and responsiveness, by which I mean a responsiveness not to the politicians of the day, but to the medium and long term interests of citizens generally. The debate about the regulation or responsiveness of the new, internet-based news media has not been a feature of Hutton. It will, surely, have its day in some future scandal.

The great danger for journalism is that it adopts a casual attitude towards these issues, laughing them off with *Private Eye* aside, or a blustering defence of the principle of a "free press."

Journalists need to understand that they are accountable to the societies in which they work and that those processes of accountability are in constant and necessary evolution. That is at the heart of the ethical contract between journalists and the publics they serve and it as at the heart of the tangled web which Lord Hutton must now help us unweave.

The themes in this contribution are considered further in *Journalism: Truth or Dare?*, by Ian Hargreaves, published by Oxford University Press in 2003.

Note

1 David Randall: The Universal Journalist. London, Pluto Press, 2000 p 13.

Chapter 20

In Search of Ethical Business Leadership: Time to Mix Our Metaphors?

Ken Peattie

Introduction – An Unfolding Crisis in Business Ethics?

The unfolding Parmalat scandal in Italy is just the latest in a series of incidents that have shone a spotlight on the behaviour and ethics of top business leaders. Founder Calisto Tanzi is currently in jail, accused of having falsified the company's accounts for many years. Twenty eight other Parmalat executives are also due to stand trial alongside him. This follows on the heels of Enron, WorldCom, Global Crossing, Equitable Life and several other sorry tales. In Germany, several business leaders have appeared in court in connection with bonus payouts during the $180bn Mannesmann takeover by Vodafone, including Deutsche Bank's Chairman, Josef Ackermann and former Mannesmann Chief Executive Klaus Esser. In America 2004 seems set to be remembered as a year of celebrity business leader trials. Martha Stewart, America's lifestyle queen, has been found guilt of conspiracy, making false statements and obstruction of justice. Bernie Ebbers, former Chief Executive of bankrupt telecoms company WorldCom, has appeared in court to answer charges of fraud, conspiracy and making false statements. Scott Sullivan, Ebbers' former Chief Financial Officer at WorldCom, has already admitted similar charges. John Rigas, the founder of Adelphia Communications, is one of several who have appeared in court charged with illegally removing one billion dollars from the company. In May the former Wall Street banking star Frank Quattrone, formerly of Credit Suisse First Boston, was found guilty of obstructing justice and witness tampering. A depressing pattern seems to be emerging.

Some might argue that such scandals are nothing new, and that there have always been business leaders who have failed in their ethical duties towards shareholders and other stakeholders in order to enrich themselves. One can go back to the Dutch East India Company of 1622 (which can be viewed as the prototype of the modern international company), to find protesting shareholders on the dockside of Amsterdam, handing out leaflets complaining about management secrecy and self-enrichment at the expense of shareholders. Their campaign did lead to action by the government of the day, who moved swiftly to ban such pamphleteering, but they also pledged to improve information for shareholders and strengthen shareholder influence over public companies. Recent events suggest that perhaps not as much has changed in the past few hundred years in the field of corporate governance as might have been hoped.

The US government and others have sought to downplay the seriousness of recent events by presenting them as isolated incidents, at odds with the vast majority of businesses that are well-run by responsible and ethically-minded individuals. There is some research evidence to support such an argument. Eighty percent of 1,498 managers surveyed categorised their firms as highly ethical (Posner and Schmidt, 1987), and most people reported themselves as unlikely to engage in unethical activities at work (Eastman et al., 1996). However, such self-reporting is not necessarily conclusive. Survey respondents consistently perceive their own ethical standards to be higher than those of their peers or others in their immediate working environment (e.g. Cole and Smith, 1996; Ford and Richardson, 1994).

Even if unethical behaviour is confined to a minority of companies, this argument does not appear to be reassuring the general public. A 2002 CNN/Time survey revealed that 72% of US adults did not believe that recent business scandals are isolated incidents, but viewed them as evidence of a systematic pattern of deception among those running major companies. Such findings have potentially serious ramifications. Trust is a vital component of a healthy economy and business culture. If investors cannot trust the information they are given by companies, it will hamper investment. This could contribute further to the emerging pensions crisis, if people do not believe that such financial investments are secure, because they fear being left in the same situation as those pensioners depending on Enron, Global Crossing or Equitable Life. If consumers do not believe the information that is provided for them on issues relating to the socio-environmental performance of business, this will also cause problems. It will hold back the development of markets for more ethical and environmentally sustainable goods and services. This is something that governments around the world are depending upon to act as a spur for the development of fairer and more sustainable economies and societies. If a culture of cynicism about the conduct of business continues to develop, it may also create a vicious circle of lowered expectations about the ethical conduct of business, which in turn leads to less ethical conduct amongst those running companies.

In the wake of the recent generation of business scandals, there has been a wide-ranging search for solutions. Tougher laws on corporate governance, greater independence for auditors, wider adoption of codes such as the Global Reporting Initiative or Good Corporation's guidelines, greater powers for non-executive directors, harsher penalties for corporate wrong-doing and more corporate ethics officers are among the solutions that have been suggested. All of these can play a valuable part, but none of them addresses the question of why senior business leaders are drawn into unethical behaviour in the first place. Research into why people engage in unethical activities often cites factors such as time pressure, or pressure to achieve demanding targets. Such factors hardly seem explanatory since they would appear to face most people in business situations, only a minority of whom respond with unethical behaviour. Other factors cited include the influence of the company's leadership and its corporate culture, group dynamics and norms.

The importance of leadership is a recurring theme within the business ethics literature, and top executives have been shown to have a great impact when it comes to establishing the ethical tone of an organization (Wiley, 1998). However, if ethical leaders help to inspire ethical organisations, who will inspire those leaders? How can we develop business leaders for this new millennium who can embrace and demonstrate an ethical approach to running businesses, and help to turn the tide of dwindling trust in business? These are important issues, that may require some original and imaginative approaches if 'business ethics' is to avoid becoming regarded by the general public as nothing more than an oxymoron.

The Role of Business Education

Working within a University, it is perhaps natural to wonder whether there are fundamental flaws in the way in which we educate the business leaders of the future, and in the ideas that underpin their view of how a company should be run. Research evidence suggests that business students typically have relatively low expectations about the ethics of businesses and managers. Students believe they must adopt a 'winning is everything' philosophy at work (Pressley and Blevins, 1984), and perceive managers as more concerned with economics than ethics (Alam, 1995), and focused more on financial goals than social and employee-oriented goals (Beggs and Lane, 1989). Students, when role-playing as managers, typically rate social responsibility criteria, both individually and collectively, among the least important determinants of organisational effectiveness (Kraft, 1991; Kraft and Singhapakdi, 1995).

One popular development over recent years has been the introduction of Business Ethics as a university course. Several studies have suggested that such courses provide significant improvements in students' ethical sensitivities (Duizend and McCann, 1998; Carlson and Burke, 1998; Gautschi and Jones, 1998), although others have found little or no evidence of improvement (Wynd and Mager, 1989; Glenn, 1992). As with many other areas of education, this suggests that it is not whether something is taught, but how well it is taught, that matters. In terms of post-graduate business education, the MBA curriculum appears to have a value neutral impact for the majority of students (McCabe et al., 1994). Where Business Schools do include teaching on business ethics, it has been criticised for being too strongly based around 'sterile ethical theories' from textbooks, with insufficient attention paid to the real-life ethical dilemmas managers face in business (Derry and Green, 1989). Business schools have also been criticised for their relatively slow response to some key socio-ethical issues which now confront society and businesses, such as pressure to develop more sustainable economies and businesses (Coopey, 2001).

A weakness in much of the research into the effectiveness of business ethics teaching is that it concentrates on business ethics as a stand-alone subject. What is usually ignored, is the extent to which the principles being taught within business ethics are reinforced or contradicted by other aspects of the business curriculum. This led me to consideration of my own discipline of strategic management and the degree to which it reinforces or hampers the process of promoting business ethics. Strategic management is typically treated as an over-arching integrative discipline that provides a holistic-counterbalance to other management subjects, which focus on individual business functions and disciplines. For business degrees that lack a dedicated business ethics course, it is also a popular place in the curriculum to address ethics. Strategic management places considerable emphasis on issues such as leadership and stakeholder analysis, and in recent years issues of corporate social responsibility have begun to feature much more strongly. It therefore provides an apparently logical and suitable 'home' for business ethics issues within the management curriculum. However, there are a number of aspects of conventional strategic management, and the way that it is taught, which provide potential barriers to the development of a more ethical and sustainable approach to business. This article will examine two of the most fundamental components of strategic management thinking from this perspective. Each involves the application of a metaphor to a key stakeholder role, and they are both so commonly used that they are rarely either noticed or challenged. Yet each potentially acts as an obstacle to the development of a more ethically orientated way of thinking about business and business leadership.

The Trouble with 'Strategy'

Strategic management is, logically enough, concerned with strategy. When we begin to educate future managers about strategy, the word itself is often the starting point. 'Strategy' comes from the Greek word 'strategos', which originally had a relatively narrow meaning referring to the role of an army commander, but later evolved to refer to 'the art of the general'. By the time of Alexander the Great it had broadened to mean 'the skill of employing forces to overcome opposition and to create a unified system of global governance' (Evered, 1980). Curiously, some two thousand years later, such a definition seems less military in its connotations and more like an excerpt from a job description for the manager of a trans-national corporation.

In developing a strategy discipline for the commercial field, management academics have borrowed freely from the military science developed by generals such as von Clauswitz and Sun Tzu. This has provided us with a vocabulary of management strategy peppered with references to targeting, outflanking, retreating, attacking and defending. Standard strategy texts reflect this, particularly the early editions of The Strategy Process (Quinn et al., 1988) which are illustrated by the campaigns of Alexander, Napoleon, MacArthur, Mountbatten and the German and French armies of 1914. Whole books have been dedicated to the parallels between military and corporate/marketing strategy (notably James, 1985, and Ries and Trout, 1992), as have articles in leading academic journals (Kotler and Singh, 1981, Parks et al., 1994). This was taken to extremes in one article published in Long Range Planning (Ginter and Rucks, 1984), which portrayed a business enterprise as a virtually perfect reflection of a war machine.

The danger in this ancestry is that we risk accepting a philosophy of strategic management in which concepts of aggression, eradicating 'the enemy' and disregarding the environmental and social costs and consequences, are seen as 'natural' and accepted as readily as in the field of military science. In practice, despite its widespread usage, an army provides a poor metaphor for a business (Peattie, 1990; Rindfleisch, 1996). As Cannan (1929) pointed out 'Economic competition is not war, but rivalry in mutual service'. The warfare analogy might seem appropriate to those engaged in oligopolistic competition, but try to imagine one of the 20,000 players in the European shoe industry defining who the 'enemy' is and where the 'battlefield' lies. Monopolists would also struggle to view themselves as akin to an army, except perhaps as an army of occupation, which lacks the usual sense of a noble struggle. The complexities of modern business relationships also make the military metaphor seem redundant. In key global industries such as cars, telecommunications, computers, aerospace, and financial services, the companies involved increasingly co-operate with their competitors through numerous strategic alliances. Such relationships do not suit the concepts of all-out aggression which typifies warfare and make business strategy formulation today much more akin to diplomacy as an activity.

Despite all the shortcomings of the military metaphor, it has become deeply rooted in the practitioner and academic view of corporate and marketing strategy, so that 'the existing strategy literature appears to present a one-sided, overly conflictual view of competitive interaction. Considering the extensive military experience of many post-war corporate executives and the positive feelings toward the military in the wake of World War II, practitioner embracement of this metaphor is not surprising. Unfortunately for many firms, marketing-as-warfare may have produced a host of unintended consequences for both themselves and their customers' (Rindfleisch, 1996).

The relevance of this for business ethics perhaps lies in the two maxims 'The first casualty of war is truth' and 'All is fair in love and war', which are both indicative of the relationship between militarism and issues of ethics and truthfulness. In an era when people are more than ever concerned with the ethics and trustworthiness of firms, it seems ironic to model them on organisations for whom propaganda, secrecy and the suppression or distortion of truth are considered legitimate and often vital. It also seems a classic example of the type of business thinking and scholarship, which those approaching the discipline from a feminist perspective criticise for being centred on masculine concepts like aggression and determinism. The metaphor certainly suffers from some of the classical biases associated with a male-dominated approach to social phenomena (Stevenson, 1990). These include a concentration on masculine dominated sectors of life; the use of paradigms, concepts, methods, and theories which reflect men's rather than women's experiences; and the use of men and male lifestyles as the norms in interpreting social phenomena. A thorough feminist critique of the military metaphor in strategic management would require an article of its own. Space considerations mean that this article can do little more than highlight the feminist perspective on the military metaphor as yet another convincing argument to consign it to the past.

The Marketing Concept – Enthroning the Consumer

Another metaphor, which acts as a fundamental building block within the strategic management discipline, is that of 'consumer sovereignty'. It resides within the 'marketing concept', that the basic aim of a business it to create profit through an integrated effort to achieve customer satisfaction. The marketing concept is so widely endorsed and accepted that it has become a 'motherhood' espoused by virtually all companies (even if fully implemented by relatively few) and rarely subject to any real theoretical scrutiny (Houston, 1986). The metaphor of the customer as a monarch, and the rallying-cry that 'the customer is king', is fundamental to marketing and to free-market economics. As Mulhern (1992) notes 'while neo-classical economic theory assumes consumer sovereignty, the marketing concept proclaims it by explicitly orientating a company toward the satisfaction of consumer wants.'

This metaphor, like that of the company as war-machine, is so widely used that in practice it is rarely explicitly considered or challenged. There are however several rather curious dimensions to it:

Monarchies that are more than symbolic are rare in the modern era. The decline of monarchies during the last thousand years suggests that as a system it is not in itself sustainable. Citizens are generally unwilling to have decisions made on their behalf by an individual whom they have not nominated to represent their interests.

Monarchs in the past have often been able to wield power without responsibility. History provides plenty of examples of monarchies tainted by cruelty, selfishness and a willingness to destroy the lives of others on a whim. This is not to say that monarchs are necessarily bad rulers, but the absolute power of the monarch can have the power to corrupt absolutely.

Monarchs can be vulnerable to manipulation by advisors who isolate them from the realities of their kingdoms and effectively control them through the use of selective information.

Faith in the concept of consumer sovereignty also has the potential to act as a barrier to the creation of more ethical and sustainable businesses for several reasons. Firstly, it allows companies to devolve responsibility for their actions to the customer. Companies have frequently defended environmentally or ethically sub-optimal strategies on the basis that 'it is what the customer wants'. McDonalds did this in defending their decision to replace polystyrene 'clamshell' hamburger boxes in America with less-recyclable paper and plastic burger wraps. This was in response to continued, but misplaced, objections from consumers who did not realised that the clamshell boxes were no longer a source of CFC pollution. Volvo, a company that could justifiably claim to be among the greenest of all the car manufacturers, also raised this defence when it found itself under attack for continuing to equip its cars with large engines (Rothenberg et al., 1992).

Close allegiance to the wants of the consumer can also lead to the neglect of the needs of other stakeholders. This is perhaps most obvious when discussing an issue like car safety. This is framed in terms of air-bags, side-impact bars, reinforced roll-cages and anti-whiplash seats. Car-safety ratings in magazines like Which? are strongly influenced by the weight of the vehicle. These are all issues specific to driver safety. As cars become heavier, the driver becomes increasingly safe, but pedestrians, cyclists and anyone else in their path become increasingly endangered. Making the driver increasingly insulated from any negative consequences associated with dangerous driving could also arguably lead to less cautious driving and a reduction in overall road safety. One important aim of sustainable development is to more equitably distribute the benefits and costs of economic activity. Consumer sovereignty as a concept encourages relatively blinkered attention to be paid to those receiving the benefits of economic activity, with little attention paid to the impact on non-consumers. Since only roughly one fifth of the world's population has the discretionary spending power necessary to qualify as a member of the 'consumer classes', the extent to which economic progress is guided by the wants of affluent consumers can be viewed as inequitable and unethical, as well as ultimately unsustainable (Durning 1992).

Even within the consumer society, advertising aimed at a minority of wealthy consumers can still reach many more people who are unable to afford the product or service in question. Since those unable to afford a product are not a part of 'the market', they are simply ignored by marketers. It is delivering satisfaction to the customer that is the raison d'être which underpins the marketing philosophy and the focus of marketing strategy. However, the 'collatoral damage' of dissatisfaction amongst people who can be made to desire a product by marketing communications, even if they can never afford it, goes unrecorded and unconsidered.

A third problem with consumer sovereignty is that it is entirely expressed in terms of consumer wants rather than consumer needs. Therefore cigarette companies can market a product that will ultimately kill their customers if used as directed (assuming nothing else kills them first), and defend it on the basis of individual freedom of choice and on satisfying the wants of the consumer. Similarly in the design of cars, the issue of safety consistently lost out for decades to the more explicit consumer desire for speed and style. Mulhern (1992) calls for a new vision of the marketing concept orientated more towards consumer welfare, and less towards consumer wants.

The image of the customer as sovereign seems intuitively attractive. It suggests that as consumers we all have some power to influence the way in which society and the economy develops, and that we can do some good through the exercise of our spending power. The reality is more reminiscent of Bertolucci's *The*

Last Emperor in which a theoretically all-powerful monarch leads an existence carefully structured and confined to maintain the illusion of power and to keep the monarch separated from the realities of life.

Conclusions – Do Metaphors Really Matter?

Is it really important that the discipline of strategic management is saturated with the vision of the strategist as an army commander in the service of their consumer sovereign? For the most part it has been largely ignored, and for many people the exact choice of words used to describe things is not considered particularly important. It is easy to dismiss the question as esoteric, and 'academic' in the most negative sense of the word (although for any people who believe that a rose by any other name would smell as sweet, a few minutes spent discussing the issue with someone from the worlds of journalism or advertising could prove educational).

In recent years however, social scientists have become increasingly interested in the power of the metaphors we use to shape both thought and action. A metaphor is 'a figure of speech in which a term or phrase with a literal meaning is applied in a different context in order to suggest a resemblance' (Sackmann, 1991). Many metaphors are so commonly used, including both 'market' and 'customer', that they have become 'dead metaphors' whose metaphorical roots have been forgotten (Palmer and Dunford, 1996). The pervasiveness of metaphors and their ability to translate the complex and unfamiliar into something familiar and simple to grasp, mean that philosophers, linguists and social scientists are increasingly agreed that they are fundamental to structuring our view of the world and how we behave within it (Lakoff and Johnson, 1999). Whether we use them consciously, or without thinking, metaphors can be shown to play powerful roles in how we create and perceive business organisations and their behaviours (Grant and Oswick, 1996; Morgan, 1986).

In the field of management, the analysis of the metaphors we use has been very popular within the organisational behaviour literature, particularly relating to organisational change and leadership (for a review see Palmer and Dunford, 1996). It can also have very practical applications. For example, it has been shown that the metaphors used to express the identity of an organisation can influence the extent to which employees identify with that organisation, their job satisfaction and self-esteem (Dutton et al., 1994). The emphasis within the organisational behaviour arena is primarily on the internal world-view within the company (see for example Morgan, 1986). The more externally focused strategic management and marketing disciplines have been less enthusiastic about metaphor analysis, although Arndt (1985) produced an early exploration of the use of alternative metaphors in marketing.

During the last decade, alternative metaphors have begun to emerge in both the practice and study of corporate and marketing strategy. They are potentially important because, as Lakoff and Johnson (1999) suggest, 'New metaphors have the power to create a new reality.' If we are to develop more ethical and sustainable businesses, what metaphors should be used for the corporate strategist and the consumer, to replace the images of general and king? Rindfleisch (1996) provides a detailed criticism of the military metaphor, and suggests the use of alternative metaphors such as organisms, games and even marriage. Oliver (1999) sees the metaphors of warfare and games within corporate strategy as distasteful and limiting, and instead suggests parallels with cuisine, with the strategist creatively combining ingredients like a chef. Other metaphors that have been suggested range from a potter's wheel to improvisational jazz. Davis (1991) has suggested that the demands of environmental management create a need for an 'orchestral' style of management with the strategist 'conducting' skilled teams of individuals. When concerns about the environmental impacts of companies are discussed, an obvious source of strategy metaphors comes from biology and ecology (Clippinger, 1999). Although such an approach has grown in popularity, particularly with the increasing interest in the field of industrial ecology, it can also lead to problems. Ecological metaphors can easily slip into misplaced pseudo-Darwinian concepts of competition, and biological metaphors also suffer from a range of limitations (see Rhenman, 1973).

In relation to the consumer, it is important to understand that the customer (in most markets) is not a single individual with a single will that can be obeyed absolutely. Consumers are more like an electorate who, through their purchasing behaviour, endorse the products and activities of individual companies. Some consumers will respond positively to the company's offering, others will not. Some may be loyal and enthusiastic customers, some may patronise the firm as the least bad option, while others may decide to register a protest purchase with a rival. Such a view of consumers would allow companies to consider themselves more like potential or appointed representatives seeking to attract and serve this electorate. This could encourage firms to broaden their perspective and to take on more responsibility for customer and stakeholder welfare. This may seem very different to the approach used by many companies, but in markets such as professional services and in many technical industrial markets, there is a culture in which the company takes some measure of responsibility for the customer and for solving their problems. A government may be elected by a minority, but they must govern for all of society. Similarly, a company may only be endorsed directly by a minority of citizens, but that should not prevent them from considering the interests of all. By treating consumers as a democratic electorate towards whom they have a responsibility, firms would be encouraged towards more openness and communication on social and environmental issues (although this perhaps represents a rather idealised, open and 'spin free' view of democracy).

One alternative to following the path of military science to understand business leadership, is to seek parallels to management strategy in the field of social anthropology. Akin and Palmer (2000) did this to an extent in using metaphors of 'Shamen', 'Priest', 'Magician', 'Medicine Man' and 'Mystic' to typify styles for organizational change agents. Similarly, instead of viewing the strategist as an army general, we could view them as analogous to a leader within a hunter-gatherer tribe. Such tribes lead a sustainable existence in harmony with their environment, and although they may engage in hostilities with other tribes, a tribal leader is responsible for a much wider range of strategic decisions than the purely military (although there is some debate among social anthropologists as to whether warfare tended to exist among tribal groups before economic and technical development encouraged the expansion of tribes and their territories once original carrying capacities were exceeded). One interesting example comes from the Comanche Indians of North America whose bands were led by a Peace Chief, 'usually a man known for his kindness, wisdom and ability to lead by influencing other men. Although a war record was important, peace chiefs were not chosen from among the most aggressive or ambitious men' (Peoples and Bailey, 1994).

The idea that modern society can learn from tribal societies was popularised nearly 30 years ago in Carlos Castenedas' 'Journey to Ixtlan' (1975) and revisited by Maybury-Lewis's 'Millennium' (1992). Pre-agricultural tribal societies have many elements that perhaps make them worth modelling companies around, beyond the fact that they are usually environmentally sustainable. They are usually egalitarian, with leaders selected on the basis of personal qualities and individual merit. They are generally stable and robust units, Coon (1971) stresses that nearly all tribal extinctions are related to outside intervention, usually in the form of contact with 'more developed' peoples.

Castaneda's book encapsulated the philosophy of the Yaqui Indians (although it can also be viewed as a vivid warning about the dangers of dabbling with psychotropic mushrooms!). This philosophy contains many principles that seem relevant to the role that business leaders will have to play if we are to create more ethical and sustainable businesses. The book outlines the philosophical steps involved in becoming a Yaqui 'Man of Knowledge'. Space precludes considering these in detail here, but some idea of their relevance for strategy can be gained by considering a few such as: 'Stopping the world', and 'Disrupting the routines of life' which refer to the need for re-evaluation and for fundamental change; 'Erasing personal history' and 'Losing self-importance' explain how to escape the restrictions of experience and ego; 'Assuming responsibility' is self explanatory and 'Becoming a Hunter' explains the principles of living in harmony with the environment – 'A hunter uses his world sparingly and with tenderness, regardless of whether the world might be things, or plants, or animals, or people, or power. .... he's not squeezing his world out of shape. He taps it lightly, stays for as long as he needs to and then swiftly moves away without leaving a mark.' This work is just one example, but it suggests that instead of looking to the likes of von Clauswitz and Sun Tzu for inspiration, strategic management could find an entirely different source of role models and wisdom about leadership to learn from.

One curious observation about these kinds of ideas, is the response that they elicit from those involved in strategic management practice and scholarship. When discussing such an idea within a conference or workshop, it is interesting how many people will use a word like 'ridiculous'. Why should the idea of a tribal leader as an inspiration for business leadership seem 'ridiculous' by people who accept the idea of a military leader as a role model and source of inspiration without question? This response perhaps says a great deal about the prejudices that we have learned, and the values that are buried so deeply that we are scarcely aware that they exist. Another observation is that some people seem to interpret this argument as a misplaced paean to an idyllic but mythical pre-industrial way of life. This article is not meant to suggest that we should return to a tribal way of life. It aims to show that there are other social systems besides armies from which we can learn potentially valuable lessons in leadership. This is particularly true if we are to develop more ethical, sustainable and effective leadership for the future.

A recurring theme in the debate about developing more sustainable and ethical business organisations for this new Millennium, is that we need to break out of old patterns of thought and action to allow ourselves to develop innovative ways to produce, consume and manage. It is in the search for innovation and new insights that the application of alternative metaphors is so valuable, because they allow an organisation to develop a fresh perspective on itself and its environment (Morgan, 1993). Such an approach is reflected in the many contributors to the collection edited by Allen et al. (2001), which discusses some of the challenges involved in creating new forms of more sustainable organisations in terms of 'metaphors for change'.

The introduction to the book 'Millennium' suggests that 'Tribal cultures have been systematically destroyed because they hinder the exploitation of the Earth and human beings. But we humans evolved as tribal beings; it may be that the survival of the human race depends upon the acknowledgement of our tribal origins.' Our survival may also be aided by the consideration of our tribal origins as a source of inspiration in terms of the metaphors we use for business leadership in the future. It is perhaps not entirely coincidental that in the commercial world, it is one of the greenest and most ethically-orientated companies, Body Shop, which consistently refers to its corporate culture as being 'a tribe'. If our approach to strategic management came to mirror the role of the Comanche Peace Chief, in ensuring their tribe's long-term security and prosperity, rather than reflecting the Western War Lord's quest for short term domination at all costs, then perhaps the discipline could help to develop a more sustainable future for itself and for the World.

References

Akin, G. and Palmer, I. (2000), "Putting Metaphors to Work for Change in Organizations", *Organizational Dynamics*, Vol. 28 (3), 67-80.

Alam, K.F. (1995), "Attitudes Towards Business Ethics of Business Students in Malaysia", *Journal of Business Ethics*, Vol. 14 (4), 309-313.

Allen, P., Bonazzi, C. and Gee, D. (2001), Metaphors for Change: Partnerships, Tools and Civic Action for Sustainability, Greenleaf: Sheffield.

Arndt, J. (1985) "On Making Marketing Science More Scientific: The Role Of Orientations, Paradigms, Metaphors, And Problem Solving", *Journal Of Marketing*, Summer, 11-23.

Beggs, J.M. and Lane, M.S. (1989), "Corporate Goal Structures and Business Students: A Comparative Study of Values", *Journal of Business Ethics*, Vol. 8 (6), 471-478.

Cannan, E. (1929), A Review of Economic Theory, P.S. King & Sons: London.

Carlson, P.J. and Burke, F. (1998), "Lessons Learned from Ethics in the Classroom: Exploring Student Growth in Flexibility, Complexity and Comprehension", *Journal of Business Ethics*, Vol. 17 (11), 1179-1187.

Castaneda, C. (1974), Journey to Ixtlan, Penguin: Middx.

Clippinger, H.J. (1999), The Biology of Business: Decoding the Natural Laws of Enterprise, Josey-Bass: San Fransisco.

Cole, B.C. and Smith, D.L. (1996), "Perceptions of Business Ethics: Students vs. Business People", *Journal of Business Ethics*, Vol. 15 (8), 889-896.

Coon, C.S. (1971), The Hunting Peoples, Penguin: Middx.

Coopey, J. (2001), Sustainable Development: A UK Business School Blind Spot?, *BAM News*, Winter 2001/2002, p. 12.

Derry, B. and Green, R.M. (1989), "Ethical Theory in Business Ethics: A Critical Assessment", *Journal of Business Ethics*, Vol. 8 (7), 521-533.

Durning, A.T. (1992), How Much is Enough? *Earthscan*, London.

Duizend, J. and McCann, G.K. (1998), "Do Collegiate Business Students Show a Propensity to Engage in Illegal Business Practices?", *Journal of Business Ethics*, Vol. 17 (3), 229-238.

Dutton, J.E.,. Dukerich, J.M and Harquail, C.V. (1994). "Organizational images and member identification", *Administrative Science Quarterly*, 39, pp. 239-263.

Eastman, K.L., Eastman, J.K. and Eastman A.D. (1996), "The Ethics of Insurance Professionals: Comparison of Personal Versus Professional Ethics", *Journal of Business Ethics*, Vol. 15 (9), 951-962.

Evered, R. (1980), So What Is Strategy?, Working Paper, Naval Postgraduate School, Monterey.

Ford, R.C. and Richardson, W.D. (1994), "Ethical Decision Making: A Review of the Empirical Literature", *Journal of Business Ethics*, Vol. 13 (3), 205-221.

Gautschi, F.H. and Jones, T.M. (1998), "Enhancing the Ability of Business Students to Recognize Ethical Issues: An Empirical Assessment of the Effectiveness of a Course in Business Ethics", *Journal of Business Ethics*, Vol. 17 (2), 205-216.

Ginter, P.M. and Rucks, C.R. (1984), "Can Business Learn From Wargames", *Long Range Planning*, Vol. 17 (3), 123-128.

Glenn, J.J. (1992), "Can a Business and Society Course Affect the Ethical Judgment of Future Managers?", *Journal of Business Ethics*, Vol. 11 (3), 217-223.

Grant, D. and C. Oswick (Eds.), Metaphor and Organizations. Sage Publications: Thousand Oaks, California.

Houston, F.S. (1986), "The Marketing Concept", *Journal of Marketing*, Vol. 50 (2), 81-87.

James, B.G. (1984), Business Wargames, Abacus Press, London.

Kotler, P. and Singh, R. (1981) "Marketing Warfare In The 1980s", *Journal Of Business Strategy*, Winter, 30-41

Kraft, K.L. (1991), "The Relative Importance of Social Responsibility in Determining Organizational Effectiveness: Student Responses", *Journal of Business Ethics*, Vol. 10 (7), 179-188.

Kraft, K.L. and Singhapakdi, A. (1995), "The Relative Importance of Social Responsibility in Determining Organizational Effectiveness: Student Responses II", *Journal of Business Ethics*, Vol. 14 (4), 315-326.

Lakoff, G. and Johnson, M. (1999), Metaphors We Live By (2nd ed.), University of Chicago Press: Chicago.

Maybury-Lewis, D. (1992) Millennium: Tribal Wisdom and The Modern World, Viking: New York.

McCabe, D.L., Dukerich, J.M. and Dutton, J.E. (1994), "The Effects of Professional Education on Values and the Resolution of Ethical Dilemmas: Business School vs. Law School Students", *Journal of Business Ethics*, Vol. 13 (9), 693-700.

Morgan, G. (1986), Images of Organization, Sage, London.

Morgan, G. (1993), Imaginization: The Art of Creative Management, Sage: Thousand Oaks, California.

Mulhern, F.J. (1992), "Consumer Wants and Consumer Welfare", in Allen, T.C. et al (eds) Marketing Theory and Applications, 1992 AMA Winter Conference Proceedings, 407-12.

Oliver, R.W. (1999) "Strategy as sports! War! Food?", *The Journal of Business Strategy*, Vol. 20 (5), 8-10.

Palmer, I. And Dunford, R. (1996), "Conflicting Uses of Metaphors: Reconceptualizing Their Use in the Field of Organizational Change", *The Academy of Management Review*, Vol. 21 (3), 691-708.

Parks, B., Pharr, S.W., and Lockeman, B.D. (1994) "A Marketer's Guide To Clausewitz: Lessons For Winning Market Share", *Business Horizons*, July-August, 68-73.

Peattie, K. (1990), "Pretending to Understand Business Policy", *Management Education and Development*, Vol. 21 (4), 287-300.

Peoples, J. and Bailey, G. (1994), Humanity (3 rd ed), West Publishing: St. Paul, Minn.

Posner, B.Z. and Schmidt W.H. (1993), "Values Congruence and Differences between the Interplay of Personal and Organizational Value Systems", *Journal of Business Ethics*, Vol. 12, 341-347.

Pressley, M.M. and Blevins, D.E. (1984), "Student Perceptions of 'Job Politics' as Practiced by Those Climbing the Corporate Career Ladder", *Journal of Business Ethics*, Vol. 3 (2), 127-138.

Quinn, J.B., Mintzberg, H. and James, D.C. (1988), *The Strategy Process* (2nd ed), Prentice-Hall: Englewood Cliffs, NJ.

Rindfleisch, A. (1996), "Marketing as Warfare: Reassessing a Dominant Metaphor", *Business Horizons*, Vol. 39 (5) 3-11.

Ries, A. and Trout, J. (1986), *Marketing Warfare*, McGraw-Hill: New York.

Rhenman, E. (1973), *Organization Theory for Long Range Planning*, London: Wiley.

Rothenberg, S., Maxwell, J. and Marcus, A. (1992), "Issues in the Implementation of Proactive Environmental Strategies", *Business Strategy and the Environment*, Vol. 1 (4), 1-12.

Sackmann, S. (1989), "The Role Of Metaphors In Organization Transformations", *Human Relations*, June, 463-485.

Stevenson, L. (1990), "Some Methodological Problems Associated with Researching Women Entrepreneurs", *Journal of Business Ethics*, Vol. 9, pp. 439-446.

Wiley, C. (1998), "Re-examining Perceived Ethics Issues and Ethics Roles among Employment Managers", *Journal of Business Ethics*, Vol. 17 (2), 147-161.

Wynd, W.R. and Mager, J. (1989), "The Business and Society Course: Does It Change Student Attitudes?", *Journal of Business Ethics*, Vol. 8 (6), 487-491.

Chapter 21

Only Connect – Broadband Provision and Social Inclusion

Ian Kenway

The term 'digital divide' is now firmly established in the rhetorical canon of both politicians and social commentators. However, its alliterative catchiness may lead to obfuscation rather than illumination unless some effort is made to differentiate the various understandings of the term. At least three can be identified at the outset. First, the term can refer to the divide between those who either own or have easy access to information and communication devices whose technologies operate digitally and those who do not have such access or ownership. Secondly, the term can refer to the divide between those who are knowledgeable, skilled and competent in the application and adaptation of information and communication technologies (ICT) and those who are lacking in the same for whatever reason. Thirdly, the term can refer to the divide between those who are able to communicate efficiently with other people through digital technologies and those who are handicapped in such endeavours through limited connectivity or bandwidth.

Clearly these separable understandings should normally be viewed as mutually contingent or intermodulatory insofar as the digital divide more often than not encompasses all three. Overcoming the digital divide must be about the development of appropriate ICT skills. However, these increasingly require not just access to the technologies in terms of equipment, but also in terms of connectivity so that people can achieve greater levels of creative endeavour and productivity through the efficient sharing of information and critical comment.

Unfortunately the provision of broadband, both in the UK and elsewhere, has too often been portrayed in the consumerist primary colours of technical one-upmanship or lifestyle enhancement for individuals rather than rendered in the more subtle and varied shades of regional, area or neighbourhood benefit which ought to characterise any serious debate about how socially inclusive communities can be created and maintained. In short, serious discussion about broadband (i.e. one that is ethically articulate) should not in the first instance start with technical or economic questions about how ICT infrastructures can be developed most effectively, but rather about how relatively (and in some instances gravely) deprived communities and disadvantaged individuals can be given greater power to organise and determine their lives.

In May 2001, Anna Diamantopoulou, EU Commissioner for Employment and Social Affairs, in an address at the European Parliament, adumbrated the particular dangers and challenges which accompany the emergence of 'E-Society':

The harsh reality is that a new a sort of class system is emerging in Europe. Between those who have access to this technology, and the skills to use it. And those that don't. Between the 'digital-haves' and the 'digital-have nots'. This was a key message from a recent Eurobarometer survey. That the spread of the information society has been hampered by gaps. Gaps between countries and regions. Between the sexes. Income gaps. Age gap...More and more women are using the Internet. But we still have a long way to go to match the US, where distribution is equal. This two-tier situation cannot continue. The 'E' in 'E-Society' does not and cannot stand for Exclusion...The new knowledge economy offers a wealth of opportunities to integrate and empower socially vulnerable groups: women, the disabled, older people, the unemployed, people living in remote and marginalised area...Helping overcome the traditional barriers of distance and mobility. Distributing knowledge and training resources in a more creative way. And on a more equal basis. Generating new, more responsive, and more user-friendly, networks, services and assistance. And, of course, giving the excluded a platform to voice their own needs and concerns. In a society and economy driven more and more by information, we cannot allow people to remain excluded. Internet access and digital literacy are becoming a must for finding and retaining a job. Providing socially vulnerable groups with the right tools, skills and ongoing training makes clear economic sense...We need to make sure that we harness the full potential of our greatest asset: people.[1]

While it may be relatively easy to dismiss the broad-brush of such language, it would be unwise not to heed the warnings or to dismiss the accompanying desiderata as merely 'idealistic Eurospeak'. Indeed in the eighteen months since Diamantopoulou's address , a growing number of voices in the UK are beginning to raise critical questions about how far the current UK Government is, at least in practice, actually 'signed up' to the idea of E-Inclusion in terms of the roll-out of broadband in the UK. While there is clear evidence that real opportunities were seized in the mid-90s in developing strategies for E-Inclusion, there is a growing feeling abroad that the progress that was achieved in that period is being undermined by several factors governing the provision of broadband in the UK.

Much is sometimes made of the technical difficulties in delivering ADSL broadband to those who live on the periphery of converted exchanges e.g. the need for subscribers to be located no more than 6.0 km from an upgraded exchange (a restriction marginally relaxed recently from an earlier 5.5 km requirement[2]) or the difficulties in developing and implementing alternative technologies in regions of extreme rurality where the problem of low population densities is often compounded by relatively inhospitable terrains. However, the inertia currently afflicting the roll-out of broadband in UK is not ultimately one of technological adequacy but of ideological commitment.

In this context, it is perhaps interesting to examine the rôle of the Office of Telecommunications (Oftel) in determining the specific modes and, hence, rates of broadband roll-out in the UK. Leaving aside the question of its regulatory function and effectiveness in other areas of telecommunications, it can be cogently argued, both theoretically and empirically, that Oftel has seriously misunderstood or misinterpreted its rôle in the area of broadband provision. Instead of serving the interests of the whole UK community best by ensuring that all regions and areas have reasonable access to high-speed internet connectivity, it has developed instead a strategy in which the fundamental needs of communities are essentially subservient to a wide spectrum of commercial 'tests' which emerge from the prism of free market ideology.

Let us be more specific: it is not a matter of coincidence that the word 'community' or the phrases 'social inclusion' or 'social exclusion' (or, indeed, their cognates) do not appear anywhere in the December 2001 publication Delivering a competitive broadband market – Oftel's regulatory strategy for broadband. In the Introduction, Oftel sets out its rôle in these terms:

There are a number of different players involved in creating the UK's broadband market. These are the industry – to provide both the infrastructure and technology needed to deliver broadband services, as well as the content of these services. Oftel – to ensure a coherent regulatory framework that allows competition in the delivery of broadband services at all levels of the supply chain. The Government – who have a number of initiatives to stimulate the take up of broadband amongst consumers, the public and small business sectors. And most important of all, the consumer – who will make their own choices over the services they want to receive and how they want to receive it. A competitive broadband market gives consumers a greater choice of how they receive broadband services, what they receive and the price they pay for them[3]...Oftel's primary focus is to meet the needs of consumers through promoting competition at all levels of the value chain. Oftel's objectives can be translated to the broadband arena through: a) effective and sustainable competition in the provision of broadband access and services (evidenced by no operators having significant market power in broadband markets); b) swift and firm corrective action in the event of anti-competitive practices; c) a high level of consumer awareness of the nature of broadband services and choices available; and d) a regulatory framework which is conducive to further investment in broadband and roll-out to remote areas of the country.[4]

Later in the same publication Oftel observes:

> If a broadband delivery '*gap*' were [my italics] identified, Oftel would aim to assist the Government as necessary in identifying and applying any measures to meet the reasonable needs of consumers outside areas addressable through commercial means. In so doing, Oftel would aim to ensure that any measures are technologically neutral and, as far as possible, have no detrimental effect on the development of competition in general.[5]

The free market approach here is glaringly obvious with its direct and naïve appeal to consumers 'abstracted' from the communities in which they actually live and work with no reference whatsoever to the history and, more importantly, the current social and economic realities affecting those communities. What appears paramount instead is the active promotion of 'effective and sustainable competition' between providers; in short the regulatory goal must always be directed in the first instance not to addressing supply distortions between different communities, which clearly have the potential to introduce or exacerbate social or economic inequalities, but in simply providing a level playing field at all times between competing suppliers and, where applicable, between competing technologies as well.

According to Haring, Rohlfs and Shooshan, whose report Propelling the Broadband Bandwagon was commissioned for United Kingdom Office of Telecommunications and Office of the E-Envoy, broadband is more 'demand-constrained' than 'supply-constrained'. What is interesting is the way this triumvirate of principals of Strategic Policy Research, a US-based research foundation, equate connectivity with commodity. In short the paradigms they adopt in their paper, not least in their distinction between 'bandwagon' and 'non-bandwagon' technologies, are provided almost exclusively by the various modalities by which domestic electronic products are sold to and adopted by consumers. While cable and satellite TV and mobile telephony (excluding SMS text messaging) are cited as non-bandwagon technologies, broadband is seen as a bandwagon technology whose market precursors and/or competitors are such products as TV broadcasting/HDTV, VCR-videocassettes, home PCs and CD-players.[6]

Four factors are cited by Haring, Rohlfs and Shoostan as determining the 'the pace of new technologies in bandwagon markets', namely: (i) 'Demand must reach critical mass, or the product cannot succeed' (ii) 'Once critical mass is achieved, demand for bandwagon products is subject to positive feedback. That is, growth in demand tends to stimulate further growth' (iii) 'A valuable standalone application – that is, an application that has substantial value, even when the user set is small – reatly helps (but does not guarantee) achievement of critical mass'; and (iv) 'With complementary bandwagon effects, expectations may play a significant role. In particular, purchase of the platform product is often based, in part, on the consumer's expectations regarding the availability of the complementary products in the future'.[7] While it would be difficult to resist the relative significance of these factors, it is not completely clear whether or not broadband can be regarded exactly in the same terms as TV broadcasting/HDTV, VCR-videocassettes, home PCs and CD-players which require new rather than merely upgraded 'peripheral hardware'. Talk about 'a valuable standalone application' is also irrelevant in this context. So too in many respects (at least in this particular context) is the extended excursus that Haring, Rohlfs and Shoostan make in their paper regarding intellectual property and copyright issues as they relate to the uploading and downloading of media content via the internet.

As in Oftel's 'before "Delivery" and after "market"' – Oftel's regulatory strategy for broadband, Haring, Rohlfs and Shoostan studiously eschew any talk about communities (except in connection with Napster!) let alone issues specifically relating to social inclusion/exclusion. Instead they see broadband as not only best provided by market forces but actually as its true engine and absolute value:

Adam Smith's theory of economic growth emphasized the 'division of labour' (what we would now refer to as 'productive specialization'), and he famously argued that growth through the division of labour was limited by 'the extent of the market.' He thus favoured the extension of markets overseas and the expansion of trade as operational means of extending market boundaries and, thereby, the scope available for further division of labour. Within Smith's framework, the reason the great improvements in maritime navigation and the subsequent development of the steam engine and rail transportation were important was that they increased the size of economically relevant markets and thereby fostered greater productive specialization. In the first Industrial Revolution, improvements in transportation played a key role in expanding the effective breadth of economic markets and thus affording greater scope (and incentives) for enterprise competition, economizing behaviour and productive specialization. In the Information Age, it is improvements in the availability of decision-relevant information and the ability to communicate that are driving advances in economic productivity via the same means. Expanding access to information is what is removing/expanding market boundaries and thereby improving the efficiency with which markets operate.[8]

More tellingly, the specific problems of rural communities are addressed, as in Oftel's published regulatory strategy, only tangentially by Haring, Rohlfs and Shoostan, government intervention being considered as a concession rather than as a necessity. Of the latter they somewhat grudgingly opine:

There *may* [my italics] exist a role for governmental subsidy of broadband network deployments in rural and other areas, where private investment cannot be economically justified but public investment may nevertheless be deemed to be economical.[9]

However, it is precisely in rural communities that the limitations of a pure market approach to broadband become most acutely apparent. In December 2002, the Countryside Agency published a series of research notes based on the ASPECT Final Synthesis Report, itself drawing upon on a two-year long European study, which focused 'on how ICTs can help ameliorate social exclusion particularly in rural areas'. According to the Agency:

The report suggests that rural areas currently suffer from a deficit in advanced telecommunications infrastructure as a result of a lack of investment by telecommunications companies, based on a perceived lack of demand in rural areas. There is a need, therefore, to tackle both sides of the supply and demand equation. The report suggests that the public sector will need to intervene to ensure supply. Either through working in partnership with the telecommunications companies or local/regional authorities establishing their own networks. In either case public investment will be required. The report suggests that there is currently an asymmetry in knowledge of ICTs between the private and public sectors and that mechanisms need to be put in place to narrow that gap. It also suggests that intervention will be required to stimulate demand. It considers a number of demand stimulation measures in the areas of economic development, public service delivery and community development, drawing on 'good practice' examples from the study.[10]

The current situation in mid-Wales provides a useful example if not actually an object lesson in how the general unavailability of broadband in rural regions is beginning to undermine the innovative and trailblazing initiatives which took place in the mid-1990s, initiatives which indeed were seen as something of a beacon for other parts in the UK in the early days of Blair's premiership.[11] Certainly the participation in 1996 of Powys County Council (the largest unitary authority in Wales) along with the Development Board for Rural Wales and the University of Wales, Aberystwyth in the EC-wide TIERRAS project (Telematics Applications Programme) augured well in terms of the relevant regional authorities' commitment 'to supporting telematics services as part of their overall social and economic development strategies'.[12] Not surprisingly the context and constraints facing all four participants in TIERRAS (namely authorities representing the regions of Midi-Pyrenées, Emilia-Romagna and Illes Balears as well as rural Wales) led to a variety of pioneering initiatives. In the case of rural Wales 'an emphasis was put on plans to expand the network (linking three rural counties) and the number and quality of access points'.[13]

In 2001 Telecentres Powys (perhaps the most successful enterprise in Wales to come out of the TIERRAS project) was able to boast that Powys had 30 public ICT facilities with 120 volunteers to service the network.[14] In addition Telecentres Powys 'had created 8 jobs, assisted over 330 community businesses and 290 community groups and trained over 500 people in previous 18 months'.[15] Moreover its aims were significant and overarching, namely:

> To address the issues of social inclusion in an era of increasing technology.
> To address issues of access to technology in remote areas for the purposes of training and awareness of technology.
> To provide access to technology for rural businesses and community groups.
> To provide technical and strategic support to community ICT facilities in rural Powys.
> To access funding on behalf of community organisations.
> To be a catalyst in the development of economic activity in the field of ICT in Rural Powys.
> To act as the 'ICT glue' in a wide [range of] community initiatives.[16]

However, in the Final Evaluation Report of the TIERRAS project (1998) a warning note is sounded about the sustainability of the project despite the way in which the latter 'gained enormously from extensive partnerships'.[17] In particular 'the absence of a clear lead strategic partner often threatened the momentum of telematics related initiatives'.[18] Such scepticism about the future is summarised in these terms: 'it remains to be seen whether the RandD work under TIERRAS and the infrastructure investments under the ERDF [European Rural Development Fund] will have sufficient programmatic momentum to ensure sustainable innovative applications in areas such as education, business support, labour market information and so on [original text corrected]'.[19]

The reference to 'infrastructure investments' is the critical one because it is precisely in this particular area that momentum has been lost in recent years, especially in second half of the last quinquennium. Currently only one non-coastal population centre in mid-Wales, Newtown, is actually able to benefit from ADSL broadband. In the third week of September 2003 the situation was as follows[20]:

Exchange Name:	Brecon
Last Update:	Tuesday, September 23, 2003
Trigger Point:	350
Registrations:	174 (49%)
Predicted Trigger Date:	February, 2004
Exchange Name:	Llandrindod Wells
Last Update:	Wednesday, September 24, 2003
Trigger Point:	350
Registrations:	148 (42%)
Predicted Trigger Date:	May, 2004
Exchange Name:	Hay-on-Wye
Last Update:	Wednesday, September 24, 2003
Trigger Point:	Not Set
Registrations:	96
Exchange Name:	Presteigne
Last Update:	Friday, September 19, 2003
Trigger Point:	Not Set
Registrations:	53
Exchange Name:	Knighton
Last Update:	Wednesday, September 24, 2003
Trigger Point:	Not Set
Registrations:	49
Exchange Name:	Builth Wells
Last Update:	Thursday, September 18, 2003
Trigger Point:	Not Set
Registrations:	48

Table 21.1 Distribution of broadband access in mid-Wales 2003

None of these population centres can be described as areas of extreme rurality though obviously they represent and service surrounding areas which may be accurately described in such terms. As can be seen from the above table, only two of the communities identified are seriously on the way to getting broadband; the remainder have as yet been assigned 'trigger points'. Perhaps there is more irony here than tragedy. Brecon may host a vibrant arts scene including an International Jazz Festival, Llandrindod Wells may be 'the venue of choice' for all-Wales local government groups and voluntary organisations, Hay-on-Wye may boast the greatest number of bookshops in the world and a global festival which, in Bill Clinton's colourful phrase, is nothing less than 'the Woodstock of the mind', Presteigne may accommodate a first rate Festival of Music and the Arts described by critic Roderic Dunnett of The Independent as having 'the pulse on contemporary music', Builth Wells may offer a permanent home for the Royal Welsh Show and Knighton and Rhayader promote the respective splendours of Offa's Dyke and the Elan Valley, yet because all their permanent populations are relatively small and their industrial and commercial activities dispersed and limited when set against the wider backcloth of agriculture and tourism, none of them are enjoying, as yet, the benefits of high speed internet connectivity. Indeed some may have to wait for a very long time, if not perhaps indefinitely as some extreme pessimists have suggested.

There are in fact a whole range of complications and confusions here. For example registrations for ADSL broadband almost certainly do not accurately reflect the intrinsic level of interest in high-speed internet connectivity but rather the general level of awareness about its potential benefits and its likely availability. BT's enthusiasm for local campaigns (usually spearheaded by a small number of 'enthusiasts') to stimulate demand through registrations of interest is at best inefficient and at worst a means of thwarting excessive demand in order to limit commercial risk or unfair competitive advantage. Clearly many more people are interested in broadband across the UK (and are willing to pay for it at the commonly advertised ADSL rates) than those who formally take steps to register an interest. Anecdotal evidence suggests that such interest may indeed be substantially greater in rural rather than urban/suburban areas because of the perceived benefits. However campaigns for promoting the registration of interest are less easily mounted and sustained in areas with small and dispersed populations. In addition such campaigns are also not helped by the apparent lack of transparency with which BT determines the setting of 'trigger points' (i.e. number of registrations of interest within an exchange area) which can justify commercially the upgrading of local exchanges. In the third week of September 2003, a dozen exchanges in the UK had not been assigned a trigger point even though 250+ people had registered an interest and in one instance the number actually exceeded 500.[21]

Substantial parts of mid-Wales, however, actually lie beyond the reach of conventional ADSL or cable technologies. Two alternatives are satellite and wireless. However, each of them requires substantial capital investment. In 2002 the Welsh Development Agency introduced a Satellite Broadband Subsidy Scheme, as part of the Broadband Wales programme, for SMEs located in areas where no alternative connection to broadband was available.

However the level of assistance for successful applications is limited to 50% of total cost (not exceeding £1,500) for one year only. In the case of wireless, current developments in mid Wales build on the Llwybr*Pathway initiative in

1997 to establish a Multi Agency Rural Area Network (MARAN). In December 1999 Powys, Carmarthen and Ceredigion County Councils, as partners of the Llwybr*Pathway, forged a five-year partnership with MLL Telecom Ltd to develop a managed wireless network with a view to overcoming the problems traditionally associated with developing cost-effective bandwidth to rural areas. However, despite goodwill and enthusiasm there has been in many respects a significant disjunction between the vision behind MARAN and its practical, ongoing implementations. Neither the commercial interests of telcos and associated companies nor the wider and inevitably constrained budgetary concerns of local authorities are specifically designed to serve local communities, let alone small enterprises or individuals, impartially or indeed particularly well. According to Mark Shucksmith:

Rural areas and people subject to restructuring need strong support from national government and the EU, as well as from regional agencies and the private sector. But formal, 'top-down' programmes alone are insufficient: policies must be formulated, implemented and managed to facilitate local people to use their own creativity and talents. Too often, external agendas, formal requirements for partnership working, competitive bidding regimes, short-term funding and existing power structures limit the effectiveness of regeneration initiatives.[22]

More specifically those with the greatest technical knowledge about developing ITC infrastructure for the wider region are not necessarily at, or perhaps even near, the driving wheel of those directorates tasked with stimulating economic and community regeneration. In addition senior executive officers often lack confidence in this area either through inexperience or relative indifference to the technical issues involved. Finally fundamental policy decisions are often not scrutinised with sufficient rigour by council members because they, too, frequently lack genuine and sustained experience in what is often relatively novel territory.

The 'invisibility' of poverty in rural areas has often been commented upon. However while this may still be true 'phenomenologically', it is nevertheless becoming somewhat easier to assess its scale and depth empirically. 'Rural Deprivation in Powys'[23] and Powys County Council's complementary 'Poverty in Paradise – a Profile of Powys,'[24] for example, examined a wide range of relevant data and were able to demonstrate that both average wages and incomes in the County were very low relative to the rest of the UK which, in turn, directly reflected the high rates of seasonal and part-time employment as well as self-employment. In addition they also investigated 'the higher costs of living in Powys following from its geography, settlement patterns and sparsity of population,'[25] 'the vulnerability to poverty of certain groups'[26] and 'some of the circumstances associated with poverty in Powys such as ill-health and poor housing.'[27] To such a catalogue of deprivation and disadvantage must now be added as a matter of considerable concern and urgency the widespread unavailability of broadband in the region.

According to a Local Futures Group report for IBM in 2002:

> Rural areas present particular challenges to public sector policymakers in the UK at the moment. The triple blows of BSE, foot and mouth and the downturn in

> tourism has exacerbated other, more long term decline in primary industries and heightened the need to create a more diversified and high value economy in the countryside. Given the problems of thin demand and dispersed markets – broadband solutions will almost certainly have to be publicly led, at least in part and in many areas of the UK, wireless initiatives such as those pioneered in Powys, mid-Wales, will form part of the picture. Given the centrality of public sector institution in the economic life of the countryside, it is to be hoped that mobile information and communications – from transport information and flood alerts to the state of footpaths – forms part of the e-governance agenda of more and more local authorities in the near future. This will of course have to be matched by high quality infrastructures of skill and business support and by a commitment to both experimentation and evaluation of ICT initiatives. But the parlous sate of many of our rural areas and the need for a step change in their economic performance suggest that the time for radical experiments is now.[28]

However, it may be asserted with a reasonable measure of confidence that the future of broadband in rural areas does not ultimately depend on radical experiments per se, but in the political will to find sufficient levels of investment to establish basic levels ICT infrastructure developed through a variety of partnerships and emergent technologies across the UK. One suspects that such a political will only be galvanised when issues of social exclusion/inclusion are systematically viewed from the perspective of telematics as much as from more traditional ones. Indeed the future mapping of social exclusion/inclusion needs to become in this respect far more sophisticated. At the moment the current Welsh Index of Multiple Deprivation is based on six measurable but weighted 'domains of deprivation', namely: Income 25%, Employment 25%, Health 15%, Education 15%, Housing 10% and Geographic Access to Services 10%. Two further domains have been proposed for inclusion in the Index – Crime and Physical Environment – but so far these have not been incorporated apparently due to 'insufficiency of data'. Future reviews of theoretical reliability and validity of the Index need to address again the omission of Crime and Physical Environment but a third domain also needs to be added which might be headed as 'Telematics/Connectivity'.

Those who are insistent that the roll-out of broadband must ultimately be governed by commercial interests consistent with a fundamentally 'free market' approach (notwithstanding all the encouraging and encouraged rhetoric about partnerships and innovative schemes) need to demonstrate how in practice such a philosophy can actually address root problems of social exclusion, not least those that manifest themselves peculiarly in rural areas. The burden of proof, in this respect, lies with BT, Oftel and ultimately with national government itself. At the moment there is growing body of evidence to suggest that current 'policy' is actually compounding the existing factors of social exclusion in low wage/income economies. Why should rural communities which already suffer from pitiful road and rail 'connectivity' and poor access to health, educational and criminal justice resources[29] also be deprived from a major resource in terms of developing a lively knowledge economy to supplement agriculture and tourism, both of which are themselves undergoing substantial change and restructuring? The rate of roll-out of broadband is critical here. SMEs (including farms) and self-employed professionals (architects, lawyers, doctors, teachers etc.) are beginning to discover that they simply do not have the degree of connectivity to work or compete effectively with other parts of the UK let alone elsewhere in the world. In short this is not about the near-instant display of content-rich web pages or downloading rap videos 'in a trice'. At stake, rather, are people's continuing livelihoods and the way in which local communities can stay alive, even 'against the odds'. Indeed it might be reasonably argued that the slow and erratic roll-out of broadband in the UK has probably already introduced historic distortions in the UK economy between different regions and areas. These are likely to intensify unless there is a major reassessment and shift in 'policy'.

Only when individuals and groups can communicate effectively with each other can they properly exploit their own creativity and talents and develop at the same time, whether consciously or not, more hospitable and sustainable forms of polis. In the third millennium digital literacy cannot be merely an optional extra for those who wish to participate fully in civil society, nor can the imperative for governments to ensure high-speed connectivity for all their tax-paying citizens be shirked; the normal passport to genuine empowerment and democratic action lies, as many already know, not just in the efficient exchange of information but also informed and critically tested opinion. 'Only connect' – but sometimes it seems as if it is politicians and policy makers rather than the electorate who are searching for the plugs and sockets!

Notes

1 AOL Conference on Social Inclusion in the E-Society, European Parliament, 29 May 2001.
2 According to a news bulletin by BT in September 2003, this development will increase 'the proportion of people who can receive broadband in enabled areas from approximately 94 per cent to 97 per cent'.
3 *Op. cit.*, 1.2.
4 *Ibid.*, 2.1.
5 *Ibid.*, 3.23.
6 Haring, Jeffrey H. Rohlfs & Harry M. Shoostan, *Propelling the Broadband Bandwagon*, Strategic Policy Research, April 2002.
7 *Ibid.*, p. 62f.
8 *Ibid*, p. 109, n 182.
9 *Ibid.*, Executive Summary, p. 2.
10 'Information Communication Technology (ICT) and Rural Inclusion', Research Notes, CRN 52, Countryside Agency, December 2002.
11 In December 1999 five local authorities – Powys County Council, Suffolk County Council, Three Rivers District Council, Bristol City Council, and Hampshire County Council – were invited to meet the Prime Minister at the opening of the refurbished Local Government House (formerly Transport House) in London to demonstrate how new technology could improve service delivery and involve citizens more effectively in decision-making.
12 TIERRAS Deliverable 6.2 – Final Evaluation Report, p. 4.
13 *Ibid.*, p. 8.

[14] Powys County Council website *Empowering people through information technology – Telecentres Powys* (uploaded/updated June 2001).

[15] *Ibid.*

[16] *Ibid.*

[17] *Op. cit.*, p. 9.

[18] *Ibid.*

[19] *Ibid.*

[20] Data provided by BT via ADSLGuide (www.adslguide.org.uk).

[21] G. Wearden, *ZDNet UK*, September 23, 2003.

[22] 'Social Exclusion and Change in Rural Britain' (Powys Conference 'Poverty and Social Exclusion: A Rural Issue', 5 Oct 2001), p. 11.

[23] *Rural Deprivation in Powys*, School for Policy Studies, University of Bristol, December 1997.

[24] *Poverty in paradise: a profile of Powys*, Powys County Council, 1997.

[25] *Ibid.*

[26] *Ibid.*

[27] *Ibid.*

[28] *Op. cit.*, extract in *Sector Report: Broadband Britain* (netimperative, October 2002), p. 18.

[29] According to the 2001 Powys Draft Objective 2 and Transitional Local Action Plan, 'Because Powys shares much of its eastern boundary with Shropshire and Herefordshire, there is a perception that the county is reasonably close to major markets for goods and services. This is illusory. Powys has no motorways, no mainline rail services and no scheduled air services. Much of the road network is below modern standards in terms of widths and/or alignments. Regular public transport services are few and far between…In the north west, the county extends almost to the west coast of Wales, near Machynlleth, from where a journey to London typically takes between 4¼ and 5¼ hours by train, depending on departure time. By way of comparison, it takes 3 hours by train from Newcastle upon Tyne to London and 4-4½ hours from Edinburgh to London…Because of the county's rurality and sparsity of settlement, accessibility to basic services is generally difficult and involves lengthy journeys, usually without public transport. There is no General Hospital and 40 mile journeys by ambulance are commonplace. There is no Higher Education establishment in Powys. Over half of the adult population lives more than 5 miles from a Job Centre. The 'accessibility' indicator in the Welsh Index of Multiple Deprivation (2000) showed that 85% of wards in Powys rank in the lower 50% of all wards in Wales when it comes to access to basic services and that 50% of Powys wards are amongst the worst off (i.e. in the lowest 15% of all wards in Wales).'

Postscript

This article was written in September 2003 and first published on the CCELS website in October. Since January 2004, the author has been collaborating with the Cardiff Centre for the Business Relationships, Accountability, Sustainability and Society (BRASS) on the OSKaR Project 'Access to the Knowledge Economy: Overcoming the Digital Divide in Wales'. More recently he has been appointed as Honorary Research Fellow in Ethics and ICT at Cardiff University.

In September 2003, Michael Eaton took up his position as Director of the Broadband Wales Unit. The current projection is that by the end of 2004 over 80% of Wales will have access to ADSL broadband. In April 2004, BT announced that it would roll out a further 135 ADSL converted exchanges by the summer of 2005 so that broadband will be available to approximately 95.5% of Welsh households within a year. At the end of May 2004, the telephone exchanges of Brecon, Hay on Wye and Llandrindod Wells had been activated, Builth Wells was 'Ready for Service' in September 2004 and Knighton and Presteigne had reached 85% and 42% respectively of their appointed trigger levels.

In December 2003, the World Summit on the Information Society (WSIS) took place in Geneva. Unfortunately the event was poorly reported in the UK press. The adopted *Declaration of Principles* clearly recognises the part that high speed connectivity can play in overcoming the Digital Divide: 'A well-developed information and communication network infrastructure and applications, adapted to regional, national and local conditions, easily-accessible and affordable, and making greater use of broadband and other innovative technologies where possible, can accelerate the social and economic progress of countries, and the well-being of all individuals, communities and peoples. Policies that create a favourable climate for stability, predictability and fair competition at all levels should be developed and implemented in a manner that not only attracts more private investment for ICT infrastructure development but also enables universal service obligations to be met in areas where traditional market conditions fail to work.''

The responsibilities of Oftel were incorporated into Ofcom in January 2004. Although there has been significant progress in the rollout of broadband in Wales during the past nine months, the author remains uneasy about the fact that telecommunications policy in the UK, not least in terms of the current regulatory framework governing broadband, has so far failed to attract extensive and mature political debate. The signal failure to view high speed connectivity as an *essential utility,* rather than as a desirable but ultimately demand-led asset, has structural and strategic implications for economic regeneration and social inclusion; this is true not only for isolated rural communities, but also for the United Kingdom considered as a whole.

PART III
HUMAN RIGHTS

Chapter 22

Human Rights – What Hope? Human Dignity – What Scope?

Roger Brownsword

Introduction

The Enlightenment view that "rational individuals would build a reasonable society thanks to the resources created by science and technology" - and, concomitantly, the belief in "progress", in the sense of a "parallelism between scientific and technological achievements on the one hand, and abundance, freedom and happiness on the other" - no longer goes unchallenged.[1] Appeals to "progress" are no longer taken on trust. In place of a willing embrace, proponents of new technologies must overcome scepticism and ambivalence.[2]

Yet, at the turn of the twenty-first century, even sceptics might have found reason to celebrate the progressive tendencies of science and technology. For, the future looked hi-tech; and the future looked bright. Many of the Millennium people were already experiencing the benefits of life in the information society; the sequencing of the human genome was more or less complete; and, for tomorrow's people, a raft of new technologies promised significant improvement to the quality of life - for example, nanotechnology with its promise of smaller and smarter solutions, pharmacogenomics with its promise of tailored drugs, robotics with its promise of tireless performance of tiresome tasks, and so on.[3]

Even at its most progressive, though, technology is capable of both use and abuse. Thus, opening an international Round Table of Ministers of Science in October 2001, the Director-General of UNESCO, Koïchiro Matsuura, spoke of the group's firm commitment to international solidarity in scientific progress, and to safeguarding human rights and human dignity from the misuse of science and technology, particularly in the life sciences.[4]

This has now been said and repeated so many times that I take it as axiomatic that bioscience and biotechnology should be regulated in such a way that human rights and human dignity are fully respected.[5] In this light, this paper asks two questions: first, whether recognised international commitments to human rights are likely to be fulfilled in practice; and, secondly, whether there is any conceptual space for human dignity (which is another way of asking how we understand the relationship between human rights and human dignity). Or, in principle, are human rights and human dignity independent constraints, each setting its own limits for the legitimate pursuit of science and technology; and, in practice, what prospect is there of such constraints (however understood) being respected?

The paper is in three parts. In the first part, in response to the first question, it is suggested that, in a global and globalising context, there are plenty of reasons to be concerned about the prospects for human rights. Quite apart from the high profile human rights violations associated with the global war on terror, and the various "emergencies", political as well as economic, that invite a pragmatic (temporary) displacement of human rights, there are threats of a much more routine (and less visible) nature. In particular, with the growth of functionally specialised agencies, there is a tendency towards "collateralism" – that is, a culture that, in practice, treats human rights as secondary considerations; there is the tendency to allow scientifically constructed risk-profiles to set the terms for debates concerning the safety and acceptability of particular technologies; and there is a tendency in some places towards "incrementalism" on the part of regulators – that is, a regulatory culture that favours (a) a permissive default position once safety concerns have been addressed and (b) moving forward from the initial permissive position. As for the development of global markets, while they present more options and an expansion of consumer autonomy, this is not an unqualified good if it means that local regulation, sensitive to human rights, can be by-passed or, indeed, subverted.

In the second part, responding to the second question, it is suggested that, where human dignity is viewed as the underpinning for human rights (articulating the triple demand that the capacity for human choice be respected, that the choices so made be respected, and that the conditions and context for meaningful exercise of human choice be promoted and preserved), then human rights and human dignity prosper or perish together. By contrast, where human dignity is deployed in the way that we find it in the so-called dignitarian alliance,[6] then the governing value that human dignity must not be compromised represents an ethic *in opposition* to human rights. It follows that we have an offer from the dignitarian alliance that will give human dignity its own distinct conceptual space. However, if we take up this offer, we will add to the challenges to which the cause of human rights is already exposed.

In the third and final part of the paper, it is submitted that, if we are to improve the prospects of human rights, they need all the help that human dignity can give. The underlying support of human dignity (its triple demand) needs to be more effectively articulated. However, such an articulation not only bears on the actions of regulators (and, in turn, those whose actions are regulated for the better fulfilment of human rights), it has important, but not obvious or easy, implications for the sustainability of the kind of context that is presupposed by the vision of a flourishing community of rights – that is, a context which encourages members to develop their own sense of identity as well as their sense of being authors of their own destinies. If the technological sophistication that envelops tomorrow's people undermines this sense of identity, self-governance, and responsibility, the inadvertent damage to human dignity will be as serious as any damage that could be done to the cause of human rights and human dignity by the intentional or reckless disregard for such constraints.

What Hope for Human Rights?

The paper commitments of the international community suggest a widespread consensus in support of human rights. With the best part of 150 states now party to the Covenant on Civil and Political Rights and its twin Covenant on Economic and Social Rights, this is an encouraging start. To say that the international community is constituted by acceptance of an international bill of rights has some credence. Moreover, in Europe, there is a developed jurisprudence of human rights giving the constitutive general principles a regional interpretation.

Of course, as Christian Tomuschat argues in his recent book, *Human Rights: Between Idealism and Realism*,[7] it takes more than paper commitments and more than mechanisms of enforcement and adjudication to create a genuine culture of human rights. As he concludes:

> Human rights must permeate the whole texture of a given society, and human beings must understand that they must claim and uphold their rights, on the one hand, and that they must also be prepared to recognize the rights and entitlements of their fellow citizens. Governmental authority is a powerful instrument for the enforcement of collective decisions, adopted in the name of the nation, but it does not constitute a panacea for the creation of a state of affairs where all human rights are fully secured to everyone.[8]

Accordingly, when the Director-General of UNESCO proclaims the group's commitment to respect for human rights, when he insists that we should not be blinded by the science, this is by no means a lone voice. Rather, it echoes the international consensus that human rights are to be taken seriously.

In practice, the human rights record of the international community leaves a lot to be desired. Writing (pre 9/11) in the Millennium year, Anne-Marie Slaughter aptly remarked that "[t]he compression of distance and the dissolution of borders that drives globalization has proved far more efficient at producing global markets than global justice."[9] Nevertheless, she, too, saw encouraging signs in the willingness of national judges to learn from the human rights expertise available worldwide. Post 9/11, however, with the global war on terrorism throwing up one human rights atrocity after another, we might surmise that we are more practised at preaching than at practising what we preach.

So, what hope is there for human rights? This is such a large question that it is difficult to know where to begin, let alone where to end. Is this a question about human rights in general or some in particular (namely, those most likely to be violated by the abuse of biotechnology – and, if so, which human rights are these?). Are we posing this question in relation to the world as a whole or only some parts of it (namely, those parts where biotechnology has its greatest impact)? And, what is the time-frame for this question? Clearly, there is too much here for one section of a short article. Let me, therefore, point to some of the threads that would have to be pulled together to offer any kind of textured answer to a question that focused on the prospects of human rights in relation to new technology in general and biotechnology in particular.

The Global War on Terror

It is the global war on terror that most urgently prompts the thought that the game is up for human rights. In this context, it is fairly easy to write a gloomy prognosis for political and civil human rights. The script runs something like this. On the one side, terrorism is defined by its insouciance towards innocent life and human rights; whether terrorism strikes in Madrid or Manhattan, respect for human rights is simply not part of the credo. On this side, if the knowledge and power that comes with modern bioscience and biotechnology can be applied in ways that aid the "cause", it will be so applied regardless of how this impacts on human rights and human dignity. Hence, the nervousness in the West about the possibility that biological weapons might fall into the "wrong" hands (if, indeed, there are any right hands for such weapons). On the other side, the proponents of human rights seem to be incapable of prosecuting their own "cause" without violating their own publicly declared commitments to respect for human rights and human dignity. On this side, if resources made available by modern biotechnology were seen as an effective and "necessary" response to acts of terror, how confident could we be that they would be deployed with full regard to their impact on human rights and human dignity? At the lower end of the scale, this reservation might reflect a concern for privacy and confidentiality (for example, where intelligence agencies rely on biometric databases)[10] running up through more serious concerns about the deprivation of liberty and, ultimately, the protection of innocent human life.

Arguably, the damage being done to human rights by this global war is not limited to those nation states that are engaged on the front lines. For, as a number of commentators have remarked, the cause of human rights is not assisted when those who most loudly proclaim its virtues see fit to opt out, overtly or covertly, when the circumstances are perceived as so demanding. Thus, as Helena Kennedy has recently written:

> The nature of a government's response to terrorism within its borders will depend on the type of violence, its history and roots, its seriousness, the extent to which it has community support and the effect on the international community's respect for human rights. Sensitive political judgements have to be made. The way in which mature legal systems deal with subversion or attack has global implications: toleration of infringements of civil liberties gives poor signals to those nations which are struggling to establish democracies. It also gives succour to tyrants who have little interest in the rule of law or the pursuit of justice.[11]

In this light, and specifically with reference to the detention policies adopted on both sides of the Atlantic post 9/11, those who allege that "the example being set by the US and the UK is being used to legitimise repression internationally on an ever-increasing scale"[12] would seem to have a point.[13]

Taking a longer view, however, we might set to one side the war on terror and its negative consequences for human rights and human dignity. Granted, this is a very large deficit to set to one side. Nevertheless, let us suppose that we treat this episode as an exceptional case, if only for the sake of argument, what then?

Crisis Management

It would be unrealistic, surely, to imagine that the global war on terror will generate the final, or the only kind of, emergency or crisis. This will hardly be the last security crisis; and nor is security the only kind of emergency – for example, in countries as far apart as Australia and Argentina, there have been recent emergencies concerning, in the former case, immigrants and asylum seekers and, in the latter, the economy and the value of the currency.[14] In both cases, and characteristically where there is an "emergency", human rights are displaced. Sometimes, displacement will be a matter of great reluctance; at other times, it will be opportunistic (the emergency serving as a pretext); sometimes it will be self-generated; at other times, it will be brought about by external pressure (such as the conditionalities imposed by the IMF in relation to Argentina).[15]

Again, though, emergencies are, by definition (and the narrower we keep the definition the better), exceptional. Perhaps, we must accept that the international commitment to human rights needs some slack, some margin of appreciation, to accommodate the exceptional cases. If so, the better indicators for the prospects of human rights, at any rate in the longer run, are those features of regular and routine global practice. When business is more or less as normal, what do we find?

Collateralism

If it is just a fact of life that there will be inevitably bumpy periods for human rights, we can detect more of a standing problem arising from a tendency towards what Sheldon Leader has termed "collateralism".[16] This concerns and characterises a more subtle displacement in the work of the burgeoning international agencies (particularly those agencies whose function is to promote trade or commerce). Collateralism captures a culture that tends towards specialised institutional interests being given a disproportionate weight where decisions calling for a balancing of considerations fall to be made. This is not to say that human rights are not taken seriously by such institutions – far from it, some rights might even be treated as having fundamental importance. However, the effect of policy informed by the collateralist mind-set is that adjustments and balances tend to favour those values (or values expressed as rights) that run with the grain of the institutional goals. What makes this process so insidious is that, from the agency's perspective, it is perfectly natural to be guided by precisely those considerations that give the body its specialised governance function and its distinctive identity.

If we wanted an illustrative example in the field of the biosciences, the view of the patent community in Europe would be almost a textbook example of collateralism. For that community, which is centred on the European Patent Office, even though a morality clause is explicitly written into its regulatory framework,[17] it is the granting of patents that defines its function. Accordingly, we see the concern with human rights marginalized in cases like Relaxin;[18] and then altogether excluded by the ECJ in the Netherlands challenge to the legality of the patent Directive.[19]

The import of collateralism for the activities of any person or body that is dedicated to scientific progress is obvious. Even where respect for human rights and human dignity is accepted as a legitimate consideration, it is not the dominant or driving consideration. It does not define risk and it does not determine responsibility. The birth of bioethics testifies to the failure of science to respect the limits set by human rights and human dignity (indeed, to the egregious failure of science to observe these constraints); but, even with ethical review incorporated into scientific thinking, collateralism signifies that such limits are never secure. Collateralism warns us, in Tomuschat's terms, that we are not yet dealing with a genuine culture of human rights.

Risk-Profiles

Regulators need to tailor their interventions to the perceived risk-profile presented by a particular technology. Is the relevant risk that the technology might go wrong or that it might be abused; or does the risk only really materialise if the technology works? Are we talking about low risk or high risk? In principle, the elaboration of a risk-profile for a particular technology should draw on the following considerations:

- the *kind* of harm (physical, environmental, social, economic, moral, political, and so on) to which the risk pertains;[20]

- the *severity and scale* of the harm if the risk eventuates; and

- the *probability* of the risk materialising.[21]

In practice, the judgments that we make depend on which of these considerations we take into account, how much weight we give to them, and which considerations we emphasise. So, for example, Martin Bauer is able to say that "technically", nuclear technology is low-risk,[22] meaning that "[n]uclear power is characterized by high damage potential with relatively low probability."[23] As for biotechnology, Bauer claims that the risks "are still largely unknown"[24] – which, no doubt, is correct in relation to some kinds of harm; but, for those who oppose the technology on moral or religious grounds, the risks are already perfectly clear.

The efforts of UNESCO notwithstanding, there is a tendency to see risk in terms of physical and environmental safety only, to characterise the risk as low (rather than high) by reference to the probability, and to reverse the precautionary principle for the purposes of expressing the bottom-line safety judgment. Once the technology has been pronounced safe, the weight of "expert" scientific opinion makes it difficult for dissenting voices to be heard and arguments concerning the protection of human rights are immediately collateralised.

Incrementalism

Closely related to collateralism, we find a tendency towards incrementalism in some regulatory thinking. By this, I mean that, where the default position is permissive unless there is a real concern about safety (which goes back to the question about the risk-profile), then each time a new (permissive) regulatory step is mooted, the baseline is given by existing regulation and its acceptance. Regulators do not go one step forward and two steps back; they only go forward (with the science). So, for example, when the House of Lords Select Committee on Stem Cell Research[25] was confronted with objections to the very idea of the use of human embryos for research, it was not prepared to go behind the baseline position in which it is accepted that, where necessary, human embryos may be used for research.[26] Even in the work of the specialist Nuffield Council on Bioethics, we might detect some traces of incrementalism[27] – and, if policy recommendations are to be taken seriously, this is perhaps understandable: famously, the political world does not like to engage reverse gear. It follows that incrementalism not only militates against turning back, with each new step there is incremental support for the next step to be taken.

If we put together collateralism and incrementalism, we can see that the international bioethical axiom, with which we started, offers little resistance to the push that comes from the biosciences. For, if human rights and human dignity are treated as collateral considerations, the constraints will be minimal; the science and technology will proceed; as it proceeds, the baseline will shift in its favour and incrementalism will hold it in place. It is like watching a tower block erected one level at a time, each level secured, and with no more than marginal delay or intervention for safety checking or concerns about human rights.

Global Markets

The fate of human rights (or, at any rate, some human rights) might, however, be judged rather differently. The story here is a more upbeat one, suggesting that the development of global markets with an emphasis on consumerism and choice will facilitate access to bioproducts and services that humans are entitled to have as a matter of right. Benighted regimes will no longer be able to deny their citizens the freedom to take advantage of the world's technological advances; global markets will help deliver affordable medicines to the Third World; and new technologies will make it possible to overcome disease, squalor, and starvation in the poorest countries.

From a regulatory perspective, the difference between global markets and local markets can be put in the following way. In a one-jurisdiction local economy, regulators will determine whether a particular kind of trade or business is lawful. If it is lawful we have, so to speak, a white market; if it is unlawful, there might or might not be a black market existing outside the law. However, when the setting changes to that of two jurisdictions, suppliers in one jurisdiction and purchasers in another, there is the further possibility of a grey market – that is, the particular kind of trade or business is lawful in one jurisdiction but unlawful in the other. Obviously, the impact of grey markets is particularly significant because, other things being equal, we can expect suppliers to supply from jurisdictions where their activities are lawful and purchasers, who can only procure (if at all) in a black market locally, to look to such grey market providers. Resolute individuals, asserting their rights to reproductive autonomy or to family life, or to some version of privacy, have already beaten this path – Diane Blood[28] and, currently, the Hashmis[29] and the Whitakers[30] spring to mind – and the HFEA anticipates that its proposed restriction on access to sex selection services will elicit similar stories.[31] Whether or not the efforts of such grey market players is viewed as a good or bad thing for human rights involves some quite complex judgments about the rights that they are asserting and the impact of their actions on the rights of third parties. However, whatever the merits, these are again fairly unusual cases and we might learn more from the routine rather than the exceptional.[32]

Such a (routine) case is that of insurance. For tomorrow's people, there is likely to be a much higher level of awareness of one's own genetic make-up. It will not be a case of being aware that there is a family history of a particular disorder, one will know whether or not one has the relevant gene(s) for that disorder as well as for other disorders. In other words, tomorrow's people will routinely know whether or not they are high-risk persons for particular insurance purposes. Anticipating this development, and with a view to protecting high-risk parties, in some jurisdictions, regulators have already prohibited insurers from requiring applicants to undergo genetic tests or to make use of genetic information. In other jurisdictions, regulators have not so reacted. And, in the result, we have a grey market (similarly for employment). What is likely to happen? In *Genes and Insurance*,[33] Marcus Radetzki, Marian Radetzki and Niklas Juth argue that those regulatory regimes that have taken a protective approach are unlikely to have their intended effect of shielding those whose genetic make-up would otherwise disadvantage them in the insurance market. Indeed, it is contended that the consequences of adopting such an approach might lead to the destabilisation of the pool through the process of "adverse selection" culminating in its collapse when it can no longer bear the weight of its high-risk burden. How so?

In the first instance, the attitudes of three key stakeholders seem to be critical. Those who are high-risk parties will normally wish to sustain the pool under its protective regulatory conditions (because it is to their economic advantage to do so); those who are low-risk will wish to revise the regulatory terms on which the pool operates so that premiums or contributions paid by individuals more faithfully reflect real risk profiles or, failing this, they will wish to exit the pool in order to join a pool with more favourable terms; and, depending upon a number of economic variables, the insurance companies might or might not prefer the pool to be run under protective terms or on terms that allow for premiums to be set on sophisticated differential terms. Given this, although there might be some occasional abuses of a protected scheme by those who know that they are high-risk, it seems to me that the major impulse for change (and the most likely source of destabilisation) will come from *low-risk* stakeholders who would prefer to participate in a pool where premiums are adjusted in line with disclosed risk profiles.[34]

However, whether or not low-risk stakeholders will actually leave the pool depends upon a number of variables about which we can be rather less certain. First, there is the question of how much genetic information we have and just how informative such information actually is in telling an insurer about the risk that an applicant represents if covered by a particular type of insurance. Let us assume that tomorrow's people know more than enough to give low-risk parties a reason to disclose. Secondly, for low-risk applicants to have access to insurance pools that are regulated in accordance with standard rules for disclosure there must of course be pools of this kind and applicants must be able to access them. For present purposes, we are assuming a grey market and, thus, the opportunity to access such pools. A third variable concerns the extent to which low-risk parties display inertia in sticking with their existing pools. Again, on our assumptions, even sluggish consumers of insurance are likely to be moved to transfer to another pool in order to cash in their low-risk advantages. Admittedly, there needs to be a degree of confidence about the prospects and security of the new pool; but, in ten to fifteen years' time, consumers should be perfectly comfortable with shopping around for insurance services that are distance-sold in electronic environments. Fourthly, there is the question of whether insurers who operate in protected schemes *and who have an interest in sustaining such schemes*, can either impose costs against exit that deter low-risk members from leaving or devise incentives for staying within the pool. For example, if there are significant premium discounts for insured parties who keep their policies, low-risk and high-risk, with a single insurer, the drift away from protectively regulated schemes might be arrested. Finally, other things being equal, short-term economic considerations encourage low-risk members to move out of protected schemes. However, if the longer-term effect of this drift away from such schemes is to jeopardise the viability of insurance clubs that serve high-risk members, then those persons who are both low-risk (for one type of insurance) and high-risk (for another) might see that their short-term calculation is in tension with their longer-term reliance on high-risk pools.

Having said this, it seems reasonable to assume that, other things being equal, low-risk members will take their business away from insurance pools that are subject to a regulatory regime that operates to their financial disadvantage. As a pool progressively becomes a club for high-risk members, premiums necessarily will rise – and, indeed, as insurers understand what is happening to the pool, they might well inflate premiums in anticipation of the higher risks that they now realise they are covering. With membership becoming more expensive, even high-risk insured parties might have to drop out; and, in due course, dwindling membership might threaten the viability of the scheme so that the few remaining members are treated as uninsurable.

Is this a positive or a negative for human rights? From the standpoint of those low-risk individuals who assert their economic freedom to buy insurance at a more attractive rate, this seems like a positive. However, if the effect of such actions is to shift the financial burden to the remaining higher-risk members of the pool, this is a negative *if the transfer of the burden infringes the human rights of the latter*. Again, this is a complex debate; but it is at least arguable that high-risk members should not be disabled through genetic circumstances beyond their control from having access to essential medical facilities and the like. For the regulators to restore a human rights compliant situation, they need to pursue some other kind of strategy (such as blocking off access to grey markets; or taxing the low-risk parties who access grey markets in order to subsidise the high-risk members; or making public provision for an average insurance package with a white market allowing for the purchase of additional cover).

This is a story that we could replicate for any number of products or services associated with modern biotechnology. In the short term, the gains for individual autonomy seem obvious. Whether or not human rights are longer term winners or losers is less clear. Plainly, there is a good deal of unfinished business here; and, even in this paper, it is a matter to which we will return.

Taking Stock

Human rights face three levels of challenge: first, from those who are openly opposed to such values; secondly, from governments that are willing to set aside their human rights commitments when confronted with the extra-ordinary and the exceptional; and, thirdly, from a range of very ordinary modes of decision-making (collateralism and its cognates) that either suppress or subordinate human rights considerations. In the longer run, there is little hope for human rights unless those who purport to be committed to such values really do believe in them.

What Scope for Human Dignity?

Will human dignity fare any better than human rights? If we answer this "It might" or, equally, "It might not", this presupposes that human dignity is distinguishable from human rights. However, if human dignity is viewed as the underpinning for human rights, it largely re-inforces the demands made in the name of human rights. Human rights and human dignity, so viewed, stand or fall together – ex hypothesi, human dignity can fare neither any better nor any worse than human rights. By contrast, if we adopt the position of the dignitarian alliance, then human dignity has its own ethical space *in opposition* to human rights, human dignity and human rights each has its own trajectory, and each will experience its independent highs and lows.

As is well-known, respect for human dignity goes to the very heart of the Universal Declaration of Human Rights, 1948, and its partner Covenants on Economic, Social and Cultural Rights, 1966, and on Civil and Political Rights, 1966. In these historic instruments, each Preamble provides that "recognition of the inherent dignity and of the equal and inalienable rights of all members of the human family is the foundation of freedom, justice and peace in the world"; and Article 1 of the Universal Declaration famously proclaims that "All human beings are born free and equal in dignity and rights." What this amounts to is the claim that each and every human being has inherent dignity; that it is this *inherent* dignity that grounds (or accounts for) the possession of *inalienable* human rights; and that, because all humans have dignity, they hold rights equally. So understood, the injunction to respect human dignity is much more than a demand that we commonly make in contexts where we detect demeaning or degrading treatment, or where we are trying to give weight to an interest in privacy, it is the infrastructure on which the entire superstructure of human rights is constructed.

Human dignity undergirding human rights makes a triple demand. First, there is the demand that one's capacity (as an agent) for making one's own free choices should be respected. Generally, this speaks against societies that are organised on paternalistic, authoritarian, or status-like lines. To be sure, there are difficult cases where it is unclear whether, say, a young person has the developed capacity (*Gillick*-competence, as it were) for self-determination; but, for the most part this is a clear demand.[35] Secondly, it follows that there should be respect for the choices that one so makes. When human rights theorists argue for, say, the right to "death with dignity", we should understand the claim not so much as the right to die but the right to choose death over life (or certain sorts of life support); it is the right to choose (whatever the choice) that matters. Finally, a third demand is that there should be respect for the context and conditions that are essential if one is to operate as a responsible source of free and informed choice, as a self-governing, self-directing agent. It follows that the context needs to be protected against the reduction of right but also the reduction of responsibility.

Against this conception of human dignity, we have the view developed by the dignitarian alliance. It shares the conceptual axiom that human dignity must not be compromised, but its particular conception is not rights-based and not as assertive of individual autonomy. It is an "alliance" because there is more than one pathway to this ethic – Kantian and communitarian as well as religious. So, for example, if we were to express the dignitarian perspective in communitarian terms, we would say that human dignity is a good which must not be compromised by our actions or practices and that any action or practice that compromises this good is unethical irrespective of welfare-maximising consequences (contrary to utilitarian pragmatism) and regardless of the informed consent of the participants (contrary to human rights thinking).

The influence of the dignitarian alliance can be seen both at home[36] and abroad, notably in regional and international accords such as the Convention on Human Rights and Biomedicine 1997, UNESCO's Universal Declaration on the Human Genome and Human Rights,[37] and the EC Directive on the Legal

Protection of Biotechnological Inventions.[38] Insofar as such declarations in favour of human dignity simply reinforce the demand that human rights should be respected, they say little that is new. However, as Deryck Beyleveld and I have suggested elsewhere,[39] it is in these most recent appeals to human dignity that we find the new turn in bioethics.

Somewhat confusingly, both the dignity-based human rights perspective and the perspective articulated by the dignitarian alliance can claim to be rooted in the writing of Immanuel Kant.[40] For, in Kant's work, we find not only the idea that humans have intrinsic dignity (albeit duty-driven rather than rights-driven)[41] but also that human dignity has no price and that humans owe themselves a duty of self-esteem. In these seminal remarks, modern writers find support for a variety of supposed applications of Kantian morality, including the claim that commercialisation of the human body is an affront to dignity (by putting a price on something that is beyond price). However, commodification of the human body – whether in the form of commerce in human organs or tissue, prostitution, surrogacy for profit, or patenting human genes – is just one of a number of practices that are regularly cited as instances of human dignity being compromised. Typically, the dignitarian alliance also condemns sex selection and positive (eugenic) gene selection, germ-line gene therapy, embryo research and abortion, euthanasia and assisted suicide, genetic discrimination, and (perhaps top of its current list) human reproductive cloning. The list, though, is hardly closed; and there surely will be additions as technology opens up new bio-options and opportunities.

One way of trying to disentangle the dignity-based view of human rights from the perspective of the dignitarian alliance is to fix on two different reference points for human dignity. One reference point is the idea that human dignity speaks to what is special or specific about humans, that is to say, what is intrinsically and universally distinctive about humans. This reference point is to be contrasted with the idea that human dignity speaks less to what is special about humans qua humans and more to what is special about a particular community's idea of civilised life and the concomitant commitments of its members.[42] Here, appeals to human dignity draw on what is distinctively valued concerning human social existence in a particular community – indeed, on the values and vision that distinguish the community as the particular community that it is and relative to which the community's members take their collective and individual identity. Whereas the former tends to be closely associated with the human rights perspective and the aim of giving individuals the opportunity to flourish as self-determining authors of their own destinies, the latter (as expressed by the dignitarian alliance) combines a (Kantian) view of what is distinctive about humans (their dignity) with views about what defines life as civilised (and, thus, respectful of human dignity) in a particular community.[43]

The dignitarian alliance, as we have said, has sought to turn back the biotechnological tide on several fronts, *inter alia* opposing the patenting of human gene sequences (or copies thereof),[44] the licensing of embryonic stem cell research,[45] and permitting tissue typing of embryos for the sake of saviour siblings.[46] In each case, the alliance rejects the pragmatic-utilitarian argument that the promotion of general benefit justifies biotechnologically-friendly regulation as it rejects the arguments made from the human rights perspective in which the primacy of autonomy and the justificatory significance of consent are relied on. For the alliance, the utilitarian pragmatists and the proponents of human rights are, quite simply, coming from the wrong place – the only place to come from is one in which it is understood (in just the way that the alliance understands it) that human dignity must not be compromised.

In the light of this analysis, it is easy to see how human dignity can be given scope. However, to give it scope, as a competing principle, is to diminish hope for human rights. Is there any way that we can maintain the hope of human rights while giving human dignity some scope?

Hope and Scope

It is submitted that, if we are to improve the prospects of human rights, they need all the help that human dignity can give. The triple demand of human dignity (that the capacity for human choice be respected, that the choices so made be respected, and that the conditions and context for meaningful exercise of human choice be promoted and preserved) needs to be more effectively articulated. However, such an articulation not only implies a level of restraint and respect on the part of regulators (understood broadly, as encompassing state, organised commerce, and the professions), it also implies that regulatees should be sensitive to the way in which their individual choices impact on the context. In other words, it is imperative that the human rights constituency re-discovers the significance of human dignity, not so much as giving straight line support for individual choice, but as concerning the context that is required before a community of rights can flourish.

In what ways might individual choice corrode the context that all agents need? We have seen already how, cumulatively, the choices made by rational economic individuals can destroy a viable insurance pool. And, a similar story about environmental pollution is too well-known to require rehearsal. However, the corrosion of the context that we are contemplating now cuts much deeper. We are talking about such "human" characteristics as a sense of personal identity, a sense of personal responsibility and, where things go well, a sense of personal achievement. And, this is the paradox – to assert our individual autonomy is to assert our own personality, to take responsibility for our actions, to be the authors of our own lives; and, yet, the suggestion is that by doing just these things, we might endanger the very context that gives meaning to our quest for autonomy. So, the function of human dignity in underpinning human rights is not just to prompt autonomous action but to draw out the conditions that make it possible to sustain an autonomous form of life.

The principle of restricting autonomy in order to prevent some indirect consequential damage to human rights is, as we have said, reasonably clearly understood (albeit controversial in application in particular cases, physician-assisted suicide being a textbook example).[47] For example, in the *Laserdrome* Decision,[48] the Federal Administrative Court in Germany was concerned that "playful killing" at the Laserdrome (a shooting arcade) tended to trivialise violence and might, thus, weaken respect for the well-being of other agents. Against this consideration, the fact that participation was voluntary and the consent of the players mutual was irrelevant.[49] Similarly, a legal regime might intervene to prevent cruelty to animals for fear that agents might otherwise become de-sensitised to the infliction of physical damage in a way that might then be copied across to transactions with fellow agents. Clearly, such slippery slope arguments need to be handled very carefully; any such proposal for restricting autonomy needs to be very carefully examined; and whatever restriction is imposed, it must be necessary and proportionate. So much is familiar. However, what we are now contemplating is something that cuts deeper. What precisely is it that the contextual dimension of human dignity alerts us to?

Attempting to tease out the strands of human dignity as a contextual phenomenon is not straightforward. Ronald Dworkin begins to get to grips with this idea when he rightly remarks that the "boundary between chance and choice is the spine of our ethics and our morality" and that "any serious shift in that boundary is seriously dislocating."[50] He continues:

> If we were to take seriously the possibility that we are now exploring – that scientists really have gained the capacity to create a human being having any phenotype that they or their prospective parents choose – then we could chart the destruction of settled moral and ethical attitudes starting at almost any point. We use the chance/choice distinction not simply in our assignments of responsibility for situations or events, for example, but in our assessments of pride, including pride in what nature has given us.[51]

Although Dworkin maintains that it would be a confusion to suppose that "even the most dramatic shifts in the chance/choice boundary somehow challenge morality itself",[52] he emphasises that it is in relation to the assignment of personal and collective responsibility that "the danger of moral insecurity seems greatest."[53] What this seems to imply is that, genetic engineering notwithstanding, we can continue to operate with morality (qua an act morality) that characterises certain acts, practices, or states of affairs as morally required, morally permissible, or morally prohibited; but the more that our genetic make-up is neither a matter of chance nor the product of *our own* choice, the less room that there is for agent morality (that is, for judgments holding a particular agent responsible for acting in immoral ways).

Trying to appreciate the significance of this contextual backdrop, neither over-stating it nor under-estimating its importance, is not easy. However, let me highlight three troubling and puzzling elements: first, a sense of personal identity (never an easy concept at the best of times); secondly, a sense of personal and collective responsibility; and, thirdly, a sense of respect for others.

First, there is personal identity, the sense that we each have of who we are. According to Susan Greenfield, the technologies of the Twenty-First Century will be all around us (quite literally), blurring the boundaries between our real and virtual selves, our real and virtual environment, ourselves and others, and at the same time enabling us to know a great deal more about ourselves (whoever we are). In this context, she says:

> The basic thesis of this book is that new technologies will have an all-powerful and unprecedented influence on our highly impressionable neuronal connections since, for the first time ever, they will be the sole source of all experience. The prospect becomes even more serious with the potential advent of invasive technologies, which could eventually drive and contrive the configurations of connections directly....
> ....By incessantly stimulating neuronal connections into certain highly constrained configurations, the new technologies might jeopardize the very existence of human nature, permanently.[54]

Paradoxically, then, as technology seems to put us ever more in control, it is technology that is taking control over us. Tomorrow's people might, thus, encounter double trouble, having difficulty in identifying who they are (because they have spent too much time in virtual surroundings) while, at the same time, losing control over what they might be.

Secondly, there is the matter of responsibility. For Jürgen Habermas,[55] like Bill McKibben,[56] it is genetic engineering (or, at any rate, genetic enhancement) that is the door to keep firmly shut. The point about genetic enhancement (or positive genetic engineering) is not that it might fundamentally alter the extent to which we have "free will" and the extent to which the predicates for human responsibility are met, but that it might affect our perception of such matters. To the extent that the idea of free will rests on a phenomenology of choice and responsibility, genetic modification could make a huge difference to the way in which we perceive ourselves, our "achievements", and our "failures". If we come to see our genetic make-up as a programme that runs us, it will be tempting to think (against free will and responsibility) that we could not have acted otherwise; and, where our particular genetic make-up has been specified by others, if there is any responsibility left in the world, it seems to be with the specifiers rather than ourselves.[57] In other words, genetic enhancement threatens to alter the context by either undermining notions of free will and responsibility or by inviting the transfer of responsibility.

If individuals can no longer make much sense of their personal responsibility for their own actions and omissions, then surely this will weaken, too, their sense of collective responsibility. In a flourishing community of rights, it will be accepted that there is a collective responsibility to make compensatory provision for those who are disabled, through no fault of their own, from functioning as agents. However, if agency is itself a devalued commodity, agency-deficits no longer seem such urgent cases for compensation – and, anyway, the idea that the community has a collective responsibility to put this or anything else to rights is no longer meaningful.

Thirdly, there is the sense of respect that regulates our interactions with others. Now, here is a radically different thought.[58] Let us suppose that regulators, judging that what has been traditionally thought to work does not in fact work, increasingly look for hi-tech or designed solutions.[59] Modern biotechnology becomes not only a regulatory target but also a regulatory tool. Initially, the technology will be employed within the framework of traditional legal modes of regulation. The technology might be designed to discourage non-compliance or to improve the chances of detection, or both; it might be pretty crude (for example, speed bumps or other traffic calming measures within restricted areas) or it might be more sophisticated (for example, CCTV, smart cards, tracking devices, forensic data bases, and so on). No matter how sophisticated the technology, however, there is always the option of non-compliance and always some chance that one will not be detected.

Next, the technology will be improved to the point where, although the regulatory mode remains recognisably legal, non-compliance will be detected and the application of the designated sanction is guaranteed. We can imagine an "all-seeing" 24/7 surveillance technology that enables the regulators to monitor our every action. If we fail to comply, we will be seen – and, in conjunction with database and recognition technology, we will be identified. We can elect non-compliance but we do so in the certain knowledge that we will pay.[60]

Human rights concerns will be voiced as regulators adopt more intrusive monitoring apparatus. However, the decisive step will come when regulators rely on a regulatory pitch that makes no attempt to engage with the practical reason of their targets; when legal, social, and financial modes give way to "techno-regulation";[61] when rules and regulations give way to technologically secured results; in the ideal-typical case, when compliance is guaranteed because non-compliance is not an option. How so? Possibly, this could be by a technical fix to the environment – for example, by taking cash as we know it out of the economy and replacing it with electronic money (which, admittedly, might simply replace one kind of crime with another) – or by a technical fix to human biology (employing programmes of genetic screening and selection) or by a combination of controlling interventions applied to human predisposition and our particular environment. With techno-regulation, there is no such thing as the perfect crime; criminality is no longer an option.[62] In place of authentic respect for others, we have a controlled environment that guarantees a certain pattern of behaviour – we have conduct simulating respectful consideration of others but without actually expressing respect. Techno-regulation, we might say, brings down the curtain on human dignity.[63]

In each of these cases, an apparently benign choice in favour of a technology has a profound and cumulative impact on the context that gives meaning to a community of rights. The process is an insidious one. Moreover, in a culture that is committed to individual autonomy, the exercise of choice is hard to resist. Above all, we need to be alert to this danger because it arises precisely where the technology works, not where it fails.

Conclusion

The aspiration that biotechnology should be used only in ways that respect human rights and human dignity is a laudable one. In practice, human rights is challenged in all sorts of ways – by governments in exceptional circumstances as well as routinely by global institutional design, by everyday discourse and regulatory practice, and by dealings in global markets. In principle, too, human rights is challenged. For much of the Twentieth Century, utilitarianism was the main opposition. However, modern biotechnology has prompted a new dignitarianism that, ironically, contests human rights on its own axiom of respect for human dignity. To fend off this latter challenge, it is important that the conception of human dignity that underpins human rights is more clearly and visibly articulated. The dignitarians must not be allowed to acquire all rights on the concept by adverse possession. However, such articulation of human dignity will generate some restraints on autonomy. Even in the human rights paradigm, choice is not an unqualified good. My choices need to be sensitive to your choices; and we both need to ensure that the choices that we make today do not compromise the context that will continue to give meaning to a community of rights to be populated by tomorrow's people.

Notes

1 Alain Touraine, "The Crisis of 'Progress'" in Martin Bauer (ed), *Resistance to NewTechnology* (Cambridge: Cambridge University Press, 1995) 45 at 51.

2 See Dorothy Nelkin, "Science Controversies: The Dynamics of Public Disputes in the United States" in Sheila Jasanoff, Gerald E. Markle, James C. Petersen, and Trevor Pinch (eds), *Handbook of Science and Technology Studies* (Thousand Oaks, California: Sage Publications, 1995), 444.

3 Susan Greenfield, *Tomorrow's People* (London: Allen Lane, 2001).

4 *Bioethics: International Implications* (UNESCO, 2003).

5 The ongoing work of UNESCO in relation to an international declaration on bioethics underlines this axiom. In October 2003, the General Conference of UNESCO having resolved that preparatory work on a "Declaration on Universal Norms on Bioethics" should continue, it was agreed that it was "opportune and desirable to set universal standards in the field of bioethics *with due regard for human dignity and human rights* and freedoms, in the spirit of cultural pluralism inherent in bioethics" (32C/Res. 24) (emphasis added). The first draft of the Declaration, published in June 2004, is peppered with references to human rights and human dignity; and one of the general principles (headed "Human Dignity, Human Rights and Justice") reads: "Any decision or practice in the field of bioethics [at all levels] shall be made in the respect (sic) of the human dignity (sic) and in accordance with the universal principles of justice, human rights and fundamental freedoms." In a second draft, prepared for discussion at the Eleventh Session of the IBC in Paris in August 2004, the emphasis on respect for human rights and human dignity persists. So, for example, the declared aims include "to ensure the respect for human dignity and the protection of human rights and fundamental freedoms..." and "to recognize the great benefit derived from scientific and technological developments whilst ensuring that such development occurs within the

framework of ethical principles that respect human dignity and protect human rights and fundamental freedoms, and to prevent practices contrary to human dignity."

6 See Roger Brownsword, "Bioethics Today, Bioethics Tomorrow: Stem Cell Research and the 'Dignitarian Alliance'" (2003) *17 Notre Dame Journal of Law, Ethics and Public Policy* 15.

7 Christian Tomuschat, *Human Rights: Between Idealism and Realism* (Oxford: Oxford University Press, 2003).

8 Ibid., at 321.

9 Anne-Marie Slaughter, "Judicial Globalization" (2000) 40 *Virginia Journal of International Law* 1103, at 1103. Compare Touraine, note 1 above, at 46:

Our world appears to be integrated as a world market, but the counterpart of this globalization is the more and more aggressive defence of personal and collective identity. Instead of living in a cosmopolitan world, as some people pretend we do, we live in a dualized world in which not only North and South are more and more distant from each other, but where rich and poor districts of the cities are more and more separated universes and in which most individuals are split between their participation in a globalized world and their consciousness of individual and collective identity.

10 See, e.g., Owen Bowcott, "Biometrics – Great Hope for World Security or Triumph for Big Brother?" *The Guardian*, June 18, 2004, page 3.

11 Helena Kennedy, *Just Law* (London: Chatto and Windus, 2004) at 61.

12 Louise Christian, "Guantanamo Bay: A Global Experiment in Inhumanity" *The Guardian*, January 10, 2004, page 24. Moreover, the bad example set extends beyond detention without trial; seemingly, evidence obtained in clear breach of the Rule of Law (namely, under torture) will be admissible provided that local agents were not complicit in such an abuse, see the majority decision of the Court of Appeal in *A & Others v Secretary of State for the Home Department* [2004] EWCA Civ 1123.

13 Compare, too, the criticisms and concerns recently voiced by the parliamentary Joint Committee on Human Rights; see Nigel Morris, "Terror Laws Used Unfairly on Muslims Warn MPs", *The Independent*, August 5, 2004, page 5, and Alan Travis, "Blunkett Faces Revolt on Internment", *The Guardian*, August 5, 2004, page 5.

14 On the Australian case, see Michael Head, "The Global War on Terrorism: Democratic Rights under Attack" in Roger Brownsword (ed), *Human Rights* (Global Governance and the Quest for Justice: Volume IV) (Oxford: Hart, 2004) 11; and, on the Argentinean case, see Sabine Michalowski, "Human Rights in Times of Economic Crisis: The Example of Argentina", ibid, at 33. For an historical overview and a biting critique of judicial deference to executive assessments of 'emergencies' and their needs, see Keith Ewing, *The Futility of the Human Rights Act* [2004] Public Law 829.

15 For a general critique of IMF policy, especially the conditionalities imposed, see Joseph Stiglitz, *Globalization and its Discontents* (London: Penguin, Allen Lane, 2002).

16 Sheldon Leader, "Collateralism" in Roger Brownsword (ed), *Human Rights* (Global Governance and the Quest for Justice: Volume IV) (Oxford: Hart, 2004) 53.

17 See Article 53(a) of the European Patent Convention; and Article 6 of Directive 98/44/EC on the Legal Protection of Biotechnological Inventions.

18 HOWARD FLOREY/Relaxin [1995] EPOR 541. On which, see Roger Brownsword, "The *Relaxin Opposition* Revisited" 9 *Jahrbuch für Recht und Ethik* (2001) 3.

19 *Netherlands v European Parliament and Council of the European Union*, Case C-377/98. For comment, see Deryck Beyleveld and Roger Brownsword, "Is Patent Law Part of the EC Legal Order? A Critical Commentary on the Interpretation of Article 6(1) of Directive 98/44/EC in Case C-377/98" [2002] IPQ 97.

20 See, e.g., Sheila Jasanoff, "Product, Process, or Programme: Three Cultures and the Regulation of Biotechnology", in Martin Bauer (ed), *Resistance to New Technology* (Cambridge: Cambridge University Press, 1995) 311; and this question arises pervasively in Martin W. Bauer and George Gaskell (eds), *Biotechnology – the Making of a Global Controversy* (Cambridge: Cambridge University Press, 2002).

21 On these second and third considerations, see Martin Bauer, "Resistance to New Technology and its Effects on Nuclear Power, Information Technology and Biotechnology", op cit note 20 above, 1, esp at 8-11. See, too, the Nuffield Council on Bioethics, *Genetically Modified Crops: the Ethical and Social Issues* (London, 1999) at 8: "it is always possible, in principle, to distinguish between the two distinct questions of 'how bad?' and 'how likely?' That is, we can and should separate the reasons for regarding an outcome as evil from the likelihood of its occurrence."

22 Op cit, note 21 above, at 8.

23 Ibid., at 19.

24 Ibid.

25 HL Paper 83(i) (Report) and 83(ii) (Evidence) (London: HMSO, Feb 27, 2002). See, for comment, Roger Brownsword, "Stem Cells, Superman, and the Report of the Select Committee" (2002) 65 MLR 568.

26 Ibid, esp at 4.21.

27 See e.g. *Stem Cell Therapy: the Ethical Issues – A Discussion Paper* (2000); but some topics (e.g. the use of animals for research) perhaps invite a less incrementalist approach.

28 *R v Human Fertilisation and Embryology Authority, ex parte Blood* [1997] 2 All ER 687.

29 See *R (Quintavalle on behalf of Comment on Reproductive Ethics) v Human Fertilisation and Embryology Authority* [2002] EWHC 2785 (Admin); [2003 EWCA Civ 667.

30 Like the Hashmis, the Whitakers, sought authorisation from the HFEA for a tissue-typing test on their embryos (their son, Charlie, suffering from the rare blood disorder, Diamond Blackfan anaemia, and needing a saviour sibling). However, the Authority refused because the test would not be carried out in conjunction with PGD—this particular blood disorder not being one for which there is a genetic marker (and thus not a disorder that would be identified by PGD). Accordingly, the Whitakers were forced to go (perfectly lawfully) to the United States for the tissue-typing but without a covering licence from the Authority. The perseverance of the Whitakers paid off when they returned to the UK to celebrate a successful donor birth. But the story is still running: in July 2004, in response to a case on all fours with that of the Whitaker family, the full 18-member HFEA announced its intention to relax the restriction that barred the way to authorising free-standing tissue-typing. The Chair of the HFEA, Suzi Leather, explained that, in the light of the latest evidence, the Authority was satisfied that there was no increased risk to the embryo arising from the tissue-typing procedure. See, Sarah Boseley, "Green Light for 'Designer Babies' to Save Siblings" *The Guardian*, July 22, 2004, page 1.

31 See, *Sex Selection: Options for Regulation* (November 12, 2003), para 130.

32 For comment on the merits of the Hashmis' (and the Whitakers') applications, see Roger Brownsword, "Reproductive Opportunities and Regulatory Challenges" (2004) 67 MLR 304.

33 *Genes and Insurance* (Cambridge: Cambridge University Press, 2003). Some of what I say in this section draws on my review in (2004) 15 KCLJ 175.

[34] In identifying low-risk parties as the key source of instability, I recognise that I am departing from what I think is the orthodox view that it will be unconscionable profit-taking by high-risk insured that is the real problem. However, there are various ways that insurers can limit their exposure to this kind of opportunism and, with the appropriate safeguards in place, the real problem then lies with low-risk parties. For an appreciation of both high-risk and low-risk sources of difficulty, see Ronald Dworkin, *Sovereign Virtue* (Cambridge, Mass.: Harvard University Press, 2000) Ch. 13.

[35] See *Gillick v West Norfolk and Wisbech Area Health Authority* [1985] 3 All ER 402. For discussion of the difficulties in identifying those who have such a capacity, see Deryck Beyleveld and Roger Brownsword, *Consent in the Law* (Englewood Cliffs, NJ: Prentice Hall, 2004) esp. Ch 4.

[36] Cf Hilary and Steven Rose, "Playing God" *The Guardian* July 3, 2003, p. 25 (harvesting eggs from aborted foetuses and the erasure of "the human dignity claims of the potential child").

[37] Adopted at the 29th Session of the General Conference, November 11, 1997.

[38] Directive 98/44/EC; OJ L 213, 30.7.98, 13.

[39] Deryck Beyleveld and Roger Brownsword, *Human Dignity in Bioethics and Biolaw* (Oxford: Oxford University Press, 2001).

[40] See, in particular, I Kant, *The Metaphysics of Morals* (translated and edited by Mary Gregor) (Cambridge, Cambridge University Press, 1996) (first published 1797) at 209.

[41] For the significance of this distinction, see Deryck Beyleveld and Roger Brownsword, "Human Dignity, Human Rights, and Human Genetics" in Roger Brownsword, W.R. Cornish & Margaret Llewelyn (eds.), *Human Genetics and the Law: Regulating a Revolution* (Oxford, Hart Publishing, 1998) 69; and Deryck Beyleveld and Roger Brownsword, op cit, note 39 above.

[42] This same point might be made by drawing on Ronald Dworkin's distinction between values that are derivative (in the sense of a conception of human dignity that is related to the interests of particular persons) and values that are detached (in the sense of a conception of human dignity that is not related to the interests of particular persons but that reflects the intrinsic value of some action or state of affairs). Originally, see Ronald Dworkin, *Life's Dominion* (London: Harper Collins, 1993); and, more recently, see "Playing God: Genes, Clones, and Luck" in *Sovereign Virtue* (Cambridge, Mass.: Harvard University Press, 2000) Ch. 13.

[43] Again, see Touraine, note 1 above, passim.

[44] See, e.g., HOWARD FLOREY/ Relaxin [1995] EPOR 541; and, for commentary, see Roger Brownsword, "The *Relaxin Opposition* Revisited" (2001) 9 *Jahrbuch für Recht und Ethik* 3.

[45] See Roger Brownsword, "Stem Cells, Superman, and the Report of the Select Committee" (2002) 65 MLR 568.

[46] See *R (Quintavalle on behalf of Comment on Reproductive Ethics) v Human Fertilisation and Embryology Authority* [2002] EWHC 2785 (Admin), [2003] EWCA Civ 667. For discussion, see Roger Brownsword, "Reproductive Opportunities and Regulatory Challenges" (2004) 67 MLR 304.

[47] See, further, Roger Brownsword, "The Cult of Consent: Fixation and Fallacy" (2004) 15 KCLJ (forthcoming).

[48] BVerwGE 115 (2001) 189. I am indebted to Pat Capps (University of Bristol) for drawing this case to my attention.

[49] This is to be contrasted with the well-known *Peep-Show* Decision BVerwGE 64 (1981) 274, where the thinking is right in line with that of the dignitarian alliance: see Deryck Beyleveld and Roger Brownsword, op cit, note 39 above. For commentary, see Shayana

Kadidal, "Obscenity in the Age of Mechanical Reproduction" (1996) 44 *American Journal of Comparative Law* 353.

50 Ronald Dworkin, *Sovereign Virtue* (Cambridge, Mass.: Harvard University Press, 2000) 444.

51 Ibid, at 445.

52 Ibid, at 446.

53 Ibid, at 445.

54 Lawrence Lessig, *Code and Other Laws of Cyberspace* (New York: Basic Books, 1999), at 258-259.

55 Jürgen Habermas, *The Future of Human Nature* (Cambridge: Polity Press, 2003).

56 Bill McKibben, *Enough: Genetic Engineering and the End of Human Nature* (London: Bloomsbury, 2003).

57 Similarly, see Dworkin, note 50 above, at 445.

58 This draws in part on Roger Brownsword, "What the World Needs Now: Techno-Regulation, Human Rights, and Human Dignity" in Roger Brownsword (ed) *Human Rights* (*Global Governance and the Quest for Justice*, Volume IV) (Oxford: Hart, 2004) 203.

59 On the new criminology of control, and the conditions under which it has developed, see David Garland, *The Culture of Control* (Oxford: Oxford University Press, 2001). As Garland remarks, the new situational approach "aims to embed controls in the fabric of normal interaction, rather than suspend them above it in the form of a sovereign command" (129); and such a strategy offers "an approach to social order that is, for the most part, amoral and technological" (183).

60 See, e.g., Clive Norris and Gary Armstrong, *The Maximum Surveillance Society: The Rise of CCTV* (Oxford: Berg, 1999) Ch. 10.

61 On the ideas of regulatory pitch and mode, see Roger Brownsword, "Red Lights and Rogues: Regulating Human Genetics" in Han Somsen (ed), *Biotechnology and Regulation* (forthcoming); and for detailed comment on the deep significance of regulatory pitch, see Roger Brownsword, "Code, Control and Choice: Why East is East and West is West" (2005) *Legal Studies* (forthcoming).

62 Cf Lawrence Lessig, *The Future of Ideas* (New York: Random House, 2001) at 249:
Technology, tied to law, now promises almost perfect control over [artistic] content and its distribution. And it is this perfect control that threatens to undermine the potential for innovation that the Internet promises. To resist this threat, we need specific changes to re-establish a balance between control and creativity. Our aim should be a system of sufficient control to give artists enough incentive to produce, while leaving free as much as we can for others to build upon and create. For scepticism about perfect technological control, see Charles Fried, "Perfect Freedom, Perfect Control?" (2000) 114 *Harvard Law Review* 606, 628.

63 See, further, Roger Brownsword, "Code, Control and Choice: Why East is East and West is West" (2005) *Legal Studies* (forthcoming).

Chapter 23

Harmonising Human Rights in Europe

Rick Lawson

Introduction

'Harmonising Human Rights in Europe' is a subject that is bound to raise two opposite emotions. One the one hand, the very term 'harmonisation' hints at the imposition of Euronorms by anonymous un-elected bureaucrats who seek to do away with the rich diversity that characterises Europe. Even in contemporary Europe it could be argued that there are relatively few common standards in the field of morals, ethics and religion and there is little point forcing alien norms upon societies and individuals. On the other hand, those take this view do have to face the question why levels of protection should be different, depending on where one lives. Would it be acceptable if torture or the death penalty were retained, or minorities persecuted, in some European countries? If *The Little Red Schoolbook* is freely available in Denmark, France, Germany and the Netherlands, why should it be banned in Britain? Isn't it the essence of human rights, as the Universal Declaration of Human Rights (1948) states, that all human beings are born free and equal in dignity and rights?

Of course the European Court of Human Rights, in Strasbourg, is very well aware of the tension between local particularities and the universal ambition of fundamental rights. The aim of this short contribution is to indicate how the Strasbourg Court seeks to draw the balance in practice, and to make some comparisons with the practice of the Court of Justice of the European Communities in Luxembourg. We will conclude by suggesting some future developments.

The European Convention of Human Rights

General Background

The European Convention on Human Rights (ECHR) was adopted 1950 in the framework of the Council of Europe. It contains a fairly limited set of 'classic' human rights and fundamental freedoms, such as the right to life, the prohibition of torture and the right to a fair trial.[1] Over the years, additional rights, such as the right to protection of property, have been added through protocols. What started as a project between ten mainly Western European States was joined by States in Central and Eastern Europe after the fall of the Berlin Wall. The Convention now embraces the Russian Federation and countries such as Armenia and Azerbaijan. In short, it has developed into 'a constitutional instrument of European public order (ordre public) for the protection of individual human beings'[2] to which 46 States have committed themselves – that is, all European States except Belarus (which does not satisfy the Council's requirements in terms of democracy and respect for the rule of law). Over 800 million individuals enjoy the protection offered by the Convention, from Reykjavik to Wladiwostok.

The main feature distinguishing the Convention from other international human rights instruments is its supervisory mechanism. Both individual victims and States parties to the Convention may bring complaints to the European Court of Human Rights in Strasbourg. The Court's judgments have binding force, and the Council of Europe's Committee of Ministers supervises their execution in practice. If the Court finds that there has been a violation of the Convention, it may afford just satisfaction to the victim – including compensation of material damage, moral damage and legal costs. The Court operates on a full-time basis. In 2003, it registered over 38,000 fresh complaints. In the same year it delivered some 800 judgments and took over 17,000 admissibility decisions.

'...the Court cannot but be Influenced by the Commonly Accepted Standards ...'

The Court's jurisprudence contains many examples of cases where considerable weight was given to the (perceived) existence of common standards in Europe. In most of these cases the 'dissident' State was forced to conform to these standards. A leading case in this area is Tyrer, concerning the use of judicial corporal punishment in the Isle of Man. When the Manx authorities pointed out that the local population was actually in favour of the retention of corporal punishment, the Court observed:

The Attorney-General for the Isle of Man argued that the judicial corporal punishment at issue in this case was not in breach of the Convention since it did not outrage public opinion in the Island. However, even assuming that local public opinion can have an incidence on the interpretation of the concept of 'degrading punishment' appearing in Article 3, the Court does not regard it as established that judicial corporal punishment is not considered degrading by those members of the Manx population who favour its retention: it might well be that one of the reasons why they view the penalty as an effective deterrent is precisely the element of degradation which it involves. As regards their belief that judicial corporal punishment deters criminals, it must be pointed out that a punishment does not lose its degrading character just because it is believed to be, or actually is, an effective deterrent or aid to crime control.

Above all, as the Court must emphasise, it is never permissible to have recourse to punishments which are contrary to Article 3, whatever their deterrent effect may be. The Court must also recall that the Convention is a living instrument which, as the Commission rightly stressed, must be interpreted in the light of present-day conditions. In the case now before it the Court cannot but be influenced by the developments and commonly accepted standards in the penal policy of the member States of the Council of Europe in this field.[3]

Ever since Tyrer the Court has underlined that the Convention is a 'living instrument' which must be interpreted in accordance with 'present day conditions'. In order to determine what these 'conditions' are, the Court follows a comparative approach, seeking to identify common standards in the laws and practices of the European States. It should be added that this process is not always very transparent – the Court only rarely indicates the factual basis for its assertions that common standards do exist – nor is it applied consistently: the Court may or may not refer to developments in Europe. Having said that, the 'living instrument' doctrine has greatly contributed to the effectiveness of the European Convention as an instrument for the protection of very basic rights. Many examples could be cited here: cases involving gay rights (*Dudgeon v. UK, Norris v. Ireland, Modinos v. Cyprus*), differences of treatment between 'illegitimate' and 'legitimate' children (*Marckx v. Belgium*), or the abolition of the death penalty (*Öcalan v. Turkey*).

Not surprisingly, applicants often seek to persuade the Court that there is a new standard which should lead it to rule in their favour. The Court is not always willing to go along, as was demonstrated by a recent series of cases concerning the provision of camp sites and facilities for travellers:

> The applicant urged the Court to take into account recent international developments, in particular the Framework Convention for the Protection of Minorities, in reducing the margin of appreciation accorded to States in light of the recognition of the problems of vulnerable groups, such as gypsies. The Court observes that there may be said to be an emerging international consensus amongst the Contracting States of the Council of Europe recognising the special needs of minorities and an obligation to protect their security, identity and lifestyle (...), not only for the purpose of safeguarding the interests of the minorities themselves but to preserve a cultural diversity of value to the whole community.

However, the Court is not persuaded that the consensus is sufficiently concrete for it to derive any guidance as to the conduct or standards which Contracting States consider desirable in any particular situation. The Framework Convention, for example, sets out general principles and goals but signatory states were unable to agree on means or implementation.[4]

Judgments like these may be disappointing for the individual applicant, but at the same time they do invite others to bring new cases before the Court in the future and argue that the standards have changed in the meantime. A successful example is offered by Christine Goodwin, the last in a series of British cases on the legal recognition of transsexuality:

While the Court is not formally bound to follow its previous judgments, it is in the interests of legal certainty, foreseeability and equality before the law that it should not depart, without good reason, from precedents laid down in previous cases (...). However, since the Convention is first and foremost a system for the protection of human rights, the Court must have regard to the changing conditions within the respondent State and within Contracting States generally and respond, for example, to any evolving convergence as to the standards to be achieved (...). It is of crucial importance that the Convention is interpreted and applied in a manner which renders its rights practical and effective, not theoretical and illusory. A failure by the Court to maintain a dynamic and evolutive approach would indeed risk rendering it a bar to reform or improvement (...).

The Court observes that in the case of Rees in 1986 it had noted that little common ground existed between States, some of which did permit change of gender and some of which did not and that generally speaking the law seemed to be in a state of transition (...). In the later case of Sheffield and Horsham, the Court's judgment laid emphasis on the lack of a common European approach as to how to address the repercussions which the legal recognition of a change of sex may entail for other areas of law such as marriage, filiation, privacy or data protection. While this would appear to remain the case, the lack of such a common approach among forty-three Contracting States with widely diverse legal systems and traditions is hardly surprising. In accordance with the principle of subsidiarity, it is indeed primarily for the Contracting States to decide on the measures necessary to secure Convention rights within their jurisdiction and, in resolving within their domestic legal systems the practical problems created by the legal recognition of post-operative gender status, the Contracting States must enjoy a wide margin of appreciation. The Court accordingly attaches less importance to the lack of evidence of a common European approach to the resolution of the legal and practical problems posed, than to the clear and uncontested evidence of a continuing international trend in favour not only of increased social acceptance of transsexuals but of legal recognition of the new sexual identity of post-operative transsexuals.[5]

It is interesting to see that the Court allows itself to be influenced by international trends. Especially the Canadian Charter of Rights and Freedoms and the jurispudence of the Canadian Supreme Court have inspired the Strasbourg Court on more than one occasion.[6] In the long run this could contribute to the universal – and not just European –'harmonization' of human rights.

The Margin of Appreciation

The reader will have noted that the Court referred repeatedly to the 'margin of appreciation'. This concept was introduced in the mid-1970s. It refers to a certain latitude, an area of discretion that the Court is willing to leave to domestic authorities, for instance because these authorities are in principle better placed than the European Court to assess whether or not there is a 'pressing social need' capable of justifying interference with one of the rights guaranteed by the Convention. The margin tends to be especially wide (and the Court's scrutiny is correspondingly less intensive) in cases that involve 'sensitive' issues such as the protection of national security, socio-economic policies and so on. The margin also plays a prominent role in the area of morals and religion:

As in the case of 'morals' it is not possible to discern throughout Europe a uniform conception of the significance of religion in society; even within a single country such conceptions may vary. For that reason it is not possible to arrive at a comprehensive definition of what constitutes a permissible interference with the exercise of the right to freedom of expression where such expression is directed against the religious feelings of others. A certain margin of appreciation is therefore to be left to the national authorities in assessing the existence and extent of the necessity of such interference.[7]

Thus, the Court observed in 1996 that blasphemy laws are increasingly rarely applied and that several States have recently repealed them altogether. In the United Kingdom only two prosecutions concerning blasphemy had been brought in the last seventy years and strong arguments have been advanced in favour of the abolition of blasphemy laws. However, the Court noted, the fact remains that 'there is as yet not sufficient common ground in the legal and social orders of the member States of the Council of Europe to conclude that a system whereby a State can impose restrictions on the propagation of material on the basis that it is blasphemous is, in itself, unnecessary in a democratic society and thus incompatible with the Convention'. Accordingly the British authorities were left a wide margin of appreciation in deciding whether material was actually blasphemous and which penalty was appropriate.[8]

Preliminary Conclusion

How can one reconcile these various judgments? Sometimes the Court forces States to change their laws and conform common European standards; sometimes the Court defers to the views of the national authorities. Three rules of thumb may be defined. First, if there is a clear consensus in Europe, with only very few States dissenting (or lagging behind), than Strasbourg will be inclined to leave only a narrow margin of appreciation. If practice is varied, the margin will be wider. However, and this is the second rule, the more intimate the nature of the right involved (or: the more the treatment complained of affects human dignity), the narrower the margin of appreciation – even if there are no clear common European standards. The third rule of thumb is only very new; it may have been introduced in May 2004. In the case of Hirst v UK the applicant was prevented from voting at any parliamentary or local election as he was serving a prison sentence. The Court fist noted the divergences existing in the law and practice within Contracting States. At one end of the spectrum, there are some 18 countries in which no restrictions are imposed on prisoners' rights to vote; in some 13 countries prisoners are not able to vote, due to operation of law or lack of enabling provisions; and between these extremes in the remainder of Contracting States loss of voting rights is tailored to specific offences or categories of offences or a discretion is left to the sentencing court. This lack of clear consensus, the Court found, 'underlines the importance of the margin of appreciation afforded to national legislatures in laying down conditions governing the right of franchise'. However – and the following phrase contains the new element that makes Hirst such an interesting case:

> That said however, the Court does not consider that a Contracting State may rely on the margin of appreciation to justify restrictions on the right to vote which have not been the subject of considered debate in the legislature and which derive, essentially, from unquestioning and passive adherence to a historic tradition.[9]

The EU and the 'Harmonisation' of Fundamental Rights

General Background: The EU and Fundamental Rights

The EU is known to harmonise anything – what about human rights? A first response would be that there are no directives or regulations seeking to harmonise human rights; nor is there any power to do so in the EC Treaty, the EU treaty of the new Constitutional Treaty for Europe. Unlike the Council of Europe with its European Convention of Human Rights, the EU is not a human rights organisation.

Having said that, it should be noted that the Court of Justice of the European Communities (ECJ) in Luxembourg accepted already in the early 1970s that it is bound by fundamental rights.[10] According to settled case-law, fundamental rights form an integral part of the general principles of law, the observance of which the Court ensures. For that purpose, the Court draws inspiration from the constitutional traditions common to the Member States and from the guidelines supplied by international treaties for the protection of human rights on which the Member States have collaborated or to which they are signatories. The ECHR has special significance in that respect. Most cases concern allegations that European institutions have violated fundamental rights – such as Connolly on the freedom of expression of EU civil servants, or Roquette Frères where the ECJ accepted that the Brussels Commission must comply with the requirements of the right to respect for private life when searching business premises.[11]

These cases in a way feature the 'harmonisation' of human rights: the ECJ seeks to develop and apply common standards that bind the European institutions. As a sort of codification of the existing situation, the Charter of Fundamental Rights of the EU was adopted, as a political document, in Nice in December 2000.[12] The Charter contains a wide variety of rights: civil and political rights, economic, cultural and social rights. Its text reveals a certain amount of ambiguity: some provisions are expressly directed to the EU; others are not addressed to any authority in particular but relate to policy areas where the Union has little or no competence. Be that as it may, the Charter combines classic and innovative provisions, from the prohibition of slavery to the right to good administration – in short, it is an attempt to formulate the 'state of the art' in human rights.

The EU and Respect for Fundamental Rights at the Domestic Level

Now to what extent does all this affect the Member States? There is certainly a 'spill over' effect. The ECJ decided in the late 1980s that the general principles of Community law, including fundamental rights, do not only bind the institutions, but also the Member States where they implement Community law.[13] It later added that the same applies if Member States restrict the common market freedoms (free movement of workers, of services, of goods, of capital): any such restriction should be in conformity with human rights.[14] The ECJ later adopted a more general formula, as a result of which the present state of the case-law can be summarised as follows:

> ... according to the Court's case-law, where national legislation falls within the field of application of Community law the Court, in a reference for a preliminary ruling, must give the national court all the guidance as to interpretation necessary to enable it to assess the compatibility of that legislation with the fundamental rights whose observance the Court ensures.[15]

It is worth observing that it may be easier, and therefore more attractive, for individual applicants to try and get their human rights claim before the ECJ than before the European Court of Human Rights: any court, even at first instance, can refer preliminary questions to the Luxembourg Court, whereas Strasbourg can only be accessed after a lengthy process whereby all domestic remedies are exhausted. The individual may not be bothered too much by the fact that an authentic interpretation of the ECHR can only be obtained in Strasbourg: he will happily rely on any 'European' ruling in his favour. And if the ECJ happens to rule against him, he can always exhaust domestic remedies and try his luck in Strasbourg. One might object that this accumulation of applications will lead to very long procedures – but the possibility already exists and is actually being used by individuals.[16]

The result is a constant flow of cases, usually through the preliminary rulings procedure, where it was alleged that national authorities violate human rights. A well-known example is Grogan which involved the Irish prohibition of information about abortion facilities abroad.[17] But many other examples can be added: Demirel on the German decision to expel the spouse of a Turkish worker, Cinétèque on the French restrictions of the sale of videotapes of films, Konstantinidis on the way in German authorities transcribed a Greek name, Kremzow on the consequences for a criminal conviction of the finding that the trial had been unfair – and more recently cases such as Carpenter and Baumbast on the free movement of persons and their family members, Österreichischer Rundfunk and Lindqvist on the right to privacy, Booker Aquaculture on the absence of financial compensation following the destruction of fish infected by a contagious disease, and Karner on the compatibility with the freedom of expression of Austrian restrictions on advertisement.[18] It should be noted that, much like the Strasbourg Court, the ECJ is prepared to leave the national authorities a margin of appreciation when balancing interests.

It is conceivable that these individuals cases may be supplemented by infringement procedures (Article 226 EC), whereby the Commission prosecutes a Member State for failing to respect fundamental rights that falls within the field of application of Community law.[19] Apart from specific obligations under Community law to respect fundamental rights (such as the prohibition of discrimination of Articles 12 and 13 EC), a more general legal basis to take action against domestic violations can be found in Article 7 Treaty on European Union (TEU). This provision allows for measures against Member States if there is a serious and persistent breach of the fundamental values on which the EU is based, notably human rights. The procedure of Article 7 TEU was enhanced by the Treaty of Nice, following the crisis surrounding the participation of the right-wing FPÖ in the Austrian government. Action may now be taken if there is 'only' a serious risk that things may go wrong in a Member State. The arrangement of Article 7 TEU returns in Article I-59 of the Constitutional Treaty.

Back to the ECJ and its role vis-à-vis the Member States in the field of fundamental rights. The newest fashion in this branch of jurisprudence is that Member States invoke fundamental rights in order to justify policies which might otherwise be deemed incompatible with EU law. An early example was offered by the Dutch 'media cases' where the Netherlands government sought to rely on Article 10 ECHR (freedom of expression) in order to defend restrictions applying to broadcasting corporations.[20] More recently the Austrian Government successfully invoked its obligations under Article 11 ECHR (freedom of association) in order to justify its permission for a demonstration on the public highway which hampered the free movement of goods.[21] And in October 2004 the ECJ accepted that German authorities prohibited the commercial exploitation of 'laser games' on the ground that these games, to the extent that they simulate the killing of human beings, are incompatible with human dignity, as protected by Article 1 of the German Constitution.[22]

Preliminary Conclusions

If one examines the developments in this area so far, the overall trend would seem to be one of growing acceptance that the EU has a legitimate interest in securing adequate respect for human rights in its Member States – either through judicial procedures before the ECJ or through political pressure on the basis of, eventually, Article 7 TEU. Yet another sentiment emerged when the EU Charter of Fundamental Rights was negotiated. Article 51 (1) of the Charter (Article II-111 (1) of the Constitution) provides:

> The provisions of the Charter are addressed to the institutions, bodies, offices and agencies of the Union with due regard to the principle of subsidiarity and to the Member States only when they are implementing Union law.

The formula 'when they are implementing Union law' reflects current practice only to a very limited extent. Was it a mistake to which no consequences should be attached, or is a deliberate attempt to roll back the existing case-law of the ECJ? Many of the cases mentioned above did not concern the implementation of EU law, but related to very diverse situations which were considered to fall 'within the field of application of Community law'. It remains to be seen if the ECJ will adapt its jurisprudence and follow the more narrow wording of Article 51 (1) Charter.

A 'purely legal' answer would be that the ECJ is under no obligation to do so: on the basis of Article I-9 (3) of the Constitutional Treaty it could simply continue to review national measures 'within the scope of Community law'. But beneath the surface there are other issues: should the EU develop its own human rights policy in order to actively promote human rights in the Member States? Do the EU institutions have a role to play in supervising domestic compliance with human rights standards? Can they take measures, or should they be able to do so, if a Member States violates human rights? Should the capacity of the Union to involve itself with domestic human rights be limited to situations were violations threaten to disturb the internal market? Or should any violation of human rights be a concern to the Union? If so, how does this relate to the activities of the Council of Europe, and in what way will this affect the position of the European Court of Human Rights? What is the impact of the introduction of European citizenship, the creation of an 'Area of Freedom, Security and Justice', and the incorporation of the Charter? In short: should the EU develop into a human rights organisation?

Some Concluding Remarks

At present there is no serious 'threat' of harmonisation – if a threat it is – there is space for diversity, albeit not unlimited. Both the Strasbourg Court and the ECJ are prepared to leave a fairly wide margin of appreciation to national authorities, although the margin is more narrow if there are common European standards or if human dignity is really at stake, or again if a practice merely derives from unquestioning and passive adherence to a historic tradition. The present writer does not believe that these are unreasonable or unpractical principles.

But it might be worthwhile to pay attention to a very different process. What we might see in the coming years is not a 'top-down' imposition of European norms on innocent societies – but rather a 'bottom-up' call for uniformity. Behind this is what one might call, with a certain degree of exaggeration, a modest clash of civilisations. Spouses who have contracted a same-sex marriage in the Netherlands may wish to travel to another Member State with the aim to continue their marital life there. Pregnant women who wish to obtain an abortion will travel from Ireland to Great Britain. Soft drugs which are freely available in one Member State will be sold to citizens from other Member States that pursue a zero tolerance policy. How should we react to these situations? Refuse to recognise legal relationships that are lawful in other EU Member States? Prosecute individuals for acts committed in other Member States that were perfectly lawful there, but are regarded as crimes in their home State?

To many, the essence of Europe is the diversity of its nations. One of the challenges facing the Union is to strike the right balance between preservation of national identity, also in the sphere of human rights, and securing overall compliance with minimum standards to an extent that the Union can actually function. Neither present EU law nor the EU Constitution give guidelines on how to deal with these and other consequences of diversity, which the free movement of persons makes visible. On the short term, one may develop ways to secure a 'peaceful co-existence' of different societies – lawyers would perhaps think of a 'private international law of human rights'. But in the long run, as a common 'legal space' in Europe develops, it seems inevitable there will be a call for harmonisation of human rights.

Notes

1 For a recent description, see e.g. Jacobs & White, *The European Convention on Human Rights* (Oxford UP, 3rd ed., 2002, by C. Ovey & R.C.A. White).

2 ECtHR, 23 March 1995, *Loizidou v. Turkey (prel. obj.)* (Series A, vol. 310; Appl. No. 15318/89), §§ 75 and 93. Judgments were officially published until 1996 in the *Series A*, and since 1996 in the *Reports*. All decisions and judgments can be found, in full text, at www.echr.coe.int by using the very accessible 'hudoc' search engine.

3 ECtHR, 25 April 1978, *Tyrer v. UK* (Series A, vol. 26; Appl. No. 5658/72), § 31, emphasis added.

4 ECtHR, 18 Jan. 2001, *Jane Smith v. UK* (Appl. No. 25154/95), §§ 100-101.

5 ECtHR, 11 July 2002, *Goodwin v. UK* (Reports 2002 VI; Appl. No. 28957/95), §§ 74, 85, emphasis added.

6 See for instance ECtHR, 5 Nov. 2002, *Allan v. UK* (Appl. No. 48539/99), and 4 Dec. 2003, *M.C. v. Bulgaria* (Appl. No. 39372/98).

7 ECtHR, 20 Sept. 1994, *Otto Preminger v. Austria* (Series A, vol. 295-A; Appl. No. 13470/87), § 50.

8 ECtHR, 25 Nov. 1996, *Wingrove v. UK* (Reports 1996-V; Appl. No. 17419/00).

9 ECtHR, 30 March 2004, *Hirst v. UK* (Appl. No. 74025/01).

10 ECJ, Case 11/70, *Internationale Handelsgesellschaft* [1970] ECR 1125, § 4; Case 4-73, *Nold* [1974] ECR 491, § 13. For an overview, see B. de Witte, 'The Past and Future Role of the European Court of Justice in the Protection of Human Rights', in Ph. Alston (ed.), *The EU and Human Rights* (Oxford UP, 1999), pp. 859-897.

11 ECJ, Case C-274/99 P, *Connolly v Commission* [2001] ECR I-1611, § 37; Case C-94/00, *Roquette Frères* [2002] ECR I-9011, § 25.

12 *OJ* 2000, C 364. On the Charter, see J.-Y. Carlier & O. de Schutter, *La Charte des droits fondamentaux de l'Union européenne* (Bruylant, 2002); W. Heusel (ed.), *The Charter of Fundamental Rights and Constitutional Development in the EU* (Bundesanzeiger, 2002); P. Eeckhout, 'The EU Charter of Fundamental Rights and the Federal Question', in *CMLRev.* 2002, pp. 945-994; J.W. Sap, *Het EU-Handvest van de Grondrechten – De opmaat voor de Europese Grondwet* (Kluwer, 2003); J. Meyer

(Hrsg.), *Kommentar zur Charta der Grondrechte der Europäischen Union* (Nomos, 2003).

13 ECJ, Case C-5/88, *Wachauf* [1989] ECR p. 2609, § 19.

14 ECJ, Case C-260/89, *ERT* [1991] ECR p. I-2925, § 43.

15 ECJ, Case C-71/02, *Karner* (n.y.r., judgment of 25 March 2004), § 49, emphasis added.

16 For an example (apart from *Bosphorus* etc., mentioned above), compare ECJ, case C-206/91, *Koua Poirrez* [1992] ECR p. I-6685, with ECtHR, 30 Sept. 2003, *Koua Poirrez v. France* (Appl. No. 40892/98).

17 ECJ, Case 159/90, *Grogan* [1991] ECR p. I-4741.

18 ECJ, Case 12/86, *Demirel* [1987] ECR, p. 1417; Joined Cases 60-61/84, *Cinétèque* [1985] ECR p. 2627; Case C-168/91, *Konstantinidis* [1993] ECR p. I-1191; Case C-299/95, *Kremzow* [1997] ECR 1997, p. I-2629; Case C-60/00, *Carpenter* (n.y.r., judgment of 11 July 2002); Case C-413/99, *Baumbast* (n.y.r., judgment of 17 Sept. 2002); Joined Cases C-465/00, C-138/01 and C-139/01, *Österreichischer Rundfunk* (n.y.r., judgment of 20 May 2003); Case C-101/01, *Lindqvist* (n.y.r., judgment of 6 Nov. 2003); Joined Cases C-20/00 and C-64/00, *Booker Aquaculture a.o.* (n.y.r., judgment of 10 July 2003); Case C-71/02, *Karner* (n.y.r., judgment of 25 March 2004).

19 On that issue see COM(2003)606final, p. 8 *et seq.*

20 ECJ, Case 353/89, *Commission v. the Netherlands* [1991] ECR I-4097. See also Case C-377/98, *Netherlands v. Parliament and Council* [2001] ECR p. I-7079. On the latter case see esp. the Opinion of AG Jacobs, § 197: '...the rights invoked by the Netherlands are indeed fundamental rights, respect for which must be ensured in the Community legal order. The right to human dignity is perhaps the most fundamental right of all, and is now expressed in Article 1 of the Charter of Fundamental Rights [....]. It must be accepted that any Community instrument infringing those rights would be unlawful'.

21 ECJ, Case C-112/00, *Schmidberger* (n.y.r.; judgment of 12 June 2003).

22 ECJ, Case C-36/02, *Omega Spielhallen* (n.y.r.; judgment of 14 October 2004).

Chapter 24

Ugly, Deformed and Grubby: The Common Law and Human Rights[1]

Luke Clements[2]

The English common law springs from the font of the rich man's insecurities. It is a vast watercourse that powers his mills, irrigates his fields and defines the moat that keeps him in his castle and the poor man at bay. The common law is concerned with the retaining of property, with the preservation of privilege and above all, the status quo. From it springs the principles of larceny, of trespass, of defamation, of confidentiality, of precedent, of deference.

Human rights law issues from a different source – that of moral concern for victims – slaves and prisoners of war, Jews and Gypsies, underclasses and outsiders. For them it provides sustenance – but it generally flows weakly – in drought, hardly at all. At times and in places however it is in spate – *après la deluge* – at Nuremberg; The Hague; Rwanda.

The common law has learned tolerance – it accommodates many tributaries – it has acquired the knack of cohabitation – at sharing its course; thus with equity it was said that the 'two streams of jurisdiction, though they run in the same channel, run side by side, and do not mingle their waters'.[3]

Five years ago, the Human Rights Act 1998 opened the sluices and introduced Convention rights into our common law system. Since then the waters have undoubtedly mingled and we are now assured that human rights have fully permeated our domestic legal channels. Lord Woolf has suggested that the 'extremely smooth implementation'[4] of the Convention into domestic case law stems from the compatibility of the two systems – that the 'values to which the European Convention on Human Rights gives effect are very much the same values that have been recognised by the common law for hundreds of years'.

This perception fills many with concern: that the judiciary are willing victims of a cognitive illusion: that notwithstanding the changed nature of the law – its course, its destination remains unchanged. The fear being that judges still think within the same common law paradigm – still articulate cases in black letter terms – terms that are intrinsically weighted in favour of the rich man.[5] A fear that many of the distinctly unpleasant values underpinning the common law remain – having merely assumed a new alias – changed their name, but still rule the same.

Gypsies are an interesting subject group with which to test the extent to which the Act has changed traditional common law notions: Gypsies trouble land owners; they are a one of the most socially excluded groups within the UK,[6] they are vilified minority persecuted by the Nazis – a persecution that prompted the drafting of the European Convention on Human Rights. There is evidence that the Human Rights Act 1998 has made very little difference to the hardships they endure – not least the one third that have nowhere legal to live. An ESRC funded study, undertaken by Cardiff Law School, for instance, considered the extent to which the 1998 Act had modified local authority responses to Gypsies.[7] It concluded that little had changed – save that there had been a concerted effort to ensure that eviction policies remained robust. In relation to the chronic 'access to land' problems Gypsies' experience the research suggested that authorities had consciously decided to take no action to make their planning policies more benign – that in this context (in stark contrast to their active review of their eviction procedures) 'not being proactive' was the most attractive local authority option.

If the approach of the statutory agencies has not been revivified by the Human Rights Act 1998, then what of the courts? One small (but revealing) example of this problem can be found in the use of a common law principle *ex turpi causa non oritur actio*. It is of interest, since in equity it is mirrored by a similar doctrine encapsulated in the maxim 'he who comes to equity must come with clean hands'. *Ex turpi causa non oritur actio* is generally interpreted in modern text books as meaning 'no cause of action may be founded upon an illegal cause'. However it is commonly (and more accurately) interpreted as proscribing actions arsing out of a 'base or shameful causes'. Many a true word is spoken in Latin. *Turpe* translates as 'shapeless, unsightly foul, deformed, ugly, base, nauseous'. Ugliness is in the eyes of the beholder – and a principle that denies access rights to the law, for people whose cause is deemed to be unsightly or ugly or base and to people who come with dirty hands – is of interest to lawyers concerned about the rights of poor and otherwise socially excluded people – people for whom the common law has not traditionally been framed – Gypsies for instance.

British Gypsies have been bringing complaints concerning their lack of sites to the European Commission and Court of Human Rights for almost 20 years. Over this period the Court has endeavoured to find a way of articulating this injustice in the language of the Convention. In *Buckley v. UK* (1996)[8] the Court gave the Government the benefit of the doubt – on the basis of its assurances that it was trying to resolve the problem. This approach was not without its critics. Judge Pettiti, one of the dissenting judges, referred to the incremental nature of the injustices suffered by Gypsies. In his opinion, it was particularly problematic for courts to identify in black letter law terms injustices that arose out of a 'deliberate superimposition and accumulation of administrative rules (each of which would be acceptable taken singly)' – the net effect of this practice being that it became 'totally impossible for a Gypsy family to make suitable arrangements for its accommodation, social life and the integration of its children at school'. This situation has been described by Liégeois[9] as 'an accumulation of handicaps ... the combined effects of [which] transform nomadism into vagrancy'.

Vagrancy is of course a criminal offence.[10] If the state (through the obfuscation or incrementalism) is able to criminalise a way of life, it can subsequently resist any claims of injustice by pleading *ex turpi*. Thus in *R v.*

Hereford and Worcester County Council, ex parte Smith (1993)[11] the applicant, a Gypsy, whose way of his life had become impossible because of systematic ditching of his traditional roadside stopping places by the local authority, applied for a declaration that this activity was unlawful. Although as a matter of strict highway law his case was unanswerable the Court of Appeal rejected the claim, relying on *ex turpi* – because the applicant's purpose in seeking the declaration was to facilitate his way of life (ie stopping on roadside waste) which was also technically unlawful.

Although this case occurred prior to the implementation of the Human Rights Act 1998 – there are grounds for believing that the concept of *ex turpi* has simply migrated into human rights jurisprudence without – it appears – any critical analysis.[12] In 2001 the European Court of Human Rights considered the complaint of *Chapman v. UK* (2001).[13] The applicant was under threat of eviction from land she owned because she lived there in breach of planning control. It is at least four times more difficult for a Gypsy to obtain planning permission than a non-Gypsy, and as a consequence about 30% of them are homeless (notwithstanding a long standing duty on local authorities to provide adequate accommodation for Gypsies). The court rejected her complaint – relying in no small measure on her illegality. This approach was castigated by Judge Bonello. In his opinion the failure of the law to provide adequate accommodation for the applicant had effectively 'entrapped' her into breaking the law: there was simply no logical reason why a 'a human rights court should look with more sympathy at the far reaching breach of law committed by the powerful, than at that forced on the weak'.

Is it the case, therefore, that the human rights jurisprudence has been so muddied by its confluence with the common law, that to all intents and purposes the Convention has lost its vitality. If actions cannot be founded on base or ugly or deformed causes, who is it that decides what is base or ugly or deformed? Is the government free to define illegality and defend itself by criminalising an oppressed group's way of life? Is the doctrine of deference now so deeply rooted that the courts must unquestioning accept such a designation?

Of course questions of this nature exploit, in part, a false dichotomy. All law (human rights or otherwise) depends for its articulation on judges who will almost always have been nurtured by a common law or civil law tradition. Such judges are chosen primarily for their brilliant analytical minds – and not for their powers of social insight or for their wisdom or their judgment (in its broader sense). Judges are drawn to black and white contestations that are amenable to black letter law solutions. The problems of socially excluded people do not come in such convenient packages. As Wexler observed 'the law school model of personal legal problems, of solving them and returning the client to the smooth and orderly world in television advertisements, doesn't apply to poor people'.[14] Judges become exceedingly unsettled if invited to look at events preceding a single discreet episode: to ask, for instance 'why was the Gypsy trespassing?' Judges invariably refuse such invitations; explaining that their craft cannot withstand such turbulent waters – that to venture there would be to stray into political territory: in short they defer and declare the issue non-justiciable.

Quo vadis justice when the government has the ability, by playing with the levers of social control.[15] to render a minority's way of life unlawful? What role is there for a legal system that defers in such cases, either explicitly or implicitly by recourse to *ex turpi*?

In the last five years we have not seen a conflict of laws of the order that should have occurred had there been a true confluence of these two legal systems. This absence of turbulence has been misinterpreted by the judiciary as evidence of an underlying compatibility between the two systems – one based on the inviolability human life and the other on the sanctity of property. A true resolution will only occur when the courts cease to think the common law way – cease to use common law doctrines (such as *ex turpi*) to stifle conflict.

Notes

1 This paper derives from an earlier consideration of the topic, which appeared as L. Clements (2002) *Dirty Gypsies — ex turpi causa and Human Rights*. Human Rights. Dec 2002 204-212. London Jordans.

2 Reader in Law, Cardiff Law School.

3 See Polden, P. (2002) *Mingling the Waters* in Cambridge Law Journal 61(3) November 2002 p575, at 575 where this famous statement is cited as follows 'W Ashburner *Principles of Equity* 2nd edition (London 1933), p.18. It is probably derived from Lord Westbury's speech in Parl. Debs. 3rd s. vol. 201 col. 1573 (30 May 1870).'

4 Lord Woolf LCJ (2003) *On the occasion of the opening of the judicial year at the European Court of Human Rights* 23rd January 2003 accessible at www.dca.gov.uk/judicial/speeches/lcj230103.htm.

5 'Although the system might administer the system impartially, justice itself is partial' Bankowski & Mungham (1976) *Images of Law* Routledge & Kegan p.9.

6 Gypsies and Travellers constitute the single largest category of people (numerically) deemed to be 'at very high risk of social exclusion' – *Breaking the Cycle: Taking stock of progress and priorities for the future. A report by the Social Exclusion Unit*, Sept 2004, Office of the Deputy Prime Minister, London: para 1.61.

7 Economic and Social Research Council funded research – reference R000239238; see L. Clements & R. Morris (2004) 'The Millennium blip: local authority responses to the Human Rights Act 1998' in Halliday, S. & Schmidt, P. (eds) in *Human Rights Brought Home: Socio-Legal Studies of Human Rights in the National Context*. Oxford: Hart Publishing.

8 23 E.H.R.R. 191.

9 Gypsies and Travellers, J-P Liégeois (1987) Council of Europe, p.111.

10 Vagrancy Act 1824.

11 Court of Appeal 7 April 1993 Lexis; a case considered by Beale, A. & Geary, R. *Abolition of an unenforced duty* N.L.J. 1995, 145(6679), 47-48, 61.

12 See in this respect L. Clements (2002) op cit.

13 (2001) 33 E.H.R.R. 399.

14 Wexler, S. (1970) *Practising Law for Poor People*; The Yale Law Journal. Vol. 79: 1049, 1970.

15 Townsend, P. (1979) *Poverty in the United Kingdom*: London, Penguin.

Chapter 25

Holding Multinational Corporations Accountable for Breaches of Human Rights

Celia Wells and Juanita Elias

Can a corporation commit a crime? Can a corporation violate human rights?[1] It is hard enough to conceptualize the 'corporation' for the purposes of developing legal and moral accountability at the best of times. The fate of some of the world's largest corporations underlined that difficulty in a stark way. In what senses did Enron and WorldCom exist? One day (one year) Enron was the subject of the biggest investigation undertaken by Human Rights Watch,[2] the next it had 'disappeared' in a cloud of debts.

These corporate scandals highlight two important distinctions: that between corporate and white collar crime, and that between corporate and directorial responsibility. As to the first, the Enron and other scandals disclose some white collar (that is offending *against the company itself*) as well as corporate crime (that is crime affecting consumers, employees and others). The second distinction subdivides the field of corporate crime into the accountability of the *corporate entity* and the accountability of individual directors and officers for that crime.

Many corporations, like states, have the resources and power both to perpetrate and to escape responsibility for abuse. While most of us would like to sign up to reduce human rights violations, the means of achieving that reduction remain elusive.

Three core questions emerge in relation to multinational corporations: what legal avenues are possible? what principles of accountability can be used? and what models of complicity can be applied?

Context: Corporate Regulation in an Era of Globalization

Many people believe it is necessary to bring multinational corporations under the authority of international human rights frameworks. Traditionally international law conforms to a state-centric view of world politics. States are viewed as the primary actors in the international system, with international law acting to regulate relations between states.[3] Challenges to the role and primacy of the state in world politics has, however, fundamentally altered the role and function of international law.

International law has expanded, but is increasingly focused, through concerns about human rights, with the individual.

This strengthening international legal commitments to human rights can be seen as another aspect of the multi-faceted nature of globalization.[4] States have lost authority to supranational bodies at the same time as they have privatized many of their domestic functions.[5] But it is economic globalization that is generally presented as the major challenge to state sovereignty. The challenge comes in particular from financial speculation in deregulated currency markets and the growing economic power of multinational corporations. States are more likely to attempt to attract international capital rather than to try to regulate it.[6] In a globalized economy, firms (especially those in manufacturing) can move easily across borders and evade boycotts and sanctions.[7] The diminishing centrality of the state in world politics is accompanied by the rise of Multinationals as rival sources of power and influence in the world. We cannot take the term 'MNC' as legally uncontested or unproblematic.

The OECD Guidelines for Multinational Enterprises use the following definition :

> ...companies or other entities established in more than one country and so linked that they may co-ordinate their operations in various ways. While one or more of these entities may be able to exercise a significant influence over the activities of others, their degree of autonomy within the enterprise may vary widely from one multinational enterprise to another. Ownership may be private, state or mixed.[8]

This reflects the more fluid organization and structure of many modern companies with strategic alliances with other producers, seeking economies of scale in manufacturing.

With intergovernmental aid now largely overtaken by foreign direct investment, the temptation for host countries to attract investors with minimal human rights standards is often difficult to resist.[9] Human rights abuses can occur whether the outsourcing takes place via wholly or partly owned subsidiary or through use of supply contracts. It is the ability of MNCs to operate across national borders and outside the effective supervision of domestic and international law that makes them important actors ripe for greater investigation under international laws. MNCs often act in concert with host states, in suppressing local populations, forcibly moving them, or forcibly requiring their labour – this is known as 'militarized commerce'.

Holding Corporations to Account

First it is useful to look at the framework of legal possibilities. While the most direct legal response to such violations would be through a criminal or civil action in the host country, it does not take much insight to see that it is unlikely that a state that itself abuses human rights would prosecute such cases or be receptive to civil litigation. This has led to the pursuit of legal redress in the home country of the multinational complicit in the host state's human rights abuses. For example, the litigation arising from the activities of Cape plc and Thor Chemical Holdings, both companies domiciled in the UK but operating in South Africa, and ATCA (Alien Tort Claims Act) cases in US.

While the UK cases focused on procedural questions, ATCA has provoked debate of substantive issues. ATCA cases are pursued under customary international law. Under customary international law, natural persons (individuals) have a duty not to violate fundamental or peremptory norms (including piracy, aircraft hijacking, forced labour, genocide, war crimes and crimes against humanity). This has led some to conclude that:

> To the extent that individuals have rights and duties under customary international law and international humanitarian law, multinational corporations as legal persons have the same set of rights and duties.[10]

ATCA is an example of a national jurisdiction treating corporations in the same way as natural persons with regard to international customary law.[11] This is less surprising in the USA where corporate liability for criminal offences is well established.

The federal Alien Tort Claims Act 1789 gave to US district courts

> original jurisdiction of any civil action by an alien for a tort only, committed in violation of the law of nations or a treaty of the United States.

It converts a violation of the international law of nations into a domestic tort actionable in federal courts. In its modern incarnation, ATCA has been held to apply to private actors in relation to international crimes of genocide, war crimes, and crimes against humanity.[12] In 1992 Congress endorsed the use of US civil law (including ATCA) against those who use torture and extra-judicial killing.[13]

Increasingly ATCA is being used to pursue corporations rather than individuals. Cases are brought on behalf of non-US citizens; one filed recently is a huge class action on behalf of all those alive during and affected by the apartheid regime in South Africa between 1948-1993. But it is the Unocal litigation, launched in 1996, that is likely to determine the liability principles. Unocal, in a joint venture with Total S.A., and the Myanmar (Burmese) government, undertook to extract oil and build a pipeline. The case against UNOCAL is brought on behalf of Burmese citizens who allegedly suffered torture, assault, rape, loss of their homes and property, forced labour, and other human rights violations at the hands of the military.[14] The tentacles of the Unocal litigation have spread far and wide through the State and federal legal systems in what has been, even by US standards, longwinded process. In summary:

1. A landmark ruling in 1997 (U.S. federal district court in Los Angeles) that corporations and their executive officers can be held legally responsible under ATCA for violations of international human rights norms in foreign

countries, and that U.S. courts have the authority to adjudicate such claims.

2. A federal appeals court panel ruling in September 2002 that the case could proceed to trial because evidence was presented that Unocal provided substantial assistance to the military.[15] At issue is how much assistance is required to trigger a corporation's liability for abuses perpetrated by another, in this case by the Burmese military. Is it sufficient to prove that Unocal knowingly assisted or does there have to proved some element of control by Unocal over the host state's actors?
3. A full constitutional challenge to ATCA on which a Supreme Court ruling is expected in the summer of 2004.[16]
4. A state trial in California that is currently (May 2004) concerned with establishing whether there is a legal link between the actions of overseas subsidiaries and California based parent company Unocal.

ATCA cases being litigated in other states include one against Exxon,[17] and the one we have already mentioned on behalf of South Africans seeking $50billion from Citigroup, UBS and Credit Suisse for the 'blood and misery' the companies allegedly caused by doing business with SA's apartheid regime. The companies are said to have profited from loans to Pretoria between 1985 and 1993 while the UN embargo on trade was in force.[18]

The point here is that ATCA is a threat - a smoking gun - which could explode in the face of an MNC at some point. While these cases show that breaches of human rights obligations do not necessarily have to be characterized as crimes, the normative nature of the standards makes crime the closest analogy. A number of points can be made about using tort, civil claims. ATCA is there and, as the constitutional challenge evidences, is a clear cause concern to the US government and to multinational corporations. This makes it a useful strategic option not least for drawing attention to specific human rights allegations. But is it the optimal mechanism? Significant problems in translating ATCA jurisprudence to national or international fora include: different regimes for civil damages (punitive damages in the US blur the crime/tort distinction); corporate liability for crime is problematic in many jurisdictions; and reliance on US domestic legislation is inappropriate as an international response.

Deploying criminal law against multinationals for their activities abroad is also fraught with difficulties. This is the background to the many calls for a formal international framework to deal with MNC complicity, such as this from Andrew Clapham.

> A legally binding convention that is enforceable in practice needs to be formulated to ensure proper multinational accountability, capturing the supply-chain, not just subsidiaries. This convention must be applied internationally and, in a development of international law, apply to corporations as well as states.[19]

Two elements that would need to be addressed in such a convention are corporate liability principles and complicity principles. The notion of corporate responsibility for crime is far from universally accepted.[20] Even in jurisdictions where it exists, its theoretical and doctrinal development is immature and quite varied. Applying these developments to multinationals will present further difficulties of course, even if the question were their direct responsibility for offences committed by their subsidiaries or contractors further down increasingly diffuse supply chains. Those arguing for a more developed doctrine of complicity often fail to consider this problematic foundation.

Principles of complicity are drawn mostly from criminal law and, are generally based on proof of knowledge, something that has proved difficult in the development of corporate liability. We are going to use the example of the International Criminal Court, although it does not yet have jurisdiction over legal persons/corporations, only natural persons. The ICC is concerned with the most egregious of wrongful conduct, genocide, crimes against humanity, war crimes, and aggression.[21] It does not take too big a leap of imagination to extend international criminal law to multi nationals. Corporate liability for crime has increasingly appeared on the agenda in many jurisdictions over the last 10 years. Additionally, it is not so difficult to conceive a corporation as the subject of international law. While the mind-set of the criminal lawyer is to think about individuals, that of the international lawyer was for a long time to think about states/a group entity, albeit of a special kind. But the ICC and other War Crimes Tribunals specifically address the crimes of individual human agents. Thus it might be said that national law is going corporate and international law is going individual. Indeed the Rome Statute contained in its *draft* form a clause extending jurisdiction over legal persons.

But there are still many problems. Those who advocate the accountability of MNCs in international law tend to be much stronger in their arguments of why this would be a good thing than in their arguments of how this can be achieved. In particular they tend to skate over the problems of attributing mental elements to corporations. Models of corporate accountability range from the broad agency principle (applied in the US federal courts) under which the corporation is responsible for anything any of its employees does, to the very narrow identification doctrine that applies in the UK for mens rea offences – where liability arises only through the culpability of an individual director. There are also some developing third way models using corporate culture as the route to accountability.

Bearing those in mind, we want now to look at some complicity schemes that might be used in this field. We are thinking of liability of the corporate entity but there may be individuals within the corporate structure who act unlawfully and, while the Rome Statute does not address corporations as such, it can of course be applied to individual directors.[22] It is more likely that the violations result from a corporate policy or decision, rather than being attributable to any one individual's conduct. An example would be where a company enters into a contract with a state to build a pipeline, or a dam, and negotiates the suspension of human rights laws as part of its terms (as appears to have occurred with the consortium constructing the

Baku-Tblisi-Ceyahn pipeline and the Turkish government).[23] It is this type of corporate participation that may prove the harder to capture.

Commonly a taxonomy of three types of involvement is used to describe corporate complicity with abusive states: direct, indirect and beneficiary complicity.[24] *Direct* complicity would include cases of joint participation, for example if Unocal had supplied personnel to work with the Burmese military. *Indirect* complicity comprises those situations where the multinational corporation's activities help to maintain a regime's financial and commercial infrastructure.

Beneficiary or third-order involvement describes the way that businesses silently exploit the regime, benefiting from lower wage costs because of poor conditions or discriminatory practices, for example. Human Rights Watch suggests that corporate complicity covers:

> Situations in which '[a] corporation facilitates or participates in government human rights violations. Facilitation includes the company's provision of material or financial support for states' security forces which then commit human rights violations that benefit the company.'[25]

One writer describes this as 'collapsing' the distinction between direct and indirect complicity.[26]

The South African Truth and Reconciliation Commission uses a similar but not entirely congruent scheme of first-, second- and third-order involvement in sustaining apartheid policies.[27] First- order complicity covers the specific case of those who assist in the design or implementation of human-rights-violating policies. A question might arise as to the role of lawyers whose clients participate in such negotiations.[28] Second-order complicity appears to encompass those who knew that their products would be used to assist in repression, such as the manufacture of torture instruments.

What is needed is a model of complicity that is not so restrictive as to be ineffective except against the most egregiously bad multinational corporations but neither so inclusive that it will be politically unacceptable except to the most ethically compliant states. This is the threshold question - what is the minimum level of involvement and or knowledge before liability is triggered?

The Rome Statute (setting up the International Criminal Court) is a useful starting point since its principles have been accepted by the international community. Article 25 more or less adopts the common law. The three routes to liability under the general principles of Article 25 roughly cover instigation, assistance and joint enterprise. It relies on knowledge, purpose and aim - all of which are difficult to apply to a corporation. Much would depend on the attribution principle to be adopted. While civil law and common law jurisdictions have similar principles in relation to complicity this, as we have already said, is not so in relation to corporate attribution. In coming closer we doubt rather that they will come to a consensus that takes the broadest model possible. If the Corpus Iuris draft is anything to go by this is likely to be some version between agency and identification. (Corpus Iuris is the attempt by EU to establish a common framework for dealing with financial crime etc in member states). Draft Article 13 states that offences can be committed by corporations 'provided the offence is committed for the benefit of the organisation by some organ or representative of the organisation, or any person acting in its name and having power, whether by law or merely in fact, to make decisions.'

In the context of this paper, commander or superior liability also provides a significant line of *analogous* argument. Under the Rome Statute the rules are slightly different for civilian than for military commanders but in both cases they are wider than the general complicity principles in Article 25 because they include liability for failure to act. Common elements are:

(i) the crimes concerned activities that were within the effective responsibility and control of the superior; and

(ii) the superior failed to take all necessary and reasonable measures within his or her power to prevent or repress their commission or to submit the matter to the competent authorities for investigation and prosecution;

In the case of civilians this failure to exercise control leads to liability only where:

(iii) the superior either knew, or consciously disregarded information which clearly indicated, that the subordinates were committing or about to commit such crimes.

But for military commanders the provision does not require proof of knowledge or wilful blindness, it is enough that the defendant 'knew or, *owing to the circumstances at the time, should have known* that the forces were committing or about to commit such crimes…' [Art 28].

Perhaps some version of this could be adapted for corporations?

To Conclude

Our task in this paper was to explore ways in which multinational corporations could be brought to account for human rights violations in which they are complicit. It is worth re-stating the obvious point that corporations owe their status in law *to law*. From this it follows that they should be challengeable in law. The cultural, social, and political changes associated with the development of highly interdependent global economies helps to explain the rise in debate about corporate liability.

International law can effect change through demands on states to regulate corporations. Some of the problems in asking states to control multinational corporations include: the reluctance of host states to cut off the hand that feeds them, problems of jurisdiction in home state litigation, and more generally the difficulty in pinning down the legal personality of a multinational corporation.

Establishing the complicity threshold – problematised in ATCA cases – is perhaps less of an issue than finding agreement on corporate attribution. We need in effect both: complicity and attribution principles that reflect the reality of state and corporate structures of decision-making. Before an effective regime can be developed it will be necessary to drive through a company culture or organizational principle of attribution.

Notes

1 See Tamara Egede and Celia Wells *An Annotated Bibliography The Accountability of Multinational Corporations in International Human Rights Law* (2003) http://www.brass.cf.ac.uk/Civil%20Rights%20Bibliography/contextandpurpose.html.

2 Human Rights Watch The Enron Corporation: Complicity: The Dabhol Power Corporation (January 1999) www.hrw.org/reports/1999/enron/.

3 A. Cassese, *International Law* (2001), at 3.

4 David Held, *Violence, Law and Justice in a Global Age* (2001), Social Science Research Council Essays on Globalization after September 11, Nov 5th, p 1.

5 International Council on Human Rights Policy (ICHRP) *Beyond Voluntarism: Human Rights and the Developing Legal Obligations of Companies* (2002), at 10. See also Kamminga and Zia-Zarifi 'Liability of Multinational Corporations under international law: an introduction' in Kamminga M and Zia-Zarifi S. (eds) *Liability for Multinational Corporations under International Law* (2000), 5.

6 For example, S. Strange, *States and Markets* (1988), P. Cerny, *The Changing Architecture of Politics: Structure, Agency and the Future of the State* (1990), p. 237. R. Roscrance, 'The Rise of the Virtual State', *Foreign Affairs*, July/Aug 1996.

7 Willets, 'Transnational Actors and International Organizations in World Politics', in J. Baylis and S.Smith (eds), *The Globalization of World Politics: An Introduction to International Relations* (2001), at 364.

8 As amended in 2000, www.oecd.org/daf/investment/guidelines/mnetext.htm.

9 Kamminga and Zia-Zarifi, *above* note 5, at 2.

10 Ramasastry 'Corporate Complicity: From Nuremberg to Rangoon, An examination of Forced Labour Cases and their Impact on the Liability of Multinational Corporations 20 *Berkeley Jnl of Int Law* (2002) 91, 96.

11 Ramasastry above, p.101.

12 *Filartiga v Pena-Irala* 630 F. 2d 876 (2d Cir. 1980); *Kadic v Karadzic*_70 F.3d at 244 (2d Cir. 1995).

13 Torture Victims Protection Act 1992.

14 *Doe I v Unocal Corp* 963 F.Supp 880 (C.D. Cal 1997).

15 110 F.Supp. 2d 1294, 1296 (C.D.Cal. 2000); *John Doe v. Unocal corp*. Nos. 00-56603, 00-57197, 00-56628, 00-57195, 2002 WL 31063976 (9TH CIR. Sept 18, 2002).

16 *Sosa v. Alvarez-Machain* US Supreme Court No 03-339.

17 *Doe v Exxon Mobil Corporation*, FEDERAL District Court for District of Columbia, 01-1257, claim filed by International Labor Rights Fund, 11 June 2001, alleging human rights abuses in Aceh, Indonesia, www.laborrights.org/projects/corporate/exxon last accessed 5 May 2004.

18 *Time* 1 July 2002, p 16.

19 *Mail & Guardian* [South Africa], 19 April 2002.

[20] Stephens notes that the extension of ATCA jurisdiction to corporations is undoubtedly a reflection of the 'common acceptance of the concept of corporate crime [in the US], Stephens 'Corporate Accountability: International Human Rights Litigation against Corporations in US courts' in Kamminga and Zia-Zarifi (eds) above note 5, 209 at 220.

[21] Rome Statute of the International Criminal Court, adopted by the United Nations Diplomatic Conference of Plenipotentiaries on the establishment of an International Court on 17 July 1998, Article 25(1), Art 5.

[22] Schabas 'Enforcing International Humanitarian Law: Catching the Accomplices' 83 *International Review of the Red Cross* (2001) 439.

[23] Monbiot 'Trouble in the Pipeline' *The Guardian* 3rd September 2002. http://politics.guardian.co.uk/columnist/story/0,9321,785316,00.html accessed 24 September 2002.

[24] Danish Human Rights and Business Project, *Defining the Scope of Business Responsibility for Human Rights Abroad (2001)* www.humanrights.dk.

[25] In the Enron report, above note 2.

[26] Ramasastry, above note 10.

[27] South African Truth and Reconciliation Commission Report, Volume Four, Chapter Two, Business and Labour 1998.

[28] Kamminga and Zia-Zarifi wryly comment that they could attract no lawyers representing major MNCs to participate in the Colloquium on which their book is based, above note 5, at 15.

PART IV
COMMENTARIES

Chapter 26

The Health Professional and the Dying Patient

Mark Fish

The debate over the health professionals' role in relation to the dying patient continues. The British Medical Association (BMA) recognizes (not condones) four categories of medical action at the end of life:

1) Alleviation of pain and distress.
2) Non-provision or withdrawal of treatment, which may be life-prolonging, but is not in the patient's best interest.
3) Physician-aided suicide by providing the means or advice to enable suicide.
4) Active medical intervention to end life, commonly termed "euthanasia" (which literally means a gentle and easy death).[1]

At the present time, physician assisted suicide and euthanasia are not legal in the United Kingdom and not condoned by the BMA. During the last year there have been two high profile cases that have been debated in the general media and highlighted ongoing campaigns to legalise assisted suicide and, by association, euthanasia. A recent survey conducted by the Nursing Times has questioned the neat distinction between the categories of distress-relief and euthanasia. In May of 2002, Diane Pretty died 3 days after her challenge had been rejected in the European Court of Human Rights. In the UK she had been seeking immunity from prosecution for her husband if he helped her to commit suicide and had argued that being required to go on living through the advanced stages of motor neurone disease was contrary to the Human Rights Act of 1998.

In January 2003 Reginald Crewe, also suffering from motor neurone disease, flew to Switzerland, accompanied by his wife, to end his life by intentionally drinking a dose of barbiturate sufficient not only to make him sleep, but also to stop his respiration and end his life. The medically staffed organisation that facilitated the process is called Dignitas, and their slogan is, "to live with dignity and to die with dignity". There is no equivalent in the UK. as anybody in this country who aids suicide is liable to prosecution and imprisonment, whether health care professionals or not. Mr Crewe's wife was clearly frustrated that her husband "could not have ended it in his own country" with medical assistance and within the law.

An attempt at law reform began in the House of Lords in February 2003 with the Compassion in Dying Bill.[2] This would provide for a competent adult suffering from terminal disease or incurable physical illness to request medical assistance in dying. Lord Joffes highlights the need for the terminally ill to be able to exercise greater choice.

As well as patient dignity, the appeal to autonomy is frequently used by advocates of physician assisted suicide and euthanasia. Opponents to legalisation include groups as diverse as the BMA, representatives of the disabled, and the Catholic Church. They fear that even a limited change in the legislation may profoundly change society's attitude to the vulnerable, and could ultimately lead to an extension of the practice of euthanasia beyond those who sought it; a "slippery slope", as the director of Disability Awareness in Action has said. Both the Catholic Church and the BMA have reminded us of eugenics programmes in Nazi Germany. There is a fear that the continually evolving relationship between the public and profession, as well as patient and doctor (in an already fragile condition post-Shipman), would be further undermined if the doctors' role were obfuscated to include assistance in suicide. It is not inconceivable that the elderly could become afraid to be admitted to a bed-short NHS hospital.

The arguments put forward by the proponents of assisted suicide and euthanasia invariably centre around the all too real plight of the terminally ill individual, and the inability for them and their carers to exercise their autonomy within the law. Opponents, whilst acknowledging their predicament, feel that the risks to society, especially to the vulnerable, are too great if the doctors role were to include facilitation of death. For the moment, health professionals are not left to resolve these conflicting imperatives of autonomy and justice.

Both Reginald Crewe and Diane Pretty suffered from motor neurone disease – generally a relentlessly progressive condition which can eventually leave the subject unable to speak, move voluntarily, or swallow safely, usually in clear consciousness. Mrs Pretty had stated that she feared the choking and asphyxia caused by her disease. Mrs Crewe asked, "why should you have to suffer, right through to the end?"

Palliative care teams do allow patients to die with dignity. Traditionally, these services provide for patients with terminal cancer. Resources are presently not directed to extend provision to countless other patients with for example terminal heart failure, end stage chronic obstructive airways disease, or neurological disease. We should not even be contemplating legislating to allow physician assisted suicide until such services are uniformly and sufficiently available. Perhaps, as the BMA states, there might be fewer patients seeking to end their lives prematurely if they felt assured of a pain-free end.

A recent poll in the Nursing Times found that about 1 in 20 of the 1000 nurses surveyed believed that colleagues are quietly helping terminally ill patients to die, and revealed some anxiety about whether "that last dose" of opiate constituted euthanasia. By the principle of double effect, it is ethical to prescribe medications, most often opiates and anxiolytics, to a dying patient if the intention of the treatment is to alleviate pain and distress, even if the "side-effect" is to hasten death. If the intention in the prescription were to expedite death, then that same action becomes unethical. The doctor may be put in a difficult position if he or she is asked by relatives, nursing staff, or the patient themselves to put them "out of their misery". The prescriber needs to be clear in their own mind and in communication with patients, relatives and staff as to the rationale and effects of treatment. Nursing staff, as well as doctors, share the responsibility of judicious administration of such medications, especially if such prescriptions appear on the "as required" side of the drug chart. The Royal College of Nursing does "not think it is the right time for a change in the Euthanasia laws" and the editor of the *Nursing Times* describes this as a "grey area". Until recently many health professionals have exercised their compassion in this "grey area" but this may become increasingly problematic.

March 2003

Notes

1 Medical Ethics Today: Its Practice and Philosophy. From the BMA's Ethics, Science and Information Division. Published by the BMJ publishing group. 1993 (reprinted 1998)

2 The 2003 "Compassion in dying" bill fell due to lack of parliamentary time. A modified version "The Assisted Dying for the Terminally Ill Bill" was introduced to the House of Lords in 2004.

Chapter 27

Legitimate Authority, Just Cause, and the Decision to Invade Iraq

Gregory Reichberg

Few political decisions are as weighty as the decision to go to war. This is doubly true of the present war, which was not thrust on the United States and its allies as a matter of strict necessity. Rather it is the outcome of a strategic choice. And like every other choice this has an inherently ethical dimension. True, some hard-core realists might argue that war by its nature falls outside of ethics; it must be decided, they say, on purely political or military grounds. And, from the opposing perspective, committed pacifists might argue that to opt for war is always morally wrongful, especially where, as in this case, the war is not purely defensive. Hence there is no need, they would say, to deliberate about the ethics of the case. Yet for all those whose moral commitments lie somewhere in the middle, the decision for and against the proposed war was not a simple one. At the very least it required a modicum of ethical reflection.

Ethical reflection on war has a long history that reaches back to the ancient Greeks. Yet it wasn't however until the mid-sixteenth century that a systematic treatise on the subject was written – the De jure belli ("On the Law of War") by Spanish philosopher Francisco de Vitoria.[1] This was followed by several works of similar cast – most famously Francisco Suárez's De bello ("On War") – culminating in the epochal work by Hugo Grotius De jure belli ac pacis ("On the Law of War and Peace"). Central to all of these was the idea that ethical theorizing about war could be organized according to a set of conditions that must be fulfilled if resort to armed force (jus ad bellum) is to have moral warrant. Some of these conditions speak to principled issues of right, while others focus on matters of prudential concern. The former were taken up under the headings of "legitimate authority," "just cause," and "right intention," and the latter were termed "last resort," "proportionality," "reasonable hope of success," and "open declaration." All of these conditions have been the subject of heated debate ("last resort" most especially) in the period leading up to the Iraq invasion. Within this limited space I will discuss only the first two of these conditions – legitimate authority and just cause – and the relation between them.

The classical just-war theorists operated with a distinction between defensive and offensive war. A defensive war was defined as a reaction to armed attack. Self-defense was viewed as an inherent human right, that could legitimately be appealed to by sovereign nations, lesser republics, and even private individuals.

No special higher authorization was needed to avail oneself of force in order to repel armed attack. This broad latitude (with respect to the authority condition) was counterbalanced by the very limited scope of what might count as justifiable self-defence. Only an attack underway, or one just completed (and likely to be renewed) might warrant a response of armed self-defence. The likelihood of a future attack could legitimate a defensive reaction ("pre-emptive strike") only when it could be shown that the attack was imminent and left the victim state "no choice of means"[2] other than armed reaction. Using armed force preventively, solely to eliminate an adversary's ability to inflict future harm was deemed illicit: it would mete out punishment for crimes not yet committed, nor even planned, but merely possible, and would make fear a principle of action in international relations, thereby opening a Pandora's box of anticipatory first strikes. This was stated most pointedly by Grotius when he asserted how "untenable is the position, which has been maintained by some, that according to the law of nations it is right to take up arms in order to weaken a growing power which, if it becomes too great, may be a source of danger.... That the possibility of being attacked confers the right to attack is abhorrent to every principle of equity.".[3]

Significantly, the logic of preventive war is one of two formal rationales that the United States government has put forward to justify the initiation of armed hostilities against Iraq.[4] It is alleged that this country is in possession of weapons of mass destruction (WMD) that represent a future danger to the United States and the entire region. Even putting aside the factual question of whether Iraq indeed possesses WMD, still, on principled grounds it must be said that preventive war is not an acceptable form of self-defence within just-war ethics. This same exclusion is embodied in recent international law. The 1945 Charter to the United Nations (Art. 51), describes the right self-defence as applicable "if an armed attack occurs," a phrase that mainstream jurists interpret restrictively as defining the sole circumstance in which the right of self-defence may be exercised.[5] Aware of this discordance with the traditional doctrine of self-defence, proponents of the Bush administration view have argued that the unprecedented risks posed by WMD require us to re-draw the boundaries of what may count as legitimate self-defence. The argument has been made that this concept must accordingly be broadened to allow the U.S. and its allies to engage in armed preventive action.[6] However, to its detractors, this argumentation is nothing more than a form of special pleading[7] that conceals the weak ethical and legal credentials of the new doctrine.

In addition to self-defence, classical just-war teaching allowed for some forms of offensive war: to redress past wrongs, to punish the violation of sworn truces or treaties, or to protect the rights of third parties. Excluded were wars undertaken for territorial aggrandizement, political domination, economic interests, etc. In any event, it was recognized that offensive war, as a war of choice, not of necessity[8] (since it is not a reaction to an armed attack that is imminent or ongoing), could only be chosen by the top leadership of the supreme political unit: the sovereign commonwealth. No lesser groupings, and certainly not private individuals, could have the legitimate authority to initiate such a course of action, even if they otherwise possessed a just cause.[9]

The imposition of a strict authority condition on offensive war is still operative today, in international law, although the standard for what counts as legitimate authority has been set even higher than in the time of the classical just-war writers. Whereas they sought to remove offensive war from the hands of all but the highest rulers (this right being denied to lesser princes and lords), international law has placed this authority squarely within the ambit of the UN Security Council (SC).[10] This is wise, since only a strict procedure of multilateral decision-making could possibly check the grave disorder that would be introduced into the international system by an unrestricted right of offensive war, even at the service of a just cause. As it now stands, no single sovereign state has the right to authorize the employment of armed force for purposes other than strict defence. The scope of offensive action (or "enforcement action" in the language of the UN Charter, chap. VII) accorded to the SC is broad, in some respects considerably broader than what the earlier just-war tradition would allow, since it encompasses even forcible preventive measures.[11] Nevertheless, this broadening is purchased by the exclusion of any unilateral offensive action on the part of individual states. It is precisely this restriction that the U.S. and its military coalition partners have violated by proceeding to war without the needed SC mandate.

True, there have been occasions in the recent past when the international community has countenanced a flexible reading of the authority condition (e.g., NATO's Kosovo airwar), yet these exceptions have enjoyed a multilateral consensus that is clearly absent in the present case. The Bush administration's assertion that it has just cause to attack Iraq in order to enforce "all relevant United Nations Security Council resolutions"[12] regarding that country is disingenuous, since it is violating a central rule (no offensive military action without express SC approval) of the very same body whose resolutions it purports to uphold. The claim that no new SC resolution was needed to commence the invasion of Iraq (since resolution 1441 had already threatened serious consequences should Iraq fail to abide by the terms of the resolution), is likewise disingenuous. The condition of legitimate authority is required not only to execute military action in favour of a just cause, but also for the very determination of the just cause itself, i.e., a specification of what particular wrongful actions actually warrant an armed response.[13] Hence, the determination that Iraq was sufficiently in breach of resolution 1441 so as to merit the sanction of armed invasion, was a matter to be decided by the entire SC, not one or several of its individual members. In fact, it is clear that had the SC been presented this March with a proposal to invade Iraq, it would have voted down the resolution.

This focus on legitimate authority may seem overly legalistic. In reality, however, it cuts to the core of just-war ethics. Military force can be made to serve the ends of justice only when it is channelled into the right hands. For this reason legitimate authority was placed at the very head of Thomas Aquinas's seminal list of criteria of the just war,[14] which has served as the starting point for all subsequent endeavours in the field.

April 2003

Notes

1 See Gregory M. Reichberg, "Philosophy Meets War" in The Classics of Western Philosophy, edited by Gracia, Reichberg, & Schumacher (Oxford: Blackwell Publishers, 2003), pp. 197–204.

2 This is from "Webster's formula" (1841–2), written apropos of the Caroline incident of 1837, which nicely sums up earlier ethical reflection on self-defence, and has since served as a benchmark for legal thinking about pre-emptive strikes. The full formula states that, for a claim of self-defence (especially pre-emptive defence) to be legitimate, there must be shown "a necessity of self-defence, instant, overwhelming, leaving no choice of means, and no moment for deliberation." It is also affirmed that the action must also involve "nothing unreasonable or excessive; since the act, justified by the necessity of self-defence, must be limited by that necessity, and kept clearly within it" (from the correspondence of U.S. Secretary of State D. Webster with British envoys, cited in Yoram Dinstein, War, Aggression and Self-Defence, 3rd edition [Cambridge: Cambridge University Press, 2001], p. 219).

3 Hugo Grotius, De jure belli ac pacis libri tres, trans. Francis W. Kelsey (Oxford: Clarendon Press, 1925), bk. II, chap. 17, p. 184.

4 In "Text of a Letter from the President to the Speaker of the House of Representatives and President Pro Tempore of the Senate," dated March 21 2003 (on the official website of the White House, www.whitehouse.gov), President George W. Bush wrote that "further diplomatic and other peaceful means alone will neither adequately protect the national security of the United States against the continuing threat posed by Iraq, nor lead to enforcement of all relevant United Nations Security Council resolutions regarding Iraq."

5 On this see Bruno Simma, et. al., The Charter of the United Nations: A Commentary, vol. 1, pp. 794–796, 803–804. Jurists are divided on the question whether or not Art. 51 was meant to restrict the pre-existing customary right of anticipatory self-defence, as expressed most notably in Webster's formula. This debate has little bearing on the present discussion, however, since the customary law as expressed by Webster would not permit preventive strikes against other states, of the sort undertaken by the U.S. coalition against Iraq.

6 In the National Security Strategy of the United States of America, September 2002 (released September 20, 2002; see www.whitehouse.gov, for the full text) it is stated that "Given the goals of rogue states and terrorists, the United States can no longer rely on a reactive posture as we have in the past. ... We must adopt the concept of imminent threat to the capabilities and objectives of today's adversaries. ... The greater the threat, the greater is the risk of inaction – and the more compelling the case for taking anticipatory action to defend ourselves.... To forestall or prevent such hostile acts by our adversaries, the United states will, if necessary, act preventively" (my emphasis) (excerpted from chapter 5). From this statement it is clear that the new security strategy promotes a doctrine of preventive, rather than pre-emptive war. Yet, by using the latter term to designate what is in fact signified by the former, it has obscured the novelty of the 2002 National Security Strategy. An attempt to re-think international law in order to make room for this new doctrine of prevention, may be found in Walter B. Slocombe, "Force, Pre-emption and Legitimacy," Survival 45/1 (2003): pp. 117-130. For a selection of essays (pro and con) on preventive war and the new U.S. Security Strategy, see The Washington Quarterly 26/2, "Is Prevention Necessary?", pp. 75–145.

7 Proponents of this broadening assume what must in fact be proven, namely that "WMD and terrorism pose threats unanticipated by traditional international law" (Anthony

Clark Arend, "International Law and the Preemptive Use of Military Force," in The Washington Quarterly, op. cit., pp. 89–103, on p. 97). This assertion is not self-evident. Careful historical thinking needs to be done on the purportedly unprecedented character of WMD and terrorism, and counter-examples should be vigorously investigated

8 Suárez employs the terminology of choice and necessity in his De bello, section 4, §10 (English translation in Selections from Three Works [Oxford: Clarendon Press, 1944], p. 823) as part of his discussion of the prudential condition of "reasonable hope of success." Since defensive wars are thrust on a party, the standard of what may count as a reasonable expectation of victory is set much lower than in a war undertaken offensively, wherein the attacking party has the freedom to decide when and indeed whether to initiate an armed conflict. It should be noted however that in either case (offensive or defensive war) the condition of "last resort" would still be applicable, although the modalities would differ.

9 Suárez thus remarks that "he who makes war without the authorization in question, even if he has, in other respects, a just title for so doing, nevertheless incurs the sanctions imposed on those who wage war unjustly" (De bello, section 2, §6 [op. cit., p. 809]).

10 Article 2(4) of the Charter states that "All members shall refrain in their international relations from the threat or use of force against the territorial integrity or political independence of any state...." The Charter recognizes only two exceptions to this renunciation of armed force in interstate state relations: self-defence under article 51, and enforcement measures mandated by the SC (Art. 42).

11 This is implied by the wording of article 1 of the UN Charter which states that the first purpose of the United Nations is "To maintain international peace and security, and to that end: to take effective collective measures for the prevention and removal of threats to the peace....." In article 42 it is likewise stated that the Security Council "may take such action by air, sea, or land forces as may be necessary to maintain or restore international peace and security." The full text of the Charter may be found on the official website of the United Nations, http://www.un.org/aboutun/charter/index.html.

12 This is the second official reason for war advanced by President Bush in his letter to the U.S. Congress (see above, note 4). The humanitarian objective (liberation of the people of Iraq from the regime of Saddam Hussein, with the goal of introducing a democratic rule of law) is not mentioned in the above notification to Congress, nor was this put forward for debate in the SC.

13 Article 39 of the Charter thus states that "The Security Council shall determine the existence of any threat to the peace, breach of the peace, or act of aggression and shall make recommendations, or decide what measures shall be taken in accordance with Articles 41 and 42, to maintain or restore peace and security."

14 See Summa theologiae, II-II, q. 40, a. 1: "In order for a war to be just, three requirements must be fulfilled. First, the authority of the sovereign by whose command the war is to be waged..." This may be found online at http://www.ccel.org/a/aquinas/summa/SS/SS040.html#SSQ40OUTP1

Chapter 28

Severe Acute Respiratory Syndrome (SARS) – An Odd New Challenge

Norman Vetter

Severe acute respiratory syndrome (SARS) is a respiratory illness that has fairly recently been reported in Asia, North America, and Europe. It appears to have originated in Southern China, whence it spread to Hong Kong and from there, by air travel, to many countries of the world.

The illness usually begins with a fever a temperature greater than 100.4°F [>38.0°C]). The fever is sometimes associated with chills or other symptoms, including headache, general feeling of discomfort and body aches. Some people also experience mild respiratory symptoms at the outset.

After 2 to 7 days, SARS patients may develop a dry, non-productive cough that might be accompanied by or progress to the point where insufficient oxygen is getting to the blood. In 10 percent to 20 percent of cases, patients need mechanical ventilation. The proportion of people dying of the illness meeting the current WHO case definition for probable and suspected cases of SARS is around 3%. Most patients identified have been previously healthy adults aged 25-70 years. A few suspected cases of SARS have been reported among children (=15 years).

The incubation period for SARS is typically 2 to 7 days; however, isolated reports have suggested an incubation period as long as 10 days. Patients without the initial fever are thought not to be infectious, which is why the presence of fever at airports and other exit and entrance points is felt to be so important.

At present we do not know the best treatment. People have tried anti-virals and steroids, sometimes with other antimicrobials. In the absence of controlled clinical trials we do not really know what is effective. Early information from laboratory experiments suggests that ribavirin does not inhibit virus growth or cell-to-cell spread of one isolate of the new coronavirus that was tested. Additional laboratory testing of ribavirin and other antiviral drugs is being done to see if an effective treatment can be found.

However, traditional public health measures can effectively prevent even a new infectious disease without specific treatment being available. These measures consist of close surveillance, accurate diagnosis and reporting and careful isolation of close contacts. In this way the disease has no-where else to spread.

Worldwide the number of new cases continues to fall. By 9 June there were 8421 reported probable cases and 784 deaths, compared with 8384 cases and 770 deaths the week before. Local transmission was now occurring only in Toronto –

Canada reported 31 new cases in the week to 9 June – and in parts of China and Taiwan.

Taiwan celebrated a decision by the World Health Organization to lift the SARS travel warning for the island in mid June 2003. Strict screening measures are still in place in Singapore despite its removal from the WHO list of SARS affected areas.

The spread of the disease suggests the virus to be of relatively low infectivity, but quite high severity. SARS is also strange because of the possible existence of super-spreaders, who infect many of their contacts. It has been suggested that a proportion of the population has an acquired resistance to the new virus, having already been exposed to another, relatively innocuous, virus that provides immune protection. It is possible that the proportion of humanity immune or partially immune to SARS could be as high as, say, 95% if the second virus were a very common one, e.g. one of the coronaviruses that causes the common cold.

This could also explain super-spreaders. There may be a majority of people who have previously met the common related coronavirus, and consequently have a degree of immunity to SARS, and a minority who have not met it, and have no immunity. The second group would get the disease in a severe form and excrete quantities of infectious material, these may be the super-spreaders.

In the last three decades we have seen several viral: ebola, AIDS, SARS and bacterial; TB, epidemics when we might have expected the eradication of infectious disease in developing countries. There are a number of theories about why this should be so. Developing countries have grown somewhat blasé about asepsis and aseptic techniques, especially good hand washing. Both housewives and doctors tend to rely on killing the germs, with potent antiseptics and antibiotics rather than a good clean-up to give no room for them to multiply. As a result strange bugs come to light by the process of evolution as their environment changes, especially if that environment wipes out their harmless competitors (it may kill 99% of household germs, but what will the 1% get up to). Other people have blamed the widespread use of vaccines; again leaving the field free for new agents. A gullible few always believe such things to be a mistake or a terror act of leakage of viral mutant from research or other laboratories or interplanetary infection.

Very recently it has been suggested that a similar virus, in that it reacts similarly to tests aimed at identifying it, has been around for some years. It is possible that the coronavirus causing SARS is an old friend who became grouchy in the last few months.

Whatever the reason, and it may be just part of life's rich tapestry, the rapid and relatively cheap movement of humans using long distance flights makes spread simple and puts us all in range. Good old-fashioned public health methods were developed before the microbial theory was born, so it is well used to dealing with the unknown and seem to be working for SARS.

June 2003

Chapter 29

Designing Donors

Shaun D. Pattinson

Introduction

Recently two couples sought permission from the Human Fertilisation and Embryology Authority (HFEA) to select embryos for tissue-compatibility with an existing child. One couple was granted permission and the other was not. Both had an existing child whose only hope of a cure for a serious and potentially fatal blood disorder was a transplant of stems cells from someone with matching tissue. No suitable donors had been found, so both couples sought to conceive a child for this purpose. If successful, stems cells could be taken from the blood in the umbilical cord of this specially created donor child and used to treat their sick child.

Applying its publish policy (see HFEA 2001; 2002), the HFEA gave the Hashmis permission to create and tissue type embryos in the hope of giving birth to a healthy baby whose stem cells could cure their sick son, Zain. Zain suffers from beta thalassaemia. In contrast, the Whitakers were refused permission to create and tissue type embryos for the purpose of creating a donor for their son, Charlie. Charlie suffers from Diamond-Blackfan Anaemia (DBA).

What was the difference? The HFEA pointed to differences in the type of blood disorder suffered by the two sick children (see HFEA 2001; 2002). Zain's condition was hereditary, whereas Charlie's condition was not. This meant that any child conceived by the Hashmis was itself at risk of developing the relevant disorder, whereas it was extremely unlikely that any child conceived by the Whitakers would suffer from the relevant disorder.

In terms of the procedures requested, both couples wished to create and biopsy embryos. However, the Hashmis wished to conduct a prior test on the biopsied material before it was tissue typed; this material was first to be subjected to preimplantation genetic diagnosis (PGD).[1] Thus, the Hashmis wanted to do more testing on the material removed from the embryos than the Whitakers (who were assured that their embryos would be free of DBA without the need to biopsy). This short paper will argue that although the HFEA has the legal authority to regulate these two cases in this way, it was wrong to do so.

The Legal Competence of the HFEA

There has been a string of recent cases challenging decisions made by the HFEA.[2] One of these was a challenge to the decision of the HFEA granting permission to the Hashmis, brought by Josephine Quintavalle on behalf of Comment on Reproductive Ethics (CORE): R (On the Application of Quintavalle) v HFEA [2002] EWHC 2785 (High Court); [2003] EWCA Civ 667 (Court of Appeal).[3]

Under the Human Fertilisation and Embryology Act 1990, it is unlawful to "use" an embryo created outside the body except under licence from the HFEA (s.3(1)(b)).[4] Treatment licences may, however, only be granted for activities that the HFEA considers "necessary or desirable" for the purpose of providing "treatment services" (Sch 2, para 1(3)), defined as services "for the purpose of assisting women to carry children" (s.2(1)). In the High Court, Maurice Kay J held that tissue typing could not be authorised by HFEA. In his words,

> The sole purpose of tissue typing is to ensure that any such child would have tissue compatibility with its older sibling. I do not consider that it can be said to be "necessary or desirable" for the purpose of assisting a woman to carry a child. The carrying of such a child after implantation would be wholly unaffected by the tissue typing. (para 17)

The judge expressly refused to comment on whether his decision rendered PGD generally unlawful (para 16).[5] It clearly rendered the treatment sought by the Hashmis (and, by implication, the Whitakers) unlawful.

Maurice Kay J's decision was, however, reversed by the Court of Appeal. The Court of Appeal read the legislation purposively, adopting an ambitious non-literal construction reminiscent of the recent House of Lords decision in the first Quintavalle case (R (On the Application of Quintavalle) v Secretary of State for Health [2003] UKHL 13). All three judges read "assisting women to carry children" to encompass assisting women to produce "a child with stem cells matching a sick or dying sibling" (per Lord Philips, para 48. See also para 89, Schiemann LJ; and para 133, Mance LJ). "Assisting women to carry children" was thereby read as assisting a woman to carry the child that she wants to carry. This rendered it necessary to consider whether tissue typing fell within the list of treatment services that could be permitted under the Act (see Sch 2, para 1(1)). Once again unanimous, the Court of Appeal held that these techniques were licensable under Sch 2, para 1(1)(d), which permits practices designed to secure that embryos are in a suitable condition to be placed in a woman or to determine whether embryos are suitable for that purpose.

The word "suitable" was held to take its meaning from the context. It follows that the HFEA does have the legal competence to grant or deny permission to both the Hashmis and the Whitakers. Indeed, Mance LJ expressly addresses the HFEA's decision with regard to the Whitakers (in para 132). The HFEA's discretion must, however, be exercised in accordance with the Act's other requirements, including the requirement in s.13(5) that account be taken of the welfare of the resultant child and "any other child who may be affected by the birth". Having the lawful jurisdiction to draw a distinction between the Hashmis and Whitakers does not, however, imply an ethical basis for doing so.

Ethical Discussion

Is there a morally relevant distinction between the two cases? There is if the performance of the biopsy is a prima facie wrong outweighed by a countervailing consideration in the Hashmi case that does not apply in the Whitaker case. According to Suzi Leather, Chair of the HFEA, performing a biopsy on an embryo that is to be implanted is a prima facie wrong because "we don't know what the longterm consequences of that will be for the child being created" (quoted in Guardian 2003). Why is this wrong outweighed in one case but not the other? The HFEA holds the view that in the Hashmi case the embryo benefits from the biopsy, whereas in the Whitaker case the embryo does not. As a spokesperson for the HFEA put it:

> We have to look at the benefit for the embryo, not just the sibling...HFEA policy states that women are allowed to have treatment only for the benefit of the embryo. (Quoted in Wright 2003)

This distinction is specious; it is premised on a false attribution of benefit.

In both cases the biopsy is to be performed so that the embryos can be tested. If the test is favourable, an embryo is thereby selected for implantation. If the test is unfavourable, that embryo is to be destroyed. It might seem plausible to claim that all embryos selected for implantation are thereby benefited in the sense that they are allowed to develop into a child. However, this view is not as straightforward as it first appears. If it were always the case that a selected embryo thereby benefits, then any and every selection process would be a benefit to the selected embryo no matter how damaging the selection process was to it. Imagine, for example, an evil scientist who decides, on a mere whim, to implant whichever embryos survive being subjected to a small amount of acid. Any surviving embryo is likely to have been damaged by this unnecessary selection process. Surely we are not committed to the view that it has nonetheless benefited because it has at least been selected. Although the selected embryo is better off than the embryos destroyed by the acid, it is not better off relative to other possible scenarios leading to its implantation. Since the biopsy is potentially damaging, the HFEA can plausibly hold the view that all forms of testing requiring a biopsy are a prima facie wrong to the embryo. (This, of course, assumes that the embryo has direct moral status, i.e. is morally valuable by virtue of its characteristics rather than by virtue of its relationship to another being.) Indeed, where the embryo is created with the intention of subjecting it to a biopsy, the whole process can be said to be characterised by an intention that is prima facie immoral.

Does anyone benefit from the selection process requested by the Hashmis and Whitakers? In both cases, successful tissue typing followed by implantation and the birth of a suitable donor will benefit the parents and the sick sibling. This is, of course, the purpose of the enterprise. The benefit to the parents and sick siblings is identical in both cases. What about the embryos? Is an embryo selected for its tissue-compatibility thereby benefited? And does the Hashmi embryo gain an additional benefit by being selected when shown to be free of a serious life-threatening genetic disorder? The notion of benefit to the embryo needs some unpacking. Moral benefit is the opposite of moral harm. Elsewhere I have argued that to suffer a moral harm one must have been made worse off relative to one's alternatives.[6] Conversely, to gain a moral benefit one must have been made better off relative to one's alternatives.

Since the HFEA seeks to rely on the benefit to the embryo to distinguish biopsying for tissue typing from biopsying for PGD followed by tissue typing, they are claiming that embryos selected for the absence of this life-threatening blood disorder are thereby benefited. Is this so? PGD will be used here to identify those embryos with the gene for DBA, it will not change the disorder status of the selected embryo. If gaining a moral benefit presupposes being made better off relative to one's alternatives two things follow. First, no embryo that is rejected following PGD is thereby benefited unless being allowed to develop is worse for it than being destroyed. It is questionable whether being allowed to develop can ever be worse for an embryo than being destroyed, but, even if it could, beta thalassaemia is not incompatible with an enjoyable life. Suffering from beta thalassaemia is in no way a state worse than death. Second, no embryo that is implanted following PGD is benefited any more than it would be benefited by being allowed to develop following any other potentially damaging selection procedure. As stated above, if the biopsy poses risks to embryos, then an embryo implanted following a biopsy would have been better off had it been implanted without a biopsy.

In addition, there is no difference between the parents' intentions towards the future donors. Both the Whitaker and the Hashmi case are characterised by the same future intentions towards the child. In both cases the intention is to raise the child within the family after blood has been taken from its umbilical cord for use to treat a sick sibling. Even if extracting cord blood from a newborn was an immoral act (which would be difficult to claim given the non-invasive nature of the procedure), both cases would be characterised by the same immoral intention. It follows that the interests of the future child do not distinguish these two cases.

Thus, since developing into a child with DBA is not worse for an embryo than being destroyed, the Whitaker case has not been adequately distinguished from the Hashmi case. In both cases, the biopsy is a prima facie wrong to the embryo (on the assumption that the embryo has direct moral status), and, in both cases, a successful biopsy could benefit the parents and sick sibling by saving the sibling's life. Any factor capable of outweighing the prima facie wrong in the Hashmi case applies with equal force to the Whitaker case.

Conclusion

Following the Court of Appeal's decision in the Hashmi case, the Hashmis are attempting IVF followed by biopsy for what is now the third time. Last year the

Whitakers travelled to the US for treatment and in June this year Mrs Whitaker successfully gave birth to a baby that was tissue-compatible with her sick child. If the HFEA's decision was justifiable this instance of reproductive tourism would be a cause for concern. However, since the HFEA has not provided a morally relevant distinction between these two cases, its policy must be regarded as unethical.

July 2003

Appendum

In July 2004, a year after this article was first posted on the CCELS website, the HFEA changed its policy and removed the need for the selected embryo to be at risk of the relevant condition (see HFEA 2004). A number of other articles had been published criticising the old policy (see eg Sheldon and Wilkinson 2004). By the time that this article is re-published, the House of Lords is likely to have heard the appeal from the Court of Appeal's decision in the Quintavalle case.

Notes

1 PGD can be used in a wide sense to encompass tissue typing or in a narrow sense whereby it is restricted to preimplantation testing for genetic disorders. I have used it in its narrower sense so that the two types of test are described by different terms. This approach is used by the HFEA in its press releases (see HFEA 2001) and by the Mance LJ in R (On the Application of Quintavalle) v HFEA [2003] EWCA Civ 667, para 101.

2 Examples include challenges to the HFEA's decision to restrict the number of embryos capable of being implanted into a woman (R (On the Application of Assisted Reproduction and Gynaecology Centre) v HFEA [2002] EWCA Civ 20), and the HFEA's refusal to release information about an anonymous sperm donor to the resulting child (Rose v Secretary of State for Health and the HFEA [2002] EWHC 1593).

3 The HFEA's decision in the Hashmi case has also been denounced by the House of Commons Select Committee on Science and Technology as "going beyond the scope of its own public consultation" on PGD (2002, para 25). The Committee was of the view that public consultation is vital and "democracy is not served by unelected quangos taking decisions on behalf Parliament" (ibid, 13). While there is a need to reconsider the procedure for such decision making (especially the appointment procedures for membership of the HFEA), these concerns are not addressed in this paper.

4 Indeed, the Act imposes a licensing requirement on the
(a) creation of an embryo outside of the body (ss.3(1)(a) & 1(2));
(b) storage or use of embryos outside the body (ss.3(1)(b) & 1(2));
(c) storage of gametes (s.4(1)(a)); and
(d) use of gametes, unless "services are provided for the woman and man together" (s.4(1)(b)).

5 However, Maurice Kay did read the phrase "for the purpose of assisting women to carry children" as restricted to purposes addressing "impaired ability to conceive or to carry a child through pregnancy to full term and birth" (para. 17). The implication of doing so is

that PGD is only lawful where the genetic condition for which the technique is applied affects the viability of the embryo including its vulnerability to miscarriage.

6 That is, one cannot be in a harmed position unless it was possible to be in a non-harmed position. I have argued for this conclusion both from rights-based perspectives generally (see Pattinson 2002b) and from a specific rights-based moral theory (see Pattinson 2002a).

References

Guardian (2003), "The Price of Life: Review the Law on Embryo Selection." *The Guardian*, Friday 20 June, 23.

HFEA (Human Fertilisation and Embryology Authority). (2001), "HFEA to allow tissue typing in conjunction with preimplantation genetic diagnosis", press release, 13 December 2001. (2002) "HFEA confirms that HLA tissue typing may only take place when preimplantation genetic diagnosis is required to avoid a serious genetic disorder", press release, 1 August 2002. (2004), "HFEA Agrees to Extend Policy on Tissue Typing", press release, 21 July 2004.

House of Commons Select Committee on Science and Technology (2002), Developments in Human Genetics and Embryology. 4th report. (London: HMSO). (Also available as a pdf file: http://www.parliament.the-stationery-office.co.uk/pa/cm200102/cmselect/cmsctech/791/791.pdf).

Pattinson, S. D. (2002a) Influencing Traits Before Birth (Aldershot: Ashgate). (2002b) "Reproductive Cloning: Can Cloning Harm the Clone?" 10(3) *Medical Law Review* 295–307.

Sheldon, S. and Wilkinson, S. (2004), "Hashmi and Whitaker: An Unjustifiable and Misguided Distinction?" 12(2) *Medical Law Review* 137–163.

Wright, G. (2003), "Call for Debate Over 'Designer Baby' Laws." *The Guardian*, Thursday 19 June.

Chapter 30

Separating Conjoined Twins: The Case of Ladan and Laleh Bijani

Stephen Wilkinson

On 8th July 2003 Ladan and Laleh Bijani, Iranian conjoined twins aged 29, died in Singapore following a separation operation which lasted more than 48 hours. In this short essay, I offer an overview of some of the many ethical issues raised by this and similar cases.[1]

The Case Against Separation

In 1996, the Bijani sisters travelled to Germany "to try to persuade doctors there to operate on them"[2] but were turned away by German doctors "who said the risks were too high".[3] Were the German doctors right? Was the separation operation ethical given that it was so dangerous? Obviously, all surgery involves some risk and so a crucial question in this case is – just how dangerous was separation?

Views about this vary and, as a philosopher rather than a clinician, this is not an issue that I can resolve. However, it certainly seems that some members of the surgical team believed the chances of success to be low. For example, one is reported to have said that the operation never had a reasonable chance of success, that "the team made a 'great deal of effort' to try to talk the twins out of it",[4] and that "the sisters each [had only] a 50-50 chance of survival".[5] While another claimed that "doctors had begged them not to undergo surgery to separate their fused heads", because it was so dangerous, but that "both women insisted that the operation should go ahead".[6] So there was a strong prima facie case for not carrying out the operation even if the twins demanded it, since the doctors' reasons for begging them not to undergo surgery were equally reasons for refusing to provide it, as the German doctors had done.

Possible Justifications

Given that it was so dangerous, how might the operation be justified? There are three main possibilities:

(a) to lengthen the life of one or both twins;
(b) to improve the quality of life of one or both twins;
(c) to respect the twins' autonomy by complying with their considered wishes.

Insofar as it is possible to tell from the news reports, justification (a) didn't apply to the Bijanis. So in this respect, as in many others, their case was markedly different from Re A (Children), which dominated the news media in late 2000. In Re A the courts were faced with a stark choice between two unpalatable alternatives: separate in an attempt to save Jodie's life but in so doing end Mary's life, or refrain from separating and leave both twins to die within a relatively short period of time.[7] In the Bijani case however there was no question of sacrificing one to save the other, for (if left conjoined) their lives would not have been in imminent danger.

Quality of Life

(b) was one of the justifications actually given for separating Ladan and Laleh. A leading doctor at the Raffles Hospital in Singapore put it as follows:

> ... we had to weigh up quality of life against risk ... We have to be convinced that the present quality of life is so poor that this huge, this immense surgery is justified and should be performed. So, over the last few months seeing them almost everyday, observing reactions of people around them, strangers, children, adults, I think quality of life is a serious issue which warrants the undertaking of this surgical procedure.[8]

There's clearly nothing wrong in principle with subjecting patients to risk in order to improve their quality of life and cases in which this happens are ubiquitous. What's distinctive about the Bijani case is the degree of risk, which raises the question of whether the expected improvements in quality of life were really enough to justify this. Perhaps we can get some (albeit inadequate) sense of the quality of life implications of conjoinment by imagining what it would be like to become permanently fused to another person. I suspect that most all of us would greet that prospect with horror and regard it as "a fate worse than death", or at least think that it would be worth risking death in order to be separate again. But these matters are really imponderables which leads me (along with many others) to conclude that the best way of dealing with the quality of life issue (for competent adults) is to let the twins decide for themselves whether this justifies the risk, since only they really know how bad conjoinment is for them.

This of course takes us straight to justification (c), but before moving onto this it is worth first mentioning a possible inconsistency in the view expressed by the surgical team. As was noted earlier, we have heard that doctors "begged" Ladan and Laleh not to go through with the surgery. But this seems not to sit very easily with the view that there is a quality of life justification for the operation. For if, all things considered, the doctors really believed that quality of life considerations justified the risk (which is what was claimed) then shouldn't this also be a reason for not dissuading Ladan and Laleh?

Autonomy and Consent

I turn now to (c), the idea that the risk can be justified by reference to the autonomous (and otherwise valid) consent of the twins. One interesting theoretical issue here is whether it is respect for autonomy per se that is doing the justificatory work, or whether autonomy is important principally because (as suggested above) the twins are the only people who can make accurate judgments about their quality of life. In other words, is complying with their wishes simply the most effective means of acting in their best interests, or does it have its own independent moral significance? This distinction would become practically important if one or both of the twins wanted something that their doctors deemed to be substantially against their interests. For example, we can imagine a case in which one twin wanted altruistically to "sacrifice herself" in order to improve the other's quality of life. Here, the question of whether the doctors should go along with her request on pure "respect for autonomy" grounds, even though it's probably against her interests, would arise.

More practical issues are raised by a story in the Observer, according to which:

> The twins adoptive mother ... said Laleh was particularly fearful of the operation and begged her sister to abandon the idea of separating themselves. "She was terrified and crying. But Laden was adamant."[9]

This suggests two related difficulties. First, how can we be sure that the twins are validly consenting given that it is very difficult for them to have private individual consultations with healthcare professionals? In particular, how do we know that coercive or manipulative pressure isn't being brought to bear by one twin on the other? Perhaps one way around this problem, if it were technically possible and could be done without causing too much distress, would be to use a blindfold and headphones on one twin while talking to the other. Second, what ought we to do if one twin wants separation but the other doesn't? Although the situation in which this arose would be terrible for all concerned, I suspect that the ethical and legal answers to this will be pretty straightforward in the vast majority of cases: namely, it would be both wrong and unlawful to proceed with a separation operation if one of the twins had expressed a valid refusal. There is however an interesting question about whether we ought to view the principle of valid consent as inviolable even in very extreme situations: for example, where the refusing twin will die anyway in a matter of hours and where the only way of saving the other twin is to separate immediately.

Conclusion

One notable feature of the Bijani twins' case is that many of the issues raised don't specifically concern conjoinment. Most obviously, the question of to what extent a patient can be subjected to a risk of death in order to attempt to improve her quality of life is one which can and does arise in many other contexts. Similarly, questions about the extent to which patients should be thought of as authoritative when making quality of life judgments are ubiquitous. The Bijani twins' case then is markedly different from some other widely discussed cases of separation, notably Re A, because in the Bijani case there was no question of "sacrificing" one twin to save the other.[10]

August 2003

Notes

1 For a more thorough consideration see Sally Sheldon and Stephen Wilkinson, Separating conjoined twins: the legality and ethics of sacrifice, Medical Law Review, 5 (1997), pp. 149-171.

2 John Aglionby & Dan de Luce, "A spark of hope, then twins lose fight for normal life", Guardian, 9th July 2003.

3 John Aglionby, "Twins joined at head to risk surgery", *Guardian*, 3rd July 2003.

4 Robin McKie, "Separate at last, the twins who died for a dream", *Observer*, 13th July 2003.

5 John Aglionby, "Twins' two-day operation underway", *Guardian*, 7th July 2003.

6 Robin McKie, "Separate at last, the twins who died for a dream", *Observer*, 13th July 2003.

7 The twins were called Jodie and Mary for the purposes of the court case only. See Sally Sheldon and Stephen Wilkinson, "On the sharpest horns of dilemma": Re A (Conjoined Twins)', *Medical Law Review*, 9 (2001), pp. 201-207.

8 BBC News Online, "Conjoined adult twins begin op", 6th July 2003.

9 Robin McKie, "Separate at last, the twins who died for a dream", *Observer*, 13th July 2003, p. 16 – my emphasis

10 I am grateful to Sally Sheldon for her helpful comments on a previous draft.

Chapter 31

Brain Research and Neuroethics

Martha J. Farah, Paul Root Wolpe and Arthur Caplan

In the past year "neuroethics" has begun to command the attention of neuroscientists, ethicists and journalists. Ethical questions associated with new knowledge of the human brain have received extensive coverage in the popular press with cover stories in The Economist and The New Scientist. There has also been a burst of discussion in the scientific literature (e.g., Caplan, 2003, 2004; Caplan and Farah, 2003; Farah, 2002; Farah, Illes et al., 2004; Farah and Wolpe, 2004; Illes, 2003; Rose, 2002; Roskies, 2002; Wolpe, 2003), and a number of professional conferences have recently focused attention of the field. The current capability of neuroscience to monitor and alter brain function has profound ethical implications, which scientists and the public have only begun to examine.

New Knowledge, New Ethical Challenges

Recent progress in neuroscience has been fuelled by a combination of methodological and theoretical advances. The most obvious factor responsible for the current explosion of knowledge is functional neuroimaging. This set of methods, particularly positron emission tomography (PET) and functional magnetic resonance imaging (fMRI), has allowed the observation of patterns of activity throughout the brain as humans engage in different mental processes (Aguirre, 2003).

The introduction of molecular biology techniques into neuroscience has been responsible for an equally important revolution in understanding the neurochemistry of thought. The past ten years have seen an acceleration in the ability to identify and control, with ever more specificity, the molecular mechanisms of human cognition, feeling, and action (Barondes, 2003).

Finally, there have been important theoretical advances in the behavioural sciences. Intelligent, motivated behaviour results from the interplay of multiple systems for cognitive and affective information processing, and it is these systems, rather than the observable behaviour, that map most directly onto the brain. With the decline of behaviourism and the ascendance of cognitive science, models of human information processing now exist that provide the needed level of psychological analysis for mediating between behaviour and the brain. Recent computational and evolutionary analyses of human behaviour have also informed theorizing about mind-brain relations (Gazzaniga, Mangun and Ivry, 2003).

Enhancement of Normal Brain Function

An especially controversial ethical issue at the heart of neuroethics is whether and when it is ethically permissible for normal healthy individuals to use medical and biotechnological means to enhance their mental functioning. While people have always tried to enhance their functioning in one way or another through ingestion (alcohol, caffeine), new drugs are appearing that greatly increase enhancement potential. On college and high school campuses, the illicit use of Ritalin (methyphenidate) is not uncommon for purposes of increasing attentional focus when studying (Farah, 2002; Farah, Illes et al., 2004; Wolpe, 2003). Medications that are effective in improving the mood of individuals with depression are sometimes also used as "mood brighteners" by nondepressed people (Kramer, 1993). New drugs are also appearing that allow persons to go without sleep for longer periods of time apparently without as many untoward side-effects as current drugs such as caffeine or methamphetamines.

Several novel drugs for improving memory in dementia are currently in clinical trials, and at least some of them appear to enhance the memory of normal healthy subjects (Farah, 2002; Farah, Illes et al., 2004). As our understanding of the neurochemistry of cognition and emotion improve further, we can expect newer drugs with ever more specific effects. The reduction in side effects will in turn entice greater numbers of people to enhance their brain function pharmacologically.

Methods of neurocognitive enhancement are not restricted to pharmacology, although at present the nonpharmacologic methods are too rudimentary for enhancement of function in healthy humans. Transcranial magnetic stimulation (TMS), used experimentally in the treatment of psychiatric disorders, might one day be used to activate or inhibit specific cognitive systems for purposes of enhancement. Brain-machine interfaces being developed to augment memory and control robot arms might, in the even more distant future, enhance the cognition of normal individuals (Hoag, 2003).

Is enhancement right or wrong? The answer will almost surely depend on the specific type of enhancement and population, but certain principles seem to apply to the question in the abstract (Farah, 2002; Farah, Illes et al., 2004; Farah and Wolpe, 2004; Caplan, 2003, 2004; Wolpe, 2003). If the benefit to be gained is the improvement of normal function rather than the remediation of disease lower levels of risk seem appropriate especially where children are involved. If enhancement is not to be abused then the prevention of coercion by employers and schools seeking higher performing workers and students is essential. Choice must always be obtained before enhancement can be undertaken in competent adults.

In addition, there will be broader social effects of brain-based cognitive enhancement. One such effect is the socioeconomic advantage likely to accrue to groups that practice enhancement. Policies that promote equal access may prevent the exacerbation of already existing inequities in our society. Loss of diversity, stigmatizing the normal or the disabled and the commodification of human talent are other potential social effects that must be considered. Finally, we must consider the ways in which the fundamental sense of self and agency may be altered when and if neurocognitive self-improvement becomes commonplace (Farah, Illes et al., 2004; Wolpe, 2003).

Neuroimaging of Psychological States and Traits

In recent years it has been possible to correlate a surprising number of different personality attributes, attitudes, and predilections with patterns of brain activity, measured at rest or while performing a task (Canli and Amin, 2003). For example, neuroticism and extraversion are associated with distinctive patterns of brain response to emotionally pleasant or unpleasant pictures. Attitudes toward individuals of other races are associated with patterns of brain response to photographs of same and other-race faces.

Studies, while still rudimentary, have revealed suggestive yet troubling uses for neuroimaging. The likelihood that a violent criminal will act violently in the future can be estimated based on resting brain scans. Intentional deception results in a different pattern of brain activity from truthfulness. These and other examples of potentially sensitive information available from brain scans are discussed by Canli and Amin (2003) and others (Farah, 2002; Farah and Wolpe, 2004; Illes, 2003). It should be emphasized that the correlations between psychological variables and brain activity are generally not high enough to make brain scanning a useful tool for screening or assessment. However, it is also the case that some individual scans may be sufficiently distinctive that they do offer reliable information. But those seeking to detect criminal intent or to detain those who may pose a threat to the security of others may be willing to utilize information that is imperfect in lieu of anything else.

Functional brain imaging has the potential to breach the privacy of a person's own thoughts. Privacy is therefore high on the list of ethical issues raised by the new brain scanning technologies. Ironically, the more pressing social issue raised by scanning concerns its inability to measure mental or neural processing meaningfully. The aura of high tech and the impact of visual images may lead judges and juries to put more weight on evidence from functional neuroimaging than is warranted. A better public understanding of the capabilities of imaging is necessary to prevent an over-reliance on this source of information.

The neurological revolution has not drawn quite the same attention as the revolution in genetics in terms of reflection on the ethical and social challenges raised by scientific progress. It should. The chances are that changes in our brains to diagnose or enhance our behaviour will take place in our brains just as quickly as they do in our genes.

September 2003

References

Aguirre, G.K. (2003), Functional neuroimaging. In T.E. Feinberg and M.J. Farah (Eds.) *Behavioural Neurology and Neuropsychology*, 2nd edition. New York: McGraw Hill.

Barondes, S.H. (2003), "Better than Prozac: Creating the Next Generation of Psychiatric Drugs. London, Oxford University Press.

Canli, T. and Z. Amin (2002), "Neuroimaging of emotion and personality: Scientific evidence and ethical considerations." *Brain and Cognition*. 50:414-431.

Caplan, A.L. "Is Better Best?", *Scientific American*, September, 2003, 9, 104-105.

Caplan, A.L. "Nobody is perfect – But why not try to be better?" *PloS Medicine*, 2004.

Caplan, A.L., M.J. Farah, "Emerging Ethical Issues in Neurology, Psychiatry and the Neurosciences." In: *Molecular and Genetic Basis of Neurology and Psychiatry Disease*, 3rd ed., R.N. Rosenberg, et. al., (Eds) *The Molecular and Genetic Basis of Neurologic and Psychiatric Disease*. 3rd Ed. Philadelphia: Butterworth Heinemann.

Farah, M. (2002), "Emerging ethical issues in neuroscience." *Nature Neuroscience* 5: 1123-1129.

Farah, M.J., Illes, J., Cook-Deegan, R., Gardner, H., Kandel, E., King, P., Parens, E., Sahakian, B. and Wolpe P.R. (2004), "Neurocognitive enhancement: what can we do and what should we do?" *Nature Reviews Neuroscience*, 5: 421-425.

Farah, M.J. and Wolpe, P.R. (2004), "Monitoring and manipulating the human brain: New neuroscience technologies and their ethical implications." *Hastings Center Report*, 34: 35-45.

Gazzaniga, M.S., Ivry, R. and Mangun, G.R. (2002), *Cognitive Neuroscience: The Biology of the Mind*, 2nd edition. New York: Norton.

Hoag, H. (2003), "Neuroengineering: Remote control." *Nature* 423: 796-798.

Illes. J. (2003), "Neuroethics in a new era of neuroimaging." *American Journal of Neuroradiology* 24:1739-1741.

Kramer, P.D. (1993), *Listening to Prozac*. Penguin, New York.

Rose, S.P.R. (2002), "'Smart Drugs': Do they work? Are they ethical? Will they be legal?" *Nature Reviews Neuroscience*, 3: 975-979.

Roskies, A. (2002), "Neuroethics for the new millennium." *Neuron* 35:21-3.

Wolpe, P.R. (2003), "Neuroethics of enhancement." *Brain and Cognition*, 50: 387-395.

Chapter 32

Who has the Right to Determine the Fate of their Embryos?

Gillian Douglas

In *Evans v Amicus Healthcare and Others; Hadley v Midland Fertility Services Ltd and Others* [2003] 4 All ER 903, Wall J dismissed applications by two women, Natallie Evans and Lorraine Hadley, for declarations and injunctions relating to the use and storage of embryos that had been created from their eggs and the sperm of their former partners. The two men no longer wished to have children with the women, and argued that they had the right to withdraw their consent to the further use of the embryos for treatment. Wall J's decision was subsequently upheld by the Court of Appeal (*Evans v Amicus Healthcare Limited (Secretary of State for Health Intervening)* [21004] EWCA Civ 727, [2004] 3 All ER 1025). The case raises in stark form the question: which prospective parent should have the final say in such a dispute?

This brief comment focuses on the legal issues addressed in the case. Parliament has laid down, in the Human Fertilisation and Embryology Act 1990, detailed provisions governing how and when a person's consent to the use of their gametes and resulting embryos is to be required. How should these provisions be interpreted and how might this interpretation be affected by the incorporation into English law (by the Human Rights Act 1998) of the European Convention on Human Rights?

The Provisions in the 1990 Act

Schedule 3 to the 1990 Act provides that consent to use and storage must be given in writing and must specify the purposes for which the genetic material is to be used. This may be for providing treatment for the person giving the consent, or for that person with another when they are being treated together; for donation to others for treatment; and for the purposes of research (paragraph 2).

Paragraph 6(3) states that

> An embryo the creation of which was brought about *in vitro* must not be used for any purpose unless there is an effective consent by each person whose gametes were used to bring about the creation of the embryo to the use for that purpose of the embryo and the embryo is used in accordance with those consents.

Wall J held that the consent that the two claimants and their partners had given was for treatment *together* as a couple, and so any attempt by the two women alone to use the embryos would not be 'use for that purpose' nor 'in accordance with' the original consents. He considered that the treatment that the couples had been receiving together at the respective clinics came to an end when their relationship broke down and that the clinics would be in breach of their licences if they went ahead and treated the claimants in these circumstances. The Court of Appeal similarly considered that references in the Act to the provision of treatment services 'for a man and woman together' should be construed as requiring that the couple remain united in their pursuit of treatment. Once one of the parties had withdrawn his consent, the continued storage and use of the embryo fertilised with his sperm was no longer permissible.

The Right to Respect for Private Life in the European Convention on Human Rights

However, since the 1990 Act was passed, Parliament has also enacted the Human Rights Act 1998, which incorporates most of the rights enshrined in the European Convention on Human Rights into English law. The question therefore arose whether the courts' interpretation of the 1990 Act's terms must be modified to give appropriate weight to the women's Convention rights. Wall J's consideration of this issue focused on the 'right to respect for private life' guaranteed under art 8. In effect, the women were arguing that this right encompasses the right to procreate. (The categorisation of procreative freedom under this article is consistent with the American legal approach which views this as an aspect of the constitutionally protected right to privacy.) But equally, the two former partners also contended that they had a similar art 8 right *not* to reproduce.

Art 8(2) states that there shall be:

> no interference by a public authority with the exercise of this right except such as is .... necessary in a democratic society ... for the protection of the rights and freedoms of others.

This proviso enables and requires a court to determine whether an 'interference' with the exercise of the right (such as that apparently preventing the women from using the embryos once their partners' original consent had ceased to be operative, under the judge's interpretation of Schedule 3) can be justified as 'necessary' to protect the rights and freedoms of others (here, the partners' right not to become fathers). This inevitably calls for a balancing out of the respective rights of the parties concerned.

In carrying out this balancing exercise, Wall J considered that the parties' competing rights under art 8 were equal.

> An unfettered right on the claimants' part to have the embryos transferred into them would, by parity of reasoning, constitute an interference with respect of the men's art 8 rights, in the same way that any attempt on their part to insist that the claimants

> have the embryos transferred into them against their will would undoubtedly constitute an interference both with the claimants' right to autonomy over their own bodies, and with respect for their private lives. [para 184]

But with respect, it is by no means clear that the two situations are exactly equal. His Lordship's reference to the women's additional right to autonomy over their own bodies marks out the difference. We would not countenance forcing a woman to have an embryo transferred into her body because this would be a gross violation of her bodily autonomy. But the true comparison with what the women were seeking in this case would be a situation where the men wished to have the embryos transferred to a willing surrogate.

On firmer ground, it is suggested, was his Lordship's view that it is not unreasonable for a partner to say that they do not want to be the parent of a child by someone with whom they no longer wish to be in a relationship. Of course, a man is not permitted to use this argument in natural procreation – he will be regarded as the father of the child, to whom legal and moral obligations will attach, even though he never sees the mother after the act of procreation. But that is because of the extra weight we place on the mother's right to bodily autonomy; the difficulty of establishing, subsequent to the event, what the parties' procreative stances were at the time; and the public policy interest (arguably outmoded but still upheld) in attaching fathers to children. Where, as here, the embryos are in storage, they are not regarded as 'persons', and Parliament has already taken the decision that their fate (including their destruction) should be in the hands of each of those who created them, it is not an unreasonable stance for Parliament to give to the now unwilling genitor the opportunity to put a stop to the further development of those embryos into potential live children.

This is not to say that this is the *best* solution to the problem, but it is a reasonable one for a state to reach, given that there is still room for considerable divergence of opinion and practice across Europe as to how IVF and related techniques are to be regulated, thus giving each state a considerable 'margin of appreciation' in determining what rules it will apply.

The Prohibition of Discrimination

In the appeal, the Court considered the effect of art 14 as well as art 8. This article provides that the enjoyment of the rights and freedoms set out in the Convention shall be secured 'without discrimination on any ground …'. Ms Evans argued that she was being discriminated against because of her infertility, since a fertile woman, as noted above, has control over the embryo she carries. But the majority of the Court rejected this approach, considering that the Act was seeking to *help* women overcome their infertility, and stating that the only discrimination apparent was between women whose partners do and do not withdraw their consent to treatment. This, however, they justified on the same ground as finding no breach of art 8 – that the greater importance attached to continuing consent was a legitimate interference with Ms Evans' rights. Arden LJ disagreed on this point, finding that there *was* discrimination between Ms Evans and a fertile woman because the genetic father was allowed to withdraw his consent to IVF later than he could do so in ordinary sexual intercourse. Nonetheless, she too found that such discrimination was objectively justifiable for the same reasons as applied to art 8.

The Court of Appeal expressed considerable sympathy for the appellant and urged that couples in similar situations be given full opportunities to weigh what they want to happen should their relationship break down before treatment is completed. As Wall J concluded, it must be for Parliament to re-think if it concludes that the present legal outcome is not desirable. Should such a re-think take place, the legislators will have to wrestle with whether the right *not* to have one's genetic material passed on to succeeding generations is as important as the right to do so, and whether men and women really can be treated as having the same rights in this regard.

October 2003

Chapter 33

Internet Governance

Ian Kenway

Despite the comprehensive sweep of its aspirations, the World Summit on the Information Society (WSIS) held in Geneva in December 2003 under the auspices of the United Nations and the International Telecommunications Union (ITU) received relatively little informed and critical comment in the UK press and news channels, despite its attendance by more than 50 heads of state together with 6,000 other delegates. Indeed it would appear from several broadsheets that the only newsworthy item at the summit was the apparent chutzpah of President Robert Mugabe in addressing the assembly so soon after the deliberations of the Commonwealth Conference in Abuja.

However, this World Summit must be regarded as a 'slow burn' affair. Indeed it will probably only see real ignition and sparks in 2005 when it 'relocates' to Tunis. Like the earlier global conferences at Kyoto and Cancun with their respective emphases on the environment and equitable trading between nations, Geneva 2003 will be seen as the 'defining moment' when the Internet lost its youthful complexion and, at long last, entered the mature world of international law and political strife.

Despite the usual cynicism that so often marks international gatherings, Geneva 2003 closed not in disarray but with the Draft *Declaration of Principles* and *Plan of Action* being formally adopted by the assembly. Inevitably both documents display, often with little subtlety, the heterogeneous interests at play in the PrepComs and the inevitable tensions that exist between national governments, the private sector and those who regard themselves as representatives of 'Civil Society'.

'Who governs the Internet?' is a reasonable question but not one that is easily answered. On the one hand many techno-libertarians are extremely suspicious (the politest word one can use) of the intentions of national governments and international bodies in wishing to regulate the Net. On the other hand, it is also clear that some national governments view the Internet as a threat to their own political hegemony and respective fortunes. However, the issues are more complex still, since Geneva 2003 touches, at least at the level of sub-text, upon more fundamental issues such as how the global free-flow of information can circumvent and frustrate governments and, *in extremis*, actually dissolve the identity of nation States through weakening their respective boundaries. The power of the Net, however, is not unmediated. Certainly it would be wrong to regard it as some serendipitous phenomenon completely beyond the reaches of conventional political discourse. For a start it requires obvious and well-developed physical infrastructures as well as manifest intellectual empowering through appropriate networks, software and significant content production and exchange.

According to the adopted WSIS's *Declaration of Principles*: 'Everyone, everywhere should have the opportunity to participate and no one should be excluded from the benefits the Information Society offers' (*WSIS*, Geneva 2003, DP, A.4). What is less clear, however, is exactly how national governments, private enterprises and representatives of civil society can form partnerships based on genuine commonality of interest. That the Net is Janus-like cannot be disputed. e-government also pre-supposes e-opposition. Moreover for every well-intentioned hobbyist forum and innocent exchange of emails, the Net also provides a superb habitat for those drawn, whether ineluctably or by choice, towards paedophile sex, money laundering and international terrorism as well as many other activities dubious in nature but less inviting of horror tone comment.

According to WSIS: 'The Internet has evolved into a global facility available to the public and its governance should constitute a core issue of the Information Society agenda. The international management of the Internet should be multilateral, transparent and democratic, with the full involvement of involvement of governments, the private sector, civil society and international organizations' (*WSIS*, Geneva 2003, DP, B6.48). In the adopted *Plan of Action* WSIS requests that: 'the Secretary General of the United Nations [to] set up a working group on Internet governance, in an open and inclusive process that ensures a mechanism for the full and active participation of governments, the private sector and civil society from both developing and developed countries, involving relevant intergovernmental and international organisations and forums, to investigate and make proposals for action, as appropriate, on the governance of Internet [*sic*] by 2005, (*WSIS*, Geneva 2003, PA, C6.13b). In particular the group are charged with developing a working definition of Internet governance, identifying public policy issues that are relevant to Internet governance and developing 'a common understanding of the *respective* [*my italics*] roles and responsibilities of governments, existing intergovernmental and international organisations and other forums as well as the private sector and civil society'.

The issue of Internet governance, together with the Digital Solidarity Agenda, provides national governments and other interested parties with a monumental challenge. Can substantial progress be made before WSIS reconvenes in Tunis in 2005? There are many questions here. How far, for example, does the Digital Solidarity Agenda impact on issues concerning Internet governance? Who *is* in control of the Internet? Who *should* be in control of the Internet? And why are we talking about 'control' at all? Is it possible to have governance (rule of law) without heavy-handed State regulation on the one hand or the more subtle dictates of the market on the other?

According to WSIS: 'policy authority for Internet-related public policy issues is the sovereign right of States. They have rights and responsibilities for international Internet-related public policy issues...' (*WSIS*, Geneva 2003, DP, B6.49). But what does this mean in practice? From the mid-1990s onwards virtually all national governments have taken a greater interest in how the Internet is governed. This includes the management or control of their country-code top-level domain (ccTLD) as well as the continuing role of ICANN (Internet Corporation for Assigned Names and Numbers – a non-profit corporation in California) in administering the domain name system. The regulation of ISPs (Internet Service Providers) is another area where national governments are exercising greater authority. Bizarrely in the United States, where arguments for a continuing decentralised, self-regulatory approach to domain names are most articulate, the federal government has actually managed to 'guide' charitable organisations in their construction of web sites by effectively linking funding eligibility with a 'no frames design philosophy' via Section 508 of the Rehabilitation Act as amended in 1998.

WSIS talks about 'strengthening the trust framework' in connection with 'information [security] and network security, authentication, privacy and consumer protection' (*WSIS*, Geneva 2003, DP, B5.35). This undoubtedly is important but such an aspiration can only have meaning within a much deeper framework of trust in which diversity and distance are seen primordially in terms of opportunity rather than threat.

December 2003

Index

For Product Safety Concerns and Information please contact our
EU representative GPSR@taylorandfrancis.com Taylor & Francis
Verlag GmbH, Kaufingerstraße 24, 80331 München, Germany